CW01213198

DESTINY
The Life of Prince Diponegoro
of Yogyakarta, 1785–1855

DESTINY
The Life of Prince Diponegoro
of Yogyakarta, 1785–1855

PETER CAREY

PETER LANG
Oxford · Bern · Berlin · Bruxelles · Frankfurt am Main · New York · Wien

Bibliographic information published by Die Deutsche Nationalbibliothek
Die Deutsche Nationalbibliothek lists this publication in the Deutsche Nationalbibliografie;
detailed bibliographic data is available on the Internet at http://dnb.d-nb.de.

A catalogue record for this book is available from the British Library.

Library of Congress Control Number: 2014934465

COVER IMAGES:

TOP AND SPINE: 'Ein Historisches Tableau, die Gefangennahme des Javanischen Häuptlings Diepo Negoro' (An Historical Tableau, the Capture of the Javanese Chief Diponegoro) by Raden Saleh Syarif Bustaman, 1857. Illustration courtesy of the Sekretariat Kepresidenan (Presidential Secretariat), Republic of Indonesia.

BOTTOM: Javanese sketch of the fighting between Diponegoro's followers and Dutch troops at Selarong in either September or October 1825. Diponegoro's personal yellow battle pennant with his Erucokro ('Just King') symbol of crossed arrows and solar discus can be seen on the left. Taken from KITLV Or 13 (Buku Kedung Kebo), f.136r–v. Photograph courtesy of the KITLV, Leiden.

ISBN 978-3-0343-0926-4

© Peter Lang AG, International Academic Publishers, Bern 2014
Hochfeldstrasse 32, CH-3012 Bern, Switzerland
info@peterlang.com, www.peterlang.com, www.peterlang.net

All rights reserved.
All parts of this publication are protected by copyright.
Any utilisation outside the strict limits of the copyright law, without the
permission of the publisher, is forbidden and liable to prosecution.
This applies in particular to reproductions, translations, microfilming,
and storage and processing in electronic retrieval systems.

This publication has been peer reviewed.

Printed in Germany

For the younger generation of present-day Indonesia in the hope that Diponegoro's example may inspire them to honour their inheritance and serve their fellow Indonesians

'You alone are the means,
but that not for long,
only to be counted amongst the ancestors.'
— PARANGKUSUMO PROPHECY, circa 1805

'The time is out of joint: O cursèd spite
That ever I was born to set it right!'
— SHAKESPEARE, *Hamlet*, Act I, Scene V, l.v. 189–90

'Religion was not the thing at first contested for, but God brought it to that issue at last, and at last it proved to be that which was most dear to us [...]'
— OLIVER CROMWELL (1599–1658), Third Speech to the Protectorate Parliament, 22 January 1655

Contents

List of Illustrations	xi
Destiny – An Appreciation by Goenawan Mohamad	xxiii
Foreword	xxvii
Preface	xxxiii
Maps of Eastern and Central Java	xlv
PART I Youth and Upbringing, 1785–1808	1
CHAPTER I	
Diponegoro's Youth and Upbringing, 1785–1803	3
CHAPTER II	
Young Manhood: Marriage, Education and Links with the Religious (*santri*) Community, 1803–1805	25
CHAPTER III	
Pilgrimage to the South Coast, circa 1805	47
PART II The Beginning of the Ruin of the Land of Java, 1808–1812	67
CHAPTER IV	
The Beginning of Ruin: Daendels' 'New Order' and the Central Javanese Courts, 1808	69

CHAPTER V

The Old Order's Last Champion: The Origins and Course
of Raden Ronggo's Rebellion, 1809–1810 — 91

CHAPTER VI

The End of the Beginning: The Fall of the
Franco-Dutch Government and the British
Rape of Yogyakarta, 1811–1812 — 113

PART III Golden Years, Iron Years, 1812–1825 — 139

CHAPTER VII

Into a New Era: Diponegoro and the
Post-June 1812 British Interregnum — 141

CHAPTER VIII

Binding on the Iron Yoke: Diponegoro, the Returned Dutch
Administration and the Impoverishment of the South-Central
Javanese Peasantry, 1816–1822 — 169

CHAPTER IX

Waiting for the 'Just King': Diponegoro's Final Visions
and the Road to War in South-Central Java, 1822–1825 — 197

PART IV War and Exile, 1825–1855 — 237

CHAPTER X

The Last Stand of the Old Order:
Diponegoro and the Java War, 1825–1830 — 239

CHAPTER XI

Betrayal or Honourable Submission? Diponegoro's Capture at
Magelang and Journey Through Batavia, February–May 1830   271

CHAPTER XII

Surviving the Dutch Gulag: Diponegoro's Years
of Exile and Death, 1830–1855   305

Glossary of Javanese words   333

Index   343

List of Illustrations

Maps

Map 1   xlvi

Map of central and east Java showing the apanage provinces belonging to the south central Javanese courts pre-1811. Map outline taken from Louw and De Klerck 1894–1909, VI, adapted by J. Wilbur Wright of Oxford.

Map 2   xlviii

Map of the Yogyakarta area in the early nineteenth century taken from Louw and De Klerck 1894–1909, IV, showing the main roads and villages. Map outline adapted by J. Wilbur Wright of Oxford.

Map 3   4

Plan of the Tegalrejo estate and its surroundings, circa 1830, on a scale of one inch to 100 metres. Adapted from Louw and De Klerck 1894–1909, I: 'Plattegrond van de hoofdplaats Jogjakarta omstreeks 1830', by J. Wilbur Wright of Oxford.

Map 4   48

Diponegoro's pilgrimage to the south coast of Java (circa 1805), showing the main places he visited. Adapted from Louw and De Klerck 1894–1909, I, by J. Wilbur Wright of Oxford.

xii *List of Illustrations*

Map 5 92

Map of central and east Java in 1810 showing the route taken by Raden Ronggo Prawirodirjo III, chief administrator (*bupati wedana*) of Madiun (in office, 1796–1810) after his flight from Yogyakarta on 20 November 1810 until his final battle and death at Sekaran on the banks of the Solo River (Bengawan Solo) on 17 December 1810. Taken from H.J. de Graaf (ed.), *De expeditie van Anthonio Hurdt* (The Hague: Nijhoff for Linschoten Vereeniging, 1971). Redrawn and rearranged by J. Wilbur Wright of Oxford.

Map 6 306

Diponegoro's journey into exile in Manado (1830–1833) on the corvette Pollux (4-5-1830–12-6-1830) and his subsequent voyage to Makassar, where he would spending his remaining days in exile (1833–55), on the Dutch naval sloop Circe (20-6-1833 – 11-7-1833). Map drawn by J. Wilbur Wright of Oxford.

Plates

Plate 1

Charcoal sketch of Diponegoro as a young man probably made by a Yogya court artist at the time of his marriage to his first official wife, a daughter of the Yogya district head (*bupati*) of Panolan, in East Java, Raden Tumenggung Notowijoyo III (in office, 1803–11), on 27 February 1807. It is the only known sketch of the prince which shows him dressed in Javanese *kraton* style in a jacket (*surjan*) and Javanese headdress (*blangkon*). Photograph courtesy of the late Ibu Dr Sahir (great-great granddaughter of Diponegoro II), Jl. Nyoman Oka 7, Kota Baru, Yogyakarta, 1972.

List of Illustrations xiii

Plate 2

Diponegoro (dressed in black) giving instructions to his two followers, Kyai Joyomustopo and Kyai Mopid, before they set out on their pilgrimage (*ziarah*) to Nusakambangan to find the flower of royalty (*kembang Wijoyokusumo*). Diponegoro is seated under a *kemuning* [Kamboja] tree (*wit kemuning*) on his meditation stone (*selo gilang*) at his retreat (*panepen*) of Selorejo just to the north-east of Tegalrejo. KITLV Oriental MS 13, *Buku Kedung Kebo*, f.81v. Photograph courtesy of the KITLV, Leiden.

Plate 3

Sketch of a Yogya court delegation with sea-scattered offerings (*labuhan*) for the goddess of the Southern Ocean (Ratu Kidul) at Parangkusumo. From Musium Nasional (Jakarta), MS 933 DI, Ir Moens, 'Platen Album', no. 8, *Slametan Cembèngan*, 116, plate 120. Photograph courtesy of the Perpustakaan Nasional (Indonesian National Library), Jakarta.

Plate 4

Kyai Mojo (circa 1790–1849), Diponegoro's principal religious adviser during the Java War, who came from the Surakarta *pradikan* (tax-free) village of Mojo just to the northeast of Delanggu, and died in exile in Kampung Jawa, Tondano, North Sulawesi. Although he had never made the pilgrimage to Mecca (*haj*), he commanded great authority amongst Diponegoro's religious (*santri*) followers because of his intimate knowledge of the *Qur'ān* and his forceful character. Uncoloured lithograph by Jean Augustin Daiwaille (1786–1850) and Pieter Veldhuizen (1806–1841) based on a sketch by Major (later Major-General) F.V.H.A. Ridder de Stuers (1792–1881), made in Salatiga in December 1828 after Kyai Mojo had given himself up to the Dutch with over 600 of his followers, sixty-two of whom later accompanied him into exile in North Sulawesi (Minahasa). Taken from De Stuers, *Prins Diepo Negoro hoofd muitelingen op Java; Kiaij*

Goeroe van Modjo hoofdpriester; Radeen Pacha Prawiro Dirdjo opperbevelhebber (Amsterdam: Lith, Daiwaille and Veldhuijsen, 1831). Photograph courtesy of the KITLV, Leiden.

Plate 5

Posthumous portrait of Herman Willem Daendels (1762–1818), painted by Raden Saleh Syarif Bustaman (circa 1811–80) in 1838. Daendels' hand points to a map of the Mount Megamendung (West Java) section of the famous trans-Java mail road (*postweg*), the highest pass on the *postweg*, which ran from Anyer on the Sunda Straits to Panarukan in Java's Eastern Salient (Oosthoek) and which was built during his administration. Photograph courtesy of the Rijksmuseum, Amsterdam.

Plate 6

Oil painting by the Belgian artist, A.A.J. Payen (1792–1853), of the governor-general's carriage being drawn up Daendels' *postweg* with the aid of a yoke of buffalo in the Priangan highlands at Gunung Pola near Sumedang (West Java). Payen painting collection, Museum voor Volkenkunde, Leiden, no. 200/22. Photograph courtesy of the Museum voor Volkenkunde, Leiden.

Plate 7

Ali Basah Abdul Mustopo Prawirodirjo (Sentot) (circa 1808–55), son of Raden Ronggo Prawirodirjo III, chief administrator (*bupati wedana*) of Madiun (in office 1796–1810), by an unofficial wife (*garwa ampéyan*). Sentot became one of Diponegoro's most effective cavalry commanders during the Java War, but gave himself up to the Dutch in October 1829 because of the increasingly desperate military situation. Uncoloured lithograph by Jean Augustin Daiwaille (1786–1850) and Pieter Veldhuizen (1806–1841)

List of Illustrations

based on a sketch drawn by Major (later Major-General) F.V.H.A. Ridder de Stuers (1792–1881) in Yogyakarta, in April 1830, after Sentot had been given the rank of lieutenant-colonel (*overste*) and placed in charge of his own column of troops (*barisan*). Taken from De Stuers, *Prins Diepo Negoro hoofd muitelingen op Java; Kiaij Goeroe van Modjo hoofdpriester; Radeen Pacha Prawiro Dirdjo opperbevelhebber* (Amsterdam: Lith, Daiwaille and Veldhuijsen, 1831). Photograph courtesy of the KITLV, Leiden.

Plate 8

A Javanese chief in war dress, taken from Raffles 1817, I:90 facing. Photograph courtesy of the Bodleian Library, Oxford.

Plate 9

Boats of His Majesty's Sloop Procris attacking and capturing six French gunboats off the north coast of Java at Indramayu on 31 July 1811. Engraving by Charles Rosenberg (flourished mid-19th century) after a painting by the celebrated naval artist, William John Huggins (1781–1845). Photograph courtesy of the British Library, London.

Plate 10

Aquatint by William Daniell (1769–1837) of a Light Infantry Volunteer Battalion sepoy (right) and grenadier sepoy (left) who took part in the British attack on the Yogya *kraton* in June 1812 and the sepoy conspiracy of 1815. Taken from John Williams, *An Historical Account of the Rise and Progress of the Bengal Native Infantry from its First Formation in 1757 to 1796* (London: John Murray, 1817), pp. 171 and 331 facing. Photographs courtesy of the Bodleian Library, Oxford.

Plate 11

Watercolour by John Newman (1795–1818) entitled 'Javanese grandee and a servant', 1811–12. It is possible that the figure depicted is Kyai Adipati Suro-Adimenggolo, the district head (*bupati*) of Torboyo in Semarang (circa 1760–1827; in office 1809–22), the uncle of the celebrated painter Raden Saleh Syarif Bustaman, and a great friend and informant of Raffles, who provided many of the details on Javanese-Islamic law for Raffles' *History of Java* (1817). Photograph courtesy of the British Library, London.

Plate 12

Watercolour by John Newman (1795–1818) entitled 'Javanese grandee and a European', 1811–12. The European in question may have been Hugh Hope, scion of a very grand Scottish family, who served as Civil Commissioner of the Eastern Districts and Resident of Semarang (in office, 1811–12). The painting is interesting for its depiction of the spread of European ways, in this case port drinking, amongst the Javanese elite. Photograph courtesy of the British Library, London.

Plate 13

Equestrian portrait of Sultan Hamengkubuwono IV (reigned 1814–22) of Yogyakarta showing him dressed in his Dutch major-general's uniform and wearing the eight-pointed star set with diamonds of the Order of the Union (*Orde van de Unie*) given to his father, Hamengkubuwono III (reigned 1812–1814), by Daendels in May 1811 after he was appointed Regent of Yogyakarta. Portrait by the Javanese artist, Soebardjo, based on an original oil painting and completed in February 1938. Photograph courtesy of the Musium Karaton Ngayogyakarta.

List of Illustrations xvii

Plate 14

Sketches of the Chinese inhabitants of Java in the early nineteenth century by A.A.J. Payen (1792–1853). Above: a Chinese tailor and his assistant; below: Chinese men dressed with their signature top-hats, pigtails and parasols. Inventaris No.E/71 and E/78 of the Payen collection in the Ethnographic Museum, Leiden. Photographs courtesy of the Museum Volkenkunde, Leiden.

Plate 15

Huibert Gerard baron Nahuys van Burgst (1782–1858), the 'bigwig with a pair of big thick epaulettes' in De Stuers' description, who served as Resident of Yogyakarta between 1816 and 1822. Diponegoro described him in his autobiographical *babad* as a resident who 'enjoyed eating and drinking and the spreading of Dutch ways' (*karemannya mangan minum/lan anjrah cara Welandi*). Painting by Jan Adam Kruseman (1804–1862) completed in 1840 when Nahuys was serving as a member of the Council of the Indies (*Raad van Indië*) (1836–1841). Photograph courtesy of the Museum Bronbeek, Arnhem.

Plate 16

Raden Adipati Danurejo IV (in office, 1813–1847) being hit over the face with a slipper by Diponegoro as a result of an argument over the renting of royal land to Europeans. A *sentono* (member of the sultan's family) looks on. From Oriental MS 13 of the Koninklijk Instituut voor Taal-, Land- en Volkenkunde (Leiden) (*Buku Kedung Kebo*), f.55v. Photograph courtesy of the KITLV.

xviii *List of Illustrations*

Plate 17

Jonkheer Anthonië Hendrik Smissaert (1777–1832), Resident of Yogyakarta between 1823 and 1825, whose bungling and ineptitude were directly responsible for the outbreak of the Java War. One Dutch contemporary, Willem van Hogendorp, described him as a 'small, fat and shy man' (*klein, dik en verlegen*), and another, the Belgian painter A.A.J. Payen, compared him to Sancho Panza, one of the most archetypal *panakawan* (clown retainer) figures in European literature. Portrait attributed to the Dutch artist W.G.F. Heymans (1797–1868), and probably painted in 1827 after Smissaert had returned to The Hague in disgrace. From the private collection of the Baron van Tuyll van Serooskerken (Kasteel Heeze), the family of Governor-General G.A.G.Ph. van der Capellen's wife, Baroness Jacqueline Elisabet. Photograph by courtesy of the Rijksbureau voor Kunsthistorische Documentatie, The Hague.

Plate 18

Sketch of Diponegoro and his armed followers (pikemen) entering the prepared encampment at Metesih, a settlement in the Progo River just below the 'old' Residency House (Karesidenan Lama) in Magelang, on 8 March 1830, before the 'peace' negotiations with the Dutch which ultimately led to his arrest on 28 March 1830. Uncoloured litograph by the Dutch painter and lithographer, Wilhelmus van Groenewoud (1803–1842), based on a sketch made by Major (later Major-General) F.V.H.A. Ridder De Stuers (1792–1881). Print from De Stuers, *Mémoires sur la guerre de l'île de Java* (Leiden: Luchtmans, 1833), Atlas, Plate 12. Photograph courtesy of the KITLV, Leiden.

Plate 19

Charcoal sketch of Diponegoro by A.J. Bik (1790–1872). It shows him dressed in the 'priestly' garments which he wore during the Java War, namely

List of Illustrations xix

a turban, an open-necked *kabaya* (cotton shirt) and a *jubah* (loose outer robe or tabard). A sash hangs over his right shoulder and his *pusaka kris* (heirloom dagger), Kangjeng Kyai Bondoyudo (Sir Duelling Without Weapons), is stuck in his flowered silk waist band. The slightly sunken cheeks, which accentuate the prince's high cheek bones, were the result of successive bouts of malaria from which he had been suffering since his wanderings in the jungles of Bagelen at the end of the war (November 1829–February 1830). Photograph courtesy of the Musium Kota (now Museum Sejarah Jakarta).

Plate 20

Letter of Pangeran Diponegoro to Colonel (later Major-General) Jan Baptist Cleerens (1785–1850) and Major (later Major-General) Hendrik Frederik Buschkens (1795–1860), dated 17 Shaban, Anno Hijrae 1245 (14 February 1830) (Islamic calendar from the date of the flight of The Prophet AD 622 from Mecca to Medina) in *pégon* (Arabic) script dealing with the negotiations for a meeting at Remokamal in north-eastern Bagelen to discuss peace terms. Diponegoro's seal which bears the royal title which he assumed at Selarong on 1 Suro, Anno Javanico 1753 (15 August 1825) (Javanese year – lunar era inaugurated by Sultan Agung [reigned 1613–1646] in 1633), is placed in the middle of the letter and reads as follows: '*Ingkang Jumeneng Kangjeng Sultan Ngabdul Chamid Hèrucakra Kabirul Mu'minin Sayidin Panatagama [...] Rasulullah s.a.w. ing Tanah Jawi* [He who is raised as His Highness Sultan Ngabdulkamid Erucokro, the First among the Believers, Lord of the Faith, Regulator of Religion, [Caliph] of The Prophet of God, may peace be on Him, in Java]'. Letter no.208 from the H.M. de Kock private collection of the Nationaal Archief, The Hague.

Plate 21

Oil painting by the Dutch artist Nicolaas Pieneman (1809–60) entitled 'The Submission of Diponegoro to Lieutenant-General De Kock, 28 March

xx *List of Illustrations*

1830', which was commissioned by De Kock following his triumphal return to the Netherlands in October 1830. Photo courtesy of the Rijksmuseum, Amsterdam.

Plate 22

Oil painting by Raden Saleh Syarif Bustaman (circa 1811–80) entitled 'An Historical Tableau, the Arrest of the Javanese Chief Diponegoro (*Ein Historisches Tableau, die Gefangennahme des Javanischen Häuptlings Diepo Negoro*)' (March 1857), which Saleh presented as a 'Trojan horse' gift to his patron, King Willem III of the Netherlands (reigned, 1849–90). The numbers refer to key figures imagined by Saleh as being present such as no.1, Diponegoro's wife, Raden Ayu Retnoningsih, or those actually present such as no.2, Diponegoro's personal retainer (*panakawan*), Joyosuroto (Roto); no.3, the Dutch military translator for Javanese, Captain Johan Jacob Roeps (1805–40); no.4, the commander of the cavalry detachment (7th Hussars), Major Johan Jacob Perié (1788–1853); no.5, the Resident of Kedu, Frans Gerhardus Valck (1799–1842; in office 1826–30); no.6, Diponegoro's eldest son, Prince Diponegoro the Younger (born circa 1803, died post-March 1856); no.7, Diponegoro himself; no.8, De Kock; no.9, Lieutenant-Colonel Louis du Perron (1793–1855), commander of the Magelang garrison with De Kock's senior staff officer, Lieutenant-Colonel Willem Adriaan Roest (1796–1875), with the gold braided uniform collar, facing forward in the background; no.10, Major de Stuers; no.11, Major A.V. Michiels (1797–1849), commander of the Eleventh Mobile Column, who was tasked with disarming Diponegoro's troops; nos.12 and 13, possible self-portraits of Raden Saleh; no.14, Saleh's servant whispering the dramatic events in '*Ecce Homine*' mode to his master; and no.15 a member of Diponegoro's priestly 'Barjumungah' bodyguard regiment who would later migrate to East Java to found new communities populated by the prince's former soldiers. Photo courtesy of the Presidential Secretariat, Jakarta.

List of Illustrations xxi

Plate 23

Personal letter in Diponegoro's hand to his mother, Raden Ayu Mangkorowati (circa 1770–1852), written from Batavia in late April 1830 before his departure for Manado, reassuring her as to his fate and asking for her forgiveness for his faults and requesting both herself and her grandchildren to intercede with his late father, see Carey 2008:823–4. Photograph courtesy of the Koninklijke Militaire Academie (Dutch Royal Military Academy), Breda.

Plate 24

Imaginary coloured drawing of Diponegoro in Fort Rotterdam (Makassar) reading an Islamic mystical text (*tasawwuf*) accompanied by his wife, Raden Ayu Retnoningsih, and a son referred to as 'Pangeran [prince] Ali Basah' who is either having a vision of a Javanese spirit or being admonished by the prince's dwarflike *panakawan* (intimate retainer) Bantengwareng (circa 1810–58). Leiden Codex Orientalis 7398 (Snouck Hurgronje Collection), photo courtesy of Leiden University Library.

GOENAWAN MOHAMAD

Destiny – An Appreciation

Even before the outbreak of the Java War, Diponegoro could be said to have been situated between the absolute past and the ever-changing present.

His autobiographical *Serat Babad Dipanegaran* (Chronicle of Diponegoro) – a well known text in Java, takes the form of an epic poem. It was written by the prince himself during his exile in Manado (1830–33), the copy of the original manuscript rather than the original itself now being most commonly used. In it, the fighting prince, who resisted Dutch rule, refers to himself in connection with a particular passage in the legend of the Indian epic hero, Arjun.

Basically the story of Arjun, as with most shadow-play (*wayang*) stories based on the Indian epics, are situated in the absolute past – but in a somewhat different sense from that intended by Goethe in his phrase *vollkommen vergangen*, subsequently used by Mikhail Bakhtin in his discussion of the epic genre. What I mean is, it is a past which is totally untraceable yet persistent as a collective memory. It cannot actually be called the past in the historical sense: while for most people in Java the *Mahabharata* stories did once happen, the stories have no specific geographical and temporal reference.

In his autobiography, Diponegoro takes the epic figure of Arjun as an allegory for himself. Thus the *Arjuna Wiwāha* (Arjun's Wedding) epic, in the prince's view, is not something fixed statically in the absolute past. Instead, the process of Arjun's asceticism in preparation for the great Bharata War (*Bharatayudha*) is brought into the context of Diponegoro's own lived experience. It is as though he is making the epic fit the context of his own early-nineteenth-century present. It is thus located in a very specific time and place, making it real and concrete.

Of course, in such a situation, experience means lived experience of change. But this type of change occurs in two rather different ways. First, there are the chronological changes, such as those which occurred when Diponegoro was brought as a baby in arms to be viewed by his great-grandfather, Sultan Mangkubumi, or his childhood at Tegalrejo (1793–1803) under the eye of his formidable great-grandmother, and all the further changes in his life right up to the end of the Java War (1825–30) when he went down to defeat. But, there is also another meaning to these events: the changes experienced by the prince being described as the unfolding of a prophecy.

As the reader can see, Peter Carey's book uses the word 'destiny' in its English title, a word derived from the original Latin '*destinare*', meaning a 'destination'. He also uses the word 'prophecy' in his earlier 2007 publication, *The Power of Prophecy: Prince Diponegoro and the End of the Old Order in Java, 1785–1855* (Leiden: KITLV Press), of which the present work is a concise version. When prophecy or the power of divination and fortune-telling hold sway, these powers in a sense determine a man's destiny and shape what will unfold. When 'destiny' is understood in this context as a reality which has already been fixed, the future belongs to the past.

Therefore, if Carey states that Diponegoro 'looks to the future', this 'future' is not what is now understood as a form of progression. The Javanese prince who gave Ottoman Turkish names and ranks to his forces seemed really to want to offer something new to Javanese society whose dignity and very existence were being threatened by modern Dutch colonialism: a future which would be both 'Islamic' and empowered. But as Carey suggests, this future is a form of recovery or 'restoration' of an order which had indeed existed but which had been destroyed by Dutch colonial power – not something new *per se*. Imaginings about the Javanese Just King (*Ratu Adil*) and dreams about the nine apostles of Islam (*wali wudhar*), who combined spiritual and temporal powers, were both shaped by a past age, which, in Diponegoro's view, had to be brought back to life.

Even Diponegoro's 'Islamic' agenda is problematic. Towards the end of the war, bitter conflicts arose between himself and his principle supporter, Kyai Mojo, which continued when both men found themselves briefly sharing the same Minahasan (North Celebes) exile (1830–33). This was principally because the religious scholars (*ulama*) around Mojo saw that the prince wanted to restore the order and values of the Javanese aristocracy on the basis of a knightly (*satria*) rather than student of religion (*santri*) social order.

Equally important, Diponegoro did not see change as part of the external world's impingement on himself, nor that he himself might have an impact on that outer world.

There was a prophecy made by his great-grandfather, Mangkubumi, that he would be the agent for resistance against the Dutch, but only for a brief time: '... *sira srananipun / mapan iku tan dawa* ...' ('... you will be the agent / but that not for long ...'). Indeed, it would be just for five short years (1825–30). But because of Diponegoro's resistance, both Java and Dutch colonialism in Indonesia would be changed into something which would endure for many years. In his *Power of Prophecy*, Peter Carey begins with an overview presenting pre-Java War Yogyakarta as prosperous, well-ordered and a Javanese version of 'Versailles'. But then after the bitterly fought war, the situation changed: 200,000 Javanese were killed, one third of the entire population of Java 'were exposed to the ravages of war', and a quarter of all farmland damaged.

Here it seems we need to read the meaning of 'prophecy' in a different way: as an explanation for something that has happened in a person's life and community – something that is so devastating that it cannot be understood by just one or two superficial analyses. The prophecy itself can also act as a kind of ideology, namely a reordering of the way of looking at the world, especially in a conflict situation. This reordering has the potential and 'power' to move people, give them an identity, and mark who 'we' and 'they' are, thus changing the very conditions of life and society.

Peter Carey's book assiduously, sharply and sensitively, develops various perspectives and interpretations of the role of prophecy in the context of the Java War.

From these perspectives we come to understand through his research how during the great war of 1825–1830 so much had become intertwined. There are beliefs, hopes, illusions, personal vendettas, local conflicts and the arrogance and incapacity of the Dutch authorities – stories which are both 'local' and specific. But at the same time there are the changing global socio-economic conditions brought about by the new industrial technologies and the force of global colonialism in contemporary – European-dominated – international politics.

Carey thus not only manages to present a story which is both local and 'empirical', but also one which enables us to draw out some important general perspectives, even though he is not in the business of making abstractions and presenting a general picture of Dutch colonialism in Indonesia.

Carey concludes, for example, that the Java War – or 'Diponegoro War' as it is better known in Indonesia – was 'the first rebellion which occurred in one of the south-central Javanese palaces, whose origins lay in social and economic suffering, and not just the dynastic ambitions of the courtly elite'. This conclusion enables us better to understand the rise of early twentieth-century Indonesian nationalism and the support it elicited in the late Dutch colonial era from the wider population rather than just the Dutch-educated elite.

From this perspective, the rise of nationalism is rather different from that suggested by the post-war Dutch Resident of Yogyakarta, Frans Gerhardus Valck (1799–1842; in office, 1831–41), who, according to Carey, situated the 'sentiment' of proto–nationalism amongst colonized peoples in feelings of anti-foreignism and humiliation. Nationalism – and presumably also 'proto–nationalism' – in Indonesia is more than just about anti-foreignism. It arises from much broader and deeper social contradictions. Even more importantly, the 'power of prophecy' in this context ensures that the future no longer belongs to the past, but is squarely anchored in changes which will really happen in the future. These modern-day 'prophecies' are called Marxism and Socialism, as effectively translated by Bung Karno [President Sukarno, 1901–70; in office, 1945–66] and other nationalist leaders of his generation, analyses which take into account the collapse of colonialism worldwide.

Jakarta, 29 December 2013

Foreword

Why write a biography of Indonesian national hero, Prince Diponegoro (1785–1855)? In most countries, such a key figure would have been the subject of numerous biographies. Every aspect of the prince's life would have been researched in detail, his understanding of Islam and his Javanese inheritance the subject of weighty monographs. One might even have expected that his own writings, in particular his magnificent autobiography – the first in any Indonesian language – written over nine months (20 May 1831–3 Feb 1832) while in exile in Manado (1830–33), the *Babad Diponegoro* (Chronicle of Diponegoro), which runs to 1,151 pages in manuscript and which is now registered by UNESCO as a Memory of the World manuscript (22 June 2013), would have long since appeared in a copiously annotated modern text edition.

In Indonesia, however, the situation is very different: history seems to have little honour here, and the results have been painfully evident in Jakarta's abysmal handling of its East Timor adventure (1975–99) and its belated understanding of the society, politics and culture of Aceh at the northern tip of Sumatra. There is little money for research or government funds – let alone the scholarly attention and respect needed – for the preservation of manuscripts. The result is that the original *pegon* (unvocalised Arabic script Javanese) copy of Diponegoro's autobiographical chronicle in the National Library (Perpustakaan Nasional) – equivalent to Oliver Cromwell's common place book or George Washington's diary – is crumbling to dust (Carey 1981:lix–lx note 76).[1]

---

1   Since the start of the so-called 'Reform' (*Reformasi*) period in May 1998, the pace of historical losses in Indonesia has accelerated: the house built by the Dutch in Makassar in 1855–6 for Diponegoro's widow, Raden Ayu Retnoningsih, has been knocked down (2000) (Chapter XII), and the original charcoal sketch of Diponegoro made by A.J. Bik while the prince was being held at the *Stadhuis* (April 1830) (Chapter XI) has gone missing from the Museum Sejarah Jakarta collection (2006).

As for the voluminous Dutch Residency reports in the Indonesian National Archives (Arsip Nasional Republik Indonesia), the backbone of this book, few can access them given the lack of knowledge of the Dutch language in present-day Indonesia. As a result most Indonesians live in an historiographical void, more aware of the globalised pop culture of the West than their own cultural inheritance. As far as Diponegoro is concerned, it is as though the clock stopped at the time when the Dutch military historians P.J.F. Louw and E.S. de Klerck completed their magisterial six-volume work on the Java War (1825–30) (Louw and De Klerck 1894–1909) and the Rusche edition (1908–9) of the *Babad Diponegoro* was published in Surakarta before the First World War.

Since independence in 1945, only a handful of studies have appeared in Indonesian. These include Yamin (1950), Tanojo (1966), Soekanto (1951a, 1951b, 1952), Sagimun (1965), and Djamhari (2003). All have enabled Indonesian readers to learn about aspects of Diponegoro's life and times, but apart from the last, primarily a history of the Dutch *benteng stelsel* (Java War fortification system), none have been based on primary research.

It was this lack of research which originally inspired my 1975 Oxford doctorate on Diponegoro, the second part of which – a twelve-canto Surakarta court chronicle on the outbreak of the Java War – was published as long ago as 1981 (Carey 1981). Twenty-five years later, the first part appeared under the imprint of the KITLV Press (Leiden): *The Power of Prophecy: Prince Dipanagara and the End of an Old Order in Java, 1785–1855* (Carey 2007, second revised edition 2008). Within six months, a second revised edition was required so great was the interest in this much respected historical figure. A third edition was even planned. But before it could see the light of day, I moved to Indonesia (August 2008) and the KITLV Press was taken over by Brill (Leiden) as the part of the division of the venerable mother institute, the Koninklijk Instituut voor Taal-, Land- en Volkenkunde (Royal Institute for Southeast Asian and Caribbean Studies), between the Royal Dutch Academy of Sciences (KNAW) and the University of Leiden.

My move to Indonesia brought new opportunities and challenges. Like the *Tale of Two Cities*, my sojourn in Jakarta proved to be the best of times and the worst of times. While my professional work with the Indonesian Ministry of Health languished, my life as an historian prospered. With the generous support of the representative of the Royal Institute/

KITLV in Indonesia, Dr Roger Tol, and the financial backing of international and local sponsors, most notably Hashim Djojohadikusumo and his Yayasan Arsari Djojohadikusumo (YAD), my English-language *Power of Prophecy* publication was translated into Indonesian by one of the country's senior journalist historians, Pak Parakitri T. Simbolon. In March 2012, it appeared in a handsome three-volume boxed set as *Kuasa Ramalan: Pangeran Diponegoro dan Akhir Tatanan Lama di Jawa, 1785–1855* under the imprint of Kepustakaan Populer Gramedia (KPG), a branch of Indonesia's leading Gramedia publishing house.

As with the original English publication, the first print run of 3,500 copies sold out quickly and a second edition appeared (April 2012), indicating that a shortened print version of the original biography would be well received. This would also make my work accessible to a wider readership by focusing on the life of the prince rather than the political and social history of pre-Java War Yogyakarta. I was approached by KPG's senior partner – Kompas-Gramedia Books – to prepare a single-volume biography in Indonesian, an offer I immediately accepted. My only condition was that a simultaneous English-language edition could be published by Oxford-based publisher Peter Lang who had already indicated an interest. In July 2012, I met with Peter Lang's Publishing Director, Lucy Melville, and submitted a formal book proposal which, after peer review, was immediately accepted. So a simultaneous publication in English and Indonesian has become a reality. Once again I am indebted to the Yayasan Arsari Djojohadikusumo for their constant and unstinting support.

At a time of unprecedented interest in the relationship between religion and politics both here in Indonesia and in the wider Muslim world, Diponegoro's life and times may be of some significance. An historical perspective on what Merle Ricklefs has termed the 'mystic synthesis' in the Javanese Islamic tradition (Ricklefs 2007:8, 2012:11–12) is much needed. Not least, it offers an opportunity to understand the cultural origins of the world view of a remarkable Javanese Sufi Muslim in the key transitional period between Java's eighteenth-century 'old order' and the high colonial era which began with the Dutch victory in the Java War.

The preparation of this book has necessitated numerous debts of gratitude most of which have been acknowledged in my *Power of Prophecy* (Carey 2008:xix–xxii). There are some others which I need to place on record here.

In particular, I would like to thank Lucy Melville, Mette Bundgaard and Alessandra Anzani at Peter Lang, and the 'three musketeers' at Kompas-Gramedia – Pak Patricius Cahanar, Pak Mulyawan Karim, and Pak 'Pri' Supriyanto – for their unstinting help and encouragement throughout the preparation of this book. They are, however, in no way responsible for the many faults which still remain. Such a radical shortening of an original magnum opus is no easy task.

My hope is that this short biography will inspire a younger generation of Indonesians with an appreciation of their own remarkable history and encourage some to contemplate a career as professional historians. A recent estimation that those residing outside Indonesia (both non-resident Indonesians and foreigners) account for ninety percent of all scholarly articles published on Indonesia overseas may serve as a wake-up here. If true, this makes Indonesia one of the countries least effective in explaining itself to the outside world (Reid 2011). Such a situation cannot bode well for the Republic. Even if the McKinsey Global Institute's recent (September 2012) economic forecast that Indonesia will move from sixteenth to seventh largest economy in the world by 2030 (MGI 2012) proves correct, it will be a ship without a compass.

In this context, the words of Indonesia's founding president, Sukarno (1901–70; in office, 1945–67), 'Do not ever forget your history' (*Jangan sekali-kali lupa dengan sejarah*), ring truer than ever. Without a love and appreciation of their own history, Indonesia will be a rootless nation, its citizens condemned to live forever on the margins of a globalizing world without a true sense of who they are or where they are going. It is the younger generation's task to see that this does not happen. And it is for the older generation, now in leadership positions, to provide the resources to ensure that history has an honoured place in the life of the nation. In the present era of reform and national renewal, a truly civilized Indonesia demands no less.

Jakarta
1 January 2014

Bibliography

Carey, Peter (1981). *Babad Dipanagara; An Account of the Outbreak of the Java War (1825–30). The Surakarta Court version of the Babad Dipanagara with translations into English and Indonesian Malay.* Kuala Lumpur: Art Printers.

Carey, Peter (2007). *The Power of Prophecy; Prince Dipanagara and the End of an Old Order in Java, 1785–1855.* Leiden: KITLV Press [second revised edition 2008].

Carey, Peter (2012). *Kuasa Ramalan; Pangeran Diponegoro dan Akhir Tatanan Lama di Jawa, 1785–1855.* Jakarta: KPG.

Djamhari, Saleh As'ad (2003). *Strategi Menjinakkan Diponegoro; Stelsel Benteng 1827–1830.* Jakarta: Yayasan Komunitas Bambu.

Louw, P.J.F. and E.S. de Klerck (1894–1909). *De Java-Oorlog van 1825–30.* 6 volumes. The Hague: Nijhoff and Batavia: Landsdrukkerij.

MGI [McKinsey Global Institute] (2012). *The Archipelago Economy: Unleashing Indonesia's Potential.* Downloaded 18 December 2012 at: www.mckinsey.com/.../McKinsey/.../The%20archipelago%20economy/MGI_Unleashing_Indonesia_potential_Executive_Summary.ashx.

Reid, Tony (2011). 'Indonesia dan Dunia sesudah 66 Tahun (Indonesia and the World after 66 Years)'. *Tempo* (Indonesian edition), 14–20 November.

Ricklefs, M.C. (2007). *Polarising Javanese Society; Islamic and other Visions (c. 1893–1930).* Singapore: National University of Singapore Press.

Ricklefs, M.C. (2012). *Islamisation and its Opponents in Java; A Political, Social, Cultural and Religious history, c. 1930 to the present.* Singapore: National University of Singapore Press.

Rusche, Albert (ed.) (1908–9). *Babad Diponagoro; Serat Babad Dipanagaran karanganipun suwargi Kangjeng Pangeran Arya Dipanagara piyambak; Nyariosaken wiwit remenipun dhateng agami Islam tuwin dadosing prang ageng ngantos dumuginipun kakendhangaken dhateng Menadho.* 2 volumes. Soerakarta: Rusche.

Sagimun, M.D. (1965). *Pahlawan Dipanegara Berjuang; (Bara api Kemerdekaan nan tak Kundjung Padam).* Djakarta: Gunung Agung.

Soekanto, R. (1951a). *Sentot alias Alibasah Abdulmustopo Prawirodirdjo Senopati Diponegoro (Seorang Terkemuka dalam abad ke-19 dari Sedjarah Nasional Indonesia).* Djakarta: Poesaka Aseli.

Soekanto, R. (1951b). *Dua Raden Saleh, Dua Nasionalis dalam Abad ke-19; Suatu Halaman dari Sedjarah Nasional Indonesia.* Djakarta: Poesaka Aseli.

Soekanto, R. (1952). *Sekitar Jogjakarta 1755–1825 (Perjanjian Gianti-Perang Dipanagara).* Djakarta, Amsterdam: Mahabarata.

Tanojo, R. (1966). *Sedjarah Pangeran Diponegoro darah Madura: Awewaton Pèngetan Kuna*. Surabaya: Trimurti.

Yamin, Muhammad (1950). *Sedjarah Peperangan Dipanegara; Pahlawan Kemerdekaan Indonesia*. Djakarta: Yayasan Pembangunan.

Preface

The Java War as a Watershed

The Java War (1825–30) was a watershed in the history of Java and of all Indonesia.[1] For the first time a European colonial government faced a social rebellion covering a large part of the island. Most of central and east Java, and many of the north coast areas were affected. Two million Javanese, one third of the total population, were exposed to the ravages of war, one fourth of the cultivated area of Java sustained damage and about 200,000 Javanese died (Carey 1976:52 note 1).

In securing their pyrrhic victory over the Javanese, the Dutch also suffered: as well as 7,000 Indonesian auxiliaries, 8,000 of their own troops perished and the war cost their exchequer an estimated 25 million guilders (equivalent to USD2.2 billion in today) (De Graaf 1949:399). The end of the conflict left the Dutch in undisputed control of the island and a new phase of colonial rule began with the inception of Governor-General Johannes van den Bosch's 'Cultivation System' (1830–70). This proved immensely profitable for Holland netting it 832 million guilders (equivalent to USD75 billion today) between 1831 and 1877 (Ricklefs 1993:123).

The war thus marked the end of a process which had been maturing since the period of Marshal Herman Willem Daendels (1808-1811). This involved the change from the era of the Dutch East Indies Company (Vereenigde Oost-Indische Compagnie, 1602–1799; henceforth: VOC), when contacts between Batavia and the south-central Javanese kingdoms had had the nature of ambassadorial links between sovereign states, to the 'high colonial' period when the principalities occupied a clearly subordinate position to the European power.

---

1 For the purpose of this volume, the term 'Indonesia' will be used to refer to the Netherlands Indies, and 'Indonesian' to the inhabitants of the archipelago. The colonial capital will, however, be referred to as 'Batavia' throughout rather than 'Jakarta'.

A Time of Transition

This transition should be borne in mind by those who approach the early chapters of this book expecting the Dutch to loom large as the colonial masters of Java. In the late eighteenth century, the island was not a Dutch version of the British Raj. A declining power in Europe, Holland seemed to be on its way out in Java while the south-central Javanese rulers enjoyed de facto sovereignty. The fact that during the international crises of the late eighteenth century, when Java was threatened by French or British invasion, for example in October 1800, the VOC authorities in Batavia turned to the south-central Javanese rulers to help them to defend their colonial capital against foreign attack, indicated the scale of the courts' military and political independence.

The most significant of these international crises – the Fourth Anglo-Dutch War of 1780–3 – was the turning point. Faced with mounting debts, which peaked at 134 million guilders (equivalent to USD12 billion today), the VOC was declared bankrupt and its assets taken over by the Dutch state on 1 January 1800 (Boxer 1979:101–2).

Four years earlier, all Dutch possessions in the East had been taken out of the hands of the Directors of the VOC and vested in a new Committee for the Affairs of East Indies Trade and Colonies. This followed the occupation of Holland by French forces in December 1794–January 1795 when the Republic had become a satellite of the *grande nation*. This had implications for Java. As one of Holland's overseas possessions, the island was included in the policy announced by the exiled Dutch *Stadhouder* (head of state). This stated that the Republic's colonies should be handed over to the British to prevent them falling into the hands of the French. So began a twenty-year period in which Indonesia was drawn into the global conflict between Britain and France.

Fought out during the Revolutionary (1792–9) and Napoleonic Wars (1799–1802, 1803–13, 1815) in Europe, the archipelago became a battle ground on land and sea. Between 1795 and 1797, British naval forces operating from Madras and Pulau Pinang captured most of the Dutch possessions outside Java. Although returned to Holland under the terms of the Peace of

Preface

Amiens (1802), all were recaptured by the British in the seven years which followed the renewal of hostilities in Europe (May 1803).

The dire situation of the Dutch was well understood by the south-central Javanese rulers. So much so that one senior former VOC official, Nicolaus Engelhard (1761–1831), suggested after Daendels' arrival in January 1808 that the marshal's government should employ some holy men and ascetics to make favourable prophecies on behalf of the Dutch to disguise their vulnerability. In October of the same year, an unusual event at one of the regular tiger and buffalo fights staged in honour of a visiting high Dutch dignitary at the Yogyakarta court may have been interpreted as an indication that Holland would soon be placed *hors de combat* in terms of their rule in Java (Chapter IV).

The tragedy for the Javanese was that just as all the signs seemed to be pointing in the direction of a Dutch collapse, half a world away in Europe events were taking place which would change the Javanese 'old order' for ever. The twin political and industrial revolutions then tearing the *ancien régime*s of eighteenth-century Europe apart would hit Java with the force of an Asian tsunami. In the space of just four years (1808–12), the relationship between the European government[2] and the south-central Javanese rulers was transformed.

Yogya bore the brunt of these changes. In quick succession, the re-energised Franco-Dutch regime of Marshal Daendels (1808–11) and the British-Indian administration of Thomas Stamford Raffles (1811–16), forced open Yogya's eastern outlying or *mancanagara* territories (Chapter V), plundered its court and exiled its reigning monarch (Chapter VI). Following the imposition of new treaties in August 1812 (Chapter VII), the relationship between Batavia and the princely states was transformed.

The returned Dutch administration of Governor-General G.A.G.Ph. van der Capellen (in office, 1816–26) compounded this situation. Its

---

2   Since there were so many changes of colonial regime involving different European states and their nationals (Dutch, British, French, Belgians) in the period covered in this book, it has been decided for the purposes of succinctness to refer to the colonial power in Batavia as the 'European government' throughout.

desperate need for money and its profound ignorance regarding the effects of its policies on ordinary Javanese opened a high road to war in south-central Java (Chapter VIII). Adverse environmental and health conditions, in particular the May 1821 cholera epidemic and soaring rice prices, provided the triggers for the popular uprisings of July–August 1825 which accompanied Diponegoro's rebellion (20 July 1825) and the start of the Java War (Chapter IX).

Long-term Implications

For the Javanese, this five-year conflict had far-reaching implications. For perhaps the first time in their modern history a rebellion had broken out at one of the south-central Javanese *kraton* which had at its heart social and economic grievances rather than the dynastic ambitions of the court elite. The emergence of a strong charismatic leader in the person of Prince Diponegoro (1785–1855), who took the title of the Javanese Messiah or *Ratu Adil* ('Just King'), served to unite many disparate social elements under the banner of Javanese Islam.

Widespread millenarian expectations caught the imagination of the peasantry, the *santri* (students of Islam) and the court elite alike, catalysing social and economic grievances which had accumulated since the beginning of the nineteenth century. The concept of holy war (*prang sabil*), imagery from the Javanese shadow-play (*wayang*), and Javanese nativist sentiments, made up of an intense longing for the restoration of an idealized traditional order, forged a common identity amongst the prince's followers. Described as a struggle for the restoration of 'the high state of the Islamic religion in Java' (Carey 1974:285), Diponegoro aimed at restoring the moral fabric of society not just the teachings of The Prophet. In this fashion, nobles, dismissed provincial officials, religious teachers, professional bandits, porters, day labourers, tax-paying farmers (*sikep*) and artisans were brought together briefly in a common cause (Chapter X).

The Java War was thus of immense significance for Indonesia's future. The subtle interplay of economic grievances and millenarian hopes created a

Preface

movement of unique social breadth which anticipated the nationalist movement of the early twentieth century (Carey 1976:52–3). Proto-nationalist sentiments were even noted at this time by senior Dutch officials. One such was the post-war Yogya Resident, Frans Gerhardus Valck (1799–1842; in office, 1831–8, 1838–41), who had served in a number of residency postings in south-central Java between 1820 and 1841 (Christiaans 1992–93:129–30). A year before his retirement he reflected:

> [My] nearly twenty years of administrative service in various Residencies has taught me that the spirit of the ordinary Javanese is against us [...] not because we Netherlanders treat him badly, but because he is imbued with a feeling of nationality [...]. Despite all the benefits which he gets from us, he cannot suppress the wish to be governed by his own rulers and chiefs – even though they would administer him worse [than we would] [...]. He continues to see in us foreign tyrants, who in morals, customs, religion and clothing etc differ so much from his own [...]. The sight of every European reminds him of his humiliating situation [and] he cannot refrain from giving him looks of hatred or contempt whenever he feels he can get away with it without incurring punishment (Carey 2008: xiv)

This strand of Javanese 'nationalism' – if such it can be called – was born of the cultural dislocation wrought by the new European imperialism. It is one of the central themes of this book. Diponegoro was key here. A major transitional figure, he lived through the transition from the old order of late eighteenth century Java to the high colonial era of the mid-nineteenth century. In his seventy-year lifetime, he felt the full force of the twin political and industrial revolutions of late eighteenth-century Europe which ripped his south-central Javanese world apart.

Diponegoro's Significance

A traditional figure steeped in the values of pre-modern Java, Diponegoro also pointed to the future. One thinks here of his use of Javanese Islam, particularly its millenarian traditions, as a way of forging a new identity for Javanese Muslims in an era when the old Javanese order was crumbling. Diponegoro lived in a world increasingly divided between those who were prepared to accommodate themselves to the new European regime and those who saw the Islamic moral order (*agami Islam*) as the lodestar in a society which had lost its traditional moorings.

The Java War gave impetus to a process which is still working itself out in modern Indonesia: namely, the integration of Islamic values into contemporary Indonesian identity. Diponegoro's world view also came to encompass a distinctly contemporary concern with how Javanese Muslims should live in an age of Western imperial domination. For Diponegoro, unlike most present-day Indonesian Muslims, the answer seemed to lie in the waging of holy war and the development of a clear distinction between the *wong Islam* ('people of Islam'; Muslim believers), the European *kapir laknatullah* (heretics accursed by Allah), and the Javanese *kapir murtad* (apostates; Javanese who had allied themselves with the Dutch). But there was also a deep concern on the prince's part for the preservation of specifically Javanese values as expressed in language, dress and cultural codes. This can be seen most clearly in his treatment of Dutch prisoners during the Java War: they were expected to adopt Javanese dress and speak to their captors not in the reviled language of the new colonial state – 'service Malay' (Hoffman 1979:65–92) – but in the polished cadences of High Javanese (*kromo*), the medium of the court elite.

Despite his adoption of Ottoman dress and titles such as 'Ali Basah' ('The High Pasha') for his top military commanders (Chapter III, Chapter X), Diponegoro was no Islamic reformer. A traditional Javanese Muslim, the prince saw no inherent conflict between the spirit world of Java and his membership of the international *ummat* (community of Muslim believers) with its centres in the Hejaz (present-day Saudi Arabia) and Ottoman Turkey.

In the end, Diponegoro did not prevail in achieving his goal of restoring the high state of the Islamic religion in Java. Indeed, the dignity and integrity which he fought for on behalf of the Javanese *ummat* would only be achieved in outward form ninety years after his death with the declaration of political independence from the Dutch on 17 August 1945. Meanwhile, his wider moral vision of securing an honoured place for Islam in the life of the nation remains a work in progress. It is also hostage to the global conflict between what some in the Islamic community see as the 'materialistic' values of the West and what many others perceive to be the fissiparous loyalties of the worldwide Muslim *ummat*. The relationship between Islam and the state in Indonesia remains a deeply contested one today more than ever.

Diponegoro in Context

This book seeks to set the prince's life in the context of his age. The key theme of the current biography is one of transition. This provides the frame in which Diponegoro's life is to be understood. He pointed backwards towards the old Javanese order of his childhood and forwards towards the new colonial order of the post-Java War era. But this book is more than just a study of transitions. It also looks at Diponegoro's legacy as a human being. In doing so, it seeks to answer the following questions: as an Indonesian national hero (*pahlawan nasional*), Diponegoro's place in the history of his country is secure, but what of the prince's deeper values? What can we learn from such a life? What, in brief, is his wider significance?

Leave aside for a moment his noble birth, his *kraton* connections, his syncretic Muslim piety, Javanist beliefs and leadership in the Java War. What remains? What was the root of Diponegoro's genius? What makes him special?

The answer, this book suggests, lies in his sensibilities as a human being: namely, his very Javanese ability to recognise the complexity of the world yet remain utterly simple. His upbringing under the stern direction of his great-grandmother in the village environment of Tegalrejo counted for much here. There was about Diponegoro much which reflected the earthy values of village Java: one thinks here of his physical strength, his insistence on travelling on foot (and not just on pilgrimage), and his annual participation in the rice harvest on his estate lands to the south of Yogya. His canniness with money, which impressed even the penny-pinching Dutch, and the care which he took with the administration of his lands (unusual in the world of the south-central Javanese *kraton* at that time) were also remarkable. So too was his pithiness of expression, his hatred of pomposity and show, his closeness with nature and his love of animals.

There was also about Diponegoro a disarming honesty: witness his acknowledgement in his mystical vision of the Just King (*Ratu Adil*) in 1824 that he was unable to fight because he could not 'bear to see death', or, on a completely different plane, his admission in his autobiography of his abiding weakness for women whose attractions he described with a connoisseur's eye. Reading his autobiographical chronicle, it is almost as though the prince is sitting directly in front of the reader so vivid and immediate is his style of expression. It was this same vividness which so struck his German officer escort, Justus Heinrich Knoerle (1796–1833), during his conversations with the prince during the prince's journey into exile (3 May – 12 June 1830) (Knoerle 1835:172).

Such expressiveness underscores an underlying creativity, an ability to move on and create new worlds. In the context of the Islamic community, this might be thought of as a form of '*hijrah*' (purposeful journey/flight). One can cite here Diponegoro's *hijrah* from Tegalrejo to Selarong on the night of 20–21 July 1825 – curtain-raiser to the Java War – the flames of his burning residence lighting up the late afternoon sky as he 'danced' in the midst of his lance-bearing bodyguard (Chapter IX). One thinks too of the other great *hijrah* in the prince's life: his arrest by General de Kock at Magelang on 28 March 1830 which marked the beginning of his quarter century as a prisoner and exile (Chapter XI, Chapter XII), his position as 'Just King' (*Ratu Adil*) exchanged for 'two miserable, hot rooms' in Fort Rotterdam (Makassar).

This is what the leading Indonesian dancer, choreographer and creator of the 'Opera Diponegoro', Professor Sardono W. Kusumo, has called the 'flight from the physical to the intellectual'. As the prince moved from the physical realm of the Java War to the intellectual sphere of authorship, meditation and art, his creativity blossomed. This was the time when his 1,000 page autobiography was written and when he developed his calligraphic skills drawing of *daérah* (mystical diagrams) and copying the *Qur'ān*.

Those who observed these transitions spoke of Diponegoro's 'unchanging indifference, resignation or submission' (Louw and De Klerck 1894–1909, V:746), emotions which the prince himself described in more poetic terms as 'gold carried along by water' (*lir mas kintaring toyo*) (Babad Dipanegara, IV:179).

Preface

Even in loss there was humour and an ability to stand back: Diponegoro's observation to Knoerle that life was indeed a curious business when at the turn of the wheel of fate one could lose everything and be reduced to the status of a fugitive is significant here. Before the Java War, he recalled, he had had sixty grooms just to look after his horses. As a fugitive escaping the Dutch flying columns he was reduced to the support of just two *panakawan*, his inseparable clown-retainers (Carey 2008:122 note 83). Here was a man who could lose a whole world and yet retain his humanity.

Indeed, the more restrictive the outer physical space which the prince inhabited, the more spacious his inner realm became. The sheer scale of his literary outpouring in Manado and Makassar bears witness to this. There are similarities here to others such as Mahatma Gandhi (1869–1948), whose physical world was also often contracted down to a prison cell only to find the blossoming of a new inner creativity transforming his jail into an ashram (place of spiritual retreat). The spiritual depth born of a life of meditation clearly counted for much here. In Diponegoro's case, the fruits of his asceticism (*tapa*) could be seen in his appreciation of the arts and of nature, as well as his skill in reading character and personal relationships from the study of faces (*ilmu firasat*).

Diponegoro's wisdom was that of the simple man, cognisant of complexity yet utterly direct. In an age of exploitative relationships – brutal and chaotic – Diponegoro's wisdom stood out clear and unvarnished. Despite living through a 'time of madness' (*zaman edan*), he kept his integrity. Unlike his principle religious adviser, Kyai Mojo (?1792–1849), he did not become a xenophobe. Unlike his youthful army commander, Ali Basah Sentot (?1808–55), he cut no deals with the Dutch. As the present ruler of Yogyakarta, Sultan Hamengkubuwono X (reigned, 1988 to present), remarked in his speech to mark the gala performance of Sardono's 'Opera Diponegoro' in Yogyakarta for the centennial of Boedi Oetomo (Noble Endeavour), on 20 May 2008, there is no 'kraton' version of Diponegoro's history different from the national one. In the Sultan's view, the prince was no traitor to his child sovereign – Sultan Hamengkubuwono V (reigned 1822–6/1828–55) – nor to the Yogya court. His decision to go into rebellion in July 1825 was dictated by the circumstances of the time. He had no other choice. In doing so, he was true to what the Japanese samurai tradition terms 'the nobility of failure': namely, the ability to remain faithful to an ideal even though he knew that he would go down to defeat.

Organisation and Lay-out of this Book

This book is divided into four parts. The first part contains the first three chapters (I–III) which deal with Diponegoro's childhood and upbringing at his great-grandmother's estate at Tegalrejo to the northwest of Yogyakarta. His early visionary experiences during his 1805 pilgrimage to the south coast are also described here.

The second part comprises another three chapters describing Diponegoro's experience of the turbulent political events at the Yogya court which occurred between the arrival of Marshal Daendels in January 1808 (Chapter IV) and the British attack on Yogyakarta in June 1812 (Chapter VI), a period which also witnessed the short-lived revolt of Diponegoro's kinsman, the *bupati wedana* (chief administrator) of the Yogya eastern outlying provinces (*mancanagara*), Raden Ronggo Prawirodirjo III (?1779–1810; in office, 1796–1810) (Chapter V).

Following the fall of Yogyakarta on 20 June 1812, a new era dawned in relations between the colonial government and the south-central Javanese principalities. The three chapters (Chapter VII–IX) in the third part focus on Diponegoro's reactions to these changed circumstances. After the prince's all too brief 'golden age' as political adviser to his father, the third sultan, which ended with the sultan's death on 3 November 1814 (Chapter VII), Diponegoro's relations with the Yogya court deteriorated. Arguments over issues of land rent to foreign estate owners and their indemnification after the May 1823 abolition caused major frictions which pitted the prince against other senior members of the sultan's family (Chapter VIII).

The same period witnessed a steep decline in the welfare of the south-central Javanese peasantry as the post–1816 returned Dutch administration attempted to close the circle between the *rechtstaat* (rule of law) ideals of

Preface

the new Netherlands-Indies government and its need for ever larger fiscal returns. The bitterness and humiliation of these years set the fuse and opened a high road for war in south-central Java. Just how the powder-keg ignited and how Diponegoro received the mandate of his Java War leadership through a series of visions and mystical experiences which preceded the outbreak of war is the subject of Chapter IX.

The final part contains the three chapters (X–XII) which consider the war itself (Chapter X), the circumstances of Diponegoro's capture in Magelang (28 March 1830) and his journey to Batavia (28 March–5 April 1830) (Chapter XI), and his last 25 years of exile in the Celebes (Sulawesi), first in Manado (1830–33) and then Makassar (1833–55) (Chapter XII). A brief conclusion, which weighs the meaning of the prince's life, closes the book.

Those familiar with my *Power of Prophecy* will see many parallels in these pages. But the focus is now more on the figure of Diponegoro than the times through which he lived. Almost none of the 2,184 notes in the original work have been retained and all the appendices have gone. For those wishing to consult these in my *Power of Prophecy* online, there is an open access version at www.kitlv.nl/pdf_documents/asia-prophecy.pdf.

It is my hope that this short biography will serve a double purpose: namely, increase public awareness of the prince's life and times, and provide a textbook for use in senior high schools and universities here in Indonesia. That these are both sorely needed has recently been underscored by a press report on the welcome performance staged by staff and students at the Diponegoro State University in Semarang to honour the new student intake on 2 October 2012. Only nine per cent of the new students in the public health faculty apparently knew who the prince was and even fewer had any notion about the Java War (*Suara Merdeka*, 2012).

If this is indeed the case then a textbook biography would seem to be more needed than ever. The general ignorance which characterizes most Indonesian perceptions of their pre-independence history is both sobering and challenging. But, as Indonesia's first president, Ir Sukarno (1901–70; in office, 1945–67), would have put it – we must make the world anew. Nowhere is this renewal more necessary than in the field of history.

Bibliography

Babad Dipanegara (2010). *Babad Dipanegara*, 4 vols, ed. Nindya Noegraha. Jakarta: Perpustakaan Nasional Republik Indonesia.

Boxer, C.T. (1979). *Jan Compagnie in War and Peace 1602–1799; A Short History of the Dutch East-India Company*. Hong Kong: Heinemann.

Carey, Peter (1976). 'The Origins of the Java War (1825–30)', *English Historical Review*, 91:52–78.

Christiaans, P.A. (1992–3). 'De Belangrijkste Ambtenaren te Batavia anno 1837, alsmede een aantal Geïnteresseerde Officieren', *De Indische Navorscher* 6:122–36.

Graaf, H.J. de (1949). *Geschiedenis van Indonesië*. The Hague: Nijhoff, Bandung: Van Hoeve.

Hoffman, J. (1979). 'A Foreign Investment; Indies Malay to 1901', *Indonesia* 27:65–92.

Hogendorp, H. Graaf van (1913). *Willem van Hogendorp in Nederlandsch-Indië 1825–1830*. The Hague: Nijhoff.

Knoerle (1835). 'Extract uit de Gehoudene Aanteekeningen gedurende mijne Reis naar Menado', *De Oosterling* 2:135–80.

Prins, Bart de (2002). *Voor Keizer en Koning; Leonard du Bus de Gisignies 1780–1849 Commissaris-Generaal van Nederlands-Indië*. Amersfoort: Balans.

Ricklefs, M.C. (1993). *A History of Modern Indonesia since c.1300*. Basingstoke: Macmillan.

Suara Merdeka (2012). 'Gelar Kirab Budaya Undip Visualisasikan Perjuangan Diponegoro (Diponegoro University Cultural Parade Performance Depicts Diponegoro's Struggle), *Suara Merdeka* (2 October 2012).

Maps of Eastern and Central Java

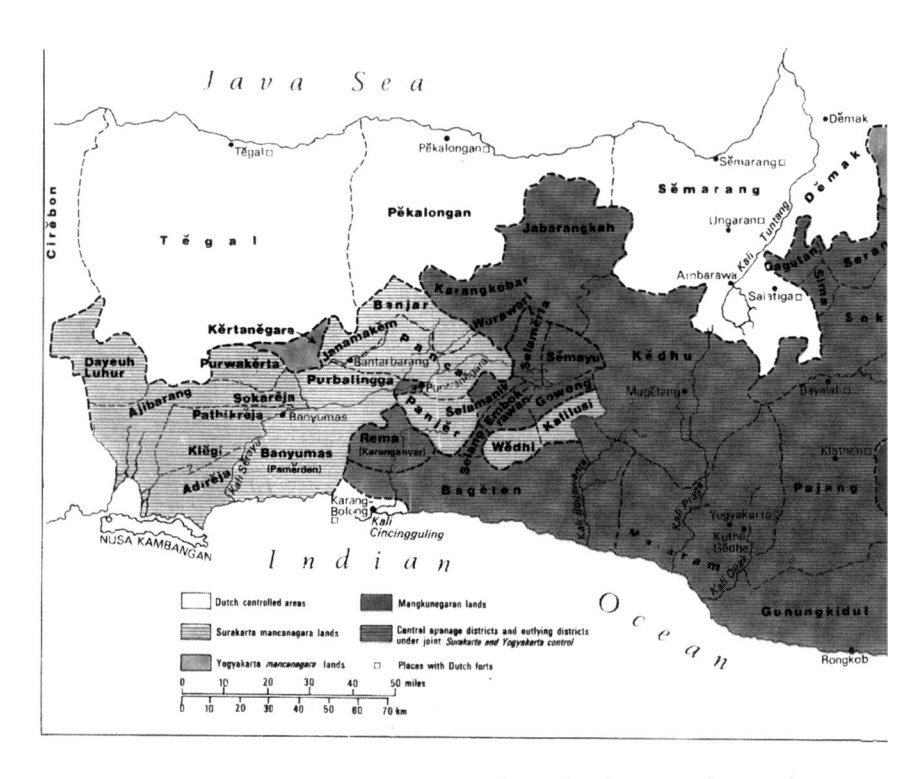

Map 1. Map of central and east Java showing the pre-1811

Maps of Eastern and Central Java

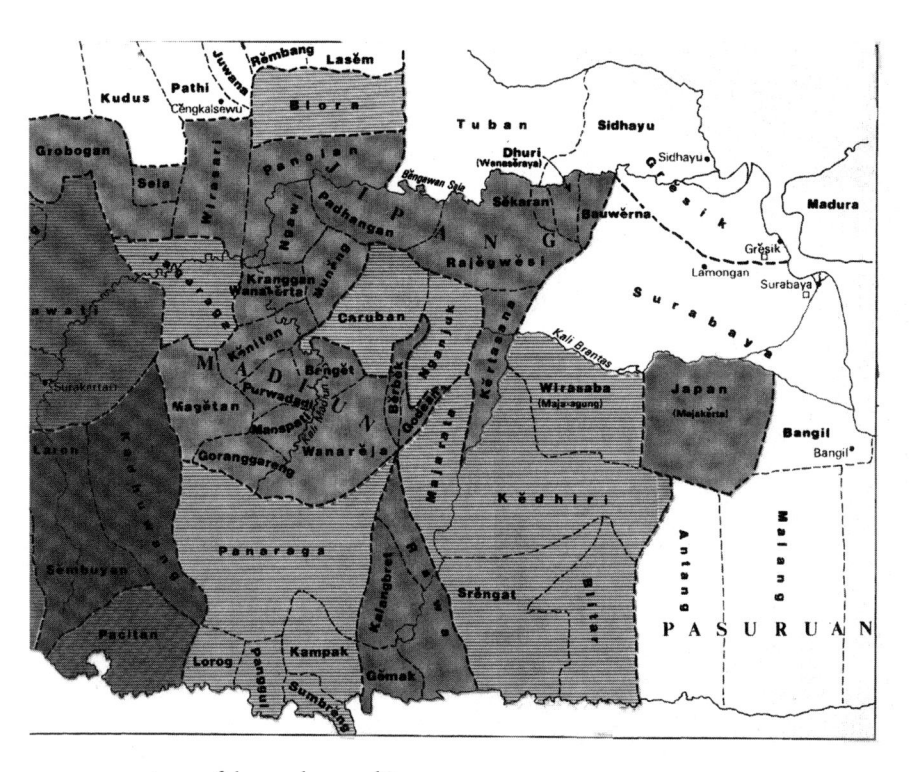

apanage provinces of the south central Javanese courts.

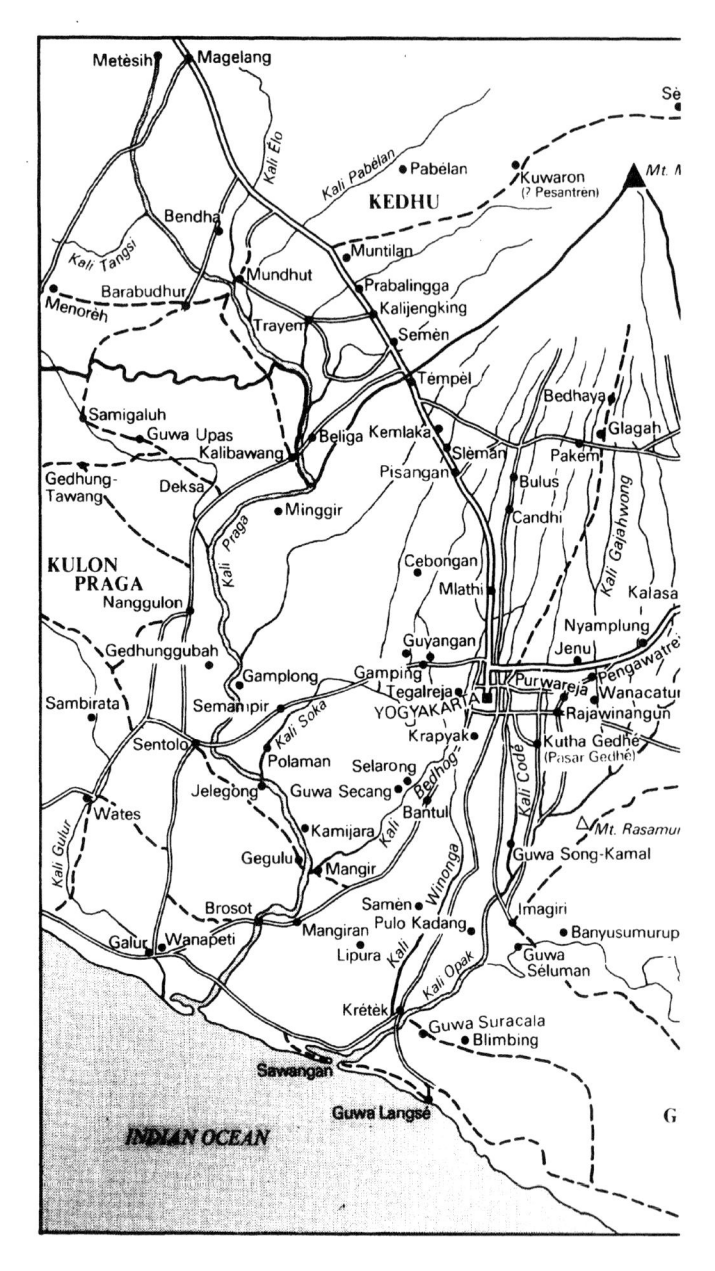

Map 2. Map of the Yogyakarta area

Maps of Eastern and Central Java   xlix

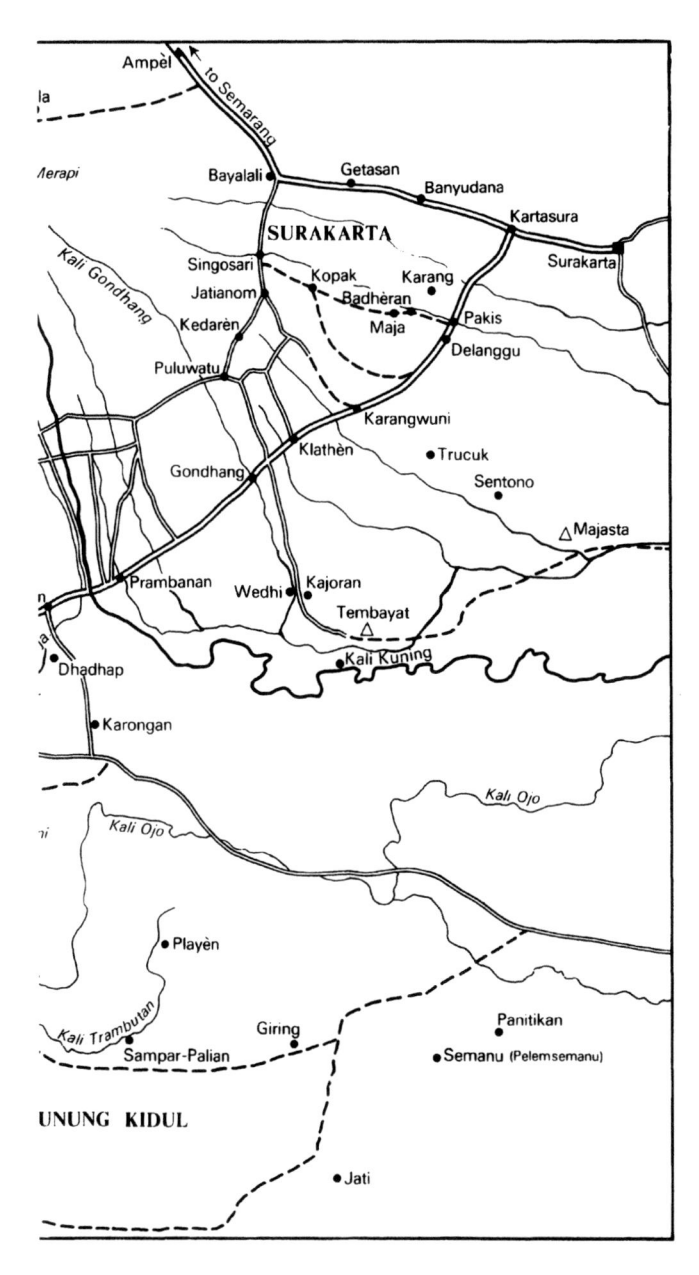

in the early nineteenth century.

PART I

Youth and Upbringing, 1785–1808

CHAPTER I

Diponegoro's Youth and Upbringing, 1785–1803

A Prophetic Birth

Diponegoro – who was given the childhood name of Bendoro Raden Mas Mustahar – was born in the Yogyakarta *kraton* on 11 November 1785 just before sunrise at the time of the fasting month pre-dawn meal (*saur*) (Babad Dipanegara, II:45). In Javanese chronology, the date of the future Java War leader's birth was especially auspicious. It fell in the Javanese month of *Sura*, the first month of the Javanese year when traditionally new kingdoms are founded and new historical cycles begin (Carey 1981:261 note 108). The day was also significant in the modern-day Javanese almanac because the combination of the day of the week and that of the five-day Javanese market week, *Jumungah Wagé* (Friday Wagé), is said to indicate a person of great fluency and power of speech, generosity of heart, and the character of a sage, but one who would also encounter great hindrances in his life because of his frank and argumentative manner (Tanojo 1966:31). Interestingly, Indonesia's first president, Sukarno (1901–70), was also a child of the dawn and the new century and saw himself as being endowed with a special destiny because of it (Adams 1965:17).

Diponegoro's father was the eldest son of the second sultan of Yogya, Hamengkubuwono II (reigned 1792–1810, 1811–12, 1826–28), by his official wife, Ratu Kedaton (circa 1750–1820), a lady of Madurese royal ancestry who was distinguished at court for her Islamic religious piety (Carey 1980:173–4, 1992:187, 382, 401 note 12). His father was a little over sixteen at the time of Diponegoro's birth, and was known as a charming young man beloved by many for his mild character and quiet sense of humour.

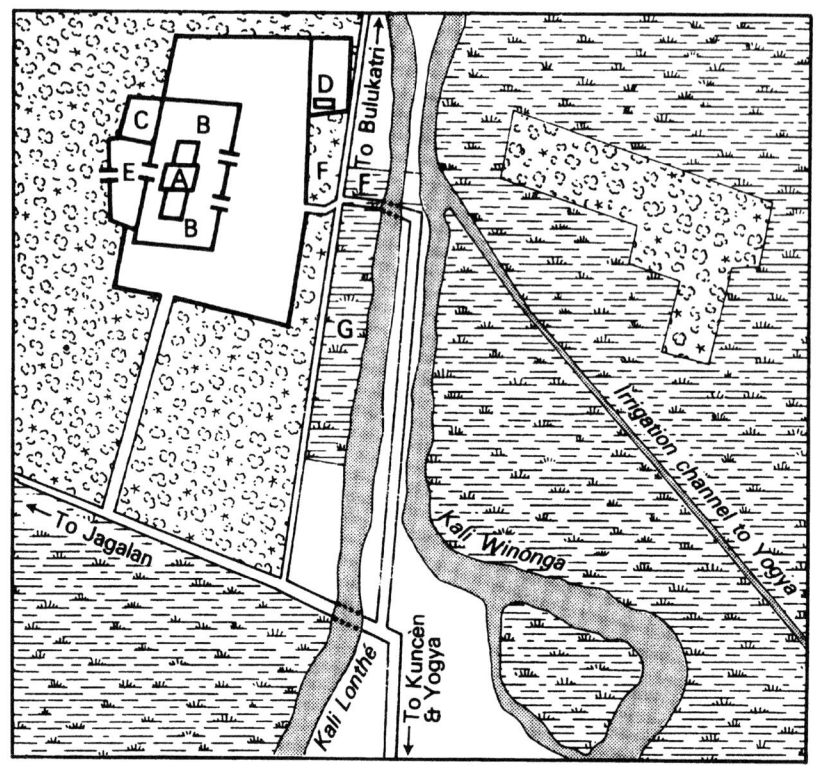

A Main *pendhapa* at Tegalreja
B Outhouse surrounding the main building
C Mosque (incomplete at the time of the outbreak of the Java War)
D Dipanagara's retreat at Sélareja and local family graves
E Gateway in the western wall of the Tegalreja estate used by Dipanagara and Mangkubumi to escape on 20th July 1825
F Village of Tompéyan (part of the Tegalreja estate) and adjacent ricefields (*sawah*)
G Ricefields known as Sawah Muntru owned by the Tegalreja estate

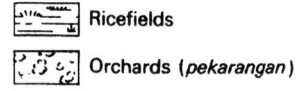

Ricefields
Orchards (*pekarangan*)
Fords

Map 3. Plan of the Tegalrejo estate and its surroundings, circa 1830.

As a keen amateur historian and a budding author in his own right, he was often called by his grandfather Sultan Mangkubumi (1717–92; reigned 1749–1792), the founder of the Yogyakarta sultanate, to read to him from old Javanese tales and histories.

It is not known how much influence Diponegoro's father had on the young prince because at the age of seven he was taken away from the *kraton* women's quarters to live with his great-grandmother at her estate of Tegalrejo, three kilometres to the northwest. But the two became close during the 1811–12 crisis, precipitated by the confrontation between the Yogya court and the colonial government, and during his father's own short reign (1812–14).

It is possible that through his father – the favourite grandchild of the ageing first sultan – Diponegoro was brought to the notice of the founder of the Yogya kingdom when he was still a baby in arms. In his autobiography, Diponegoro described how he was presented to Sultan Mangkubumi by his teenage mother. The ageing ruler had apparently foretold that he would cause the Dutch greater destruction than he had done during the Giyanti War (1746–55), but that only the Almighty knew the outcome (Babad Dipanegara, II:45). This anecdote provides an insight into the importance which Diponegoro attached to the charismatic figure of the first sultan, who would continue to inspire both himself and his court supporters during the Java War (1825–30).

The first sultan's prophecy can also be linked to another prediction in Diponegoro's autobiography ascribed to the great seventeenth-century ruler of Mataram, Sultan Agung (reigned 1613–46). This had foretold that after the death of Agung in February 1646, the Dutch would rule in Java for 300 years and that although one of the Mataram ruler's descendants would rise against them, he would be defeated (Carey 1974a:30, 2008:71). It seems almost certain that Diponegoro identified himself with this descendant, thus providing a prophetic context in which to understand his later failure against the Dutch. It would be reinforced by the enigmatic prophecy of the voice heard by Diponegoro as he slept at Parangkusumo during his pilgrimage to the south coast in circa 1805: 'You alone are the means, but that not for long, only to be counted amongst the ancestors' (Chapter III).

Female Relatives and Influences

Although Diponegoro's male forbears were of considerable significance for the young prince, his female relatives were even more important in shaping his character and outlook. This was rooted in deep religious convictions and extensive connections with the *santri* (pious Muslim) communities in south-central Java. Such connections were rather unique for a person of his birth. Both were to be critical to his style of leadership during the Java War, enhancing his personal charisma.

The fact that Diponegoro was mainly brought up in the company of strong females until the age of eighteen may also have contributed to the development of the feminine aspects of his character such as his sensitivity and intuition. These would later manifest in his gift for reading of character through the study of facial expression – what the Javanese call *ngelmu firasat* (the science of physiognomy) – and his supposed hatred of bloodshed (Chapter II).

Through his female relatives, Diponegoro could claim blood links with some of the most prominent *kyai* (country gentlemen, teachers of religion/spiritual disciplines) in Java, some of whom could trace their ancestry back to the legendary 'nine apostles of Islam' or *wali songo* of the fifteenth and sixteenth centuries. Others were renowned as religious leaders and scholars in their local communities.

Diponegoro's mother, Raden Ayu Mangkorowati (?1770–1852), an unofficial wife (*garwa ampeyan*) of the future third sultan, who gave birth to him at the age of fifteen, was descended from just such a figure: Kyai Ageng Prampelan, a revered contemporary of the first Mataram ruler, Panembahan Senopati (reigned 1575–1601). Another of her forbears was Sunan Ngampel Dento of Gresik, one of the first apostles of Islam (*wali*) in Java, who had founded an Islamic community in east Java before the fall of Majapahit (circa 1510s).

Although the evidence about his mother is somewhat fragmentary, she appears to have been born in the *pradikan* or tax-free village set aside for men of religion of Majasto close to the famous religious centre of Tembayat

Diponegoro's Youth and Upbringing, 1785–1803

in the Pajang area. Both these places had been settled by descendants and supporters of Panembahan Kajoran (?1620–79), a major opponent of the Mataram dynasty in the seventeenth century. It had remained a potential centre of opposition to the central Javanese courts right up to the time of Diponegoro's birth. The fact that the prince's father had chosen a wife from this troublesome region is a good illustration of the courts' policy of containing the threat to their authority from such religious communities by marriage alliances and tax-free land grants. These ties of family and courtly patronage were later to produce significant local support for Diponegoro during the Java War (Carey 2008:73).

Diponegoro made few references to his mother in his autobiography beyond mentioning that she was 'strong' (*kuwat*) and 'unusually beautiful' (*luwih bagus*). But he seems to have been devoted to her: between 1825 and her capture on 14 October 1829, they shared the vicissitudes of war together. As late as 1849, when the prince had been in exile for nearly twenty years first in Manado (1830–3) and then Makassar (1833–55), and his mother was nearly eighty, he received correspondence from her which caused him to hope that she might join him in exile. She declined saying that she was too old to make the sea voyage to Makassar (p.322). She apparently died of dropsy in Yogya on 7 October 1852 (Hageman 1856:412) only three years before her son passed away in Makassar (8 January 1855). Diponegoro was apparently her only child by the future third sultan (Mandoyokusumo 1977:29–33).

Another female relative who may well have helped to shape Diponegoro's outlook in his youth was his grandmother, Ratu Kedaton, a descendant of Panembahan Cakradiningrat II of Pamekasan (Madura) (reigned 1680–1707). In his autobiography, Diponegoro refers to her with respect. Her staunch attitude towards Islam, for which the Madurese are noted, may have impressed him. The *Ratu*, in the words of a Dutch Resident had 'a strong Madurese spirit which seemed to flag little in her old age'. Her husband, the second sultan, according to this same source, 'with his usual Javanese thought patterns', was completely unable to understand her (Carey 2008:74).

Unsurprisingly, she had a spectacularly volatile marital relationship with the Yogya ruler, who favoured his offspring from another queen. The fact that Diponegoro was himself one quarter Madurese through his descent from Ratu Kedaton may well have had an effect on his personality and contributed to his volatile temper and sudden rages.

Diponegoro's Guardian: Ratu Ageng Tegalrejo

Easily the most important female influence on the young prince was his great-grandmother, Ratu Ageng, sometimes referred to as Ratu Ageng Tegalrejo. A daughter of a revered *kyai* (religious teacher) from Majangjati near Sragen, Kyai Ageng Derpoyudo, Ratu Ageng could trace her ancestry on her mother's side to the first sultan of Bima (Sumbawa), Abdul Kahir I (1583–1640; reigned 1621–40) (Carey 2008:76). Her grandfather was the well respected Bimanese Islamic divine and eldest son of Sultan Abdul Kahir, Kyai Ageng Datuk Suleiman (alias Kyai Suleiman Bekel Jamus) (born 1601), who spent many years in Java studying at leading *pesantren* and married the daughter of a prominent east Javanese teacher, Kyai Wiroyudo (Amirulhaq 2012).

When Diponegoro was seven, she became his guardian. Her motives for adopting him are not discussed in the sources. Perhaps she recognised in him a certain spiritual depth which set him apart from other family members and made him fit for serious religious study. Perhaps the youth of Diponegoro's mother – still in her mid-teens when she gave birth to him – influenced the old lady's decision. But teenage brides and mothers were common in court circles at this time. Perhaps she just wanted to have the companionship of a young child as she set off to open out new lands, part of the late eighteenth-century expansion of ricefields (*sawah*) in the core regions.

Certainly the practice of 'adoption', or more accurately 'lending' children, was not unusual in Javanese society (Geertz 1961:36–41). There were many instances at this time of royal children being lent to older relatives to ensure they received an education (Carey 2008:75). Whatever the reason,

Diponegoro found himself as a pre-pubescent boy living with a remarkable woman who had a very critical view of developments at the Yogya court under the wayward and unskilful rule of her eldest son.

By all accounts, Ratu Ageng was exceedingly tough: she followed the first sultan throughout his campaigns against the Dutch during the Giyanti War (1746–1755), and gave birth to the future second sultan while her husband's forces were bivouacked on the slopes of Mount Sundoro in Kedu – hence the future second sultan's childhood name of Gusti Raden Mas Sundoro. After the foundation of Yogyakarta in 1755, she became commander of the elite female bodyguard or royal Amazon corps (*prajurit èstri*), the only military formation which impressed Daendels when he visited Yogya in July 1809 (Poensen 1905:144; Chapter V).

She was also renowned, according to one Yogya court chronicle, for her Islamic piety, taking pleasure in reading religious texts and insisting on the maintenance of traditional Javanese *adat* (customs) at court. Her unshakeable commitment to these traditional customs would pass in full measure to her great-grandson who was later described by the veteran VOC official, Nicolaus Engelhard (1761–1831), as 'in all matters a Javanese [who] followed Javanese customs' (Van der Kemp 1896:415).

By the time Diponegoro was taken away to live with her at Tegalrejo, she remained in her mid sixties an exceedingly energetic and strong-willed lady, quite redoubtable for a young boy of seven: 'in my childhood people used to make me afraid when giving an order', were the words ascribed to the prince in the Surakarta *Babad Diponegoro* (Carey 1981:78–9, 271 note 145). A similar reference can be found in Diponegoro's own *babad* (Babad Dipanegara, II:138). If Ratu Ageng did indeed occasionally act the stern stepmother, the portrait which Diponegoro draws of her in his autobiography is overwhelmingly affectionate. In two short verses, he evoked the simple life she led amongst the Tegalrejo farming communities and the numbers of *santri* visitors (Babad Dipanegara, II:45–6):

> XIV 50. [...]
> We describe the Ratu [Ageng]:
> [how] she delighted in farming
> and in her religious duties.
> She made herself anonymous
> in her profession of her love of God.

> 51. [...]
> Tegalrejo became extremely prosperous
> for many people came to visit.
> All sought food
> [while] the *santri* sought [religious] knowledge.
> There was much devotion and prayer,
> moreover, there were also farmers.

The atmosphere in which Diponegoro was brought up could not have been more different than that of the Yogya court under the second sultan. Tegalrejo's rural simplicity taught him from an early age to mix in an easy and unaffected manner with all levels of Javanese society. In the words of Willem van Hogendorp (1913:154):

> A special characteristic about Diponegoro in the view of the Javanese, who are always extremely exalted and distant in their dealings between superiors and inferiors, is that he consorts as easily with the common man as with the great ones. Because of this he has made himself much loved everywhere.

'In emulation of what the priests do', Diponegoro would later recall, 'I often went to Pasar [Kota] Gede, [Imo]giri, the south coast [Guwo Langse] and to Selarong [...] to help cut and plant *padi* [rice] which [helped] popularize the chiefs with the people' (Louw and De Klerck 1894–1909, V:744; Carey 1981:240 note 27).

Ratu Ageng's careful administrative methods and her willingness to engage in trade with the north coast and with her native Bima were emulated by him (Carey and Hoadley 2000:135–6; Carey 2008:78). We know from later Dutch accounts that Diponegoro was nearly unique amongst contemporary Yogya princes in that he derived substantial income from his lands without engaging in extortionate practices (Carey 1980:118–26). His personal wealth also helped him finance the early stages of the Java War. The Dutch Resident of Manado, where he was first exiled (1830–33), commented that he was careful with his money to the point of miserliness (Van der Kemp 1896:331; Carey 2008:78, 461) and the penultimate Governor of his Makassar years, Vreede Bik (in office 1849–52), would later describe him living 'in a state bordering on poverty' (Carey 2008:746).

The country gentry-origins of Diponegoro's female relatives were a distinct advantage when it came to his leadership role during the Java War. Not only did they relate him to influential village-based religious leaders, but they almost endowed him with a robust genes: marriages between scions of ruling dynasties and country gentry produced more enterprising offspring than the inbred alliances between families of high court nobility.

A Tegalrejo Childhood

The reasons why Ratu Ageng left the Yogya *kraton* so suddenly in the early part of the second sultan's reign are not clear. According to Diponegoro, she had become saddened and embittered by the conflicts with her children and the incessant intrigues of the court. As he put it in his chronicle (Babad Dipanegara, II:45–6):

>   XIV   49. We now tell of the Ratu Ageng
>   how she was often at odds
>   with her own sons.
>   She therefore broke away in anger and cleared new land:
>   the waste fields were opened up,
>   [and] then she settled there.
>   The distance from the town of Yogya
>
>   50. was a journey of one hour [on foot].
>   When it was ready,
>   it was called Tegalrejo ['Fields of Prosperity'].
>   [...]

It is likely that Ratu Ageng did not approve of the lifestyle of her son, the second sultan. In particular, she was grieved by his nonchalant attitude towards his religious duties: he rarely visited the great mosque, Mesjid Ageng, the official place of worship of the Yogya rulers, although he was apparently more diligent about dispatching court *santri* to undertake pilgrimages to Mecca and various holy sites in south-central Java and the north coast.

In his autobiography, Diponegoro would later reflect on the religious climate in Yogya in his youth and the way in which many of its inhabitants ignored the precepts of Islam. He was especially critical of the second sultan's three sons-in-law – Raden Tumenggung Sumodiningrat (?1760–1812), Danurejo II (?1772–1811) and Raden Ronggo Prawirodirjo III (?1779–1810), all of whom would meet violent ends. In his *babad*, he described these three as 'incorrigible sinners' (Babad Dipanegara, II:46):

> XIV 56. The three officials were all young;
> the desires of the sultan
> were greater than those of his father
> as also were [the desires] of these three officials,
> who all sinned
> against religion.
> The *pengulu* (head of the religious establishment) and
> all the people in Yogya as well,
> from the highest to the lowest, rarely followed the truth.

Ratu Ageng's disapproval of the Yogya ruler and his entourage, as well as her deep root of faith and humility – the latter a rare quality in court circles – can be seen in her deathbed speech addressed to her son before her demise on 17 October 1803:

> Sultan! The path I have to lay aside is difficult and now I feel that I am in essence no more than an ordinary person. My son, keep that in view and do not believe that, although you are now ruler, after your death you will be anything more than a common coolie (*batur*). So live accordingly! (Carey 2008:81)

Ratu Ageng's disgust at the frivolity, religious laxity and self-serving politics of the Yogya court seems to have left a lasting mark on the mind of the young prince. At the end of the Java War, he confided to Major de Stuers, his Dutch officer escort, that 'if I had continued to insist on my known demands [to be recognised as the regulator of religion] then it was out of the conviction that people at the courts did not follow the old customs as scrupulously as before [and] above all that people neglected religion' (Louw and De Klerck 1894–1909, V:744). In his autobiography he was to speak of it being 'the will of God' that 'he should follow his great-grandmother, for it was his wish to be absorbed in religion' (Babad Dipanegara II:47; Carey 2008:82).

Already in her mid-sixties when she moved to Tegalrejo in the early 1790s, Ratu Ageng led an active life almost until the end. This came at three o'clock on the afternoon of 17 October after she had whispered her trenchant last words to her son, the second sultan. She was then laid in state and buried at sunset the following day at the royal graveyard at Imogiri some five hours journey on foot to the south of Yogya. Her cortege was followed by all the members of the sultan's family with the exception of the second sultan and Diponegoro's father, the future third sultan, who only accompanied it as far as the southern *alun-alun* (Carey 2008:83).

The young Diponegoro is likely to have been amongst the family mourners who made the thirty-four kilometre round-trip journey to the royal burial ground.

Inheriting the Tegalrejo Estate

The Dutch Resident reported that both the sultan and the crown prince were very distressed at the old lady's passing. But it must have been a particularly heavy blow for the eighteen-year-old Diponegoro. He now remained alone at Tegalrejo, succeeding his great-grandmother in charge of the estate. Although he was soon to marry the daughter of a local *kyai* and was even threatened for a time with having the redoubtable Ratu Kedaton sent out to live with him, his life in Tegalrejo continued its quiet course.

What then of Tegalrejo itself? What did this estate, which went by the auspicious name of 'Fields of Prosperity', look like? By the time of Ratu Ageng's death in 1803, it was already an impressive complex including an extensive residence with gardens, orchards and ponds, one of which Ratu Ageng had fallen besides at the start of her last illness. A Dutch visitor who inspected the ruins (the residence had been burnt at the start of the Java War, Chapter IX) in the 1840s described it in admiring terms (Brumund 1854:184–5):

> The princes of Yogyakarta were apparently better lodged than at present. At least I know of no princely residence in Yogya which can compare to the earlier one at Tegalrejo. The [princes'] houses are [now] mostly of wood [and are] low, small and insignificant. Diponegoro's [residence], [however], was large, spacious, high and entirely built of stone. On both sides there ran rows of no less large and spacious stone outhouses. There [Diponegoro's] friends lodged and the priests who came to visit him. There were also his warehouses and repositories [for storing the products of the Tegalrejo estate], and the places where his immediate followers and retainers lived. The other followers lived in the village which surrounds the *dalem* [princely residence].

The same visitor went on to describe in detail the lay-out of the house itself. This included the remains of a large open-sided pavilion or audience hall and adjoining gallery suitable for shadow-puppet performances and the playing of Javanese *gamelan* orchestras, both deeply appreciated by Diponegoro (Carey 1974a: 10–16). The visitor also noticed the high stone wall which surrounded the yard of the residence and the many fruit trees (Brumund 1854:185).

Although the original residence and estate garden were laid out on Ratu Ageng's orders, Diponegoro seems to have had a hand in its later features. In his *babad*, he related how many of the buildings were improved and enlarged after his great-grandmother's death, presumably to house the increasing number of visitors, especially wandering *santri* who came to engage in prayer and religious discussion (Carey 2008:100).

According to the prince, the amount of religious observance at Tegalrejo 'exceeded that of his great-grandmother's days' (Babad Dipanegara, II:47). It was probably at this time that plans were laid to build a stone mosque at Tegalrejo, a building which had been almost completed at the time of the outbreak of the Java War. As Diponegoro would later reflect (Louw and De Klerck 1894–1909, V:744; Van der Kemp 1896:418; Carey 1992:495 note 464):

> I always had the desire to have a really fine mosque [and] I spent much money on the one I had at Tegalrejo which was very nearly completed when I had to leave [in

July 1825] [...] a mosque has always been a delight for me: one does not always have to pray in it, but it directs the heart towards religious sincerity.

Like Ratu Ageng before him, Diponegoro took an interest in the arrangement of the trees and ponds on his estate. He would later build himself a retreat at Selorejo just outside the northeast wall of Tegalrejo, where he often withdrew to meditate and pray (see Map 3). This was encircled by a moat filled with different kinds of fish. The island where Diponegoro's meditation seat was placed was planted with various types of fruit and flowering trees, including *kemuning* (Brumund 1854:192–4; Carey 1981:236–7 note 14). Ubiquitous in graveyards and holy sites, this tree with its white pungently scented flowers would have spread a 'canopy of white flowers' over the prince's head as he sat in meditation (Brumund 1854:188; Van Raay 1926–27:51). There was also a large banyan tree (*waringin*) which gave its name to the island, Pulo Waringin.

The prince took similar pains to lay out fruit orchards, vegetable gardens and shrubberies on his lands at Selarong near the cave of Secang in the Bantul district to the south of Yogya where he retreated during the fasting month (*Puwasa*) and whose facilities he greatly extended (Carey 1981:238–9 notes 20–5; Louw and De Klerck 1894–1909, I:435–7). He would later boast that 'there is nothing on earth that does not grow luxuriantly on the soil of Java' (Knoerle, 'Journal', 1830:24).

Like many Javanese, Diponegoro had a great affinity with nature: some of the most lyrical passages in his autobiography describe the retreats which he established in caves, mountain fastnesses, and fast-flowing streams. According to a Dutch report, his garden at Selarong was enclosed by a wall the height of a man. He also referred with affection to the different types of animals which kept him company during his periods of retreat and withdrawal: the fish at Selorejo, the turtles, turtle-doves, crocodiles and tigers during his jungle retreats during the Java War, and his beloved cockatoos while in exile in Manado and Makassar. Such affinity with nature and the animal kingdom, was, in the Javanese view, a reflection of the sensitivity and spiritual wholeness of a human being, a state best expressed in the descriptions of the wandering knight (*satrio lelono*) in the Javanese *wayang* (shadow-play) (Boedihardjo 1923:28; Chapter III).

Relations with the Yogya Court

Diponegoro's preoccupation with religious matters and the development of his own spiritual practice through periodic retreats and daily meditation clearly placed a strain on his relationship with the Yogya ruler and his court. By his own admission, the prince rarely attended *kraton* audiences, only coming to Yogya for the thrice yearly *Garebeg* ceremonies celebrating The Prophet's birthday (*Mulud*), the end of the fasting month (*Puwasa*), and Abraham's willingness to sacrifice his son as well as the Great Day (*Ari Besar*) of the pilgrims in Mecca (*Idul Adha*) (Groneman 1895:40; Carey 2008:87–8).

These latter attendances, Diponegoro described as a 'great sin', perhaps because the *Garebeg* were more Javanese than Islamic in character. But he forced himself to take part out of fear for his grandfather, the second sultan, and his father, the crown prince. He also related how he came to the capital on certain special occasions such as on 3 September 1805 when at the age of twenty Javanese years, he received his adult name and title of Raden Ontowiryo (Carey 2008:88), and on 27 February 1807 when he married the daughter of a Yogya outlying region *bupati*, an unhappy union to which we will return shortly (Chapter III).

The Tegalrejo Circle: Early Contacts with the Islamic Religious Communities

Diponegoro clearly grew up in an environment dominated by religious discussion. Already, during his boyhood in the *kraton*, he had mixed with *santri*. The Suranatan corps, a group of armed religious officials at the Yogya court, for example, formed part of the military establishment of the *kadipaten* (crown prince's establishment), his father's residence. There were also members of the *kaum* (firm Islamic community) in receipt of tithe (*zakat*) payments from the court who are listed in the *kraton* records as having been domiciled at both the *kadipaten* and Tegalrejo in the late 1790s (Carey 1980:170).

Ratu Ageng had also encouraged members of the Yogya religious hierarchy to visit or take up residence at Tegalrejo. Amongst these were her own *pengulu* (head of religious establishment), Kyai Muhamad Bahwi – later known as Muhamad Ngusman Basah – who had previously served as the presiding *ulama* (religious scholar) of the Suranatan mosque (the sultan's private mosque). Another was Haji Badarudin, a commander of the Suranatan corps who had twice made the Yogya court-sponsored pilgrimage to Mecca and was knowledgeable about Ottoman administrative practice in the holy cities (Carey 2008:89).

Besides the members of the court religious hierarchy, Diponegoro almost certainly met most of the key independent teachers in the Yogya region during his Tegalrejo youth. The estate was close to the four main centres for scholars of Islamic law known as *pathok negari* (literally 'pillars of the state'), namely those at Kasongan (between Selarong and Tegalrejo), Dongkelan (immediately to the south of Yogya on the Bantul road), Papringan (between Yogya and Prambanan), and Melangi just northwest of Tegalrejo (Carey 2008:90, 784–5).

Diponegoro would later (November 1827) marry the daughter of the *kyai guru* (revered senior teacher) of Kasongan, who later took the title of Raden Ayu Retnokumolo during the Java War. The prince would also have frequently passed through his future father-in-law's centre on his way from Tegalrejo to his lands at Selarong to the south of Yogya (Carey 2008:90, 768).

Of the four *pathok negari*, Melangi seems to have been by far the most important at this time. It lay just three kilometres from Tegalrejo, the land being part of the patrimony of the Danurejan family with whom Diponegoro had close family ties (Carey 2008:762–3, 781). They maintained a religious teacher at Melangi, who served as mentor to members of the Yogya court community. One of these teachers was Kyai Taptojani, whose family seems to have hailed from Sumatra. He achieved considerable local recognition as a scholar and translator of difficult Islamic texts (Carey 1974b:272–3). Diponegoro greatly respected him and received his sons into his wartime service taking care to spare his *pathok negari* at Melangi from damage during the Java War. Described as a 'prominent priest', he was said to have been in his ninetieth year when he brokered the first peace negotiations between Diponegoro's key religious adviser, Kyai Mojo and the Dutch in October 1826 (Carey 2008:90).

In the Surakarta version of the *Babad Diponegoro*, there is a passage in which Taptojani is described as having visited Diponegoro at night at the head of all the *ulama* from the tax-free (*pradikan*) areas to give him advice as to the right moment for the *Ratu Adil* ('Just King') to proclaim himself and the holy war (*prang sabil*) to commence (Carey 1981:43–7, 261 note 108). Although there is nothing in the contemporary Dutch sources to confirm that particular visitation, the links which Diponegoro maintained with Taptojani's family during the early stages of the war were of great importance.

In 1805, Taptojani had moved to the Sunan's territory following a dispute with the Yogya *pengulu* (Carey 1974b:273), but he maintained contacts with his far-flung family in central and east Java. These included prominent religious scholars residing in tax-free areas in Kedu, as well as a highly placed royal official in Madiun who had links with the famous religious boarding school (*pesantren*) at Tegalsari (Carey 2008:90–1). He was also on intimate terms with Kyai Mojo's extensive family settled in the tax-free villages of Mojo and Baderan near Delanggu, and at Pulo Kadang near Imogiri to the south of Yogya. These far-flung connections, which pivoted around Taptojani's influential position as a legal scholar and teacher, were clearly vital for Diponegoro when he appealed for support from *ulama* in Pajang, Madiun, Kedu, Bagelen and Pacitan at the start of the Java War.

The Surakarta Connection and the Santri Communities

During the time Diponegoro was reaching early manhood in Tegalrejo, Surakarta was far more important than Yogya as a religious centre. A.H. Smissaert (1777–1832), the Yogya Resident (in office 1823–1825) whose behaviour so alienated Diponegoro in the months before the Java War

(Chapter IX), would later remark that there were many more princes in Surakarta than in Yogyakarta who were known by the Dutch authorities as 'fanatical' about their religious duties (Carey 2008:93).

Another reason may have been was that there were more generous patrons of the religious communities at the Sunan's court than in the sultan's capital. Pakubuwono IV (1768–1820; reigned, 1788–1820) himself was described by the Dutch as 'a great friend of the *ulama* who can get him to do anything' (Carey 2008:91). The Surakarta *Garebeg Mulud* and *Garebeg Puwasa* ceremonies attracted droves of *haji*, *kaum* (lower ranking village religious officials) and *pradikan* (men of religion from tax-free areas) from all over Java. This was not the case in Yogya which only attracted *santri* from the immediate neighbourhood. The Sunan's greater largesse at religious feasts when compared to that of the sultan probably counted for much here.

Nor was it only the Sunan whose largesse was renowned in *santri* circles: his younger brother, Pangeran Buminoto – a 'tall, dessicated man with an officious manner' (*Lettres de Java* 1829:93) – was also known for his unstinting support of religious teachers, amongst whom was Kyai Mojo. Significantly, Diponegoro's gifted eldest son, Pangeran Diponegoro II (born circa 1803), who later took the *santri* name of Raden Mantri Muhamad Ngarip, decided after long peregrinations to sit at the feet of a Surakarta teacher, Kyai Mojo, rather than one of the many *guru* whom he had visited in the vicinity of the sultan's capital (Louw and De Klerck 1894–1909, V:744).

While Kyai Mojo's favoured position amongst the ranks of Diponegoro's religious supporters underscored Surakarta's ascendancy as a centre of religious instruction, it also fuelled latent tensions between the prince's aristocratic and *santri* followers (Chapter X). The former, nearly all Yogyanese, tended to view Kyai Mojo and his fellow Surakarta *ulama* with deep suspicion, an attitude reciprocated by the Solo *santri* (Louw and De Klerck 1894–1909, V:744; Carey 1987:279–84).

In the early 1800s all this lay in the future. At this time, the prince's personal links seem to have been largely confined to the immediate Yogya area and they remained so until the period of H.G. Nahuys van Burgst's residency (1816–22). At that time, according to Diponegoro's own testimony, he travelled out of the Yogya area for the first time, walking more than forty kilometers along back country roads to the village of Mojo to seek out his eldest son, who had by then become a pupil of the *kyai guru* (Louw and De Klerck 1894–1909, V:744; Carey 1981:261 note 110).

Soon afterwards, Kyai Mojo visited Diponegoro at Tegalrejo, arriving, according to the prince, unannounced and unbidden shortly after the prince himself had returned from one of his fasting month (*puwasa*) retreats at Selarong (Louw and De Klerck 1894–1909, V:744–5). The prince's bane and inspiration during the Java War, Diponegoro's relationship with Mojo would be fateful for both men.

Conclusion

Diponegoro's upbringing at Tegalrejo under the formidable and pious Ratu Ageng fixed the bearings for his future life. The old adage, ascribed to the Jesuits, 'give us a child until he is seven and we will show you the man' did not quite hold in Diponegoro's case since he only joined his great-grandmother at her country estate at the age of seven in around 1792–3. But even before his departure from the Yogya court it is likely that he began to feel the influences which would later shape his character and personality. The links between his father's establishment (*kadipaten*) and the court *santri* communities may have already begun to tell.

At the same time, the young prince would have certainly been influenced by the presence of his mother and great-grandmother, both offspring of prominent *kyai*. These influences would become even more pronounced during the critical 1793–1803 decade when he grew to early manhood under Ratu Ageng's watchful and discerning eye. As a prince raised in a village environment and instilled from his youth with a sense of shared identity with the rural communities, Diponegoro was unique. Thanks to Ratu Ageng, he had acquired both an intimate knowledge of the life of the Javanese peasantry as well as an entrée into the world of the rural *santri*. His understanding of Javanese society was shared by few of his contemporaries.

Is it any wonder that such a young person would have had an unusual destiny? While the prophecies supposedly uttered by the first sultan and subsequently reiterated during the prince's pilgrimage to the south coast in circa 1805 foretold tragedy – 'You alone are the means but that not for long, only to be counted among the ancestors' (Chapter III) – the shadows which these evoked still lay some way ahead. The immediate future for the eighteen-year-old, who now had sole charge of Tegalrejo, seemed bright. Living comfortably removed from the incessant intrigues of the Yogya court, and coming into his own as a young adult with a growing sense of commitment to his religious path, Diponegoro could look forward to a life of spiritual and personal fulfillment sustained by his ever widening circle of *santri* and pious *priyayi* friends. It is to these links and the formation of the prince's intellectual character and understanding of Islam that we must now turn.

Bibliography

Adams, Cindy (1965). *Sukarno; An Autobiography as Told to Cindy Adams*. Indianopolis: Bobbs-Merrill.
Amirulhaq, Dzul (2012). 'Haji Datuk Sulaiman, Pangeran Bima di Tanah Rantau; Leluhur Pangeran Diponegoro [Haji Datuk Suleiman, a Bimanese Prince in a Foreign Land; An Ancestor of Prince Diponegoro], *Babuju News*, 20 July 2012, <http://www.babuju.com/2012/07/haji-datuk-sulaiman-pangeran-bima-di-html?> accessed 5 October 2012.
Babad Dipanegara (2010). *Babad Dipanegara*, 4 vols, ed. Nindya Noegraha. Jakarta: Perpustakaan Nasional Republik Indonesia.
Boedihardjo (1923). 'Grepen uit de Wajang', *Djåwå* 2:22–8.
Brumund, J.F.G. (1854). 'Bezoek in den Vervallen Dalem van Dipo Negoro te Tegal Redjo', *Indiana* 2:181–97.
Carey, Peter (1974a). *The Cultural Ecology of Early Nineteenth-century Java; Pangeran Dipanagara, A Case Study*. Singapore: Institute of Southeast Asian Studies [Occasional Paper 24].

Carey, Peter (1974b). 'Javanese Histories of Dipanagara; The Buku Kĕdhuŋ Kĕbo, its Authorship and Historical Importance', *Bijdragen tot de Taal-, Land- en Volkenkunde*, 130:259–88.
Carey, Peter (ed.) (1980). *The Archive of Yogyakarta. Vol. I: Documents relating to Politics and Internal Court Affairs*. Oxford: Oxford University Press.
Carey, Peter (1981). *Babad Dipanagara; An Account of the Outbreak of the Java War (1825–30). The Surakarta Court Version of the Babad Dipanagara with Translations into English and Indonesian Malay*. Kuala Lumpur: Art Printers.
Carey, Peter (1987). 'Satria and Santri; Some Notes on the Relationship between Dipanagara's Kraton and Religious Supporters during the Java War (1825–30)', in: T. Ibrahim Alfian, H.J. Koesoemanto, Dharmono Hardjowidjono and Djoko Suryo (eds), *Dari Babad dan Hikayat sampai Sejarah Kritis; Kumpulan Karangan dipersembahkan kepada Prof. Dr. Sartono Kartodirdjo*, pp. 271–318. Yogyakarta: Gadjah Mada University Press.
Carey, Peter (2008). *The Power of Prophecy; Prince Dipanagara and the End of an Old Order in Java, 1785–1855*. Leiden: KITLV Press, second revised edition.
Carey, Peter and Mason Hoadley (eds) (2000). *The Archive of Yogyakarta. Vol. II: Documents relating to Economic and Agrarian Affairs*. Oxford: Oxford University Press.
Groneman, J. (1895). *De Garebeg's te Ngajogyåkårtå*. The Hague: Nijhoff.
Hageman, J.Jcz. (1856). *Geschiedenis van den Oorlog op Java van 1825 tot 1830*. Batavia: Lange.
Kemp, P.H. van der (1896). 'Dipanegara, eene Geschiedkundige Hamlettype', *Bijdragen tot de Taal-, Land- en Volkenkunde* 46:281–433.
Knoerle 'Journal' (1830). 'Aanteekeningen gehouden door den 2e Luit Knoerle betreffende de Dagelyksche Verkeering van dien Officier met den Prins van Djocjakarta, Diepo Negoro, gedurende eene Reis van Batavia naar Menado, het Exil van den genoemden Prins', Manado, 20–6–1830. MS 391 of the Johannes van den Bosch private collection in the Nationaal Archief, The Hague.
Lettres de Java (1829). *Lettres de Java ou Journal d'un Voyage en cette Île, en 1822*. Paris: n.p. [anonymous author Justinus van Schoor]
Louw, P.J.F. and E.S. de Klerck (1894–1909). *De Java-Oorlog van 1825–30*. 6 volumes. The Hague: Nijhoff and Batavia: Landsdrukkerij.
Mandoyokusumo, K.R.T. (1977). *Serat Raja Putra Ngayogyakarta Hadiningrat*. Yogyakarta: Bebadan Museum Karaton Ngayogyakarta Hadiningrat.
Poensen, C. (1905). 'Amăngku Buwånå II (Sĕpuh); Ngayogyåkarta's Tweede Sultan (naar Aanleiding van een Javaansch Handschrift)'', *Bijdragen tot de Taal-, Land- en Volkenkunde* 58:73–346.
Raay, J.V.J. van (1926–7). 'Wat de Oude Boom in den Dalem van den Javaanschen Hamlet Beleefde', *Indische Verlofganger* (1926–7):51.

Soekanto, R. (1951a). *Sentot alias Alibasah Abdulmustopo Prawirodirdjo Senopati Diponegoro (Seorang Terkemuka dalam abad ke-19 dari Sedjarah Nasional Indonesia)*. Djakarta: Poesaka Aseli.

Soekanto, R. (1951b). *Dua Raden Saleh, Dua Nasionalis dalam Abad ke-19; Suatu Halaman dari Sedjarah Nasional Indonesia*. Djakarta: Poesaka Aseli.

Tanojo, R. (1966). *Sedjarah Pangeran Diponegoro Darah Madura: Awewaton Pèngetan Kuna*. Surabaya: Trimurti.

CHAPTER II

Young Manhood: Marriage, Education and Links with the Religious (*santri*) Community, 1803–1805

First Marriage and Development of the Tegalrejo Community

In the period after his great-grandmother's death in October 1803, Diponegoro deepened his connections with the *ulama* who resided in the villages around Tegalrejo. An important development here was his marriage in circa 1802 to the daughter of a prominent religious teacher from the Sleman area to the north of Yogya. His bride, Raden Ayu Retno Madubrongto, was the second daughter of Kyai Gede Dadapan from the village of Dadapan near Tempel.

The mother of Diponegoro's eldest and most able son, Raden Mas Ontowiryo (post-August 1825, Pangeran Diponegoro II; post-1830, Raden Mantri Muhamad Ngarip), Madubrongto's offspring would later write a prophetic-historical account of his life and times – the *Babad Dipanagara Surya Ngalam* – in which his mother is described as a devout woman who took pleasure in accompanying her husband in his religious duties (Carey 2008:97).

His parents remained close until the elder Diponegoro was prevailed upon by his father to make a more prestigious 'political' marriage. The new bride was Raden Ajeng Supadmi (post-1807, Raden Ayu Retnokusumo), the possibly part-Chinese daughter of the Yogya *bupati* of Panolan, Raden Tumenggung Notowijoyo III (in office 1803–11) (Carey 2008:97–8). Their lavish 27 February 1807 nuptials are described in detail in the Residency letters. One of the Dutch Resident's official bridal presents was five feet of writing parchment, a gift which indicated a level of literacy on the part of both bride and groom (Carey 2008:98).

This second wife had only met Diponegoro three months before their marriage and their union was brief and unhappy. The prince never once refers to her in his autobiography and she probably separated from her husband at the time of the birth of their only child, the future Pangeran Diponingrat (born circa 1808). Thereafter, she remained in the women's quarters (*keputren*) in the Yogya *kraton* (Carey and Hoadley 2000: 395–6; Carey 2012, III:914). She also behaved, in the view of the younger Diponegoro, in an arrogant and unjust way towards his more lowly-born mother who died before the outbreak of the Java War (Carey 2008:98).

Besides the village-based *ulama*, Diponegoro also had friends among those in the Yogya court elite with Islamic interests. The Danurejan family were important here. One family member in particular, Raden Ayu Danukusumo, a daughter of Sultan Hamengkubuwono I and the mother of Danurejo II (in office 1799–1811), was especially appreciated by the prince being mentioned in his *babad* as his chess partner, a game he greatly enjoyed (Babad Dipanegara II:119). She was also renowned for her knowledge of Javanese-Islamic literature and facility with *pegon* (Javanese written in Arabic script), skills which Diponegoro valued highly (Carey 1992:157, 343, 489 note 425).

Other *priyayi* (high court official) dynasties with religious commitments included the Wirogunan and Kertodirjan families. Both were closely connected with the prince through service as senior officials at his father's official residence (*kadipaten*). Raden Tumenggung Wironegoro, the son of the much respected *patih kadipaten* in Diponegoro's youth, Mas Tumenggung Wiroguno (in office, 1780–1807), was a pupil of the renowned Kyai Taptojani (Carey 1981:245 note 41; Chapter I). Many of his relatives were *santri* (Carey 1981:245 note 41). Married for a time to the prince's eldest sister, he would later incur Diponegoro's wrath by conducting an affair with his stepmother, Ratu Ibu (pre-1814, Ratu Kedaton; post-1820, Ratu Ageng) (?1780–1826), the third sultan's consort (Chapter VIII).

The prince's relations with the Kertodirjan family were even closer. One family member, Mas Tumenggung Kertodirjo II, served as Yogya *bupati* in the Sukowati area (1812–21), and had many Javanese-Islamic works in his possession at the time of his dismissal in December 1821. A personal friend of Diponegoro, he subsequently took up residence at Tegalrejo and became one of his commanders in the Madiun area in 1825-6 (Louw and De Klerck 1894-1909, I:523 note 2, 559, 576; Carey 1981:284-5).

The prince also had non-Javanese *priyayi* connections at Tegalrejo. One such was Sheikh Abdul Ahmad bin Abdullah al-Ansari, an Arab from Jeddah who had married into the family of the first sultan's son, Pangeran Blitar (Nahuys van Burgst 1835-6, I:13; Louw and De Klerck 1894-1909, III:570-1; Carey 1974:35 note 116). A trader with business interests in Semarang (Carey 2008:101), he may have kept Diponegoro informed of political developments outside the principalities. As a Sharif (presumed descendant of the Prophet), he may also have exercised some religious influence over him. The Sheikh's presence at Tegalrejo in his signature white tabard and turban might have been the inspiration for Diponegoro's own Arabic-style clothing during the Java War (Chapter IX, Chapter XI).

Al-Ansari's son-in-law, also known as Ahmad, was likewise part of the prince's pre-Java War Tegalrejo circle. He would later die defending Diponegoro's headquarters at Selarong in October 1825. Raden Mas Alip (?1810-?60), one of the prince's sons, later claimed that these two Jeddah-born Arabs were amongst his father's most important councillors in the lead up to the Java War (Nahuys van Burgst 1825, 1835, I:10-14; Louw and De Klerck 1894-1909, III:560).

Unsurprisingly, Diponegoro is silent in his autobiography about another group of 'friends' whom he would turn to for support during the Java War. These were the members of the Yogya criminal underworld. They included local *jago* (literally: 'fighting cocks', thugs) and *wong durjono* (highwaymen, robbers), some of whom were 'social bandits' who robbed the rich to give to the poor (Hobsbawm 1969). Amongst these underworld figures were the ferry-crossing bandits based at Mangiran and Kamijoro on the Progo River, and the tiger hunters (*mantri tuwa buru*) of Jelegong in Kulon Progo who were ordered to prepare weapons and shelter for Diponegoro's followers after his flight from Tegalrejo (20 July 1825) (Van der Kemp 1896:390; Carey 1981:262 note 112; 282 note 197).

The prince's dealings with bandits provoked much negative comment: the Surakarta version of the *Babad Diponegoro* spoke of the prince 'mixing with the scum of the nation' (*akanthi wong urakan*), and another text, the *Buku Kedung Kebo* (Book of the Buffaloes' Watering Hole), characterised his *wong durjono* allies as 'robbers [...] not fighting men [...] just entering a market to snatch food' (Carey 1981:19, 243–4 note 36). More recently, two prominent Yogyanese – W.S. Rendra (1935–2011) and Pangeran Adinegoro, a younger brother of Sultan Hamengkubuwono IX (1912–88; reigned 1940–88), – compared Diponegoro unfavourably with his great-grandfather, Sultan Mangkubumi, who eschewed such alliances during the Giyanti War (1746–55) (Carey 2008:50, 102).

Education and Literary Interests

These then were some of the prince's friends, advisers and underworld associates during his youth and early manhood at Tegalrejo. What now of his education?

Compared with the upbringing of most of the Javanese nobility at this time, Diponegoro's intellectual development at Tegalrejo was unusual. In the view of Surakarta Residency Translator, J.W. Winter (1777/8–1839, in office 1806–20), the education of the court elite at this time was often a hit and miss affair (Winter 1902:39–40) involving a 'house' *ulama* (Islamic scholar) who would be retained by noble households to teach Arabic prayers and *Qur'ān* exegesis (Chijs 1864:212–323; Carey 2008:102).

Diponegoro's formal *pesantren* (religious boarding school)-style instruction by visiting *ulama* at Tegalrejo in the *Qur'ān* and *Hadith* (traditions of The Prophet) was altogether more impressive. And it was something he took care to pass on to his own male children, at least four of whom would gain a *pesantren* education and become ardent Muslims (Louw and De Klerck 1894–1909, V:744; Sagimun 1965:359–60; Carey 1981:lxiii note 112, 2008:103; Chapter XII).

Some of the texts studied by Diponegoro at Tegalrejo are listed in the Javanese sources. Amongst his favourites was the *Kitab Tuhfah*, a Sufi ontology on the doctrine of the 'seven grades of being' much appreciated by Javanese when speculating on God, the world and man's place in it (Drewes 1966:290-300). He was also familiar with treatises on Islamic theology and mysticism, such as *Uṣul* and *Tasawwuf*, as well as Javanese mystical poems such as *suluk*. The history of the prophets (*Serat Anbiya*) and the *Tāfsir*, a Qur'ān exegesis, likewise formed part of his literary curriculum, as did didactic works on Islamic political philosophy such as the *Ṣirāṭ as-salāṭīn* and *Tāj as-salāṭīn* (Carey 2008:103).

Another special area of interest was Muslim jurisprudence: the *Taqrīb*, *Lubāb al-fiqh*, *Muḥarrar* and *Taqarrub* (a commentary on the *Taqrīb*) were all known to Diponegoro, and he would later mention his personal collection of Javanese-Islamic law codes which had been kept for him by a friend in Yogya during the Java War (Knoerle, 'Journal', 1830:30-1). The 1812 legal reforms introduced by the interim British administration of Thomas Stamford Raffles (1811-16), which curtailed the power of the Javanese religious courts (*surambi*), troubled him deeply (Carey 1987:299-301; Chapter VIII). Such works on Muslim jurisprudence, scholastic theology, grammar and Qur'ānic exegesis were in general use for instruction in religious boarding schools (*pesantren*) in Java during this period (Van den Berg 1887:518-55). So the prince's interest in Muslim jurisprudence was perhaps not so unusual.

Besides these Javanese-Islamic texts, Javanese sources relate that Diponegoro also studied – or had read to him – works of a more moralistic and Javanese literary nature. These included edifying tales on kingship and statecraft adopted from Persian and Arabic classics such as the *Fatāḥ al-Muluk* ('Victory of kings'), *Hakik al-Modin* and *Naṣīhat al-Muluk* ('Moral lessons for kings'), as well as Modern Javanese versions of Old Javanese classics like the *Serat Rama*, *Bhoma Kāwya*, *Arjuna Wijaya* and *Arjuna Wiwāha* (Chapter VII).

Another text certainly known to Diponegoro was the *Joyo Lengkoro Wulan*, a copy of which was found at his Selarong headquarters in October 1825 (Pigeaud 1967-80, IV:86). Dealing with aspects of statecraft and epitomising the ideal education of a *satria lelono* (wandering warrior nobleman), it tells the tale of a young prince wandering (*lelono*) through Java and meeting many masters of secular, religious and arcane lore (Pigeaud 1967–80, I:230). A text with universal appeal amongst the courtly elite at this time (Ricklefs 1998:271; Ricklefs and Voorhoeve 1977: 61, reference to Yogya *kraton* text IOL Jav. 24, dated 1803), it was one which Diponegoro would emulate in his circa 1805 pilgrimage (Chapter III).

Amongst the prince's favourites was Modern Javanese *wayang* (shadow puppet) and he would make numerous allusions to characters in the Javanese show theatre in his autobiography (Carey 1974:12–37). A copy of the Purwa cycle of *wayang* plays up to the great 'brothers' war' (*Bratayuda*) was made for him in exile to educate his children (Carey 2008:105, 744; Chapter XII), as were copies of the *Serat Gandokusumo* (*Angling Driya*), the *Asmoro Supi*, a romance related to the Menak cycle, the *Serat Angreni*, an episode from the *Panji* cycle, and the *Serat Manikmoyo*, a text on cosmogony dealing with agricultural myths and *wayang* traditions (Pigeaud 1967–80, I:154; Carey 1992:495 note 466). Another favourite was the *Menak Amir Hamza*, a romanticized version of the life of the uncle of The Prophet (Carey 2008:744; Chapter XII).

Character, Intellectual Ability and Relations with Europeans

While the list of works on Islam, Javanese-Islamic law and Javanese literature reportedly studied by Diponegoro seems impressive, their bare enumeration affords few insights into the prince's character. How intelligent and discerning was he? Could he read and write? What was his understanding of Islam, and how deep was his spiritual commitment?

The answers to some of these questions can be found in two surviving holograph letters written by the prince to his mother (Plate 23) and eldest son, now kept in the Dutch Military Academy in Breda (Hollander 1877:192–6). Composed before the prince sailed to Manado from Batavia on 3 May 1830, they were entrusted to his Javanese-speaking Dutch military escort, Captain Johan Jacob Roeps (1805–40), who took them back with him to the Netherlands in July 1830. Both letters are in a bold hand but give an untidy impression with many doubled-up *aksara* (Javanese letters) and other errors (Hollander 1877:192-6; Kielstra 1885:408; Louw and De Klerck 1894-1909, I:151). Crossings out and ink blots abound. Perhaps Diponegoro simply had no sand to dry his ink. Whatever the case, the letters seem the product of an autodidact.

The records of the European officers who spent time in his company confirm this. The diary of Lieutenant Justus Heinrich Knoerle (1796-1833), military adjutant to Governor-General Johannes van den Bosch (1780-1844; in office, 1830-4), is key here (Knoerle 1835:135-80, 'Journal', 1830). Luxemburg-born and of German parentage, he accompanied the prince on his seven-week voyage into exile in Manado on the naval corvette *Pollux* (Chapter XII).

According to Knoerle, the prince appeared as 'a noble, but at the same time proud man, gifted with shrewdness, a strong [and] enterprising character, and penetrating judgement such as is rarely found amongst highborn Javanese' (Knoerle 1835:171). His lack of formal education could be seen in his 'unusually unmannerly and inaccurate' style of speech. But the force and vitality of his personality shone through in the vividness of his ideas, which were, in Knoerle's estimation, 'rich, powerful and very clear' (Knoerle 1835:172).

Diponegoro's personality impressed people after even a short meeting. At the Magelang 'peace conference' in March 1830, the Dutch supreme commander, Lieutenant-General Hendrik Merkus de Kock (1779-1845), and his staff, none of whom were initially well disposed, all spoke with praise about the prince's 'open-hearted and intelligent' character. Later, Prince Hendrik 'De Zeevaarder' ('The Seafarer') (1820-79), the sixteen-year-old son of the future King William II (reigned, 1840-9), would write of the prince's 'pleasant appearance' and speak of his character as 'still full of fire' even after four years as a prisoner in Fort Rotterdam, Makassar (Wassing-Visser 1995:246).

The prince apparently spoke some Malay, but always avoided using the language because he found it so distasteful (Carey 2008:108). He also had an excellent memory: during his conversations with Knoerle he was able to recall developments in pre-Java War Yogyakarta with great clarity and he later set down the whole of his life history in *babad* form in Manado in under nine months (May 1831–February 1832) entirely without notes, but with remarkable chronological rigour and attention to detail (Carey 1981:xxiv–xxvi).

Another facet of Diponegoro's intelligence was his ability to discern other people's characters from their facial appearance (*ngelmu firasat*). At the beginning of the Java War, he is depicted in the *Buku Kedung Kebo* using this science of physiognomy to pick his officials, army commanders (*basah*), and religious advisers, his choice of subordinates usually being successful (Carey 2008:108). He was also very careful with money, as we have noted in his estate administration (Chapter I), and which we will later see in his 1823 negotiations for the indemnification of the European land-renters in Yogya (Chapter IX), his management of his wartime finances (Chapter X) and exile allowances (Chapter XII).

The prince's judgement of European officials was likewise penetrating: Huibert Gerard Nahuys van Burgst (1782–1858; Yogya Resident, 1816–22; Plate 15), the bluff Harderwijk lawyer, administrator and 'pseudo-military' man (Louw and De Klerck 1894–1909, III:386–7; Genealogie Nahuys 2000-1:29–56), was dismissed as a person who 'merely enjoyed eating and drinking and the spreading of Dutch ways' (Babad Dipanegara, II:106). By contrast, John Crawfurd (1783–1868), the scholar-Resident of Yogya (in office 1811–14, 1816) during the British interregnum was highly praised, the prince stating that:

> He had never known any Dutch [official] endowed with the same love of his fellow man and [...] noble-hearted character as Crawfurd. [...] Crawfurd spoke about everything with his father or with himself, and he had made the Javanese language his own in under six months because the Malay language is the language of chickens which no ruler in Java wished to hear (Knoerle, 'Journal', 1830:41).

It is clear that Diponegoro had an enquiring mind and a knowledge of eclectic topics, especially Javanese history and legends. This can be seen in his Makassar notebooks which deal with *wayang* (Javanese shadow-play), Javanese mythology, legendary heroes and holy sites (Carey 1981:xxx–xxxi; p.320). In his diary, Knoerle noted that the prince talked at length about the goddess of the southern ocean (Ratu Kidul), the kingdoms of Pajajaran and Majapahit, the first sultan of Demak, Raden Patah (reigned circa 1500–18), and the late seventeenth-century Balinese mercenary-adventurer, Untung Suropati (circa 1645–1706), as well as more general topics of commerce, navigation, and European dynastic history (Knoerle, 'Journal', 1830:8, 21, 25, 32, 45). He also showed a lively interest in the Dutch corvette's maps and navigational instruments as well as the illustrations in the books Knoerle lent him on Singhalese Buddhism (Upham 1829) and the First Crusade (1095–9) (Torquato Tasso 1581) (Knoerle, 'Journal', 1830, 11, 19).

On all occasions, Diponegoro showed himself perfectly at ease in the company of Europeans. His first Dutch officer escort, Major de Stuers (1792–1881; Plate 22 no.10). De Kock's son-in-law, noting his 'genteel manners' and superior knowledge of European table etiquette (Louw and De Klerck 1894–1909, V:746).

Understanding of Islam

Diponegoro's understanding of Islam can be best assessed from his own writings, most notably his autobiographical *babad* and Makassar notebooks. Even Europeans commented favourably on his understanding of Islam. 'Diponegoro is very closely acquainted with the spirit which pervades the religious system of [The Prophet]', Knoerle noted, '[and] I believe he judges all miracles achieved by Muhammad from a fair point of view [knowing] how to distinguish [their supernatural aspects from] the [historical] circumstances in which Muhammad found himself' (Knoerle, 'Journal', 1830:46).

Diponegoro's writings, however, show that he was more a typical Javanese mystic than an orthodox Muslim reformer, something recognised early in the Java War by his principle religious adviser, Kyai Mojo, himself perhaps a Shaṭṭārīyya mystical brotherhood adherent, who remarked that the prince seemed to be striving for the mystical unity of the Sufi (Babad Dipanegara, IV:7).

Despite an impressive display of quotations from the *Qur'ān* in his Makassar notebooks, Diponegoro was not so interested in textual exegesis but in the use of *dhikr* (short prayers for the glorification of Allah endlessly repeated in ritual order) and on various forms of meditation (Carey 1981:xxx–xxxi). In the same passages where he praises the efficacy of *dhikr*, he also refers to *daerah* (diagrams for regulating breathing during prayer) and the rituals adopted by the Naqshabāndīyya and Shaṭṭārīyya mystical brotherhoods (Carey 2008:111). According to Diponegoro, the repeated use of such *dhikr* would enable the 'name of majesty' (*isim jalalah*), which is Allah, to become 'engraved' on the innermost heart (*ati sanubari*) (Babad Dipanegara, IV:98–9).

In this context, he took a mystical view of the fundamental dogma of Islam, namely *tokid* (Arabic *tawhīd*), the profession of Allah's unity and uniqueness. He considered that all man's efforts should be directed towards realising this profession of unity by denying being to all that exists, inclusive of himself, and striving after union with the Eternal and Only Being (*Kang Jati Purbaning Sukma*). The development and progress of the mystic, in the prince's view, ran from *iman* (faith) via *tokid* and *ma'ripat* (gnosis) to true *islam*, the most absolute surrender of the individual and effacement of the human personality and its being in the Divine. Significantly, he made no mention of the *sharī'a* (Islamic law) as the container for such mystical striving, precisely the sort of oversight which so struck the teachers of the Jâwah (Indonesian) community in Mecca in the late nineteenth century (Snouck Hurgronje 1931:271).

As Diponegoro put it in his autobiography (Babad Dipanegara, IV:20–1):

> XXXIII 27. *Iman* means 'acceptance'
> because man is granted life
> by God Most High.
> The meaning of *tokid* is truth
> that one has to observe
> God's ordinations [as stipulated in the law]
> be they onerous or light to fulfill.
>
> 28. *Ma'ripat* means to reject duality;
> as this body is bound to perish,
> do not take it into account.
> Its [being] is an illusion, too absurd to endure.
> Strive only after the primordial

Young Manhood: Marriage, Education and Links with the Community

Essence of the All-Pervading One.
The meaning of *islam*

29. is surrender, the avowal of man's nullity.
All comes from God,
man has only to accept humbly.
Equally in this world and the hereafter,
there is nothing but the grace of God, Lord of the Worlds,
creature being transitory.
That is my view.

30. These four together are [also] called *tokid*.
They are evidence of earnest application [to the striving after God].
[...]

For readers familiar with Javanese mystical literature, the fourfold path towards unity propounded by Diponegoro is typical Javanese *primbon* (divination almanac) material. Even the prince's repeated references to the mystical practices of the *tarekat* cannot be taken as an indication that he was in touch with the centres of the mystical brotherhoods in the Middle East. Both the Naqshabandīyya and Shaṭṭārīyya had long been established in the archipelago. By the early nineteenth century, the Shaṭṭārīyya in particular had become degenerate serving as a receptacle for many old-fashioned mystical teachings exposed in the *Serat Centhini* (1815), the great early nineteenth-century encyclopaedia of Javanese manners, history and belief systems (Ricklefs 2006:195–206).

Diponegoro thus drew on traditional sources for his religious inspiration and remained completely unaffected by the strict Wahhābī reform movement, which for nearly a decade between 1803 and 1812 controlled a large part of the Arabian peninsula and later had a profound influence the course of events in West Sumatra during the Padri War (1821–38) (Dobbin 1974:319–56). There was nothing in Diponegoro's vision which involved the creation of an Islamic society along the lines of the Padri reformers.

Nor did the prince have any problems with reconciling his experience of the Javanese spirit world with his own unshakeable commitment to Islam. Even his desire to end his days in Mecca after making the *haj* (pilgrimage) was more a way of seeking honourable retirement than a wish to imbibe the teachings of the Islamic divines (Van Hogendorp 1913:159; Knoerle, 'Journal', 1830:4, 33). Ricklefs' idea of pre-colonial Java's 'mystic synthesis' reaching its epitome in the person of Diponegoro is certainly correct (Ricklefs 2006:206–20, 2012:11–12).

Appearance, Personality and Family

Apart from the nature of Diponegoro's religious convictions, what were the main traits of his personality, appearance and character?

A sketch of the prince drawn by a Yogya court artist when he was about twenty-one years old around the time of his second marriage to the daughter of the Yogya *bupati* of Panolan in February 1807, shows him dressed in an *iket* (head-dress) and high-collared Javanese jacket (*surjan*) fastened at the neck with six gold buttons. A gold cord hangs over his shoulders on which a penknife may have been fastened and tucked into his jacket. The face is still young with tightly pursed lips, a slightly splayed nose and powerful downcast eyes (Plate 1). The sketch's whole appearance gives the impression of concentrated energy or *cahya* (internal spiritual power/ radiance). It is the only drawing from life by a Javanese artist showing the prince in Javanese dress. All other portraits are by Dutchmen (Chapter XI). They depict him in *santri* garb, the dress he adopted during the Java War and tend to give him an unwittingly European appearance (Bastin and Brommer 1979:13–14; Plate 19).

According to Dutch sources, the prince was heavy in build and of middling height (Carey 2008:115). But he had great reserves of energy and a remarkable constitution. Dutch officers tasked with tracking him down in the jungles of Bagelen at the end of the Java War were impressed by his perseverance and will-power: 'Diponegoro must be made of iron', De Kock wrote, 'when one reads the descriptions of the terrain in which he is holding out and of the shacks in which he rests his exhausted body – everything is desolate' (Kielstra 1896:298–9).

Young Manhood: Marriage, Education and Links with the Community

The prince's robust constitution and ability to endure great privations, including severe bouts of tropical malaria (Knoerle, 'Journal', 1830:7, 11, 14, 21, 39; Chapter X), made him a firm believer in traditional medical treatments. During the war, he had his own personal physician, Nurngali, whom he described as a traditional healer (*dukun*). A Muslim Bengali, he may have perhaps been a former Bengal sepoy who stayed on after the British occupation (1811–16) (Carey 1977:310, 322 note 117). Later, during his voyage to Manado, Diponegoro expressed his contempt for Western medicine (Knoerle, 'Journal', 1830:11):

> How can you speak to me about your Dutch doctors and medicines [...] [when] every day we have dead men on board this vessel who are thrown into the sea? How suspicious [you] Europeans are about [your] doctors!

In terms of physical appearance, Diponegoro could not be described as handsome in the sense that Arjuna – the *wayang* hero with whom the prince identified – is seen as good-looking in Javanese terms (Carey 1974:16). But it is likely that he had a strong personal magnetism which made him attractive to women. Diponegoro himself related that one of the main 'impeding qualities' (*sipat ngaral*) was that he was 'often tempted by women'. During the Java War, he ascribed one of his most serious defeats (Gawok, 15 October 1826) to an illicit dalliance with a young Chinese woman (*nyonyah Cina*) from Kedaren (Delanggu), who acted as his masseuse (pp.245–6).

Even in exile, he apparently boasted of his conquests: the Resident of Manado, Pietermaat (1790–1848; in office 1827–1831), reported that 'his greatest conversation is about women of whom he seems to have been a great lover' (Kielstra 1885:408; Louw and De Klerck 1894–1909, I:151). He even made an abortive attempt to marry a local Manadonese woman, the daughter of a leading Muslim citizen, Lieutenant Hasan Nur Latif (Carey 2008:119; Chapter XII).

In his pre-exile period Diponegoro had an active family life. He had four wives at Tegalrejo and several unofficial ones known in Java as *selir* (Brumund 1854:188). One of these last was attractive enough to catch the roving eye of the Dutch Assistant-Resident of Yogyakarta, P.F.H. Chevallier (1795–1825; in office 1823–1825), who lived with her for a few months before the Java War. The prince had at least ten children (six sons and four daughters) by his official wives in this period (Carey 2008:766–9; Babad Dipanegara, IV:3).

During the war, following the death of his beloved fourth wife, Raden Ayu Maduretno (?1798–1827), in late November 1827 he chose three new brides. One of these was Raden Ayu Retnoningsih (?1810–85), a daughter of the Yogya *bupati* of Keniten near Madiun and a niece of Diponegoro's 'hero' Raden Ronggo Prawirodirjo III (Carey 2008:768; Chapter VI). Still in her teens when she married Diponegoro, she was quite a beauty according to Knoerle ('Journal', 1830:8–9). Alone amongst his official wives, she accompanied him into exile where she bore him at least two sons (Carey 2008:769; p. 312, p. 320).

Although Diponegoro clearly had a great deal of personal charm and attractiveness to the opposite sex, the sources are silent about his sense of humour. European contemporaries tend to portray him as a rather dour and forbidding figure (Carey 2008:119). The prince's great-uncle, Pangeran Panular (?1772–1826), author of a major chronicle on the British period in Yogya (1811–1816), referred to the prince as 'behaving almost like a ruler' and 'making himself little liked generally' (Carey 1992:144, 327). But his testimony is contradictory. In other passages he describes his great-nephew in flattering terms as a charismatic figure with an impressive public presence, a fine way with words and an ability to relate to all levels of Javanese society (Carey 1992:119, 290; p. 149).

Diponegoro would later acknowledge that few of his *kraton* relations dared to make jokes with him (Babad Dipanegara, II:123). But he did have a light-hearted side. His clown-retainers constantly engaged him in frivolous banter and Knoerle noted that at times the prince infected those in his company with a sense of irrepressible joy (Knoerle, 'Journal', 1830:14, 20). But often the prince's humour was tinged with savage irony: during the Java War, he had the habit of sending women's clothes to his army-commanders deemed guilty of cowardice with handwritten notes pointing out that these became them better than Javanese *prajuritan* (fighting dress) (Anderson 1972:142; Carey 2008:121).

Spiritual Powers: Supposed and Real

Diponegoro's ability to place curses on people who let him down was renowned (Louw and De Klerck 1894–1909, VI:251). Even his personal belongings, such as his walking staff with its *cakra* (discus) emblem of Wisnu on the wrought iron handle, were thought to be *kramat* (supernaturally charged) (Carey 2008:116). Here was a man not to be trifled with, a spiritually powerful individual steeped in the Javanese mystic arts.

Popular belief in his spiritual powers also extended to the battlefield. He was thought to be invulnerable to bullets: although struck twice during the battle of Gawok (15 October 1826), the shots apparently left no trace on his body (Kielstra 1885:409; Louw and De Klerck 1894–1909, II:517). There was even speculation in Dutch sources that the prince wore body armour so unusual was his ability to deflect musket fire (Louw and De Klerck 1894–1909, II:517, quoting Hageman 1856).

In the section of his *babad* which deals with the Gawok incident, Diponegoro has a revealing take, being keen to stress the lightness of his wounds to reassure his wife that he had not been unfaithful to her. Javanese popular belief holds that spiritual powers like invulnerability will disappear if the individual possessing them indulges in immoral or unsuitable acts (Louw and De Klerck 1894–1909, II:517 note 1). Since he had indeed been unfaithful just before this battle when he had slept with his Chinese masseuse, he was anxious that his wife, Raden Ayu Maduretno, would not make the link his battlefield wounds and his sexual conduct (Chapter X).

Pleasures, Hobbies, Humanity and the Art of War

Diponegoro's pleasures were modest and typically Javanese. His two main ones were gardening and the keeping of song birds, especially turtle-doves (*perkutut*) and cockatoos (Chapter I). Even in exile he spent much of his time in the company of his cockatoos (Louw and De Klerck 1894–1909, I:151). He was also an avid chess player.

Chewing betel was one of his few addictions: so much so that he even reckoned the passage of time by how long it took him to masticate a mouthful of the lime, leaf and betel mixture (Babad Dipanegara, II:138; Carey 1981:277, 2008:122; Knoerle, 'Journal', 1830:19). He also smoked Javanese *rokok* (hand-rolled cigarettes made of local tobacco wrapped in maize leaves) (Knoerle, 'Journal', 1830:37) and drank wine in European company, his favourite Cape Town vintage, Constantia, being patronized by the likes of Napoleon, Jane Austen (1775–1817) and Charles Dickens (1812–70). But he never took this habit to excess (Louw and De Klerck 1894–1909, V:743; Knoerle, 'Journal', 1830:35–6). Indeed, he had his own independent interpretation of The Prophet's injunctions holding that it was not an offence to drink sweet white wine given that Europeans drank it as 'medicine' when they were intoxicated (Knoerle, 'Journal', 1830:35–6).

He was eclectic too in his culinary tastes developing a liking for freshly baked white bread during the week he spent at the Residency House in Semarang (29 March–5 April 1830). He also grew accustomed to Dutch potatoes (*kentang Welanda*) – 'exile's potatoes' (*kentang sabrang*) in the punning words of his *panakawan*, Roto – which he ate with *sambal* (chili condiment) and dried cassava as his daily fare during his sea voyages to Batavia, Manado and Makassar (Carey 2008:700).

Like many of his *kraton* contemporaries, he both made and collected jewelry. Rings and gold *kris* sheathes are specifically mentioned amongst his possessions in exile and he sent one of these – a black agate stone set in a gold band – to his eighty-year-old mother when she opened a correspondence with him in Makassar in March 1849 (Carey 2008:750; p. 322). He was also an accomplished horseman, keeping a large stable at Tegalrejo (Knoerle, 'Journal', 1830:19), expertise which stood him in good stead during the Java War.

Despite his religious zeal, Diponegoro gave Knoerle the impression that his spiritual commitment was tempered by a deep humanity. When he heard of the suicide of a Dutch sailor who had killed himself with his penknife rather than undergo punishment for a crime he did not commit, the prince expressed pity and indignation (Knoerle, 'Journal', 1830:30): 'How was it possible', he asked Knoerle, 'to punish a man of whose guilt people were unconvinced?' 'Whenever his father and himself had tried to bestow justice on Yogya subjects,' he observed, 'they had always started from the principle that no one should be punished who was not clearly convicted of committing a crime.' 'In everything Diponegoro said during the course of our conversation about this matter', Knoerle noted, 'he gave evidence of deep religious feelings. He steadfastly pitied the sailor whom he said [had] a pure heart [and] could certainly reckon on God's mercy' (Knoerle, 'Journal', 1830:30).

The prince also told Knoerle that he had never been able to bring himself to bear arms during the Java War and was revolted by the sight of battlefield carnage. He stated that he had always instructed his commanders to spare Dutch prisoners but that they had not always obeyed his orders (Knoerle, 'Journal', 1830:20–1). Later, we will see how in his visionary encounter with the Ratu Adil ('Just King') in May 1824, he begged to be excused from his summons to lead the Ratu Adil's armies because he was 'unable to fight' and 'could not bear to see death' (Babad Dipanegara, II:121; Chapter IX).

There may even have been some special pleading here on Diponegoro's part. True, Dutch prisoners were spared and some offered ranks and responsibilities, but only after they had embraced Islam (Carey 1981:259 note 106, 294 note 244). As for bearing arms, Diponegoro may not have fired a gun in anger or wielded a sabre in a cavalry charge, but he had an extensive collection of heirloom (*pusaka*) weapons, one which he always carried. These included Kyai Abijoyo, the *kris* he had inherited from his father; Kyai Nogo Siluman (The Magician King of the Snakes) and his great *pusaka*, Kyai Ageng Bondoyudo (Sir Duelling without Weapons) forged during the Java War (Chapter III; Carey 2008:813). So the idea of a weaponless prince is stretching the truth a bit, something he acknowledged at the time of his arrest at Magelang on 28 March when he spoke of his dual role as 'ruler of Java' (*Ratu Tanah Jawa*) and soldier (Babad Dipanegara, IV:181) (Carey 2008:697; Chapter XI).

Finally, he was not averse to demanding sanguinary punishments against civilian officials and others who sided with the Dutch: De Stuers relates the supposed order given by the prince in late 1825 to behead all the village chiefs (*lurah*) to the west of the sultan's capital who had assisted in the rebuilding of the main Yogya-Brosot highway, the severed heads of the *lurah* being displayed on long bamboo poles as a warning to others (De Stuers 1833:58–9; Chambert-Loir 2000:284–5).

Conclusion

Separating man and myth in Diponegoro's case is difficult. The most valuable sources are the rarest, namely Javanese *babad* written by contemporaries who knew the prince before fame or notoriety skewed his image. One such is his great-uncle's chronicle of the British interregnum (Carey 1992). But I have discovered no others. Instead, I have been forced to construct a portrait of the prince and his world from the most varied material. In doing so, I have painted a portrait of the prince which is almost like a Post-Impressionist *pointilliste* sketch, a number of tiny dots giving the illusion of depth, movement and colour but which in essence is just a *trompe-l'oeil*.

That so much of this material derives from the Java War should not surprise us given the seismic shock of that event both for the Dutch and the Javanese. But it remains inevitably coloured – if not flawed – by hindsight. The fact that since Indonesian independence in 1945, Diponegoro has become an official Indonesian 'national hero' (10 November 1973), his name gracing the main thoroughfares of many Indonesian towns, as well as the Indonesian Army's Central Java division, makes the task of the contemporary historian even more difficult. A flawed and all too human prince is certainly not in accord with 'national history'. But this book is about historical realities not contemporary myth-making.

It is now time take up once again the prince's own story as he set out for one of the most significant journeys of his life, his pilgrimage to the south coast in circa 1805 and his mystic encounters with the guardian spirits of Java and its greatest rulers. These encounters would provide further perspectives on the prince's future as a born leader in changed times, a leader who would also be counted among the ancestors even if only for such a brief and tragic time.

Bibliography

Anderson, B.R.O'G. (1972). *Java in a Time of Revolution, Occupation and Resistance, 1944-1946*. Ithaca, London: Cornell University Press.
Babad Dipanegara (2010). *Babad Dipanegara*, 4 vols, ed. Nindya Noegraha. Jakarta: Perpustakaan Nasional Republik Indonesia.
Bastin, J. and B. Brommer (1979). *Nineteenth-century Prints and Illustrated Books of Indonesia*. Utrecht, Antwerp: Spectrum.
Berg, L.W.C. van den (1886). *Le Hadhramaut et les Colonies Arabes dans l'Archipel Indien*. Batavia: Landsdrukkerij.
Brumund, J.F.G. (1854). 'Bezoek in den Vervallen Dalem van Dipo Negoro te Tegal Redjo', *Indiana* 2:181-97.
Carey, Peter (1974). *The Cultural Ecology of Early Nineteenth-century Java; Pangeran Dipanagara, A Case Study*. Singapore: Institute of Southeast Asian Studies [Occasional Paper 24].
Carey, Peter (1977). 'The Sepoy Conspiracy of 1815 in Java', *Bijdragen tot de Taal-, Land- en Volkenkunde* 133:294-322.
Carey, Peter (ed.) (1980). *The Archive of Yogyakarta. Vol. I: Documents relating to Politics and Internal Court Affairs*. Oxford: Oxford University Press.
Carey, Peter (1981). *Babad Dipanagara; An Account of the Outbreak of the Java War (1825-30). The Surakarta Court Version of the Babad Dipanagara with Translations into English and Indonesian Malay*. Kuala Lumpur: Art Printers.
Carey, Peter (1984). 'Changing Javanese Perceptions of the Chinese Communities in Central Java, 1755-1825', *Indonesia* 37:1-48.
Carey, Peter (ed.) (1992). *The British in Java, 1811-1816; A Javanese Account*. Oxford: Oxford University Press.
Carey, Peter (2008). *The Power of Prophecy; Prince Dipanagara and the End of an Old Order in Java, 1785-1855*. Leiden: KITLV Press, second revised edition.
Carey, Peter (2012). *Kuasa Ramalan; Pangeran Diponegoro dan Akhir Tatanan Lama di Jawa, 1785-1855*. Jakarta: KPG.
Carey, Peter and Mason Hoadley (eds) (2000). *The Archive of Yogyakarta. Vol. II: Documents relating to Economic and Agrarian Affairs*. Oxford: Oxford University Press.

Chambert-Loir, Henri (2000). 'Le Chagrin d'un Belge; Le Journal de Campagne du Comte Édouard Errembault de Dudzeele durant la Guerre de Java', *Archipel* 60:267–300.
Chijs, J.A. van der (1864). 'Bijdragen tot de Geschiedenis van het Inlandsch Onderwijs in Nederlandsch-Indië aan Officiële Bronnen ontleend', *Tijdschrift voor Indische Taal-, Land- en Volkenkunde (TBG)* 14:212–323.
Dobbin, C. (1974). 'Islamic Revivalism in Minangkabau at the turn of the Nineteenth Century', *Modern Asian Studies* 8–3:319–56.
Drewes, G.W.J. (1966). 'The Struggle between Javanism and Islam as Illustrated by the Sěrat Děrmagandul', *Bijdragen tot de Taal-, Land en Volkenkunde* 122:309–65.
Hageman, J.Jcz. (1856). *Geschiedenis van den Oorlog op Java van 1825 tot 1830*. Batavia: Lange.
Hobsbawm, E.J. (1969). *Bandits*. London: Weidenfeld and Nicholson.
Hogendorp, H. Graaf van (1913). *Willem van Hogendorp in Nederlandsch-Indië 1825–1830*. The Hague: Nijhoff.
Hollander, J.J. de (1877). 'Twee brieven van Dipå Negårå', *Bijdragen tot de Taal-, Land- en Volkenkunde* 25:192–6.
Huyssen van Kattendijke-Frank, Katrientje (2004). *Met Prins Hendrik naar de Oost: De Reis van W.J.C. Huyssen van Kattendijke naar Nederlands-Indië, 1836–1838*. Zutphen: Walburg.
Kemp, P.H. van der (1896). 'Dipanegara, eene Geschiedkundige Hamlettype', *Bijdragen tot de Taal-, Land- en Volkenkunde* 46:281–433.
Kielstra, E.B. (1885). 'Een en ander omtrent Dipo Negoro', *De Gids* 2:407–35.
Kielstra, E.B. (1896). 'Eenige Personen uit den Java-oorlog', *Tijdspiegel* 53:290–301.
Knoerle 'Journal' (1830). 'Aanteekeningen gehouden door den 2e Luit Knoerle betreffende de Dagelyksche Verkeering van dien Officier met den Prins van Djocjakarta, Diepo Negoro, gedurende eene Reis van Batavia naar Menado, het Exil van den genoemden Prins', Manado, 20–6-1830. MS 391 of the Johannes van den Bosch private collection in the Nationaal Archief, The Hague.
Knoerle, J.H. (1835). 'Extract uit de Gehoudene Aanteekeningen gedurende Mijne Reis naar Menado', *De Oosterling* 2:135–80.
Louw, P.J.F. and E.S. de Klerck (1894–1909). *De Java-Oorlog van 1825–30*. 6 volumes. The Hague: Nijhoff and Batavia: Landsdrukkerij.
Nahuys van Burgst, H.G. (1825). 'Proces-Verbaal van Radeen Mas Alip', 3–8–1825, UBL BPL 616, Port 9 no.2.
Nahuys van Burgst, H.G. (1835–6). *Verzameling van Officiële Rapporten betreffende den Oorlog op Java in de jaren 1825–1830, voorafgegaan door eenige Aanmerkingen en Mededelingen omtrent denzelven, benevens eene Memorie over de Verhuring of Uitgifte van Landeryen aan Europeanen*. Deventer: Ballot. Four vols.

Nes, J.F.W. van (1844). 'Verhandelingen over de Waarschijnlijke Oorzaken, die Aanleiding tot de Onlusten van 1825 en de volgende jaren in de Vorstenlanden gegeven hebben', *Tijdschrift voor Nederlandsche Indië* 6:112–71.

Palmer van den Broek, W. (1873–77) (ed. & trans). 'Geschiedenis van het Vorstenhuis Madoera uit het Javaansch Vertaald', *Tijdschrift voor Indische Taal-, Land- en Volkenkunde (TBG)* 20:241–301, 471–563, 22:1–89, 280–310, 24:1–169.

Pigeaud, Th.G.Th. (1967–80). *Literature of Java; Catalogue Raisonné of Javanese Manuscripts in the Library of the University of Leiden and other Public Collections in the Netherlands.* The Hague, Leiden: Nijhoff. Four volumes.

Rees, W.A. van (1867). *Toontje Poland; Voorafgegaan door eenige Indische Typen.* Arnhem: Thieme. Two volumes.

Ricklefs, M.C. (1998). *The Seen and Unseen Worlds in Java, 1726–1749; History, Literature and Islam in the Court of Pakubuwana II.* Sydney: Allen and Unwin, Honolulu: University of Hawaii Press.

Ricklefs, M.C. (2006). *Mystic Synthesis in Java; A History of Islamization from the Fourteenth to the Early Nineteenth Centuries.* EastBridge, Norwalk: Signature Books.

Ricklefs, M.C. (2012). *Islamisation and its Opponents in Java; A Political, Social, Cultural and Religious history, c. 1930 to the present.* Singapore: National University of Singapore Press.

Sagimun, M.D. (1965). *Pahlawan Dipanegara Berjuang; (Bara api Kemerdekaan nan tak kundjung padam).* Djakarta: Gunung Agung.

Schoemaker, J.P. (1893). 'De Onderwerping en Gevangenneming van Dipo Negoro Hoofd der Opstandelingen in den Java Oorlog 1825–1830', *Indisch Militair Tijdschrift* 1–6:407–91.

Snouck Hurgronje, C. (1931). *Mekka in the latter part of the Nineteenth Century; Daily Life, Customs and Learning; The Moslims of the East-Indian-Archipelago.* Translated by J.H. Monahan. Leiden: Brill, London: Luzac.

Stuers, F.V.H.A. de (1833). *Mémoires sur la Guerre de l'Île de Java.* Leiden: Luchtmans.

Tasso, Torquato (1581). *Gerusalemme Liberata.* Parma & Ferrara.

Upham, Edward (1829). *The History and Doctrine of Buddhism popularly illustrated with Notices of Kappoism or Demon worship and of the Bali, or Planetary Incantations of Ceylon.* London: Parbury, Allen & Co.

Wassing-Visser, Rita (1995). *Royal Gifts from Indonesia; Historical Bonds with the House of Orange-Nassau (1600–1938).* Zwolle: Waanders.

Winter, J.W.(1902). 'Beknopte Beschrijving van het Hof Soerakarta in 1824', G.P. Rouffaer (ed.). *Bijdragen tot de Taal-, Land- en Volkenkunde* 54:15–172.

CHAPTER III

Pilgrimage to the South Coast, circa 1805

Lelono: Spiritual Wanderings as Rite de Passage

Diponegoro's emergence into manhood was marked by a number of significant events: the passing of his great-grandmother on 17 October 1803, his investiture as Raden Ontowiryo on 3 September 1805, and his lavish *kraton* nuptials on 27 February 1807 (Chapter II). These last could be perceived as something of an official court *rite de passage* between his prepubescent years at Tegalrejo and the beginning of his young adult life as a Javanese nobleman.

Whereas for most of his contemporaries, such a young adult life might now have entailed family responsibilities around the Yogya *kraton*, for Diponegoro there was an added dimension. A second and more meaningful *rite de passage* – this time an extended form of spiritual wandering or *lelono* – loomed. This would confirm the spiritual practices of his youth and clarify his prophetic destiny. What this entailed has been well expressed by the Javanese historian Soemarsaid Moertono (1976:20–1):

> To set off on wanderings when one's age was approaching adulthood meant to obtain wisdom in the sense of finding a teacher who could guide one's development [enabling] one's powers to outstrip those of ordinary men. It also [...] entailed acquiring tranquility [...] so that on one's return one would be able to withstand all temptations. It was even occasionally a time of testing of the knowledge and wisdom which one had already acquired [through ascetic and meditative practices]. This tradition continued during the Islamic period in Java when people set off on long journeys – sometimes from [the furthest] west to [the furthest] east of Java and back again – to find esoteric knowledge at religious schools.

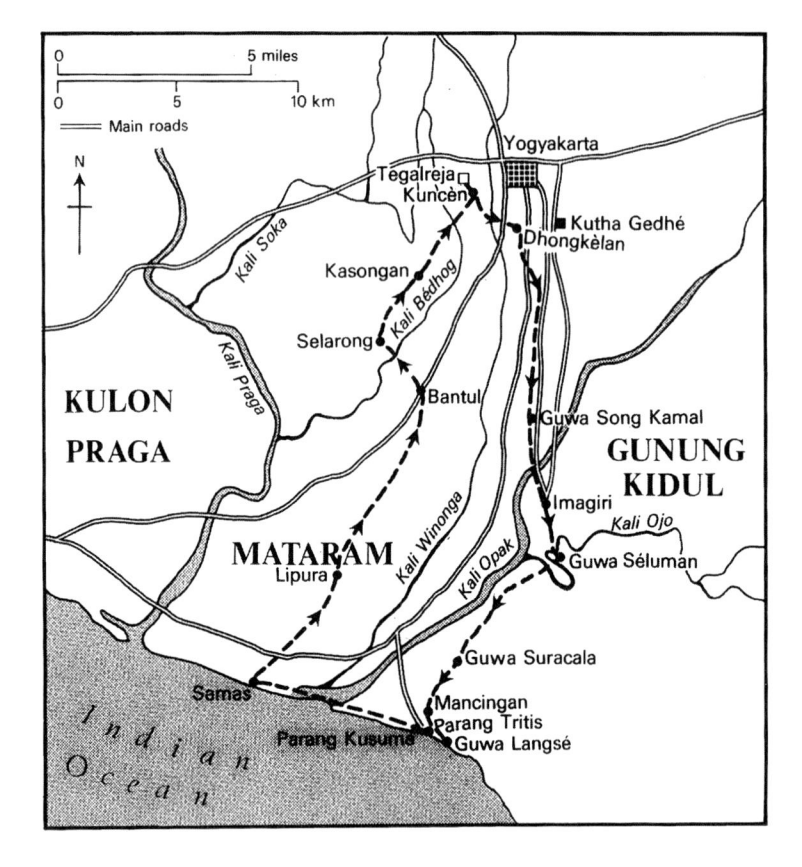

Map 4. Diponegoro's pilgrimage to the south coast of Java, circa 1805.

The first sultan, Mangkubumi, was widely regarded as the epitome of such a *satria lelono* (wandering knight) (Carey 2008:71). Another was Mangkubumi's contemporary and brother-in-arms, Raden Mas Said (Mangkunegoro I) whose his heirloom sword and court *gamelan* both bore *satria lelono* inscriptions (Carey 2008:128). Such testing journeys were the making of both the future Mangkunegoro I and Mangkubumi (Sultan Hamengkubuwono I). So it was with Diponegoro.

The exact timing of the prince's wanderings from Tegalrejo and his pilgrimage to the south coast is unclear. In his autobiography, he states that he started visiting religious schools or *pesantren* at the age of twenty (Javanese) years, hence sometime after April 1805. The next events related in his *babad* after his return to Tegalrejo from his journey to the south coast are the description of the changes in the position of the Dutch Residents (post-July 1808, ministers) introduced by Daendels' July 1808 decrees on Ceremonial and Etiquette (Babad Dipanegara, II:50; Chapter IV).

If the chronology in Diponegoro's *babad* is correct – and there is nothing to doubt it – then his journey to the south coast took place sometime before 1808. In my view, it is likely to have been even earlier, namely before his 27 February 1807 marriage after which he probably spent more time at Tegalrejo. We can thus surmise that his journey took place in circa 1805, probably early in the dry season (May–October) when travelling was easiest.

Preparations for a Pilgrimage

In preparation for his south coast journey, Diponegoro departed at the age of twenty (Javanese) years, namely around April 1805, on a series of visits to mosques and religious schools in the Yogya area (Babad Dipanegara, II:47). The importance of these visits was to complete his education as a student of religion and to identify appropriate teachers to guide his further religious development.

The prince also prepared himself for his spiritual quest by taking a new name, Seh Ngabdurahim. He used this on his wanderings to preserve his anonymity. This was derived from the Arabic Shaykh 'Abd al-Rahim (Babad Dipanegara, II:47; Ricklefs 1974b:231–2) and may have been suggested by one of his religious advisers at Tegalrejo – perhaps even Sheikh al-Ansari (Chapter II).

The adoption of such an 'Islamic' name was not so unusual amongst members of the Javanese nobility at this time: Pangeran Dipowijoyo I, a son of the first sultan changed his name to Pangeran Muhamad Abubakar in preparation for making the *haj* to Mecca in 1810 (Carey 1992:291–2, 336, 340, 400 note 5; Chapter VI). He also shaved off his hair – traditionally worn long by the Javanese nobility (Carey 1981:254 note 79, 1992:462 note 300a) – as a sign that 'he wanted to become a *santri*'.

Diponegoro and his followers followed suit during the Java War when they took Islamic names and shaved their heads in emulation of The Prophet's tonsure (*paras Nabi*) (Louw and De Klerck 1894–1909, II:497). Indeed, the prince may well have cut hair before his wanderings to *pesantren* to pass unnoticed in the communities of ordinary *santri*. He also disguised himself in simple attire so that few people would recognize him (Babad Dipanegara, II:47; Carey 2008:131). This involved exchanging his high-collared Javanese jacket, hand-drawn batik wrap-around and head-dress for standard *santri* dress: namely, the coarsely woven sarong, buttonless open-necked white coat (*kabaya*) and green or white turban (Raffles 1817, I:90; Djajadiningrat 1936:20; Plate 19). After the Java War, his eldest son, Pangeran Diponegoro II (born circa 1803), would seek to follow his example travelling around in Kedu dressed in the garb of a common farmer to emphasise his closeness with the people.[1]

When the preparations were complete, Diponegoro departed from Tegalrejo and began a typical wandering *santri* existence visiting religious schools and mosques, where he lived in the dormitories together with the ordinary *pesantren* students (Babad Dipanegara, II:47–8). It is not certain which schools he visited, but they may have included those to the south of Yogya like Gading, Grojogan, Sewon, Wonokromo, Jejeran, Turi, Pulo Kadang, Kasongan and Dongkelan, the last two *pathok negari* (Carey 2008:787–94; Map 4).

---

[1] Such demotic solidarity was regarded with deep suspicion by the Dutch. One 'Just King' (*Ratu Adil*) from the Diponegoro family was enough. He was thus exiled first to Sumenep in eastern Madura (1834–51) and then Ambon (1851–?). Diponegoro II's offspring by his wife whom he brought from Madura would be the ancestors of a whole line of Diponegoro descendants in the Moluccas (Maluku) (Carey 2008:131, 767–8; personal communication the late Mas Den Diponegoro, lineal descendant of Diponegoro II, Bekasi, 29 November 2012). The headstones (*nisan*) on both her grave and that of Diponegoro II at Batu Merah in Ambon are now so weathered that the dates can no longer be read.

Tirakat: Solitary Withdrawal and First Visions

After a time, the prince ceased visiting *pesantren* and departed far from inhabited areas to engage in asceticism and meditation (Babad Dipanegara, II:47). There now began a very crucial stage in Diponegoro's wanderings during which he sought out some of the most important shrines and holy places associated with the Mataram dynasty (Ricklefs 1974b:232). This period of withdrawal and self-negation had much of the quality of a retreat from the world (*tirakat*) of a man who wished to prepare himself for a serious undertaking (Winter 1902:87; Carey 1974a:15). It afforded an interval of solitude in which to purge oneself of *pamrih* (selfish or concealed personal motives and ambitions). In Diponegoro's case, it would also legitimate his subsequent actions through contact with his departed ancestors and Java's spiritual guardians.

Diponegoro's first vision occurred at the cave of Song Kamal in the Jejeran district to the south of Yogya (Map 4). Sunan Kalijogo, one of the nine apostles of Islam (*wali*), appeared before the prince in the shape of a man 'who shone like the full moon'. He informed the prince that it had been determined by God that in the future he would become king (*ratu*). After delivering this prophecy, the vision immediately disappeared.

The appearance of Sunan Kalijogo and his prophecy of kingship was clearly of great importance for Diponegoro. Not only was the *wali* especially revered in south-central Java as the adviser of kings and the spiritual protector of Mataram, but legend also ascribed him a key role in the area's islamisation (De Graaf and Pigeaud 1974:28–30; Solichin Salam 1963). Sunan Kalijogo's grave at Kadilangu, together with the great mosque at Demak, are still regarded by Javanese rulers as the island's two indispensable *pusaka* (heirlooms) and early-nineteenth-century court pilgrimages regularly visited both places (Carey 1980:171).

In Javanese political history, Kalijogo was also viewed as the agent who had presided over the division of Java at Giyanti (1755) (Ricklefs 1974b:233–7). But this may not have weighed with Diponegoro who saw himself as transcending such political divisions by governing the whole of Java as a *pandita-ratu* (priest-king) (Chapter IX).

The vision was also important at another level since the style of political leadership represented by Kalijogo and his eight fellow apostles (*wali*) served as an example for the prince. Like the legendary *wali*, Diponegoro would come to see himself not merely as a temporal ruler but also as spiritual overseer of the Javanese sovereigns (Carey 1974a:16–17, 21–2, 1974b:285–8). Both he and his advisers would frequently debate their example, especially those of Kudus, Demak and Giri, when striving for consensus during the war regarding their overall political and religious aims (Carey 1974a:19–22).

Descendants of the *wali* like Pangeran Serang (circa 1794–1854), or those related by marriage like his mother, the redoubtable Raden Ayu Serang (circa 1769–1855), were highly esteemed by Diponegoro. He viewed them as persons imbued with *kasekten* (inner spiritual power) (Louw and De Klerck 1894–1909, I:361–3; Carey 1981:284 note 205). There was even a rumour during the war that he would delegate some of his authority to one of the Raden Ayu's grandsons – Raden Mas Papak (Pangeran Adipati Notoprojo) – given that Kalijogo's descendants were best placed to wield spiritual power in Java (Carey 2008:133).

The vision of the revered *wali* and the support of his lineal descendants helped legitimize Diponegoro's subsequent rebellion. This process was confirmed in the prince's dream just before the outbreak of the Java War on 16 May 1825 when he met eight apostles, referred to as '*wali wudhar*', namely *wali* exercising both temporal and spiritual office, who confirmed his Just King (*Ratu Adil*) title as Sultan Erucokro (pp.219–24).

Following his stay in the Jejeran district, Diponegoro walked through the countryside to Imogiri, the royal gravesite of the Mataram rulers. There at Bengkung by the pond at the top of the great stairway leading to the royal graves, he spent a week in meditation. He then observed the Friday prayer at the mosque at Jimatan, the mosque of the keepers of the keys (*jurukunci*) known as *jimat*, who guarded the royal graveyard below the summit of Imogiri. Despite his ragged appearance, Diponegoro related that the *jurukunci* recognised him and 'paid him honour with all they possessed' (Babad Dipanegara, II:48; Ricklefs 1974b:237–8, 254–65), an indication of just how much he was admired by these religious officials. Many would later support him during the Java War (Carey 2008:786–94).

Apart from visiting the graves of his deceased relations, especially those of Sultan Mangkubumi (Hamengkubuwono I) and Ratu Ageng, Diponegoro's meditation at Bengkung was almost certainly directed to Sultan Agung (reigned 1613–46), the famous seventeenth-century Mataram ruler. Diponegoro knew that Bengkung had been Agung's special place of retreat (Babad Dipanegara, I:158), and he would visit his grave frequently, even planning his own and his favourite wife, Raden Ayu Maduretno's, burial there during the Java War (Louw and De Klerck 1894–1909, III:76, 219, V:744; *Bataviasche Courant* 44, 2–11–1825; *Javasche Courant* 143, 29–11–1828; Carey 2008:692, 2012, I:160, III:917).[2]

There is an interesting reference in a hostile Javanese source, the *Buku Kedung Kebo* (Book of the Buffaloes' Watering Hole), composed by one of the prince's foremost adversaries (Carey 1974b:259–88, 1981:xxvi–xxvii). This describes how the prince sent an intimate retainer to Sultan Agung's grave to beg for a sign. After a night spent in meditation, a dark red spot about the size of a plate appeared on the curtains surrounding the tomb. The chief *jurukunci*, Kyai Balad, then explained that this meant that God had decreed that warfare should break out in Java and that much blood would be shed (Carey 2008:135; Plate 2).

There is no mention in Diponegoro's *babad* of his having received a sign at Agung's grave, but the prince did refer to one of Agung's prophecies relating to the 300-year period of Dutch rule in Java which had a direct connection with his own life (Chapter I). He also showed his great admiration for the seventeenth-century ruler referring to him as 'a spiritual man who did as I did travelling around everywhere' and as 'a consummate Islamic ruler who established the five pillars [*rukun*] of Islam' (Louw and De Klerck 1894–1909, V:744; Carey 1974a:17).

2 According to Diponegoro's autobiography (Babad Dipanegara, IV:3), Raden Ayu Maduretno died at Kawisarjo in the Kulon Progo area on 20 November 1827 (Carey 2012, III:917). She appears to have been initially buried there, her body only being transferred to the royal graveyard at Jimatan (Imogiri) after the end of the Java War, personal communication Ki Roni Sodewo (lineal descendant of Diponegoro's son, Raden Mas Alip), Kulon Progo, 5 November 2012.

At the South Coast: Meetings with Ratu Kidul

After staying at Imogiri, Diponegoro made his way to the south coast, overnighting at the cave of Seluman near the Oyo River, home to the female spirit Genowati (Ricklefs 1974b:406 note 89 no. 85, 2006:209). He then spent a further two nights at the cave of Surocolo, also known as Guwo Sigologolo, on the left bank of the Kali Opak in the Gamelan sub-district of Gunung Kidul (Babad Dipanegara, II:48; Ricklefs 1974b:238).

Both caves have associations with the Javanese spirit world and were frequently visited by the court elite for periods of meditation and retreat (Carey 1980:112; 2008:137; Carey and Hoadley 2000:409) The first is mentioned in the *Kidung Lalembut* ('Song of the spirits') as part of the 'palace of the spirits' ruled over by the south sea goddess, Ratu Kidul, through her deputy, Dewi Genowati (Ricklefs 1974a:406 note 89 no.85, 1974b:238–9). The second is referred to in the Bima Raré series of shadow-plays describing the *wayang* hero, Bima's, exploits as a young man, during his search for the 'water of life'. While meditating there he had undergone a test by fire (Carey 2008:137; Pigeaud 1967–80, I:205). Interestingly, one of Diponegoro's heirloom *kris*, subsequently presented to King Willem I (reigned, 1813–40) as a war trophy, was identified in 1831 by the celebrated Javanese artist, Raden Saleh Syarif Bustaman (?1811–80), as Kangjeng Kyai Nogo Siluman (His Highness the Magician King of the Snakes) (Kraus 2005:280–1; Carey 2008:813).

In neither of these two caves did Diponegoro receive any visitations.

The prince then walked across the Gunung Kidul foothills to the cave of Langse which overhangs the thunderous Indian Ocean. Reached by a steep and precipitous path down the limestone cliffs and through an entrance almost at sea level, it is a place of great importance in the local cult of Ratu Kidul (Carey 2008:140). The cave and the adjacent sites of Pamancingan (Mancingan), Parangtritis, Parangkusumo and Parangwedang, a warm-water spring, are all associated with this spiritual protector and consort of the central Javanese rulers whose beauty waxes and wanes with the moon (Jordaan 1984:99–102, 107, 2006:14; Hadiwidjojo 1972:126; Carey 2008:140).

Mancingan, for example, is known as one of the eight principal residences of the spirits (*lalembut*) of Java and home of the female hermit, Cemoro Tunggal, herself closely identified with Ratu Kidul (De Graaf and Pigeaud 1974:248 note 8; Ricklefs 1974a:375 note 33). The same place is also associated with Seh Maulana Maghribī, a *wali* said to be from the Demak period, who lived and was buried at the top of one of the small hills overlooking the sea (Adam 1930:158–9).

Parangtritis, so called because of the water which gushes out of the rocks in a petrified grotto, is the spot where Senopati set out to meet Ratu Kidul in her underwater court and where on his return he encountered Sunan Kalijogo (Olthof 1941a, I:82, 1941b, I:79). An annual offering, known as the *labuhan* (from Javanese *labuh*, 'to throw into the water', Gericke and Roorda 1901, II:163), is performed each year by the sultan of Yogya to the south sea goddess from the twin rocks at Parangkusumo (Palmer van den Broek 1873–77, 24:143; Groneman 1888:13–14; Adam 1930:157–8; Plate 3). The whole site is thus deeply connected with the Javanese spirit world and still attracts visitors from all over Java.

At the time Diponegoro visited the place in circa 1805, it was already a major pilgrimage site. The second sultan made regular trips there, residing at Mancingan for days on end (Carey 2008:141). Small open pavilions, known in Javanese as *pondok*, had been constructed by the sea at Parangkusumo, Parangwedang and Parangtritis for meditation and ceremonies associated with the goddess of the southern ocean. There was also a larger wooden *pesanggrahan* (overnight residence) at Parangtritis to house the sultan and his retinue (Thorn 1815:295; Carey 2008:784). The upkeep of these structures and the grave of Seh Maulana were overseen by court-maintained *jurukunci*, referred to locally as 'people in white' (*wong putihan*) (Carey 2008:141, 784). In May 1812, a Dutch visitor noticed some of these white-garbed meditators with a young Javanese 'in a religious attitude' at Parangtritis. He was informed that people often came there to pray for things or if they were in difficult circumstances (Carey 2008:144).

Diponegoro was therefore following a well worn route when he arrived at the south coast as a young twenty-year-old. His aim was to prepare himself for a meeting with Ratu Kidul and he describes how he remained in the Langse cave for two weeks 'striving to purify his desires' (Babad Dipanegara,

II:48). As his physical and mental state grew calmer, he entered a deep meditative trance, 'a condition that cannot be described'. He was then visited by Ratu Kidul whose presence was heralded by a brilliant aura of light. The prince, however, was so deeply sunk in his meditation that the goddess realised 'he could not be tempted'. So she withdrew, promising that she would come again when the time was right (Babad Dipanegara, II:48-9; Ricklefs 1974b:239, 256).

Over twenty years would elapse before Ratu Kidul's next visitation. The Java War was then at its height and Diponegoro was encamped at Kamal on a tributary of the Progo River in the Kulon Progo district (Louw and De Klerck 1894–1909, II:346–8, V:Map; Carey 2008:144). The exact date is unclear in his account, but it seems to have been in mid-July 1826, possibly on the night of the full moon (20–21 July). The following is the description in his *babad* (Babad Dipanegara, III:42–3):

> XXV 63. [...]
> Then the sultan [Diponegoro]
> was sitting at night in his pavilion
> unattended by anyone,
> for they were all asleep.
>
> 64. He was sunk deep in meditation with his back against a pillar,
> for heavy was his heart.
> Now it is told that
> swiftly someone came.
> It was as though a falling star had descended on the pavilion.
> Immediately sitting before
> the sultan was the form of a woman.
>
> 65. Two accompanied her,[3]
> both women with a similar appearance
> which cannot be described.
> But, of the three, one
> was slightly different from those who escorted her.

---

3   These refer to Ratu Kidul's two lieutenants (*patih*), Nyai Roro (or Loro) Kidul and Raden Déwi, the tutelary spirit of Guwo Langse, Carey 2008:145.

For long the sultan did not address her,
dumbfounded he gazed,

66. and closely observed her.
She was sitting but did not touch the ground.
The sultan said softly:
'I ask [your name]
for I am quite mystified.' Ratu [Kidul] said:
'Earlier I
made a promise to your lordship

67. that in the future, when the time had come,
[I] should not fail to meet you.'
The sultan understood in his heart.
Thus were his thoughts
that perhaps her name was Ratu Kidul
for she was exceedingly young.
The sultan spoke quietly:

68. 'I now recall it.'
Ratu [Kidul] then said gently:
'If I am allowed to help
your lordship,
I beg a firm promise
that once they have all disappeared
the unbelieving devils [the Dutch],

69. you sir will intercede for me
with Allah the Almighty
that I may return again
to be a human being.
Moreover, all your army
let there be none who join the battle,
for it is I who promise

70. to [bring about] the disappearance of the devils.'
The sultan said softly:
'I do not ask your help
against my equals [fellow human beings],
for in religion there is only the assistance of the Almighty.'
Ratu [Kidul] immediately disappeared.

Ratu Kidul's visitation had a specific objective. As queen of the spirit world, she was offering Diponegoro her help on condition that he intercede with the Almighty to enable her to return to the world as a human being. It is a request which she makes to all her royal lovers. But, as Diponegoro observed, no one can change her fate. She is fated to remain in the spirit kingdoms until the Day of Judgement (*Ari Kiyamat*) (Balai Pustaka 1940:31–7; Carey 2008:147). Such is the Will of God. For all her beauty and magical power, the goddess of the southern ocean is a tragic figure as much in need of help as capable of assisting others. Certainly, Diponegoro viewed her in this light. He thus resolutely refused her offer of assistance.

What then was his purpose in relating this encounter? One explanation is that he wished to put himself on a par with Senopati and Sultan Agung, both monarchs who enjoyed a special relationship with Ratu Kidul. As we have seen, Diponegoro was especially keen to draw out parallels between himself and Agung in terms of his exercise of spiritual and temporal power during the Java War (Carey 2008:147, 642).

At another level, the prince may have referred to his meeting to stress that he had no truck with magical powers or Faustian bargains with the spirit world in his struggle against the Dutch. As a devout Muslim, he placed his faith in the Almighty. Moreover, his primary aim during the Java War was the furtherance of religion, in particular 'the raising up of the high state of the Islamic religion throughout Java' – namely the moral order as much as formal Islamic practise (Carey 1974a:285). The prince's refusal to accept help from Ratu Kidul underscores this ideal for which he would sacrifice so much.

Personally, however, he remained fascinated by the ever beautiful goddess. A Javanese to the core, he drew as much inspiration from the ancestral spirit world as from his Muslim devotions and adherence to the esoteric teachings of the Shaṭṭārīyya. This mirrored the 'mystic synthesis' which Ricklefs describes so brilliantly in his study of pre-nineteenth-century Java (Ricklefs 2006:195–220). On his journey into exile, the prince would refer to Ratu Kidul at length in his conversations with Knoerle ('Journal', 1830:25). His eldest son, Pangeran Diponegoro II, meanwhile, would emulate his encounter with the goddess in his allegorical chronicle of the Java War (Carey 2008:150).

Final Instruction at Parangkusumo and Return to Tegalrejo

After his first wordless encounter with Ratu Kidul at Guwo Langse, the prince descended to the sea shore and walked back along the beach to Parangtritis where he bathed. During his subsequent night at Parangkusumo a final visitation occurred. A disembodied voice, maybe that of Sunan Kalijogo, told him of the coming destruction of Yogya, a 'beginning of the ruin of the Land of Java' (*wiwit bubrah Tanah Jawi*) which would start in under three years' time. Instructed to change his religious name from Ngabdurahim to Ngabdulkamit, he was informed that a sign would be given him in the shape of an arrow named 'Sarutomo'. This appeared like a lightning flash piercing the stone on which he was sleeping (Carey 2008:49).

He was also enjoined to watch over his father, the future third sultan, and sternly warned not to accept the title of crown prince (*Pangeran Adipati Anom*) if it was offered by the colonial government 'for that would be definitely sinful' (Babad Dipanegara, II:49; pp. 128–9). Finally, the voice ended on this enigmatic note (Babad Dipanegara, II:49):

> XIV 80. There is no other:
> you alone are the means,
> but that not for long,
> only to be counted amongst the ancestors.
> Ngabdulkamit, farewell, you must return home!

Sultan Agung's prophecy mentioned in the first chapter, namely his prediction that the Dutch would rule in Java for 300 years after his death (1646) and that although one of his descendants would rise against them he would be defeated, may well have a connection here (Chapter I).

The implications of the other passages are perhaps more straightforward: the reference to Yogya's imminent destruction presaged the arrival of Daendels as governor-general on 5 January 1808. His subsequent humiliation of the sultan's court following Raden Ronggo's November 1810 revolt (Chapter V) would set in train a process which would culminate in the fall of the *kraton* on 20 June 1812. The British plundering of the court, the theft of its archives and the exile of the second sultan marked the real beginning of the Parangkusumo prophecy's fateful 'destruction of the land of Java' (Babad Dipanegara, II:49; Chapter VII).

Diponegoro's change of name from Ngabdurahim to Ngabdulkamit was of great significance. He would bear this moniker throughout the Java War and incorporate it in his title as Sultan Erucokro or Javanese 'Just King' in August 1825 (Carey 1981:287 note 218; Ricklefs 1974b:244). In exile he would style himself 'Pangeran Ngabdulkamit' (Knoerle, 'Journal', 1830:29; Carey 2008:152), later exchanging his princely title for that of *fakir* (religious mendicant) when he came to write his religious reflections in Makassar in 1838 (Diponegoro, 'Makassar Notebooks', II:67).

In Ricklefs' view, the prince's new name may have had a connection with Sultan 'Abd al-Hamīd I, the late eighteenth-century Ottoman sovereign (1773–87), who revived the sultanate's claims to the authority of caliph, the protector of all Muslims worldwide (Ricklefs 1974b:241, 2006:210). For Diponegoro and his contemporaries this recalled Sultan Ngrum, a name inspired by the Arabic Rūm (eastern 'Rome' or Byzantium, hence Constantinople) of Javanese legend (Ricklefs 2006:210). A Islamic universal monarch who appears in both the Aji Soko tales and the messianic Joyoboyo prophecies, he is depicted as organizing the civilising and peopling of Java and later dispatches a force to drive out foreign oppressors (Pigeaud 1967–80, III:366; Ricklefs 1974b:242–4).

The prince himself would later reproduce a version of the Aji Soko tales dealing with Sultan Ngrum's peopling of Java and ridding the island of evil spirits during his period of exile in Makassar (1833–55) (Diponegoro, 'Makassar Notebooks', I:50–3).

As a bulwark of Islamic power in the Middle East and potential protector against the expanding might of Christian Europe, the Ottoman empire was widely admired in Java (Carey 1979:217 note 93). This admiration inspired Diponegoro's use of Ottoman ranks such as '*Ali Basah*' from the Turkish 'Ali Pasha (the 'High' Pasha) (Carey 1974a:287 note 6) and Janissary regimental names for his military formations during the Java War. Thus his elite Bulkio, Turkio and Arkio troops were arranged in companies modelled on the Bölüki (from *bölük*, a squad or troop), Oturaḳi, and Ardia Janissary units of the Ottoman sultans, later reorganized as a new model army of 'trained victorious soldiers of Muhammad' (*muallem azakir-I mansuri-i Muhammadije*) under Mahmud II (reigned, 1809–39)

(Marsigli 1732:68-9; Louw and De Klerck 1894-1909, II:277; Booms 1911:34; Aukes 1935:74; Shaw and Shaw 1977, II:22-4).

The gift of the arrow Sarutomo, which came to the prince like a flash of lightning, again recalls Arjuna, the *wayang* figure with whom he most closely identified (Carey 1974a:12-16; Chapter VII). In the Mahabhārata-inspired shadow-play, the same magical weapon was associated with the Pandawa prince during his meditation at Lake Tirtomoyo (Carey 2008:153), prefiguring the period of destruction which Diponegoro would bring about in Java as foretold by the Parangkusumo prophecy. There were resonances here with Arjuna's arrow, Pasopati, which also served as the agent of destruction against demonic forces in the poem *Arjuna Wiwāha* ('Marriage of Arjuna'; Poerbatjaraka 1926:288-90).

On his return to Tegalrejo, Diponegoro fashioned the arrow head into a small stabbing dagger (*cundrik*), which he later gave to his beloved fourth wife, Raden Ayu Maduretno (Babad Dipanegara, II:49-50; Carey 2008:814). After her death in late 1827, it was melted down together with two other *pusaka* weapons to make a single heirloom *kris*, Kyai Ageng Bondoyudo (His Highness Sir Duelling without Weapons), which was used to rally troop morale during difficult stages of the war (Babad Dipanegara, III:145). It would later be buried with the prince in his grave in Makassar (Carey 2008:813; Chapter XII).

Finally, the voice's injunction to the prince to watch over his father in facilitating his accession as sultan and the stern warning to refuse the title of crown prince had immediate relevance. They both referred to the political crisis which would engulf Yogya following the arrival of Marshal Daendels on 5 January 1808. During the four-and-a-half years preceding the 20 June 1812 British attack, Diponegoro depicts himself in his *babad* playing a similar role to that envisaged in the Parangkusumo prophecy, helping to mediate between his father and his grandfather, the second sultan, and acting as a negotiator between his father and the British, resulting in the former's accession as third sultan on 21 June 1812 (Chapter VII). At the same time, he successfully deflected British attempts to appoint him as crown prince by getting them to recognize his better born younger brother – the future fourth sultan (reigned 1814-22) – as heir apparent (pp. 128-9).

Diponegoro's Parangkusumo visitation was the last of his south coast pilgrimage. His period of *tirakat* was over. Making his way back to Tegalrejo, he stopped for a short while at Sawangan, a marshy area at the mouth of the Kali Opak where the wide tidal river flows into the sea. He then went to Lipuro on the seashore close to Sawangan (Babad Dipanegara, II:49; Carey 2008:784). At Lipuro, he spent a night at Selo Gilang, the holy black stone – probably a meteorite – which is watched over by the spirit guardian Kyai Jonggo (Ricklefs 1974b:247; Carey 2008:154). According to historical legend, this stone had descended over Senopati's head as he lay asleep announcing that it was God's Will that he should become king of Java. The place thus had important associations with the founder of the Mataram dynasty and Diponegoro may have chosen it for that reason. Even today it remains a revered site where holy *kris* blades are sometimes struck (Ricklefs 1974b:247 note 59).

The following day the prince walked on to the cave at Secang situated on what after July 1812 would become his lands in the Selarong area to the west of the Kali Bedog (Carey 2008:369). Later frequented by him as a place for withdrawal and meditation, it would become his first headquarters during the Java War. The ground around the cave was later converted into a garden and a special rock chamber hewn out of the cave wall with a stone niche for sleeping. Here the prince passed the night before returning to Tegalrejo (Babad Dipanegara, II:49–50; Carey 1981:238–40 notes 20–7; Ricklefs 1974b:247).

Conclusion

Diponegoro's return from his pilgrimage in the latter part of 1805, marked the end of his spiritual apprenticeship. The period of his youth was over. He had learnt much from his great-grandmother whose self-discipline, religious devotion and ability to mix with all classes of Javanese society had shaped him. Living at Tegalrejo had also taught him the advantages of distancing himself from the Yogya court, turning him into an intensely private person, a lover of solitude and that inward peace which comes from meditation and silent reflection.

The prince was now a mature young man whose self-awareness was tempered by the insights gained on his pilgrimage. He had glimpsed the significant but fleeting role he would be called upon to play in the great events which would now unfold in his native Yogyakarta. On the eve of the Java War, he would return again to the south coast to meditate in its caves and grottos as part of his spiritual preparation for his great rebellion (Chapter IX). By then he would have received new visions which would make his destiny all the clearer.

The passages in his *babad* relating to the visions Diponegoro received on his south coast pilgrimage afford an insight into the way he perceived his place in Javanese history. Much is still obscure, but four themes stand out. The first is the importance of the historical example of the *wali* or apostles of Islam, especially Sunan Kalijogo, which prefigured his leadership style during the Java War and legitimized his rebellion. The second is the influence of Sultan Agung, whom Diponegoro viewed as the Mataram ruler most worthy of emulation. The third is Diponegoro's conscious rejection of help from the Javanese spirit kingdoms and his stress on his faith as a Javanese Muslim. Significantly, however, he remained enough a Javanese to always refer to the Almighty in his autobiography entirely by Sanskrit-derived names: *Hyang Agung* ('The Great One'), *Hyang Suksma* ('The Immaterial One') or *Hyang Widi* ('The One Who Leads') rather than the Islamically orthodox *Allah Ingkang Rabulngalimin* ('God the Forgiving One') or *Allah Tangala* ('God the Sublime').

The fourth was the prince's identification with the *wayang* hero Arjuna. A leitmotif for his life, Arjuna's role in the *Arjuna Wiwāha* tale, particularly his actions to prepare himself through asceticism to achieve invincible power in the world, had a strong resonance for Diponegoro. The prince's brief period as a Javanese Ratu Adil or 'Just King' would be linked with a time of purifying destruction similar to that carried out by the *wayang* hero in the *Arjuna Wiwāha* story. The Java War leader even had Arjuna's Pasopati arrow – incarnated for him as Sarutomo – emblazoned on his personal battle standard (see cover image).

These four themes provided the context and frame within which the prince's career would later develop. At the time of his return from his pilgrimage in late 1805 all this lay in the future. What was clear, however, was that he had returned with a clearer sense of his prophetic destiny and his place in Javanese history. But he would be called to act just as the old Javanese regime, which had defined and shaped his youth, was crumbling in the face of a new and more potent European imperial order. Unleashed by the twin industrial and political revolutions which had reshaped late eighteenth-century Europe, it would reconfigure the prince's world in ways beyond his wildest imaginings.

Bibliography

Adam, L. (1930). 'Eenige Historische en Legendarische Plaatsnamen te Jogjakarta', *Djåwå* 10:150–62.

Aukes, H.F. (1935). *Het Legioen van Mangkoe Nagoro*. Bandoeng: Nix.

Babad Dipanegara (2010). *Babad Dipanegara*, 4 vols, ed. Nindya Noegraha. Jakarta: Perpustakaan Nasional Republik Indonesia.

Bataviasche Courant [pre-January 1828, Netherlands-Indies government newspaper] 44, 2-11-1825 (report on Diponegoro's visit to Imogiri in October 1825).

Booms, A.S.H. (1911). *Eenige Bladzijden uit de Nederlandsch-Indische Krijgsgeschiedenis, 1820–1840; Uit de "Mémoires" van F.C. Gilly de Montela*. Amsterdam: Engelhard en Van Embden.

Carey, Peter (1974a). *The Cultural Ecology of Early Nineteenth-century Java; Pangeran Dipanagara, A Case Study*. Singapore: Institute of Southeast Asian Studies [Occasional Paper 24].

Carey, Peter (1974b). 'Javanese Histories of Dipanagara; The Buku Kĕdhuŋ Kĕbo, its Authorship and Historical Importance', *Bijdragen tot de Taal-, Land- en Volkenkunde*, 130:259–88.

Carey, Peter (ed.) (1980). *The Archive of Yogyakarta. Vol. I: Documents relating to Politics and Internal Court Affairs*. Oxford: Oxford University Press.

Carey, Peter (1981). *Babad Dipanagara; An Account of the Outbreak of the Java War (1825–30). The Surakarta Court Version of the Babad Dipanagara with Translations into English and Indonesian Malay*. Kuala Lumpur: Art Printers.

Carey, Peter (ed.) (1992). *The British in Java, 1811–1816; A Javanese Account*. Oxford: Oxford University Press.

Carey, Peter (2008). *The Power of Prophecy; Prince Dipanagara and the End of an Old Order in Java, 1785–1855*. Leiden: KITLV Press, second revised edition.
Carey, Peter (2012). *Kuasa Ramalan; Pangeran Diponegoro dan Akhir Tatanan Lama di Jawa, 1785–1855*. Jakarta: KPG, second revised edition.
Carey, Peter and Mason Hoadley (eds) (2000). *The Archive of Yogyakarta. Vol. II: Documents relating to Economic and Agrarian Affairs*. Oxford: Oxford University Press.
Diponegoro, Pangeran (1838) 'Makassar Notebooks', Fort Rotterdam, Makassar, library photocopy of manuscript formerly in possession of the late Raden Mas Jusuf Diponegoro and the late Raden Mas Saleh Diponegoro, Jalan Irian no.83, Makassar. 2 volumes.
Djajadiningrat, Achmad (1936). *Herinneringen van Pangeran Aria Achmad Djajadiningrat*. Amsterdam, Batavia: Kolff.
Gericke, J.F.C. and Roorda, T. (1901). *Javaansch-Nederlandsch handwoordenboek*. Amsterdam: Muller, Leiden: Brill. Two vols.
Graaf, H.J. de and Th.G.Th. Pigeaud (1974). *De Eerste Moslimse Vorstendommen op Java; Studiën over de Staatkundige Geschiedenis van de 15de en 16de Eeuw*. The Hague: Nijhoff. [KITLV, Verhandelingen 69].
Groneman, J. (1888). *In den Kedaton te Jogjakarta; Oepatjårå, Ampilan en Toneeldansen*. Leiden: Brill.
Hadiwidjojo, K.G.P.A.A. (1972). 'Danse Sacrée à Surakarta; La Signification du Bedojo Ketawang', *Archipel* 3:117–30.
Javasche Courant [post-January 1828, Netherlands-Indies government newspaper] 143, 29-11-1828 (report on Diponegoro's visit to Imogiri in November 1828).
Jordaan, R.E. (1984). 'The Mystery of Nyai Lara Kidul; Goddess of the Southern Ocean'. *Archipel* 28:99–116.
Jordaan, R.E. (2006). 'Why the Śailendras were not a Javanese Dynasty', *Indonesia and the Malay World* 34 (98):3–22.
Knoerle 'Journal' (1830). 'Aanteekeningen gehouden door den 2e Luit Knoerle betreffende de Dagelyksche Verkeering van dien Officier met den Prins van Djocjakarta, Diepo Negoro, gedurende eene Reis van Batavia naar Menado, het Exil van den genoemden Prins', Manado, 20-6-1830. MS 391 of the Johannes van den Bosch private collection in the Nationaal Archief, The Hague.
Knoerle, J.H. (1835). 'Extract uit de Gehoudene Aanteekeningen gedurende Mijne Reis naar Menado', *De Oosterling* 2:135–80.
Kraus, W. (2005). 'Raden Saleh's Interpretation of the Arrest of Diponegoro; An Example of Indonesian "Proto-Nationalist" Modernism', *Archipel* 69:259–94.
Louw, P.J.F. and E.S. de Klerck (1894–1909). *De Java-Oorlog van 1825–30*. 6 volumes. The Hague: Nijhoff and Batavia: Landsdrukkerij.

Marsigli, L.F. (1732). *L'Etat Militaire de l'Empire Ottoman; Ses Progrès et sa Décadence.* La Haye: Gosse et Jean Neaulme, De Hondt, Moentjens, Amsterdam: Uytwerf, Changuion. Two vols.

Olthof, W.L. (ed. and trans.) (1941a). *Babad Tanah Djawi in Proza; Javaansche Geschiedenis loopende tot het jaar 1647 der Javaansche jaartelling.* The Hague: Nijhoff. Two vols.

Othof, W.L. (ed.) (1941b). *Poenika Serat Babad Tanah Djawi wiwit saking Nabi Adam doemoegi ing taoen 1647.* The Hague: Nijhoff. Two vols.

Palmer van den Broek, W. (1873–77) (ed. & trans) "Geschiedenis van het Vorstenhuis Madoera uit het Javaansch Vertaald", *Tijdschrift voor Indische Taal-, Land- en Volkenkunde* 20:241–301, 471–563, 22:1–89, 280–310, 24:1–169.

Pigeaud, Th.G.Th. (1967–80). *Literature of Java; Catalogue Raisonné of Javanese Manuscripts in the Library of the University of Leiden and other Public Collections in the Netherlands.* The Hague, Leiden: Nijhoff. Four volumes.

Poerbatjaraka, R. Ng. (1926). 'Arjuna Wiwāha', *Bijdragen tot de Taal-, Land- en Volkenkunde* 82:181–305.

Raffles, T.S. (1817). *History of Java.* London: Black, Parbury and Allen. Two vols.

Ricklefs, M.C. (1974a). *Jogjakarta under Sultan Mangkubumi, 1749–1792; A History of the Division of Java.* Oxford: Oxford University Press.

Ricklefs, M.C. (1974b). 'Dipanagara's Early Inspirational Experience', *Bijdragen tot de Taal-, Land- en Volkenkunde* 130:227–58.

Ricklefs, M.C. (2001). *A History of Modern Indonesia since c.1200.* Basingstoke: Macmillan.

Ricklefs, M.C. (2006). *Mystic Synthesis in Java; A History of Islamization from the Fourteenth to the Early Nineteenth Centuries.* EastBridge, Norwalk: Signature Books.

Ricklefs, M.C. (2012). *Islamisation and its Opponents in Java; A Political, Social, Cultural and Religious History, c. 1930 to the present.* Singapore: National University of Singapore Press.

Shaw, S.J. and E.K. Shaw (1977). *History of the Ottoman Empire and Modern Turkey. Volume 2: Reform, Revolution and Republic.* Cambridge, New York: Cambridge University Press.

Soemarsaid Moertono (1968). *State and Statecraft in Old Java; A Study of the Later Mataram Period, 16th to 19th century.* Ithaca: Cornell Modern Indonesia Project.

Solichin Salam (1963). *Sekitar Wali Sanga.* Kudus: Menara.

Sumahatmaka, R.M.P. (1981). *Ringkasan Centini (Suluk Tambanglaras).* Sudibyo Z. Hadisutjipto (trans). Jakarta: Balai Pustaka.

Thorn, W. (1815). *Memoir of the Conquest of Java with the Subsequent Operations of the British Forces in the Oriental Archipelago.* London: Egerton.

Winter, J.W.(1902). 'Beknopte Beschrijving van het Hof Soerakarta in 1824', G.P. Rouffaer (ed.). *Bijdragen tot de Taal-, Land- en Volkenkunde* 54:15–172.

PART II

The Beginning of the Ruin of the Land of Java, 1808–1812

CHAPTER IV

The Beginning of Ruin: Daendels' 'New Order' and the Central Javanese Courts, 1808

Daendels' New Order

The 'beginning of the ruin of the Land of Java' had been Diponegoro's prophetic warning at Parangkusumo (Chapter III). Specifically, he had been told that this would start in just under three years' time. On cue on 5 January 1808, Marshal Herman Willem Daendels arrived in Batavia as Java's new governor-general (Stapel 1941:77). Lawyer, revolutionary, politician and career soldier, Daendels was very much a product of the French Revolution. One of the leaders of the 'Patriot Revolt' against the *Stadhouder* (1786–7) and commander of the Batavian Legion (1793), he had assisted French Republican forces in their conquest of Holland (December 1794–January 1795). As head of the Pro-French Unitarian Party, he later earned a reputation as a 'headstrong, sentimental and obstinate character' (Schama 1977:342–3). A man of few scruples, great energy and willingness to use force to achieve his ends, he was destined to make a lasting mark on the history of Java (Carey 2013).

Such character traits had recommended him to Napoleon who tasked him, as his only non-French marshal, to secure Java as a military base against the British. Fortuitously eluding British naval forces, Daendels arrived to find the island nearly defenceless and its coffers empty (Boulger 1897:90; Van Kesteren 1887:1276–7). Although his task was primarily a military one, Daendels was also vested with wide powers to reform the corrupt VOC administration, the Company itself having passed under the control of the Dutch state following its 1799 bankruptcy. The 1803 Colonial

Charter envisaged sweeping changes to the system of rule in the Indies (Day 1972:127–48) and Daendels brought to his post all the ruthlessness and determination which had marked his previous political and military career. The three years of his administration (1808–11) laid the foundations for the Dutch Indies modern colonial state (Van 't Veer 1963:107–86).

One of the marshal's primary strategic considerations in planning Java's defence was the position of the independent Javanese courts whose power and influence marked them out as potential rivals to the European government and dubious allies in the event of enemy attack. The court of Yogyakarta was the most redoubtable here: its military resources and substantial cash reserves gave it significant advantages of which Daendels was only too well aware: even before he left Holland – according to Nicolaus Engelhard (1761–1831) – he 'already had a prejudice against the sultan [...] He had the wish to make [him] feel his superiority and attack him at the first opportunity' (Engelhard 1816:257–8).

While Engelhard's views should be treated with caution given that he was a bitter critic and opponent of the marshal, it is clear that Daendels was anxious to place the relationship between Batavia and the courts on a new footing. Just over a month after taking over as governor-general (14 January 1808), he requested Engelhard to provide detailed information on the south-central Javanese kingdoms, and told him his post as Governor of Java's Northeast Coast would soon be terminated. Daendels wanted to deal directly with the Residents at the courts (Daendels 1814:Bijlage 1, Organique stukken 3).

On 25 February, he briefed the Residents on the new administration's court policy (Daendels 1814:Bijlage 1, Organique Wetten 6). The fifth article underscored the great importance Daendels attached to the honour and prestige of the new Franco-Dutch government:

> They [the Residents] should exert themselves in an impassive [*ongevoelige*] [...] way to give the rulers an impression of the power and splendour of the present royal government in Holland and of the protection of the great Napoleon, and [...] inspire them with due awe and respect (Daendels 1814:Bijlage 1, Organique Wetten 6, article 5).

Plans for Annexation of Territory in Central and East Java

In his final memorandum as outgoing Governor (14 May), Engelhard urged Daendels to 'break the connection between the courts and the north coast for good'. This should be done once a sufficiently redoubtable military force had been assembled to overawe the courts and a new boundary negotiated (Carey 2008:162). The incorporation of the districts slated for annexation – namely those areas abutting the north coast belonging to the courts redefined as government territory in the new boundary settlement – could proceed by dismissing all court-appointed *bupati* with family ties to the south-central Javanese *kraton*, precisely what the Dutch would do after the Java War (Carey 1974:276–7; Houben 1994:54–7).

The outgoing Yogya Resident, Matthijs Waterloo (in office, 1803–8), was even bolder, suggesting the annexation of parts of the core districts of Pajang, Mataram, Kedu, Bagelen and Banyumas, together with the island of Nusa Kambangan and the deepwater port of Cilacap. These western districts produced rice which the European government needed to feed its garrisons on the north coast and eastern Indonesia (Nagtegaal 1996:199–204). He also urged that the chaotic distribution of land between the courts in the core areas of the Principalities, which gave rise to so many village wars (*prang desa*) and other criminal activities, should be ended.

Together with Engelhard's final memorandum, Waterloo's letter constituted a blueprint for annexation which, if acted on, would have refashioned the political face of Java. Many of the key issues which drove the European government from this point to the end of the Java War were included, such as access to strategic resources (timber, cash crops, manpower), the security of Java's vulnerable south coast in time of war, the annexation of key rice-producing districts (Kedu, Bagelen and Banyumas), greater clarity of boundaries between Surakarta and Yogyakarta in the core regions, and tighter military and political control of the courts.

Daendels' Edicts on Ceremonial and Etiquette

While these ideas for a new territorial division of Java were being weighed, Daendels acted on his plans for a new relationship with the courts. His first move was to abolish the position of governor and director of Java's Northeast Coast which he did in person on 13 May 1808 (De Haan 1910-12, IV:78). The way was now open for direct communications between the governor-general and the Residents. It was the first step in the marshal's plan to centralize the colonial government on Batavia.

On 28 July 1808, Daendels promulgated his celebrated Edict on Ceremonial and Etiquette (Valck 1844:140; Van der Chijs 1895-7, XIV:63-5). This did away with most of the ceremonial functions previously performed for the rulers by the Residents which Daendels considered degrading (Daendels 1814:94). The Residents were instead accorded various privileges more fitting for their new positions as direct representatives of the governor-general and King Louis Bonaparte's royal government in The Hague (reigned, 1806-10).

Receiving the title of 'minister' with new uniforms and the right to carry a blue and gold state parasol or *payung* emblazoned with the arms of the king of Holland (Van der Chijs 1895-7, XIV:63-5), they were ordered not to remove their hats when approaching the ruler, who was to rise to greet them and make space immediately to his left on his throne. This would allow the Residents to sit at exactly the monarch's level. They were also instructed not to serve the ruler in menial fashion with drink and betelnut, and to observe new etiquette when saluting the ruler both inside and outside the *kraton*, the most important of which was that the minister no longer had to stop his coach when passing that of the ruler (Carey 2008:166).

The changes in ceremonial amounted to a very substantial alteration to the position of the Dutch representatives at the courts. This struck at the heart of the Javanese understanding of the Dutch presence in Java, which Ricklefs has analysed on the basis of three Javanese texts from the late eighteenth and early nineteenth centuries (Ricklefs 1974:362-413). These provide evidence that by the late eighteenth century the Yogyakarta court had legitimised the Dutch presence in west Java, roughly in the Pasundan

(Sundanese language area), by regarding them as legal descendants of the Sundanese kingdom of Pajajaran.

This kingdom was roughly contemporaneous with the great east Javanese empire of Majapahit (1292–circa 1510s) and has an obscure history, its memory being preserved in mythical fashion in the modern Javanese *babad* literature. For the Javanese, Pajajaran had two important characteristics. First, it was a 'foreign' kingdom since it lay in the Sundanese-speaking area of west Java. Second, it ruled the high mountains of the Priangan region, a place closely associated in the Javanese view with the spirit world, hence the derivation of the place name 'Priangan' from the Javanese *parahyangan* ('abode of the spirits') (Ricklefs 1974:375).

This area had important associations for the Mataram rulers given that their spiritual consort, Ratu Kidul, was traditionally described in court chronicles as a Pajajaran princess (Chapter III). This same tradition held that the Dutch too were now the lawful successors of the foreign kingdom of Pajajaran and rulers over the spiritually significant Priangan. Such legitimacy could be traced to Governor-General Jan Pieterszoon Coen's (in office 1618–23, 1627–9) foundation of Batavia in 1619 on the site of the Sundanese fishing port of Sunda Kelapa (Jayakarta). It could also be linked, in the Javanese view, with his mythical descent from another Pajajaran princess who carried the signs of royal legitimacy in the form of flaming female pudenda (Ricklefs 1974:399–413; Caldwell and Henley 2008:165, quoting Sahlins 2008).

Diponegoro clearly understood the court tradition in this way. In his Makassar exile writings (1833–55), he reflected this dichotomy between Majapahit and Pajajaran as representatives of two royal traditions in Java by relating the well-known story of the twin cannon, Kyai Setomo and Nyai Setomi, suggesting these represented the Dutch and the Javanese. In his words, Dutch-ruled Batavia 'had assumed the mantle of Pajajaran' (*Pajajaran wus ngalih kuthanira Batawi*) (Diponegoro, 'Makassar Notebooks', 1838, I:155). For Diponegoro and his contemporaries, the Dutch governor-generals after Coen – Daendels included – were senior sovereign partners in Java. But they were partners who carried no rights over the south-central Javanese kingdoms.

When Diponegoro left Magelang for Batavia following his 28 March 1830 arrest by De Kock (Chapter XI), he wrote in his *babad* that 'he was leaving Java' (Babad Dipanegara, IV:187), indicating that he considered he was travelling to a foreign kingdom. The practical expression of this political philosophy lay in the Javanese view of a dualistic hegemony on the island with the Dutch ruling the west and the Javanese supreme in the centre and east, also known as the *kejawen* (area of Javanese settlement and language).

While the south-central Javanese rulers referred to the governor-general respectfully as 'grandfather' (*ingkang eyang*), this did not indicate a close personal relationship. Quite the contrary, although he was revered as a senior ruler, he was not expected to involve himself in the affairs of the courts. On nearly all occasions when a governor-general visited the pre-Java War Principalities difficulties ensued (Ricklefs 1974:40, 373; Carey 2008:168, 525–6). A new governor-general was also expected to receive the sultan's felicitations in the colonial capital, Batavia, since this had the nature of an embassy to a neighbouring kingdom. It was certainly not an act of fealty from a vassal to a liege lord (Ricklefs 1974:247–54, 373).

In these circumstances the Dutch representative at the courts occupied a crucial position forming part of a duality. This consisted of two men, the *patih* (first minister) and the Resident who owed loyalty both to the Dutch and the Javanese. Thus the Resident was treated by the Javanese rulers as a VOC 'ambassador'. As such, he was required to fulfill certain ceremonial functions at their court. At times he even acted as their servant, hence the pouring of wine and the serving of betelnut at state receptions.

Daendels' edicts effectively destroyed this finely balanced political structure sanctioning Dutch rule in Java. If the articles of the edicts were enforced there could no longer be any pretence that the Resident was a 'joint servant' of both the European government and the ruler. The second sultan's reaction, as recorded in both Dutch and Javanese sources, was one of dismay. According to the Yogya court chronicle, he had few illusions about the seriousness of the change (Carey 2008:170):

> XVI 42. The sultan was disturbed at heart
> earnestly pondering over the difficulties.
> He already felt quietly about the future
> [that] the Dutch would rule,

> push aside his royal dignity
> [and] break his authority.
> In the end, they would gather up Java
> like gold carried along by water.

In his own *babad*, Diponegoro referred to the discussions which followed the news of Daendels' edicts in Yogya. He singled out the new seating arrangements and the right of the 'minister' (Resident) to carry a state umbrella as especially invidious (Babad Dipanegara, II:50), something which another Javanese source described as putting the Resident on equal footing with the sultan (Carey 1981:234–5 note 9).

Despite the succinctness of his references, Daendels' reforms clearly unsettled the prince. One of his subsequent war aims would be to return Java to its pre-Daendels state: in the initial ceasefire negotiations in December 1829, for example, the Dutch were given various options all linked to the pre-Daendels era: as private traders, for example, they would be required to restrict themselves to two cities on the north coast, Batavia and Semarang (Carey 1974:285–8, 2008:661; Chapter XI). Diponegoro's experience of the 1808 crisis thus shaped his long-term political philosophy.

At first a head-long conflict was avoided. The new Yogya Resident, Pieter Engelhard, a cousin of the last Semarang governor and a member of the same immensely gifted Swiss-Dutch family, was an accomplished diplomat (*wasis amicara*) who did much to temper the impetuousness and arrogance of Daendels' demands (Poensen 1905:126; De Haan 1910–12, I pt. 2:97–8). But it was clear that the changes could not long be delayed by diplomatic niceties.

The Yogya *babad* describes how immediately upon receipt of the edict, the sultan ordered his throne to be changed in order to maintain a more elevated position during state functions. This involved making his *dampar* (throne seat) narrower so that only the ruler could sit on it. At the same time, a wooden footstool was placed under it so that he would always sit higher than the Resident (Houben 1994:11), a procedure which would have near fatal consequences during Raffles' December 1811 visit to Yogya (Chapter VI).

The reactions of the Surakarta court to the 28 July edict were seemingly more accommodating: Van Braam, the Surakarta Resident (in office,

1808–10/1811), was struck by the 'astonishing difference' in the friendliness of the two courts after his mid-October 1808 Yogya visit: 'The sultan cannot speak Malay and it is difficult to converse with him', he noted, adding 'he has a wild look in his eyes [...] which indicates suspicion and fear' (Carey 2008:175). Such reports confirmed Daendels' convictions:

> '[Whereas the Sunan accepted the new ceremonial], it was quite otherwise with the Sultan of Yogya. The contempt he felt for the Dutch Government caused him to disapprove of the new ceremonial [...] and he had supposedly designed a plan to rid himself of the Dutch' (Daendels 1814:94).

So the stage was set for Yogyakarta's confrontation with the 'Thundering Governor-General' (*Gupernur-Jendral Guntur*) (Carey 1992:461 note 299), an encounter which initially the sultanate would survive rather better than the Dutch.

Military Manoeuvres: Javanese and Dutch

The problem for Daendels was that his government was bankrupt and his military forces unreliable (Louw and De Klerck 1894–1909, I:33): 'a hastily assembled rabble' as one historian put it (Aukes 1935:28). Not entirely tongue in cheek, Nicolaus Engelhard proposed that the government should hire some holy men – '*tapa*' (ascetics) – to make pro-Dutch prophecies to disguise its desperate situation (Carey 2008:177).

With the defence of the island a priority, Daendels spent much of his administration's first year strengthening his military position. He informed the sultan that he would be leaving Semarang to make a 'tour of [central and east] Java', news which brought the inhabitants of Yogya into 'uproar' (*oreg*) (Carey 2008:177) and caused the sultan to make his own military preparations, exercising his own troops and calling up levies (*prajurit arahan*) from the eastern outlying provinces. Diponegoro summed up the situation well (Babad Dipanegara, II:50):

The Beginning of Ruin

XIV 84. [...]
Then the governor[-general] came to [central] Java.
His name was General Daendels.

85. He arrived in Surakarta
[and] wished to proceed to Yogya.
But the sultan did not wish it.
For there was nothing about it
in previous custom
that a governor[-general] should come to [south-central] Java.
Although some had come to [central] Java,
they had stopped in Semarang,
or at the very furthest, had halted in Salatiga.

The prince's description fits nicely with the Yogyakarta court view of the dual division of Java in which the governor-general was expected to reside in Batavia and not involve himself in the internal affairs of central Java.

The sultan's response was predictable: he immediately ordered half his 10,000-strong military establishment to participate in a grand review at his Rojowinangun country seat to the east of Yogya on 1 June 1808 (Carey 2008:179). Diponegoro's father, the Crown Prince, was tasked with this general muster witnessed by Resident Engelhard and other Dutch dignitaries (Carey 2008:179). The young Diponegoro – then styled Raden Ontowiryo – was mobilized as commander of a fifteen-strong cavalry detachment in the Crown Prince's 763-strong troop (Carey and Hoadley 2000:296–7).

This great review at Rojowinangun would be the last set piece display of Yogya military might before the sultanate's dismemberment four years later. The prince's ominous Parangkusumo warning would have as its curtain raiser a final parade of half the gorgeously uniformed Yogya troops, an event which should have been captured in the sepia tint portraits of a court photographer like Kassian Cephas (1844–1912), or a great Woodbury and Page albumen silver print.

Instead, we must make do with Pieter Engelhard's vivid pen portrait which describes his pre-dawn meeting at the Crown Prince's residence in the north-eastern corner of the *kraton* (Carey 2008:179–81). There Engelhard was joined by nine young unmarried noblemen or *panji* – bachelor confidants of the ruler – who rode out with him to the official meeting place (*paseban*) on the northern *alun-alun* (great square). After watching the sultan's troops file out of the *kraton*, they rode the five kilometers to the ruler's country seat, where, at the midday meal Engelhard observed the Crown Prince's 'good character [and] distinguished and friendly appearance' which 'made him loved by great and small' (Carey 2008:180).

Profiting from this rare occasion when he was away from his father's jealous gaze, the Crown Prince sought to prove his pro-Dutch sentiments by insisting that his tea should be served with milk like that of his Dutch guests (d'Almeida 1864, II:79; Carey 1992:467 note 320) and crying out that his courtiers should only speak Malay on that day 'because that was the language which the sultan's friends, the Dutch, used with their people!' (Carey 2008:180). In this fashion, the politics of the new colonial era played themselves out at the level of language and taste as pro and anti-Dutch sentiments split factional alignments at the Yogya court.

Diponegoro's small squadron had been ordered to muster with the other court regiments on the great open field before the country seat to engage in two hours of military exercises and mock battles. Aimed at impressing the watching Europeans with their pikemanship and musketry skills, the assembled Javanese troops were observed to be seriously deficient in the use of their flintlocks (*snaphaan*). But their handling of their long Javanese lances was second to none, something which the British would discover to their cost during their June 1812 attack (p. 131).

While this show of force was taking place in Yogya, Daendels attempted to impress the sultan with his own display of military might. With 3,000 cavalry and mounted artillery assembled in Semarang, he invited the Yogya ruler to send some of his nobles to Semarang 'to witness the measures he was taking for the defence of Java' and 'his sentiments towards the Javanese' (Carey 2008:181). But the Yogya delegation visit (12–20 June) between was not a success. After meeting Daendels, the Yogya delegation head, Raden Ronggo, could scarcely conceal his boredom when invited to witness the marshal's troop manoeuvres (Poensen 1905:131). An incensed Daendels refused to bid him farewell or even send a message of greeting to the sultan (Carey 2008:181).

This was all very different from the reception accorded the two Surakarta court delegations in early June, visits marked, according to

Resident Van Braam, 'by the utmost friendship and respect'. The eleven-year-old son of the Surakarta ruler, Raden Malikan Saleh, the future Sunan Pakubuwono VII (reigned, 1830–58), was invested as lieutenant of cavalry, while the incumbent head of the junior Surakarta court, the Mangkunegaran, Pangeran Prangwedono (post-1821, Mangkunegoro II, 1768–1835; reigned 1796–1835), received promotion as full colonel of the king's *armée*, his 1,150-strong private force being established as an official 'legion' in emulation of Daendels' short-lived Batavian Legion (Van der Chijs 1895–7, XIV:775, XV:66; Rouffaer 1905:604–3; Carey 2008:182–4).

In this fashion, the forty-year-old Mangkunegaran ruler's position as a 'Company Prince' was given official recognition. Apart from the single case of Raden Ronggo's November–December 1810 rebellion (Chapter V), he would serve the European government loyally until his death in January 1835. Henceforth, his official dress was to be his European colonel's uniform, his hair cut short in European military fashion, his social style that of a regimental commander on constant campaign (*Lettres de Java* 1829:86; Van Hogendorp 1913:169; Carey 1992:409 note 57).

The Emergence of an Anti-Dutch Party in Yogya

Steeped as they were in the martial culture of Mangkubumi's court, the Yogya elite needed no reminding that Daendels' terrifying new order posed a challenge to their very existence. While the Crown Prince's response – as evidenced at the Rojowinangun review – had been to stress his pro-Dutch sentiments, others were deciding on a very different course. The second sultan was key here. In early August 1808, at the height of the crisis with Daendels, he had quietly reappointed a tough battlefield commander, Raden Tumenggung Sumodiningrat, to the post of First Inner Regent or *patih jero*, a key position which controlled access to the ruler (Carey 2008:188–9).

A man of high noble birth descended on his mother's side from the first sultan and on his father's from an old line of Mataram *bupati* (Carey 1980:191, 1992:419 note 94), Sumodiningrat had married one of the second sultan's daughters by his part-Madurese consort, Ratu Kedaton (Mandoyokusumo 1977:18 no. 8). This made him a full brother-in-law of two other key court officials, Raden Ronggo and the *patih* (first minister), Danurejo II, who, like himself, would lose their lives as the crisis with the European government unfolded (pp. 107–8, p. 122). Since his marriage with the sultan's daughter proved childless, he adopted Diponegoro's younger brother, Pangeran Adinegoro (post-1825 Suryengologo, born 1786), and through this sibling the prince would later inherit the dead commander's lands around Selarong (p. 62, p. 148).

Addicted to strong drink, gambling and cockfighting with common Javanese, Sumodiningrat remained in the words of Van IJsseldijk, 'the strongest pillar of the sultan's administration'. His very appearance betrayed his martial spirit, the Chronicle of the Fall of Yogyakarta referring to his moustachioed face (Carey 1992:91, 242), and the Yogya court *babad* stating (Carey 2008:188):

> I 16. His actions were like those of a *singa-barong* (a monstrous mythical lion) terrifying to behold
> [...]

The return of this pugnacious xenophobe to the sultan's inner council was immediately reflected in the court's tougher attitude to Daendels' ceremonial. On the same day as his appointment, Engelhard was reporting that the sultan had had a meeting with the senior court officials (*nayaka*) at which Sumodiningrat had counseled rejection, warning that the new ceremonial would bring humiliation on the Yogya ruler. 'This affair is still not settled', the Resident observed, 'and very much uneasiness reigns [at court].'

In fact, the council was split right down the middle with the first minister, Danurejo II, and three of the *nayaka* urging acceptance, and two other key officials remaining silent. One of these was Raden Ronggo. 'That sly fox' in Engelhard's words, 'came out of the meeting with a tearful face, indicating that he was prepared to counsel acceptance even though he was hugely embarrassed about it' (Carey 2008:189). For much of the next two and a half years until his death in rebellion in December 1810, Ronggo would be at the heart of Yogya's confrontation with Daendels.

The Beginning of Ruin

How did it happen that this still youthful man – he was still only thirty-one at the time of his death – came to play such a key role in the politics of the sultan's court and through his example become such an inspiration for Diponegoro?

The youngest and most charismatic of the sultan's three sons-in-law married to the daughters of his part-Madurese consort, Ronggo saw himself as the scion of martial ancestors whom he revered as 'warrior kings' (*ratu pinarjurit*) (Carey 2008:189). Yogyanese contemporaries regarded him as a courageous fighter: the Pakualam *babad* characterised him as 'bellicose' (*agul-agul*) (Poensen 1905:162, 179), while Diponegoro viewed him as Yogya's only 'champion' (*banteng*) (Babad Dipanegara, II:53), describing him as someone who felt a calling to die as 'a commander in battle' (Knoerle, 'Journal', 1830:16).

Strikingly handsome with a fiery temperament, Ronggo's features were later inherited by his son, Sentot (?1808–55), who would become Diponegoro's foremost Java War commander (Soekanto 1951). Through his mother, Ronggo was descended from the much admired first sultan (Mandoyokusumo 1977:12 no. 9; Carey 2008:764–5, 773), his paternal grandfather, Kyai Ronggo Wirosentiko, being Sultan Mangkubumi's most trusted army commander and founder of a celebrated line of Madiun chief regents (Ricklefs 1974:86–7). Diponegoro's guardian at Tegalrejo (Carey 2008:764–5; Amirulhaq 2012), Ratu Ageng, was Wirosentiko's sister. So the ties of blood and family with the young prince were very close.

This formidable spiritual and royal ancestry, combined with Ronggo's sudden elevation as *bupati wedana* in 1796 at the age of seventeen initially went to his head (Carey 2008:190). But the teenage chief administrator's impulsive acts of youth were soon tempered by responsibility. Subsequent Residents' reports indicate that he was a highly intelligent man who ran a good administration in Madiun and never extorted his subjects (Carey 2008:191). During the eight years (1802–10) of his residence at Maospati just across the river from Madiun, the population increased hugely (Nahuys van Burgst 1826; Carey 2008:191). He was even mentioned as 'well-disposed towards Europeans', although Daendels' actions would soon change that (Carey 2008:191).

The Javanese Buffalo Confronts the Dutch Tiger

During the early part of August 1808, as evidence of the second sultan's reluctance to accept the new ceremonial began to mount, Daendels threatened to come to Yogya with an armed force to impose his will. Accusing the Yogya ruler of a 'lack of steadfastness', he suggested that everything would be sorted out if he could come to talk with the sultan in person. But with 3,000 troops at his back Daendels' *tête-à-tête* would hardly have been a meeting of minds (Carey 2008:194–5). The diplomatic Pieter Engelhard persuaded the marshal that such a visit was unnecessary.

Meanwhile, pressure was mounting on the courts to open their extensive eastern outlying district (*mancanagara*) teak forests to the Dutch. The governor-general's newly appointed president of the Forest Administration Board, Gustaf Wilhelm Wiese (1771–1811; in office, 1808), requested the Yogya *bupati* of Padangan and Panolan, whose lands the Dutch authorities needed for timber supplies, to present themselves in Yogya to hear Daendels' instructions. Raden Ronggo was also summoned, his Madiun district being especially timber rich. Significantly, Wiese would soon be posted to Yogya as Resident (in office, 1808–10). Of the two *bupati*, the first, Mas Tumenggung Sumonegoro (Padangan), would later go into rebellion with Ronggo, and the second, Raden Tumenggung Notowijoyo III (Panolan), was Diponegoro's father-in-law. Through him, the young prince probably learnt of the political pressures now bearing down on the sultanate to open its timber reserves.

Besides securing access to hardwood, Daendels was also keen to restrict raids by the inhabitants of the eastern *mancanagara* on neighbouring government territories. The lack of cooperation between the courts over criminal investigations and the ease with which perpetrators could take shelter in adjacent *kraton* jurisdictions had convinced him that a new law-and-order agreement was necessary. On 26 September 1808, a new version of the *Angger Gunung* law code (Soeripto 1929:163–7) was signed by the two first ministers of Surakarta and Yogyakarta at Klaten. The severity of the stipulated punishments reflected the impossibility of getting law-and-order measures to work in the hopeless administrative confusion of the south-central Javanese courts. Only after the Java War, when a comprehensive land

The Beginning of Ruin 83

settlement separated the court territories for good, could such reforms be implemented (Houben 1994:17–69).

Just over a month after this agreement, another joint understanding between the courts was signed at Klaten regulating the working of the porters' guilds (Soeripto 1929:287–96). The provision of labourers to work on Daendels' trans-island highway (*postweg*) had already caused problems with the Sunan's court (p. 96), and Daendels needed access to the necessary manpower to complete his ambitious building and defence projects ahead of the seemingly inevitable British invasion.

Even with these agreements signed, the marshal had not quite finished with the courts. He wanted the respective Surakarta and Yogyakarta *patih* to greet him as incoming governor-general in Semarang so that they could present their usual 'homage' and gifts to him on behalf of their sovereigns (Carey 2008:197). He tasked his secretary-general, Hendrik Veeckens (1779–1815; in office, 1808–11), with receiving their 'homage' and making a statement regarding the recent political changes in Europe.

This contained such difficult concepts, particularly with regard to the abolition of feudalism in Europe (Schama 1977:180–1), that the official Javanese Translator in Semarang, C.F. Krijgsman (1774–1823; in office, 1803–21) (De Haan 1935:592–3; De Neve 2000:100), had problems rendering the text into Javanese (Hageman 1855–6:254). As Danurejo II and his party made their way back to Yogya with Veeckens' declaration in their hands and Daendels' compliments to the sultan ringing in their ears, they must have wondered what exactly was going on. A post-feudal Java? The happiness of subjects? The mightiest empire in the world? How to make sense of all this in the context of an 'old order' in Java which seemed so immutable?

Luckily, symbolic explanation was at hand. No sooner had the Yogya delegation returned home, than Van Braam – soon to be appointed as Daendels' deputy (De Haan 1935:507–8) – came over from Surakarta on an official visit with his wife (Carey 2008:200–1) (12–15 October). It was usual on such occasions for the court to honour their distinguished guest with a tiger and buffalo fight on the southern *alun-alun* and Van Braam was not disappointed. However, the particular fight he witnessed had an interesting denouement: in the first round of the contest, the tiger severed the leg tendons of the buffalo and then refused to fight further. In the second, when a new tiger was introduced, it jumped clean out of the ring of guarding spearmen and was killed behind the elevated platform on which the sultan was sitting with his Dutch guest. 'This situation, which had never occurred before,' Van Braam reported, 'caused the Javanese to make many conjectures with regard to me [...] and the sultan made me a compliment and said that it had occurred in my honour!' (Carey 2008:200).

Some compliment, some honour! What Van Braam did not realise was that these contests had a deeper meaning. Whereas for a visiting European dignitary like himself, a tiger and buffalo fight might have been seen as a rather gruesome form of entertainment like bear-baiting in Europe, for the watching Javanese the contests had a more profound significance. They equated the Europeans with the quick and deadly tiger and themselves with the powerful wild buffalo. Although the former was ferociously aggressive, it had little staying power and was nearly always defeated by its slower and more cautious adversary (Ricklefs 1974:274–6, 303–4, 345–6; Carey 1992:467 note 321; Houben 1994:81–2).

In this particular case, both rounds had shown the Dutch 'tiger' in a rather unflattering light: in the first, although able to move in for the kill, it had not done so. In the second, it had jumped clean out of the ring. Did this not mean that the Javanese could expect some unusual developments in terms of their Dutch adversary? At the time of Van Braam's visit, the British invasion was still three and a half years away. But when it happened, those Yogya courtiers who still recalled the October 1808 tiger-and-buffalo fight on the southern *alun-alun* might have been forgiven for surmising that it presaged a time when the once mighty Dutch and their now defunct East Indies Company would be placed completely *hors de combat* as far as their rule in Java was concerned. A new and more formidable European power would soon replace them.

A Diplomatic Incident Closes the Year of Living Dangerously

As if in presage of tragedy to come, Van Braam's last day – 15 October – in the sultan's capital was marred by an ugly diplomatic incident (Carey 2008:200–1). As the Surakarta Resident and his wife were being driven out from the Dutch fort in his carriage to make the short journey to the Residency House, his gold-and-blue *payung* (state sunshade) clearly visible, who should be riding down the main avenue but Raden Ronggo. But instead of stopping to let the high Dutch official pass as the new ceremonial demanded, the *bupati wedana* cut Van Braam dead. Here was an affront indeed.

Engelhard ever the diplomat suggested that his colleague just mention the incident to the sultan as he took his leave and ask Ronggo to make a personal apology. Ronggo's apology swiftly followed. Was this enough (*cukup*) the sultan asked in Malay? No, said Van Braam, he wanted the *bupati wedana* to make a public apology in front of the entire court. This created a sensation. Amazement was written on every face as Raden Ronggo, his own visage puce with embarrassment, intoned the formal Javanese apology in Malay. Then toasts were drunk and Van Braam departed. Scarcely a day later at Klaten (16 October) at the time of the signing of the agreement on the porters' guilds, the Surakarta Resident and Ronggo's paths crossed again. Van Braam pretended that nothing had happened, but Ronggo's face was a mask of discomfort. 'That dangerous, irascible, resentful and enterprising man who gives in to nothing', in Van Braam's words, was now the government's public enemy number one. The denouement would not be long in coming.

Conclusion

As the year 1808 drew to a close, the Yogya court may have wondered just what more lay in store for them. For Diponegoro, the beginning of the ruin of the Land of Java promised by the disembodied voice at Parangkusumo was now as real as his darkest forebodings. With each new humiliation visited on the court and with every slight made to its ruling family and officials (*priyayi*), the brash new world of Revolutionary Europe, personified by Daendels, was becoming more evident. This was not just about changing a few archaic practices, a little tinkering at the edges to bring the Dutch East Indies Company into the modern world. This was root and branch change. Henceforth, the Javanese political philosophy of two sovereigns and the reassuring divide between the kingdoms of Batavia/west Java and Java proper – the *kejawen* – would be impossible to maintain.

In everything that touched the relationship between south-central Java and Batavia, from political demands, to access to labour and economic resources, to military and defence requirements in an era of global conflict, it was clear that Java had entered a new age. And yet, it was not easy for those like Diponegoro, born when the Javanese old order was still intact, to make this shift. Much more would have to happen before such a change would be seen as either necessary or inevitable. Amongst the south-central Javanese elite, a select few would make the necessary adjustments to the new colonial order before the Java War. But by then it was too late. The time for making changes the Javanese way would have long since passed. The European government would do it for them. Daendels was just a beginning.

Bibliography

Amirulhaq, Dzul (2012). 'Haji Datuk Sulaiman, Pangeran Bima di Tanah Rantau; Leluhur Pangeran Diponegoro [Haji Datuk Suleiman, a Bimanese Prince in a Foreign Land; An Ancestor of Prince Diponegoro], *Babuju News*, 20 July 2012, <http://www.babuju.com/2012/07/haji-datuk-sulaiman-pangeran-bima-di-html?> accessed 5 October 2012.

Aukes, H.F. (1935). *Het Legioen van Mangkoe Nagoro*. Bandoeng: Nix.

Babad Dipanegara (2010). *Babad Dipanegara*, 4 vols, ed. Nindya Noegraha. Jakarta: Perpustakaan Nasional Republik Indonesia.

Boulger, D.C. (1897). *The Life of Sir Thomas Stamford Raffles*. London: Horace Marshall.

Caldwell, I. and D. Henley (2008). 'The Stranger who would be King; Magic, Logic, Polemic' in: I. Caldwell and D. Henley (eds). 'Stranger Kings in Indonesia and Beyond', *Indonesia and the Malay World*, 36:159–324.

Carey, Peter (1974). 'Javanese Histories of Dipanagara: The Buku Kedhung Kebo, its authorship and historical importance', *Bijdragen tot de Taal-, Land- en Volkenkunde* 130:259–88.

Carey, Peter (1980). *The Archive of Yogyakarta. Vol. I: Documents relating to Politics and Internal Court Affairs*. Oxford: Oxford University Press.

Carey, Peter (1981). *Babad Dipanagara; An Account of the Outbreak of the Java War (1825-30); The Surakarta Court Version of the Babad Dipanagara with Translations into English and Indonesian Malay*. Kuala Lumpur: Art Printers.

Carey, Peter (1992). *The British in Java, 1811-1816; A Javanese Account*. Oxford: Oxford University Press.

Carey, Peter (2008). *The Power of Prophecy; Prince Dipanagara and the End of an Old Order in Java, 1785-1855*. Leiden: KITLV Press.

Carey, Peter (2013). *Daendels and the Sacred Space of Java, 1808-1811; Political Relations, Uniforms and the Postweg*. Nijmegen: Vantilt.

Carey, Peter and Mason Hoadley (eds) (2000). *The Archive of Yogyakarta. Vol. II: Documents relating to Economic and Agrarian Affairs*. Oxford: Oxford University Press.

Chijs, J.A. van der (1895-97). *Nederlandsch-Indisch Plakaatboek 1602-1811*. Vol. XIV (1807-1808), XV (1808-1809), XVI (1810-1811). The Hague: Nijhoff.

Daendels, H.W. (1814). *Staat der Nederlandsche Oostindische Bezittingen, onder het Bestuur van den Gouverneur-Generaal Herman Willem Daendels, ridder, luitenant-generaal &c. in de Jaren 1808-1811*. The Hague: Van Cleef.

D'Almeida, W.B. (1864). *Life in Java with Sketches of the Javanese*. London: Hurst and Blackett. Two vols.

Diponegoro, Pangeran (1838) 'Makassar Notebooks', Fort Rotterdam, Makassar, library photocopy of manuscript formerly in possession of the late Raden Mas Jusuf Diponegoro and the late Raden Mas Saleh Diponegoro, Jalan Irian no.83, Makassar. 2 volumes.

Drooglever, P.J. (1978). 'The Netherlands Colonial Empire; Historical Outline and Some Legal Aspects', in: H.F. van Panhuys (ed.), *International Law in the Netherlands*, vol. I, pp 103-65. Alphen aan den Rijn: Sijthoff en Noordhoff.

Engelhard, N. (1816). *Overzigt van den Staat der Nederlandsche Oost-Indische Bezittingen onder het Bestuur van den Gouverneur-Generaal Herman Willem Daendels enz. enz.* The Hague, Amsterdam: Van Cleef.

Haan, F. de (1910-12). *Priangan; De Preanger-Regentschappen onder het Nederlandsch Bestuur tot 1811*. Batavia, The Hague: Landsdrukkerij. Four vols.

Haan, F. de (1935). 'Personalia der Periode van het Engelsch Bestuur over Java, 1811-1816', *Bijdragen tot de Taal-, Land- en Volkenkunde* 92:477-681.

Hageman, J.Jcz. (1856). *Geschiedenis van den Oorlog op Java van 1825 tot 1830*. Batavia: Lange.

Hannigan, Tim (2012). *Raffles and the British Invasion of Java*. Singapore: Monsoon.

Hogendorp, H. Graaf van (1913). *Willem van Hogendorp in Nederlandsch-Indië 1825-1830*. The Hague: Nijhoff.

Houben, Vincent (1994). *Kraton and Kumpeni; Surakarta and Yogyakarta 1830–1870*. Leiden: KITLV Press. [Verhandelingen 164].
Kesteren, C.E. van (1887). 'Eene Bijdrage tot de Geschiedenis van den Java-Oorlog', *De Indische Gids* 9–2:1263–1324.
Knoerle 'Journal' (1830). 'Aanteekeningen gehouden door den 2e Luit Knoerle betreffende de Dagelyksche Verkeering van dien Officier met den Prins van Djocjakarta, Diepo Negoro, gedurende eene Reis van Batavia naar Menado, het Exil van den genoemden Prins', Manado, 20–6–1830. MS 391 of the Johannes van den Bosch private collection in the Nationaal Archief, The Hague.
Lawick van Pabst, P.H. van (1826). 'Consideratiën over de Nota van den Heer [Hendrik] MacGillavry', MvK 4132, 26–8–1826.
Lettres de Java (1829). *Lettres de Java ou Journal d'un Voyage en cette Île, en 1822*. Paris: n.p. [J. van Schoor pseudonymous author.]
Louw, P.J.F. and E.S. de Klerck (1894–1909). *De Java-Oorlog van 1825–1830*. The Hague: Nijhoff, Batavia: Landsdrukkerij. Six vols.
Mandoyokusumo, K.R.T. (1977). *Serat Raja Putra Ngayogyakarta Hadiningrat*. Yogyakarta: Bebadan Museum Karaton Ngayogyakarta Hadiningrat.
Nagtegaal, Luc (1996). *Riding the Dutch Tiger; The Dutch East Indies Company and the Northeast Coast of Java, 1680–1743*. Leiden: KITLV Press.
Nahuys van Burgst, H.G. (1826). 'De Montjonegorosche-Djocjokartasche Landen', UBL BPL 616, Port.22 no.4.
Neve, R.G. de. 'De Matrilineaire Afstamming van Napoleon Gilles Charles de Neve (1916–1992)', *De Indische Navorscher* 13:100.
Pigeaud, Th.G.Th. (1967–80). *Literature of Java; Catalogue Raisonné of Javanese Manuscripts in the Library of the University of Leiden and Other Public Collections in the Netherlands*. The Hague, Leiden: Nijhoff. Four vols.
Poensen, C. (1905). 'Amǎngku Buwǎnǎ II (Sěpuh); Ngayogyåkarta's tweede sultan (naar aanleiding van een Javaansch handschrift)', *Bijdragen tot de Taal-, Land en Volkenkunde* 58:73–346.
Prawirawinarsa, Raden and R.Ng. Djajèngpranata (1921). *Babad Alit; Djoemenengipoen Tjoengkoep ing Pasaréan Koetagedé*. Weltevreden: Balé-Poestaka [Uitgave van de Commissie voor de Volkslectuur no. 462].
Ricklefs, M.C. (1974). *Jogjakarta under Sultan Mangkubumi, 1749–1792; A History of the Division of Java*. Oxford: Oxford University Press.
Rouffaer, G.P. (1905). 'Vorstenlanden', *Encylopaedie van Nederlandsch-Indië* 4:587–653.
Sahlins, Marshall (2008). 'The Stranger King', in: I. Caldwell and D. Henley (eds). 'Stranger Kings in Indonesia and Beyond', *Indonesia and the Malay World*, 36:177–99.

Schama, Simon (1977). *Patriots and Liberators; Revolution in the Netherlands, 1780–1813*. London: Collins.
Soekanto, R. (1951). *Sentot alias Alibasah Abdulmustopo Prawirodirdjo Senopati Diponegoro (seorang terkemuka dalam abad ke-19 dari Sedjarah Nasional Indonesia)*. Djakarta: Poesaka Aseli.
Soeripto (1929). *Ontwikkelingsgang der Vorstenlandsche Wetboeken*. Leiden: IJdo.
Valck, F.G. (1844). 'Overzigt van de Voornaamste Gebeurtenissen in het Djocjocartasche rijk, sedert dezelfs Stichting (1755) tot aan het Einde van het Engelsche Tusschen-Bestuur in 1816', ed. J.C. Steyn Parvé, *Tijdschrift voor Nederlandsch Indië*, 6-3:122–57, 262–88, 6-4:25–49.
Veer, P. van 't (1963). *Daendels; Maarschalk van Holland*. Zeist: Haan, Antwerpen: Standaard.

CHAPTER V

The Old Order's Last Champion: The Origins and Course of Raden Ronggo's Rebellion, 1809–1810

The Despoliation of Yogya

On 3 December 1808, the former Rembang Resident, Gustaf Wilhelm Wiese, was installed by Pieter Engelhard as 'minister' (Resident) in Yogyakarta. Introduced to the second sultan as a man 'of soft character and a true heart', the Javanese chronicles concur that during his incumbency matters proceeded 'calmly' (*tentrem*) (Poensen 1905:140; Carey 2008:205). But this hardly describes the increasingly turbulent nature of Yogya-Dutch relations as the second year of Daendels' administration dawned.

One of the first problems facing the former Rembang Resident was Daendels' demand for money. On 22 December, he wrote the Yogya ruler asking for a cash contribution 'as a sign of his attachment to the [Dutch] government'. Daendels would subsequently obtain some 200,000 Spanish dollars from Yogya, the bulk (196,320 Spanish dollars, around twenty million US dollars in today's money) taken as indemnity to pay for his army and civilian officials following Raden Ronggo's revolt (Daendels 1814: Bijlage 2, Additionele Stukken 24; Poensen 1905:135–6).

Daendels thus began a process which the British, the world's champion colonial asset strippers, completed: the despoliation of the Yogya treasury. Built up by the second sultan during the first sixteen years of his reign, it was estimated in February 1808 to exceed one million Spanish dollars – nearly a hundred million US dollars in today's money – not counting 'a very large sum in diamonds' (Carey 1992:414–15 note 80; 2008:206). During the next four years (1808–12), it would be removed from Yogya by force and diplomatic diktat.

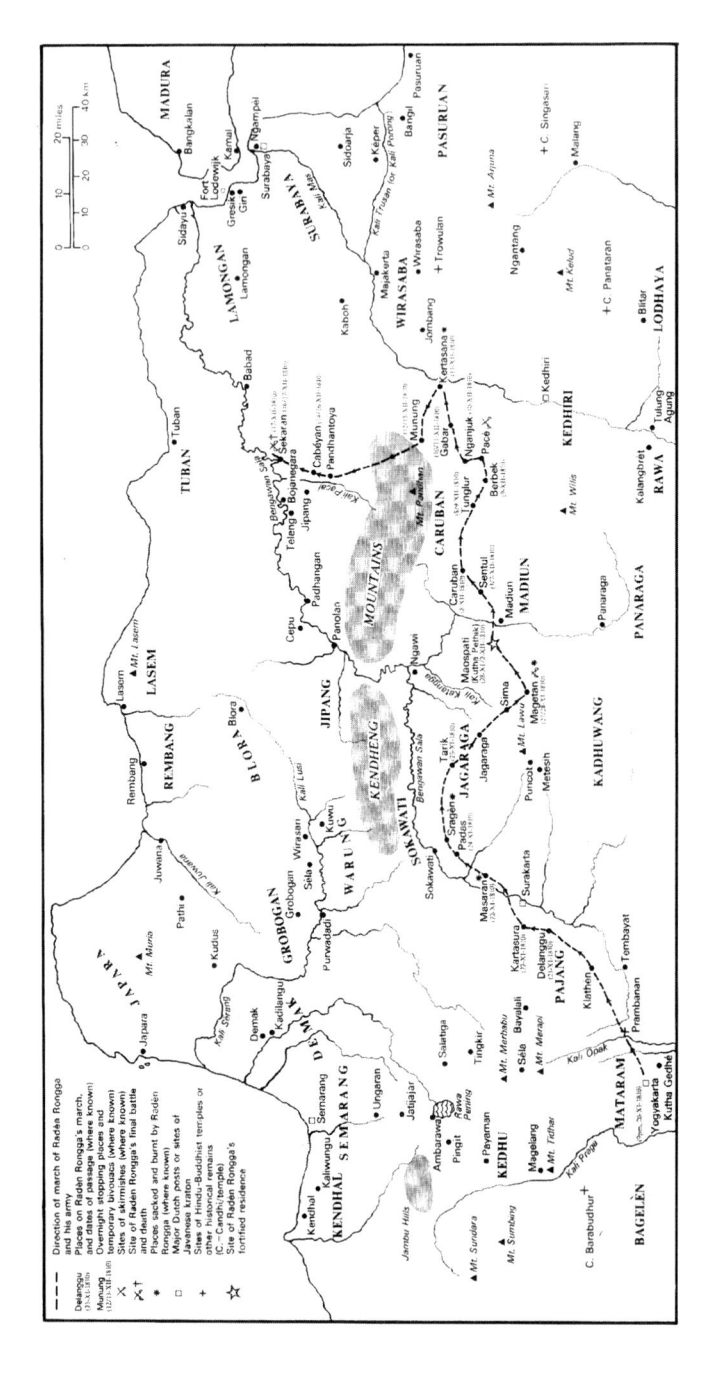

Map 5. Map of central and east Java in 1810 showing the route taken by Raden Ronggo in November–December 1810.

Plunder on this scale gave the lie to Daendels' protestations that his administration represented the new 'enlightened government' of post-Revolutionary Europe (Chapter IV). The same gap between rhetoric and reality would be the hallmark of the British administration (1811–16). Small wonder that Diponegoro would later insist in his preliminaries to his March 1830 peace negotiations that the only trade henceforth allowed with the Dutch would be one in which they paid the right market prices for Javanese products and the only land leases those which paid the going market rents (Carey 2008:663; Chapter XI).

Military Preparations and Daendels' July 1809 Official Visit

While these negotiations were proceeding, the military situation in Yogya was deteriorating. In late January 1809, in response to news of a military exercise in Surakarta, the sultan ordered all male inhabitants of Yogya to turn out for a military review. Although this order was subsequently cancelled, the tensest expectations were aroused in early April when Daendels' announced his intention of visiting the south-central Javanese courts (Carey 2008:207). Diponegoro describes how many Yogyanese went about dressed permanently in battle array (*prajuritan*) (Babad Dipanegara, II:50-1).

When the day of Daendels' official visit dawned (29 July 1809), the prince rode out to greet Daendels at Kalasan in his capacity as *kadipaten* troop contingent (*prajurit kadipaten*) commander. Together with his two of his younger brothers, Adinegoro and Suryobrongto, he was on hand to witness the governor-general's arrival in the imposing full dress uniform of a Napoleonic marshal (Babad Dipanegara, II:51).

As the first visit by a governor-general to Mangkubumi's capital (Carey 1984b:58), Daendel's arrival provoked much curiosity and interest. But the mailed fist nature of his regime was underscored by his sizeable military escort (Carey 2008:210). Efforts were made to turn his visit into a diplomatic success, however, including 'discussions' in the *kraton* and Residency on cash-crop production and agriculture, as well as the sultan's duties as ruler. There were also official visits to the royal family and tours of the sultan's hunting lodges and country estates, some of which had military purposes (Carey 2008:210).

The usual court entertainments were laid on, including a tiger spearing (*rampog macan*), a firework display, and *serimpi* (female warrior court) dances. The highlight was a mock one-hour tournament on the southern *alun-alun* conducted by forty of the Yogya ruler's cherished Amazon corps (*prajurit èstri*) (Carey 2008: 210). Daendels expressed amazement that women could ride so adroitly on horseback while handling cavalry carbines (Poensen 1905:144). Such comments were not new: previous VOC officials had been similarly impressed (Kumar 2008:11–12). But perhaps the male chauvinist governor-general did not realize that these viragos were not just for show but also had real fighting capacity as the British would later discover (Carey 1992:414 note 78; p. 142).

Despite the formal compliments and outward display of friendship, no deeper understanding was reached. Diponegoro dismissed the whole affair in a single sentence: 'there was much talk but nothing came of it' (*kathah bicara kang nora dadya*) (Babad Dipanegara, II:51). Other Javanese accounts dwell on the humiliations experienced by the sultan regarding seating arrangements, his attempt to sit higher than Daendels at the court reception having been rebuffed (Poensen 1905:142; Hageman 1855–6:255). The visit probably convinced the sultan that he should give not an inch on matters of ceremonial.

The Struggle over the Teak Trade and the Crisis in the Eastern Mancanagara

While these events were taking place in Yogya, tensions were mounting in the eastern *mancanagara* and north coast (*pasisir*) border areas. From July 1808, Daendels had applied increasing pressure on the courts to gain access to these regions' timber reserves (Chapter IV). By early 1809, his demands had broadened to include a ban on the private sale of teak across

The Old Order's Last Champion

the border into the Dutch-held *pasisir*. The marshal's establishment of a de facto timber monopoly impacted the local regents (*bupati*) who stood to lose a valuable revenue source from the Chinese-run timber felling farm (Carey 2008:211).

When they arrived in Yogya for the 27 April 1809 *Garebeg Mulud* festival, the eastern outlying *bupati* alerted the sultan to the plight of the wood-cutter forest populations, an issue commented on by Raffles in his *History of Java* (1817, I:81), where he noted that the 'size and comfort' of local houses which were 'very essentially contracted' by the closure of teak forests 'formerly open to natives of all classes'.

In this affair, the sultan sided with the forest inhabitants, stipulating that even if the forests were leased to the European government, the common people should still be allowed to sell wood to the *pasisir* (Poensen 1905:161). Coming from a ruler who had gained such a notorious reputation for his harsh fiscal policies, this was a change indeed. But it was one replicated by the *kraton* elite: J.W. Winter, the curmodgeonly Surakarta Residency Translator (in office, 1806–20), remarked that since Daendels' arrival, the princes and *bupati* of the south-central Javanese courts had discovered a new-found 'compassion' for the common man (*wong cilik* or 'little people') (Winter 1902:51).

Despite this solicitude, the forest-dwelling populations' situation continued to deteriorate. Many took to petty crime: small affrays involving inhabitants of the eastern *mancanagara* and those in the Dutch-controlled *pasisir* became commonplace. As chief administrator of the eastern outlying districts, Raden Ronggo was blamed for these incidents, a situation described by Diponegoro (Babad Dipanegara, II: 50):

> XIV 89. So gradually
> there was even more talk,
> yet it was Raden Ronggo
> who was constantly discussed.
> So they piled up
> the affairs of Raden Ronggo
> [and] he was often invited to Semarang.
>
> 90. But Raden Ronggo Prawirodirjo
> was wary:

> he understood in his heart
> that he was being picked upon
> by the Dutch,
> so he was continuously
> [and] exceedingly cautious of danger.

This sense of being picked on aroused in Ronggo a smouldering resentment which would turn into a fatalistic resignation following the early death of his beloved consort, Ratu Maduretno, in mid-November 1809.

These difficulties were soon compounded by the flight of the *pasisir* populations into the princely territories to avoid labour duties on Daendels' trans-Java post-road then being laid through the Dutch-held north coast (Joekes 1948:413–16; Carey 2008:215). Of the estimated 12,000 Javanese victims of this infamous highway (Thorn 1815:208), nearly a third would perish on this section alone (Thorn 1815:283; Van Polanen 1816:73; Joekes 1948:416). In the ensuing confusion numerous small incidents and raids occurred on villages and customs posts in government areas. The forest of Kedawung, a Yogya-administered Kedu enclave between Pekalongan and Kendal, became a base for numbers of these *wong durjono* (robbers) who preyed on north coast traffic (Carey 1980:73 note 2).

Sensing an imminent showdown with the Dutch government, the sultan extended his military defenses by using Raden Ronggo's eastern *mancanagara* workforce to strengthen the *kraton* battlements. The four main bastions were projected by between fifteen to eighteen feet, and cannon cast in Gresik and the royal gun foundries at Kota Gede for the new gun batteries (Louw and De Klerck 1894–1909, II:283 note 1; Gomperts and Carey 1994:26 note 10; Carey 2008:216).

Daendel's determination to enforce his hard-line policy was soon evidenced by his appointment of a tough new Resident, Johannes Wilhelmus Moorrees (1774–1815; in office, 9 March–24 August 1810), who had served in Banten after the 1808–9 abolition of the sultanate. No sooner had Moorrees settled into his new post in early March, however, than a new attack occurred on the Pekalongan village of Wonodadi (Schoel 1931:444; Carey 2008:217). This involved a well-known robber band operating out of the Yogya district of Tersono in the above-mentioned Kedu enclave. Daendels demanded the leader be caught.

When the inevitable happened and the robbers slipped away over the border, the district head (*demang*) of Tersono, Raden Tirtowijoyo, was summoned to Yogya. Daendels demanded he be executed, something which the Yogya ruler was loathe to do given his relationship to his favourite consort, Ratu Kencono Wulan (Poensen 1905:149–50; Carey 1980:185). Exile was suggested, but refused by Daendels. So the unfortunate official was handed over to the Resident, who sent him in chains to Semarang from whence he was taken out onto the new highway (*postweg*) and shot, his bullet-ridden body being left by the roadside at Weleri to be collected by his family for decent Javanese-Islamic burial (Poensen 1905:148–9).

The Scapegoating of Raden Ronggo

Daendels intended Tirtowijoyo's miserable end to serve as a warning to diehards in Yogya. But his tactic backfired. The time for making concessions to the Dutch had passed. The governor-general's pressure only coalesced groups in Yogya who either out of self-interest or genuine anti-European sentiments were now advocating open resistance.

Raden Ronggo was central here. Immediately following his return from the mid-November 1809 *Garebeg Puwasa* in Yogya, he had been plunged into inconsolable grief following the death of his beloved official wife, Ratu Maduretno (Babad Dipanegara, II:51; B.Ng. I:95, XXV.71). His reaction to her loss as recorded in the Pakualam *babad* was dramatic: interring her at the Ronggo family graveyard at Gunung Bancak (Maospati), he spent day and night at her gravesite, only being brought to his senses by his subordinate *bupati* (Poensen 1905:154; Adam 1940:333–4).

No sooner had Ronggo recovered from this bitter loss than he was implicated in a cross-border raid into neighbouring Ponorogo which left two dead and one mortally wounded (31 January 1810) (Carey 2008:219–20), an incident which would lead to his November rebellion.

The Surakarta ruler, who detested Ronggo, eagerly seized on the affair to complain to Daendels. His senior administrator in Ponorogo also levelled a number of additional accusations, the most intriguing of which was that Ronggo had retained a military deserter from Ponorogo to capture sets of Javanese *gamelan* (orchestras) from adjacent Surakarta territories (Carey 2008:220).

Such activities speak more of cultural kleptomania – of the kind perfected by the British – rather than the usual round of cross-border plunder. But this weighed not a whit with Daendels. He ordered Moorrees to give the sultan a letter pointing out that unless Ronggo was punished, the Yogya ruler risked the joint ire of both Daendels and Pakubuwono IV. The sultan was incensed. He saw the Surakarta ruler's actions as a way of putting bad blood between himself and the governor-general and recalled the misunderstandings which had occurred during the marshal's first year. After hearing Ronggo's report delivered during his 18 April 1810 *Garebeg Mulud* visit, he concluded that the *bupati wedana* had been well within his rights to strike down three notorious robbers (Carey 2008:221).

The 'Piling Up' of Affairs and Preparations for Ronggo's Rebellion

While Ronggo's stock continued to rise at court, the relationship between the sultan and Moorrees unravelled. In late June, as the Resident was about to leave for Semarang to confer with Daendels, his wife, Jacoba Margaretha (1787/8–1843), was held up in her carriage during a country outing by an armed band operating under the sultan's orders (Carey 2008:228). When Moorrees eventually met the governor-general, he was urged to stand firm. But Yogya-Dutch relations were now in crisis. In the ensuing deadlock, Moorrees found himself, in the words of the Pakualam *babad*, 'like an egg caught between two sharp stones' (Poensen 1905:178). His Residency was over.

On 1 September 1810, Pieter Engelhard returned to Yogya (Carey 2008:229, 809). The marshal had decided to make concessions and the sultan was allowed to receive the new Resident in the *Srimenganti* hall seated on his throne in the old style (Poensen 1905:184–5). Ever the diplomat, Engelhard was instructed to calm the sultan's ruffled feelings.

The lull was short: within two weeks of Engelhard's arrival, news came through of an attack on a Chinese tax-farmer in Demak by a band of Yogya robbers from the village of Gabus in the Grobogan-Wirosari area. Opium, cash and ornaments worth some 10,000 Spanish dollars (equivalent to one million US dollars in today's money) had been taken. Deserters from the Semarang garrison regiment against whom neither the sultan nor Ronggo had taken action, were thought to be involved. Daendels was furious. Instructing Engelhard to press for 'sensational satisfaction' (*eclatante satisfactie*), he demanded the 'complete return of the stolen goods' and the arrest of the robbers within a fortnight otherwise his troops would enter the offending Yogya territory (Carey 2008:229).

Twenty days elapsed before the sultan deigned to give Engelhard an interview. After listening to the governor-general's threats, the Yogya ruler calmly told the Resident that the sultan was content with Daendels' missive, that he would indeed give him 'satisfaction', but that he would feel 'ashamed' if the governor-general ordered his troops to enter Yogya territory. Nothing could be done, he said, until the return of the Yogya commission from Grobogan-Wirosari, prompting an exasperated Daendels to write in the margins of Engelhard's dispatch: 'I will await one more post, but then I will await the outcome of this Yogya commission no longer!' It would be a full two weeks and many more posts before the commission returned (Carey 2008:231).

Following this *kraton* meeting, Engelhard received a surprise nighttime visit from Ronggo informing him of his imminent departure for Madiun. He would remain there until after the end of the fasting month (*Puwasa*). Engelhard was suspicious: 'This seemed very strange because usually it is [at the end of] the *Puwasa* month [30 October 1810] when the *mancanagara* regents make their annual return [to Madiun] and they usually come in state to the minister [Resident] to take their leave together' (Carey 2008:232). The first steps in Ronggo's rebellion had begun.

Once back in Madiun, the still unfinished walls of Ronggo's Maospati residence were fortified with sharpened bamboo spikes and cannon. Contacts were also made with Prangwedono (Mangkunegoro II), a personal friend, who gave assurances that if his legion was deployed against him, his soldiers' guns would have no live rounds in them (Carey 2008:232). Ronggo's subordinate *bupati* were informed that he would not be appearing at court at the April 1811 *Garebeg Mulud*, Notodiningrat (1786–1858; post-1829, Pakualam II, reigned 1829–58) having warned him that the official report of the Ponorogo incursion commission would soon be received and there would be serious consequences (Carey 2008:233).

'So they piled up the affairs of Raden Ronggo', Diponegoro noted in his *babad* (Babad Dipanegara, II:50). In that month of October as the *bupati wedana* paid his last peacetime visit to his Maospati residence, the sultan was confronting four separate demands for 'satisfaction' from Daendels for cross-border incursions. By the time of the celebration of the *Garebeg Puwasa* on 30 October, relations between the Resident and the sultan had reached breaking point.

'I sense more and more that the sultan is hurrying to his fall', Daendels minuted on the back of Engelhard's dispatch relating the humiliations of the recent *Garebeg* celebrations. But he resolved to give the sultan one last chance by sending his deputy Van Braam to Yogya bearing letters demanding satisfaction from the Yogya ruler in three outstanding cases involving Ronggo, while warning him about the political ambitions of his younger brother, Pangeran Notokusumo (1764–1829; post-1812, Pakualam I, reigned 1812–29). Should this fail, the same marginal minute indicated that the marshal had made the necessary military preparations with the commander of the Semarang military division, Brigadier-General Von Winckelmann (1767–1820).

No sooner had Van Braam settled into his three-day commission (10–13 November) than a second letter arrived from the governor-general which was altogether more explosive. Its central message was to warn the sultan against his younger brother, Pangeran Notokusumo, who was said to harbour designs on the sultanate. Daendels suggested the involvement of both Raden Ronggo, who had now returned to Yogya (8 November), and Ratu Kencono Wulan, the sultan's favourite wife. To back his accusations, the governor-general included extracts about Notokusumo's ambitions from the final administrative reports of previous VOC Residents.

The marshal's aim was to place both Notokusumo and Raden Ronggo 'out of commission' by securing their handover to the European government.

The Old Order's Last Champion

Once achieved, Daendels expected no further opposition from the Yogya court since the Crown Prince could then be supported as the government's key ally. He would begin with Ronggo, whom he requested Van Braam to place 'at the disposal of the government' in Bogor to answer the cases against him (Carey 2008:237). These orders were subsequently changed: instead of Bogor, where Ronggo's 1,000-strong following could not be lodged, he should proceed direct to Batavia. Since the eastern *mancanagara* administrator would not be long for this world in Daendels' scheme of things, the size of his entourage and their long-term lodging were hardly a problem (Carey 2008:238).

To ensure the sultan's cooperation, Daendels proposed 'a large dose of fear', suggesting Von Winckelmann's Semarang troops create a feint on Yogya by spreading rumours that 2,000 Dutch soldiers were on the march and had reached Boyolali. Convinced that a hostile military force was moving south, the sultan received Daendels' letters on 10 November during a state council meeting. None of the Yogya *bupati* and princes at the meeting opposed Ronggo's removal to Bogor. Even Ronggo with swollen face had answered *sandika* ('as you order!') as the decision was taken (Carey 2008:238).

Whether the sultan was genuinely shocked by Daendels' revelations or just felt it politic to bend before the wind we may never know. Engelhard later remarked that the Yogya ruler had 'become quite another person' when reading the marshal's second letter and Diponegoro critized him bitterly for this change of heart, stating that the ruler's faint-heartedness and unwillingness to defend Ronggo had led directly to 'the destruction of Yogya' (Babad Dipanegara, II:52).

A date was now set for Ronggo's departure (26 November) and the court *gamelan* played to signify that the differences between the sultan and governor-general had been resolved (Carey 2008:239). As Van Braam rode back to Surakarta on 14 November, his Yogya colleague, Engelhard, was celebrating, signing off his dispatch to the Semarang divisional commander to stand down his troops with his own Latin epigram: *nulla salus bello, pax optima rerum* ('there is no deliverance in war, peace is the best of things') (Carey 2008:239).

Cleansing Java of Defilement: Raden Ronggo's Eastern Mancanagara Rebellion

At half past three in the morning of 21 November, Engelhard was roused early from his bed: Ronggo had departed with 300 followers for Madiun. He wrote immediately to Surakarta to ask the Sunan and Prangwedono (Mangkunegoro II) to cut off Ronggo's march. But it was too late: the *bupati wedana* had already passed Delanggu.

The following morning the sultan assembled a 1,000-strong expeditionary force under his brother-in-law, Raden Tumenggung Purwodipuro (?1766–1826), sending a circular ordering all Yogya *mancanagara bupati* to cooperate in Ronggo's capture. The royal decree specifically sanctioned Ronggo's death should he refuse to return to Yogya (Carey 2008:243), an order subsequently overtaken by further instructions stating that even if taken alive he should be killed immediately. The sultan did not want the embarrassment of the *bupati wedana* being brought back to Yogya alive, mindful of the promise made by his father, Sultan Mangkubumi, to Ronggo's grandfather, Ronggo Wirosentiko, during the Giyanti War (1746–1755), that he would never harm any of his descendants (Carey 2008:243). The sultan's refusal to honour this solemn undertaking was, in Diponegoro's view, the reason for all the ills which would befall the sultanate.

Ronggo had prepared his move in advance, using his time in Maospati in October to strengthen the fortifications of his walled residence, contact his subordinate *bupati* and come to an agreement with Prangwedono. On his return to Yogya, he had collected the necessary cash and clothing for his troops, obtaining cash and jewelry loans from the wealthy Ratu Kencono Wulan and credit from a French textile merchant to equip his followers. Together with the outstanding eastern outlying district taxes which the *bupati wedana* owed for the previous *Garebeg Mulud*, his midnight departure left the Yogya ruler and favourite consort 20,000 *ronde real* (around two million US dollars) out of pocket (Carey 2008:243–4).

The Old Order's Last Champion

Three days before his flight he had written almost identical letters to Notodiningrat and Sumodiningrat. These give an insight into his key objectives (Carey 2008:244-5):

> Younger brother Tumenggung Notodiningrat, I beg leave to inform you that I now wish to take my leave [...] to lead a roving life intending to destroy those who constantly deceive the Javanese. Even though they do this in the name of the [European] government, they too are Javanese. [...] Moreover, after my departure, it is you who must watch over the court of Yogyakarta [...] so that if I succeed in taking over the territories of the [Dutch] fortress in Yogyakarta, and of the Surakarta *kraton*, they will certainly not dare to disturb the court of Yogyakarta. Furthermore, I am absolutely not rebelling against His Highness [the second sultan] and will not exceed the royal blessings which I implore, together with the blessings of the ancestors who were warrior kings. And don't let it go so far [...] that His Highness entertains the wish to cause me misery. I urgently and deeply beseech this with all my heart and soul. For truly, I earnestly intend to take away the uncleanness from Java and will thank God all the more if I can do that which will bring good to the court and pleasure to His Highness' heart.

Purging Java from 'uncleanness' and foreign defilement were key here. But it was a purification targeted as much against pro-European Javanese as against the Dutch. Here one can find echoes of the voice heard by Diponegoro at Parangkusumo warning of 'the beginning of the ruin of the Land of Java'. But in this latter case the restoration of the moral order during the Java War was linked with the teachings of Islam, Diponegoro dismissing the Dutch and their Javanese allies as 'unbelievers' (*kapir*) and 'apostates' (*kapir murtad*) (p. xxxviii).

Despite his extensive connections with the east Javanese Islamic communities, there was nothing in Ronggo's rebellion which distinguished the 'people of Islam' from the European *kapir* and Javanese 'apostates'. Instead, the spirit of the Hindu-Javanese shadow play (*wayang*) and the ghost of Sultan Mangkubumi hovered over his enterprise, Ronggo having the conceit that he was Batara Guru, the supervising deity in the *wayang*. Drawing on the Ramayana epic for inspiration when he appointed his troop commanders in Madiun in late November, he gave his leading general the name of 'Dasamuka', a moniker for Rawana, the giant-king of Lanka (Ceylon) (Carey 2008:247).

Much like a ruler in the shadow-play (*wayang*), Ronggo also set about turning his family and followers into a court-ordered hierarchy by bestowing royal titles on his female relatives, as well as appointing his son, male cousins and *bupati* as heir apparent, first minister (*patih*) and *nayaka* (senior court counsellors) respectively. The *payung* (state parasol) makers in Madiun were worked overtime to turn out the requisite regalia: all gold for the new ruler, green with gold bands for his deputies, and blue for local officials who rallied to his cause. Maospati had become an alternative *kraton* (Carey 2008:247–8).

As for the shade of the first sultan, this was evoked by Ronggo's invocation of 'the blessings of his ancestors who had been warrior kings'. His subsequent royal title, 'His Highness the king, ruler in war (*Kangjeng Susuhunan Prabu Ingologo*) of the court of the warrior kings at Maospati now wandering to wage war' also recalled the title taken by Mangkubumi during his initial 1746 rebellion with Raden Mas Said (Mangkunegoro I) (Balé Poestaka 1939:32; Carey 2008:248).

One aspect of Ronggo's rebellion which differed markedly from that of Diponegoro was his appeal to the Chinese communities. Prior to his uprising, Ronggo had enjoyed close relations with these communities in Madiun due to his position as the sultan's chief tollgate-leaser (Carey 1984a:21–2). He also shared their deep misgivings about the threat posed to their local economic interests by the activities of European loggers. Declaring himself 'protector' of all the Javanese and Chinese who had been 'mistreated by the [European] government', he urged them to work together to 'exterminate' the Dutch officials who had undermined the prosperity and well-being of Java (Carey 1980:36–8, 1984:22, 2008:250).

His particular target were the wealthy mixed-blood (*peranakan*) Chinese communities in north coast towns like Lasem, Tuban and Sidayu, whom he hoped to enlist in attacks on Dutch garrisons between Rembang and Surabaya. Urging them to take control of the offices and posts of evicted Europeans, he instructed the Chinese to guard against possible counter-attacks (Carey 1980:37, 1984:22, 2008:250). Just two days before the European-officered flying column caught him at Sekaran on 17 December, Ronggo was appealing to the *Kapitan Cina* of Lasem and Rembang, promising them that once the Europeans had been annihilated, they would enjoy

The Old Order's Last Champion

his protection and their descendants inherit their official positions (Carey 1980:40 note 1, 1984:22 note 100).

Ronggo's appeal to the Chinese showed his shrewd understanding of their economic and social importance in the eastern outlying districts. Specific eastern *mancanagara* grievances against the Dutch played a critical role in generating local support for his rebellion. Those who had suffered most from Daendels' teak monopoly were the first to rally to him as he made his way to Madiun in the last rainy days of November. His demand that the *pasisir* areas of the north coast should once again be delivered up to the Javanese was also a goal dear to the hearts of the south-central Javanese rulers (Carey 2008:250, 290–1).

Short-lived though it was, Ronggo's attempt to involve the Chinese in his cause stands in marked contrast to the situation during the Java War. Why? The small number of Chinese tollgate keepers in the eastern *mancanagara*, when compared to the situation in south-central Java before the Java War, may account for this (Carey 2008:249–50). There was also a regional aspect: the Chinese Muslim communities on the north coast whom Ronggo courted so assiduously were precisely those who gave Diponegoro the greatest support in his struggle against the Dutch (Louw and De Klerck 1894–1909, III:444–5, 452, 525).

After 1816, Dutch fiscal oppression through the opium farm, markets and tollgates changed local Javanese attitudes towards the south-central Java Chinese whose invidious role in Dutch fiscal oppression in the pre-Java War decade provoked intense local resentment (pp. 180–3). Sexual relations and inter-marriage with those of Chinese descent, hitherto never a problem, were now seen as an issue (Louw and De Klerck 1894–1909, III:525; Carey 1984a:2, 32, 2008:617–20).

Ronggo's revolt also had significant Javanese messianic undertones which again prefigured Diponegoro's uprising. The Yogya *babad* describes how Ronggo's deputy, Mas Tumenggung Sumonegoro, received the inspiration that the *bupati wedana* should rule at the '*kraton*' of Kuta Petik in the 'kingdom' (*praja*) of Ketonggo (Carey 2008:250–1). We know from other sources that this was another name for Maospati, the place chosen by astrologers as the most auspicious location for Ronggo's new *dalem* when he moved from Madiun in the early 1800s (Onghokham 1975:60).

This suggests that Ronggo saw himself as a messianic 'Just King' or Ratu Adil (Carey 2008:250–1). The timing of Ronggo's rebellion in the Javanese year Wawu, the seventh year of the eight-year Javanese cycle, was also significant. It was seen as the appropriate time for the Ratu Adil to appear: Diponegoro also took his Erucokro title in this year (Carey 1981:261 note 108, 2008:251).

Ronggo seems to have enjoyed the tacit support of many of the south-central Javanese rulers and princes: both Pangeran Notokusumo and his son, Notodiningrat, were suspected of such collusion even before Ronggo's flight from Yogya. As soon as news of Ronggo's flight broke, Notokusumo's residence was placed under guard and orders issued both for his and his son's arrest. On 17 December, on the very day of Ronggo's death, they were sent overland to Batavia where they were held in Daendels' forbidding fortress of Meester Cornelis (present-day Jatinegara) before being transferred to Cirebon, where the marshal schemed their execution (Carey 2008:252, 276; p. 118).

The position of the sultan was also delicate. He had been very supportive of Ronggo and his complicity in the *bupati wedana*'s uprising was assumed. But the marshal's demand that Engelhard arrest the sultan along with his senior army commander, Sumodiningrat, was rejected: the Resident was not prepared to execute such drastic measures given the ruler's apparent cooperation. Diponegoro even thought the sultan had turned against his former favourite, his decision to send an expeditionary force to track Ronggo down being viewed as 'a great sin' (*kalangkung ing durakanira*) (Babad Dipanegara, II:52). In fact, this force achieved little: its commander, Purwodipuro, spent his time trading opium and engaging in currency deals (Carey 2008:252), leaving Ronggo to be hunted down by a flying column commanded by the sultan's Eurasian coachman Sergeant Lucas Leberveld (1757–?1815) (*Bataviasche Koloniale Courant* 3, 18-1-1811; Daendels 1814:Bijlage 2, Additionele Stukken 4).

Subsequently evidence came to light that far from being innocent in the affair, the sultan had plotted with Sunan Pakubuwono IV to coordinate a general uprising in the Principalities in the event of Ronggo's successfu *pasisir* attack. These details came from a respected local *kyai*, Murmo Wijoyo (?1757–1824), who had extensive contacts at both courts as a teacher, and had been a secret emissary between Surakarta and Yogyakarta (Carey 2008:253, 444–8). If this source is sound, then it is clear that the Sunan played a duplicitous role because he also denounced the sultan to Daendels for having been 'at one' with Ronggo. This general collusion of the rulers of south-central Java would be repeated in October 1811–May 1812 when the courts engaged in a secret correspondence to coordinate resistance against the British (Carey 1980:54–70; Chapter VI).

Ronggo's rebellion offered no opportunity for such collusion, however. Daendels moved swiftly to crush the uprising, disembarking 3,000 infantry in Semarang and two squadrons of cavalry and two companies of horse-drawn artillery between 2 and 6 December, and himself reaching Semarang by sea on 10 December (Carey 2008:253–4). Ronggo, meanwhile, was being relentlessly pursued. After his departure from Yogya on the night of 20–21 November he made his way under unseasonally heavy rain to his Maospati residence (see Map 5), fighting a pitched battle on the way at Magetan on 27 November where his troop commander Dasamuka was apparently killed. Arriving in Maospati a day later, he attempted to win the Yogya *mancanagara bupati* to his side, but only his long-time friend and ally, Mas Tumenggung Sumonegoro of Padangan, rallied (Carey 2008:255).

After abandoning an attack on Ponorogo, Ronggo decided to make for the *pasisir* where he hoped for the support of the local Chinese communities. This did not materialise. In the final encounter on the morning of 17 December on the banks of the Solo River, most of Ronggo's army slipped away, leaving only his deputy, Sumonegoro, his *patih*, Mas Ngabehi Puspodiwiryo, and their pennant and *payung* carriers on the field of battle (Carey 2008:256). After the first exchange of shots, a Yogya *bupati* in Leberveld's force asked what Ronggo wanted. The *bupati wedana* replied that he intended no harm to the Javanese but wished to kill all those who were being a burden on the *mancanagara* Javanese and Chinese. Thereupon he dismounted and thrust out with his pike. The *bupati* wounded him in the chest with his counter-thrust, Leberveld then ordering his foot-soldiers to finish him off. The same fate befell Ronggo's deputy, Sumonegoro. The bodies of the slain rebels were washed in the Solo River, wrapped in white linen and taken to Yogya (Carey 2008:256–7).

Once this sad cargo reached the royal capital on 21 December, the sultan ordered the corpses to be hung in open coffins at the Pangurakan crossroads near the guardhouse on the northern *alun-alun*, where the bodies of executed criminals were publicly displayed (Poensen 1905:262; Carey 1980:125–6). The young Diponegoro may well have witnessed this gruesome sight on one of his court visits. A day later, on 22 December, they were cut down and interred at the traitors' graveyard at Banyusumurup to the southeast of Imogiri (Van Mook 1972:18; Hageman 1855–56:269–70).

Conclusion

Despite the pathos of Raden Ronggo's end, his rebellion was a major event in the history of the south-central Javanese courts. Prior to 1810, notwithstanding Daendels' bluster, the balance of power had not yet swung decisively in favour of the European government. The ability of the sultan to resist the imposition of the new ceremonial and his skill in spinning out his responses to the governor-general's demands for 'satisfaction' for border incursions showed the limits to the government's power. In south-central Java proper these limits would continue until the 20 June 1812 British attack on the Yogya *kraton* when the remaining court-based militaries were finally swept aside.

In the *mancanagara*, however, the situation was different. Here Ronggo was indeed the 'last champion'. His death accelerated the transformation of these eastern outlying districts into a European-influenced economic zone. Although they couched their resistance in terms of protection for the *wong cilik* ('little people'), in particular the teak forest dwellers, their principal motivation was to preserve their economic position. Here they received the tacit support of the sultan, and, if we believe the testimony of figures like Kyai Murmo, of the Sunan and Prangwedono (Mangkunegoro II) as well.

The failure of Ronggo's eastern rebellion marked the point when the balance of power in the territories bordering the Dutch-controlled *pasisir* swung decisively in favour of the colonial government. Henceforth, these eastern outlying districts would be pulled inexorably into the European orbit. Within the space of two short decades, the whole of the *mancanagara* would be annexed by the government (Houben 1994:143–50).

The political significance of all this was not lost on Diponegoro. His admiration for Ronggo shines through in his *babad*. Here was a young Yogya nobleman, almost his contemporary, a man like himself who enjoyed strong links with the local Javanese-Islamic communities and who was prepared to go down fighting rather than die miserably as a prisoner of the European power. Here was the *satria*, the warrior prince, whom Diponegoro had in mind as an example when he confronted similar economic and political circumstances in the south-central Java before the Java War. With his close family ties to Ronggo, ties enhanced by his marriages (1814, 1828) to the *bupati wedana*'s daughter and niece (p. 38, p. 158), and the support of his teenage son, Sentot (?1808–55), it is hardly surprising that Diponegoro should have seen Ronggo as the sultanate's 'last champion'.

When the prince's turn came to step forward to defend the Javanese moral order, he would do so under the much broader banner of Javanese Islam and with a messianic appeal unmatched by that of Ronggo. But the ghost of the slain *bupati wedana* and his evocation of the 'warrior kings' of Mataram would still hover over his enterprise.

Bibliography

Adam, L. (1940). 'Geschiedkundige Aanteekeningen omtrent de Residentie Madioen', *Djåwå* 20:329–46.
Babad Dipanegara (2010). *Babad Dipanegara*, 4 vols, ed. Nindya Noegraha. Jakarta: Perpustakaan Nasional Republik Indonesia.
Balé Poestaka (1939). *Babad Gijanti; Pratélan Namaning Tijang lan Panggénan*. Batavia: Balé Poestaka.
Bataviasche Koloniale Courant (Batavia: 's Lands Drukkerij, 1810–11) 3, 18-1-1811.
Carey, Peter (1980). *The Archive of Yogyakarta. Vol. I: Documents relating to Politics and Internal Court Affairs*. Oxford: Oxford University Press.

Carey, Peter (1981). *Babad Dipanagara; An Account of the Outbreak of the Java War (1825–30); The Surakarta Court Version of the Babad Dipanagara with Translations into English and Indonesian Malay.* Kuala Lumpur: Art Printers.
Carey, Peter (1984a). 'Changing Javanese Perceptions of the Chinese Communities in Central Java, 1755–1825', *Indonesia* 37:1–48.
Carey, Peter (1984b). 'Jalan Maliabara ('Garland Bearing Street'); The Etymology and Historical Origins of a Much Misunderstood Yogyakarta Street Name', *Archipel* 27:51–63.
Carey, Peter (1992). *The British in Java, 1811–1816; A Javanese Account.* Oxford: Oxford University Press.
Carey, Peter (2008). *The Power of Prophecy; Prince Dipanagara and the End of an Old Order in Java, 1785–1855.* Leiden: KITLV Press.
Carey, Peter and Mason Hoadley (eds) (2000). *The Archive of Yogyakarta. Vol. II: Documents relating to Economic and Agrarian Affairs.* Oxford: Oxford University Press.
Daendels, H.W. (1814). *Staat der Nederlandsche Oostindische Bezittingen, onder het Bestuur van den Gouverneur-Generaal Herman Willem Daendels, ridder, luitenant-generaal &c. in de Jaren 1808–1811.* The Hague: Van Cleef.
Gomperts, A. and P. Carey (1994). 'Campanalogical Conundrums; A History of Three Javanese Bells', *Archipel* 48:13–31.
Hageman, J.Jcz (1855–6). 'Geschiedenis van het Bataafsche en Hollandsche Gouvernement op Java 1808–1810', *Tijdschrift voor Indische Taal-, Land- en Volkenkunde (TBG)* 4:333–75, 5:164–284.
Houben, Vincent (1994). *Kraton and Kumpeni; Surakarta and Yogyakarta 1830–1870.* Leiden: KITLV Press. [Verhandelingen 164.]
Joekes, L.V. (1948). 'Het Gedeelte Batang-Weleri van den Grooten Postweg op Java', *Bijdragen tot de Taal-, Land- en Volkenkunde* 104.1:413–28.
Kumar, Ann (2008). *Prajurit Perempuan Jawa: Kesaksian Ihwal Istana dan Politik Jawa Akhir Abad Ke-18.* Jakarta: Kommunitas Bambu [Original title: 'Javanese Court Society and Politics in the Late Eighteenth Century: The Records of a Lady Soldier. Part I: The Religious, Social and Economic Life of the Court', *Indonesia* no.29 (April 1980):1–46; 'Part II: Political Developments: The Court and the Company, 1784–1791', *Indonesia* no.30 (October 1980):67–111].
Louw, P.J.F. and E.S. de Klerck (1894–1909). *De Java-Oorlog van 1825–30.* 6 volumes. The Hague: Nijhoff and Batavia: Landsdrukkerij.
Mook, H.J. van (1972). *Kuta Gedé.* Jakarta: Bhratara [Original title: 'Koeta Gedé', *Koloniaal Tijdschrift*, 1926, 15–4:353–400.]
Onghokham (1975). 'The Residency of Madiun; Priyayi and Peasant in the Nineteenth Century'. PhD thesis, Department of History, Yale University.

Poensen, C. (1905). 'Amăngku Buwånå II (Sĕpuh); Ngayogyåkarta's tweede sultan (naar aanleiding van een Javaansch handschrift)', *Bijdragen tot de Taal-, Land en Volkenkunde* 58:73–346.

Polanen, R.G. van (1816). *Brieven betreffende het Bestuur der Koloniën, en bevattende eene Beoordeeling van een Werkje over dat onderwerpen uitgegeven, getiteld 'Java'; Waarbij gevoegd zijn eenige Belangrijke Authentieke Stukken welke een Nieuw Lichtverspreiden over het vorig Bestuur aldaar van den Gouverneur-General H.W. Daendels.* Amsterdam: Van der Heij.

Raffles, T.S. (1817). *History of Java.* London: Black, Parbury and Allen. Two vols.

Schoel, W.F., ed. (1931). *Alphabetisch Register van de Administratieve-(Bestuurs) en Adatrechtelijke Indeeling van Nederlandsch-Indië. Vol. I: Java en Madoera.* Batavia: Landsdrukkerij.

Thorn, W. (1815). *Memoir of the Conquest of Java with the Subsequent Operations of the British Forces in the Oriental Archipelago.* London: Egerton.

Valck, F.G. (1844). 'Overzigt van de Voornaamste Gebeurtenissen in het Djocjocartasche rijk, sedert dezelfs Stichting (1755) tot aan het Einde van het Engelsche Tusschen-Bestuur in 1816', ed. J.C. Steyn Parvé, *Tijdschrift voor Nederlandsch Indië,* 6–3:122–57, 262–88; 6–4:25–49.

Winter, J.W.(1902). 'Beknopte Beschrijving van het Hof Soerakarta in 1824', G.P. Rouffaer (ed.). *Bijdragen tot de Taal-, Land- en Volkenkunde* 54:15–172.

CHAPTER VI

The End of the Beginning: The Fall of the Franco-Dutch Government and the British Rape of Yogyakarta, 1811–1812

Introduction

In the eighteen months from Raden Ronggo's death on 17 December 1810 to the fall of the Yogya *kraton* to British-Indian troops on 20 June 1812 'the beginning of the ruin of the Land of Java' prophesied to Diponegoro at Parangkusumo would come full circle. This would see the evisceration of the south-central Javanese courts as the treaties imposed by Daendels (January 1811) and Raffles (August 1812) removed their principal fiscal and military resources. By the time of the Java War (1825–30), Diponegoro's struggle would draw on a much broader social and political constituency than just the *kraton* elite. The prince's appeal to Javanese-Islam and Javanese 'national' identity would popularize his cause in ways unimaginable to his elite predecessors such as Sultan Mangkubumi, Raden Mas Said (Mangkunegoro I) and Raden Ronggo.

This process of evisceration is the subject of the present chapter. Not only would it complete the Parangkusumo prophecy, but it would also bring to Java's shores a new and far better resourced power: Great Britain. The Javanese elite would now experience the full force of the newly emerging superpower at its imperial zenith, what historian C.A. Bayly has termed that island nation's 'imperial meridian' (1780–1830; Bayly 1989). They would also find that they had exchanged one form of colonial tyranny for another, no longer a Napoleonic Marshal this time but a 'virtual Napoleonic philosopher' and instinctive authoritarian, Thomas Stamford Raffles (1781–1826; in office, 1811–16).

The Reckoning

Even before Ronggo's death, Daendels had decided on a radical alteration of Yogya's governance. On 23 December, he summoned the Dutch Residents and first ministers to Semarang to inform them of his plans to force the sultan to resign his throne in favour of the Crown Prince. Three days later, he marched on Yogya with a force of 3,200 men. He was already at the old Mataram tollgate at Kemloko between Tempel and Pisangan when news reached him of Ronggo's death. Although there was now no need to proceed to the sultan's capital, the marshal persisted. He needed prize money and pay for his officers and men, who were deserting at the rate of seventy a day (Carey 2008:262).

The cash hand-outs would be substantial: Daendels' deputy, Van Braam, received 10,000 Spanish dollars (equivalent to 250,000 US dollars today) whereas Pieter Engelhard and the former Resident, Gustaf Wilhelm Wiese, who had both been tasked with Van Braam with drawing up the new boundary demarcation, were each 5,000 Spanish dollars (equivalent to 125,000 US dollars) better off. The commanding officer, Brigadier-General (post-1821, Lieutenant-General) Hendrik Merkus de Kock (1779–1845), later supremo of Dutch military forces during the Java War, received a similar sum (*Bataviasche Koloniale Courant*, 5, 8-2-1811).

These hand-outs constituted the first step in the impoverishment of the sultanate, a situation which would astound former VOC officials when they visited the Principalities after the Dutch restoration in 1816 (Carey 2008:263).

Daendels arrived in Yogya on 28 December and went straight to the Residency House, summoning the sultan to meet him there without paying the customary courtesy visit to the *kraton* first. Such a gross breach of etiquette cut to the quick (Carey 2008:263). Diponegoro described how preparations were made for military resistance with the ever bellicose Sumodiningrat counseling action. But the sultan was too conflicted to act (Babad Dipanegara II:53).

On 31 December, the sultan acquiesced to the governor-general's demands. He signed a proclamation giving up the administration of Yogyakarta to the Crown Prince, who would now rule as Prince Regent bearing his previous title of *Raja Putro Narendro Pangeran Adipati Anom Amangkunegoro*. Superficially, it seemed that Daendels had effected a political revolution. He immediately boasted of such to the Council of the Indies. In fact, nothing had changed. The Javanese accounts make it clear that the Crown Prince was acting with the sultan's permission. True, he now had control of the sultan's seal, presided over the council of state, and sat on the sultan's right side at the *Garebeg* ceremonies, but the centre of power remained with the old ruler who retained charge of finances and apanage lands. He also stayed on in the *kraton*, a concession accorded by Daendels at the express request of the Crown Prince. This was tantamount to permitting affairs to continue as before as the heir apparent lacked the character to gainsay his father (Carey 2008:264-5).

If Daendels' measures changed little of substance beyond humiliating the sultan, why did the latter agree to them? Perhaps the old ruler felt it was necessary to bend before the wind: the presence of 3,200 troops in Yogya probably gave him pause. But it was clear that once the opportunity presented itself, he would seek revenge against all those who had helped the Crown Prince. The disordered period which followed the collapse of the Franco-Dutch government in late September 1811 would afford him just such an opportunity as we shall see shortly.

The treaties imposed by Daendels provided for the annexation of areas bordering on government-controlled north coast districts. Some of these like Selo, burial place of the Javanese Prometheus, Ki Ageng Seselo, contained important graves and sites of court pilgrimage. There was also the issue of the *strandgeld* payments. This was the 'rent' for the north coast districts taken over by the VOC under the terms of their 1746 treaty with Pakubuwono II (reigned 1727-49) (Veth 1896-1907, II:163). Fixed at 20,000 Spanish dollars, of which Yogya received half following the 1755 Giyanti settlement (Soekanto 1952:185; Ricklefs 1974:62), the abolition was a financial blow to the sultanate. It also involved the loss of nominal sovereignty over the *pasisir* with its ancestral tombs and pilgrimage sites. In fact, the abolition removed one of the main incentives for the south-central Javanese courts' toleration of a European presence in Java.

As a concession, Daendels agreed to cede Yogya some Dutch-controlled lands around Boyolali in the east and the districts of Galuh and Cauwer Wetan in the far west. Surakarta was to receive the districts of Malang and

Antang earlier considered VOC territory (Daendels 1814: Bijlage 2, additionele stukken 27 art. 6; Ricklefs 1974:106–7). The marshal also agreed to pay the debts of the Sunan's 96,875 silver reals (USD7,000,000) debts to private individuals. But these concessions were not appreciated: Malang and Antang were still depopulated from local wars going back to Untung Surapati's time (?1645–1706) (Ricklefs 1986), and Galuh and Cauwer Wetan were renowned as bandit hideouts (Carey 2008:266).

Major changes were also introduced into the administration of Raden Ronggo's old fiefdom in Madiun, the senior administrator (*bupati wedana*) post being divided between two new appointees (Carey and Hoadley 2000:67–8, 232–6, 244–50): Pangeran Dipokusumo, who was married to a daughter of the second Ronggo (Raden Ronggo Mangundirjo, in office 1784–1790, 1794–1796), and Raden Ronggo's notoriously corrupt uncle, Ronggo Prawirosentiko (Carey 1980:189). They would remain in office until the majority of Ronggo's eldest son in 1826. Their first task was to obliterate the last vestiges of Raden Ronggo's royal pretensions: his *kraton*-style residence at Maospati was leveled and the chief regent's seat moved back to Madiun. Curiously, amidst all this administrative activity and reform in the eastern *mancanagara*, Daendels' proposed annexations were effectively ignored (Carey 2008:268–9).

What could not be ignored, however, was the very large indemnity demanded Daendels as the condition of the removal of his troops. This sum, amounting to some 196,320 Spanish dollars (USD14,000,000 in today's money), was eventually brought to the fort in silver coin from the *kraton* treasury on 4 January in sixty-six chests. Danurejo II, who oversaw this payment, was later accused of embezzling some 20,000 *ronde realen*, a charge which may have hastened his murder (Carey 2008:269–70).

Daendels' visit to Yogya thus left the sultan with a triple humiliation: a disastrous treaty, the loss of a fifth of his state treasure and an almost impossible situation at court.

The sultan's jealousy was further aroused in early May 1811 when Daendels sent the Prince Regent an order, referred to in Diponegoro's *babad* as a 'star' (*bintang*). This was the *Orde van de Unie* (Order of the Union) created as a new Dutch nobility by King Louis on 14 February 1807. It was set in an eight-pointed gold star studded with diamonds and became an immediate bone of contention at court when the *patih* persuaded the Prince Regent to wear it at the celebrations for Napoleon's birthday on 15 August 1811 (Carey 2008:270).

Incipient Civil War in Yogya

In the early months of 1811, the Prince Regent attempted to establish his own administration through the appointment of new court *bupati*, but this proved impossible. His request that his new officials be provided with the necessary ricefields (*sawah*), provoked a curt response from his father: he had no *sawah* to give them, instead his son should ask for the requisite lands from Surakarta or the Dutch-controlled districts on the north coast. All seven of these new *bupati* would later be stripped of their offices by the old sultan in May 1812 just before the British attack when British reports suggested that he intended their execution (Carey 2008:273–4).

By June 1811, rumours began to circulate that the second sultan was preparing to appoint his younger son Mangkudiningrat as heir apparent in the Prince Regent's place, a move urged by two of the old sultan's consorts, Ratu Kencono Wulan and Mangkudiningrat's mother, Ratu Mas (Babad Dipanegara, II:54). It was a tactic to bring pressure to bear on the Prince Regent (Carey 2008:274).

Resident Engelhard, meanwhile, could do little to support his protégé: he was suffering from recurrent fevers linked to his galloping TB, his health being so seriously undermined that he would immediately request the new British administration to relieve him (De Haan 1935a:543). As the royal government descended into disarray in Yogya, the number of robberies and violent attacks in the countryside around the sultan's capital increased. The old sultan's hand was thought to be behind many of these. It was an extremely effective way of unsettling his son's administration (Carey 2008:274).

Reports of the Prince Regent's troubles reached Daendels who threatened to return to Yogya with a sizeable force, but only after he had 'dealt with the English'. This was an idle threat: Daendels was in the last days of his administration and his motley army would prove no match for the 12,000 seasoned soldiers drawn from British line regiments, Bengal sepoy battalions, and Madras horse artillery being readied in Melaka for the August invasion of Java (Carey 2008:275; Hannigan 2012:67–70).

The Collapse of the Franco-Dutch Government

While Yogya stood on the cusp of civil war and the threat of invasion loomed, the former Dutch government in Java underwent its final transformation. At seven o'clock on the morning of 27 February 1811 the 'momentous and joyful' news reached Yogya of the proclamation of the annexation of Holland by France (9 July 1810). The following day a brief ceremony took place: 'Minister' Engelhard and his secretary, Hendrik Willem Gezelschap, in their full dress uniforms processed by coach to the Crown Prince's residence where all the princes and notables had gathered to hear the announcement. The Dutch flag was then lowered and the French tricolour raised as a 45-gun salute boomed forth from Fort Vredeburg (Vink 1892:444–7). Napoleon's France was now the proud ruler of Java. Henceforth all civil and military officials would be required to take an oath of loyalty to the emperor (Nahuys van Burgst 1858:46–7). But it would not be long before another flag would fly over Mangkubumi's capital.

Two members of the Yogya elite who were not at the flag-raising ceremony and for whom a change in political regime could not come soon enough were Pangeran Notokusumo and his son, Notodiningrat. Held in dungeons in Cirebon, they were in danger of their lives: Daendels had made up his mind to do away with them before they could be used by the British in the event of a successful invasion. Only the delaying tactics of the bailiff of Cirebon and former Yogya Resident, Matthijs Waterloo (1769–1812; in office, 1803–8), supported by his friend Nahuys (1782–1858), ensured that the two Yogya noblemen's lives were spared long enough for the new governor-general, Jan Willem Janssens (1762–1838; in office May–September 1811), to replace Daendels on 16 May (Carey 2008:276–8).

The End of the Beginning

Neither Notokusumo nor his son would forgive the Prince Regent for his role in their twelve-month exile. Their implacable animosity would lie at the heart of the poisoned relations between the Pakualaman and the Yogya court during the Prince Regent's reign as Hamengkubuwono III (1812–14), Pakualam I's own unhappy regency (1814–20) (Chapter VII) and far beyond into the late nineteenth century (Carey 1992:458–9 notes 286, 288).

The arrival of Janssens led to an immediate liberalisation of Daendels' administration, his honest character forming a sharp contrast to the brutality of his predecessor. A Malay text, the *Hikayat Mareskalek* ('The Marshal's Chronicle'), speaks of him as a 'gentle ruler and beloved father' (Van Ronkel 1918:872; Zaini-Lajoubert 1987), and he took several initiatives during his four-month tenure. One of these was the 20 July 1811 establishment of a new training scheme for young European administrators in Javanese known as the *élèves voor het civiele* (pupils for the civil service) later renamed *élèves voor de Javaansche taal* (pupils for the Javanese language) (Chijs 1895–97, XVI:715–17; Houben 1994:119–22). But such steps had little immediate impact given that he had inherited an insolvent administration. Although the marshal had done much to organise the island's military defences and more than double the number of local troops to 17,774 (Peucker and Van Hoof 1991:57), the government's financial situation was desperate.

A portent of the coming change were the Malay-language letters dispatched by the future British lieutenant-governor of Java, Raffles, from Melaka in December 1810 to the archipelago's rulers. These announced that the British were coming to help them make 'an end of everything associated with the Franco-Dutch regime' (Carey 2008:280–1; Hannigan 2012:66). Raffles' letter to the sultan also promised him that he would be restored to his 'full dignity' as monarch in accord with previous contracts thus overturning Daendels' recent changes. The rulers were urged not to enter into any further treaties or agreements with the Dutch. Instead, they were to await the British arrival.

Meanwhile, the British invasion took place. On 3 August, their massive landing fleet of 81 transports and ships-of-the-line appeared off Batavia and by 8 August the old town had fallen (Hannigan 2012:25–8, 72–7). Janssens entrenched himself with his troops at Meester Cornelis (present-day Jatinegara), Daendels' great redoubt to the south of his new

Weltevreden administrative centre, but it was clear that resistance would be difficult given the invaders' overwhelming military superiority (Thorn 1815:16–32; Stockdale 1812:15–17; Hannigan 2012:87–100).

News of the fall of Meester Cornelis on 26 August in a bloody battle in which the British suffered over 500 casualties and Janssens' defending force nearly twenty times more (Hannigan 2012:94–100; Carey 2008:283), was relayed to Yogya via the Semarang divisional commander on 1 September. The same dispatch brought a report that Janssens had moved his seat of government to Semarang. The death toll on the Franco-Dutch side was so high – fifty percent of their European and Ambonese troops and eighty percent of their Javanese and Madurese auxiliaries – that rumours spread that the victorious British-Indian troops had run amok (Aukes 1935:35). Their bloody actions would forever after be remembered in the name of the area near Cornelis, Rawabangke ('the swamp of the corpses', Schoel 1931:313), where the victims of the battle were promiscuously flung.

On the day of the fall of Cornelis, Lord Minto, the governor-general of India (in office 1807–13), who had accompanied the Java expedition, issued a proclamation setting forth the liberal and enlightened principles on which the new British government would be based, promising the Javanese an immediate amelioration in their condition (Carey 2008:285):

> The inhabitants of Java now touch the fortunate moment when they will be placed under the protection of a power which will keep the calamities and sufferings of war far from their shores and under the guardianship of a just and beneficent government whose principle it is to combine the interests of the state with the security, prosperity and happiness of every class and denomination of the people.

It was the curtain-raiser for a five-year interregnum which would witness remarkable changes in colonial policy, but would also see the principles so confidently proclaimed by Minto at Weltevreden sacrificed on the altar of political expediency.

Janssens, meanwhile, had regrouped his forces in Semarang. But his position was hopeless. His attempt to hold the line in central Java had more to do with personal honour than with military realities. Napoleon's last words: 'Remember, Sir, that a French general does not let himself to be taken a second time!' (Thorn 1815:103), still rung in his ears, his previous loss of Cape Colony to the British in January 1806 a blot on his escutcheon

(Thorn 1815:103). He had thus rejected Minto's surrender offer (Aukes 1935:33). But his fate was sealed. On 12 September, 1,600 British and sepoy troops, commanded by Colonel (post-1813, Major-General) Samuel Gibbs (?1775/6–1815), landed at Semarang and four days later at Jati Ngaleh near Serondol on the heights above Semarang, Janssens and his Javanese allies were comprehensively defeated (Thorn 1815:97–101; Aukes 1935:38–47).

On 18 September, at the bridge at Kali Tuntang, which Raden Ronggo had ordered destroyed at the start of his doomed rebellion (Carey 2008:248), the second and last of the Franco-Dutch governor-generals signed the articles of capitulation. All civilian officials in post under the Franco-Dutch government were allowed to offer their services to the new British administration, while those with military commissions became prisoners-of-war (Thorn 1815:101; Soekanto 1952:83–7). The British were now the undisputed masters of Java.

The Squaring of Accounts

In the wake of the Franco-Dutch government's collapse, a confused period ensued in south-central Java. Bands of robbers acting on the orders of the rulers preyed on travelers. Captain William Robison (?1775–1823), Lord Minto's *aide-de-camp*, sent to the courts to make initial contacts with the rulers noticed groups of roving bandits as he set out for Surakarta on 21 September (Carey 2008:287–8).

In Surakarta, the Sunan listed his grievances with the former Franco-Dutch administration, in particular the withdrawal of the *strandgeld* payments, the despoliation of the most important royal tomb on the north coast, that of Sunan Amangkurat I (reigned 1646–77), and the change in court ceremonial. Similar grievances were tabled in Yogya where the old sultan and the Prince Regent drew attention to the plight of Yogya inhabitants in the *pasisir* border areas (Carey 2008:288).

Like Van Braam (Chapter IV), Robison noticed the difference in atmosphere between the two courts, noting that the Sunan was 'well-disposed and pliant', but the old sultan still smarted from the indignities inflicted by Daendels. His eldest son, the Regent, was 'on the contrary more tractable and, if established beyond the control of the sultan, things should go well [...]' (Carey 2008:291), Robison's shrewd judgement foreshadowing Raffles' later policies. But for the time being, the old sultan had the upper hand.

Diponegoro described in his *babad* how the former monarch was 'overjoyed' (*geng tyasipun*) that the Dutch had been 'wiped out' (*sirna*). He could now wreak revenge on his court rivals (Babad Dipanegara II, 55). Orders were immediately given to his court *bupati* to restrict their dealings with European officials and Danurejo summoned to a morning meeting in the *kraton* (28 October). On entering the Purworetno pavilion, he was seized from behind by seven senior officials led by Sumodiningrat and an hour later strangled with white cloth, the usual method of execution for the Javanese elite as it left no marks on the body. The next day, his body was taken south for interment at the traitor's graveyard beyond Imogiri where Raden Ronggo's hacked corpse had been laid to rest just ten months previously (Carey 2008:292–3).

The short official letter informing Engelhard of the *patih*'s 'dismissal' referred to his many defects. These included besmirching the Islamic religion (*angresahi agami Islam*), demeaning the sultan's royal dignity, and violating his injunctions as sovereign (Carey 1980:76–7; 2008:293). The sultan may have had *syariah* (Islamic law) in mind in his use of the term 'Islamic religion' (*agami Islam*), but there is something larger being evoked here: Islam was being used as a shorthand for the Javanese-Islamic moral order in general, something Diponegoro would emulate during the Java War (p. 218).

The position of the Prince Regent was now desperate. With his main supporter murdered and the Resident mortally ill, he was in grave danger. In his *babad*, Diponegoro gives a graphic account of his father's plight: summoned from Tegalrejo late on 1 November, he found the great outer doors of his father's residence, the *kadipaten*, bolted and guarded by members of the 'priestly' Suranatan corps. Informing his son of Danurejo's death, the Crown Prince asked what he should do if summoned to the *kraton*. Diponegoro suggested that he not go that night, but instead allow him to accompany his father on his next official audience. He also stated that he had thrown away the bolts to the *kadipaten*'s outer doors and dismissed his father's bodyguard to avoid misunderstandings (Carey 2008:294-5).

On 5 November, the erstwhile Regent – now once again Crown Prince – made his peace with the sultan. All his male relations accompanied him, including the twenty-six-year-old Diponegoro – then styled Raden Ontowiryo – who was fast emerging as his father's chief political adviser (Carey 1992:290; 2008:373-4).

On 7 November, Engelhard reported that the differences between the Prince Regent and his father had been 'overcome' (Carey 2008:295). The ex-Regent wrote to the sultan formally relinquishing his previous position and was reinstated as Crown Prince. Raffles later commented on the extraordinary 'filial piety' of the Crown Prince at this time (Carey 1980:85 note 1). But events would soon to undermine the precarious unity of the Yogya court.

The British Attempt at Compromise and Raffles' First Visit to the Courts

On 14 November, the new British Resident, John Crawfurd (1783-1868; in office, 1811-13, 1814, 1816), arrived in Yogya with a 300-strong sepoy escort. The Scotsman was undoubtedly the most able official ever to serve in the sultan's capital. Fluent in Javanese in under six months (p. 32) and a noted horseman who allowed his bloodstock to participate in court-sponsored races (De Haan 1935a:529; Carey 1992:296, 420 note 106, 453-4 note 262, 524 note 617), he did not begin well. Ignoring Raffles' explicit instructions that he should immediately improve British-Yogya relations, and in particular that he should investigate the possibility of restoring the sultan and maintaining the Regent as Crown Prince (Deventer 1891:307-8), Crawfurd made a set against the sultan (Carey 2008:298).

A curt note of protest calculated to offend was sent with the Resident's official seal placed at the bottom rather than the usual top left-hand corner. Protesting 'all the measures' taken since 31 October, the Scotsman declined to meet the sultan for nearly a fortnight after his arrival (Carey 2008:298–9). The Yogya monarch was confused: Raffles' Melaka letter of 20 December 1810 had spoken of his being 'restored' to his full dignity as ruler. Surely this meant that the new British Government had accepted his political revolution (Carey 2008:301)? In response, he sent a joint letter with the Crown Prince telling Crawfurd not to 'meddle' in the events which had taken place since 1 November in the *kraton* (Carey 1980:77–9).

An alarmed Raffles immediately warned his subordinate: 'it must be laid down as a principle in all our dealings with the native courts that in no case must we demand what we cannot enforce in case of refusal' (Deventer 1891:313). In fact, the lieutenant-governor's demands at this time were minimal and almost as politically naive as those of his brash subordinate. In late October, he had already assured Minto that the second sultan's reinstatement seemed 'practicable [...] without endangering the tranquillity of the country', a view he reiterated to Crawfurd in early December, adding the condition that the Yogya ruler should simply write a letter of atonement for his recent actions (Carey 2008:301). Then came a remark of stunning ignorance: if he refused, Yogyakarta should be placed under Surakarta administration!

Crawfurd's first audience with the sultan took place on 26 November and passed off well, although he noticed with alarm that instead of sitting next to his father or on a stool, the Crown Prince sat on the floor with other senior officials. The second sultan's throne was also once again raised above his own seat by the insertion of a wooden bench (Carey 2008:303), the Yogya ruler being determined to return to the pre-July 1808 status quo, something which Raffles had seemingly encouraged in his Melaka dispatch.

On 16 December, the sultan's younger brother, Notokusumo, returned to Yogya from Surabaya after deeply impressing Raffles with his understanding of Yogya affairs. Seething with resentment against the Crown Prince, he was further outraged by the plundering of his residence during his absence (Poensen 1905:276–7; Carey 1992:96, 250, 404 note 30). The next six months until the fall of the Yogya *kraton* to British assault on 20 June 1812, were a period of delicate manoeuvring on the part of the future Pakualam I and the Crown Prince. The prize was nothing less than the throne of Yogya.

Preparations were now made for Raffles' first visit to the sultan's capital. On 23 December, a three-man commission led by the lieutenant-governor's able Dutch assistant, Harman Warner Muntinghe (1773–1827), with two Malay-speaking Bengal army officers arrived in Yogya to open political negotiations (Deventer 1891:313–14; De Haan 1935a:615; Carey 1980:91). They were joined by Colonel Colin Mackenzie (1754–1821), Raffles' chief engineer officer, whose expertise was required to assess the sultan's military capacity and the strength of the *kraton* fortifications (Carey 2008:307–8).

The fact that Raffles insisted on being received in Yogya with the full prerogatives and ceremonial of a visiting governor-general like Daendels during his July 1809 visit even though his rank was that of a mere lieutenant-governor heightened feelings of unease in Yogya. Was this cocky Englishman really a governor-general or just a British version of the former Dutch governor of Java's Northeast Coast?

Such preliminaries did not augur well for Raffles' visit. In fact, it nearly turned to tragedy: during the lieutenant-governor's initial meeting with the sultan on 27 December in the 'throne room' of the Residency, one of his *aides-de-camp* kicked the wooden bench away from under the Yogya ruler's silver throne so he would be forced to sit at Raffles' level. Members of the sultan's entourage then unsheathed their krises as British officers entered the room. Just in time the Crown Prince stepped between the lieutenant-governor and his father and the two men came to their senses. The situation was saved, but the incident underscored the tensions which lay just below the surface, tensions exacerbated by four years of humiliation and indignity (Carey 2008:309).

The new treaty signed between Raffles and the sultan on 28 December allowed for the return of all the lands ceded to Daendels under the 10 January treaty except for Grobogan which was reserved for Notokusumo. The *strandgeld* payments, however, were not reinstated. The tollgate and market taxes were also taken over by the government on payment of 80,000 Spanish dollars a year (Deventer 1891:318 article 6), a clause which would later open the way to much fiscal oppression by the returned post-1816 Dutch administration in the years leading up to the Java War (Chapter VIII).

The treaty would be short-lived. Neither side had any intention of abiding by it. According to the Pakualam *babad*, Raffles had assured

Notokusumo that at the onset of the next dry season (May–October) affairs in Yogya would be 'reconsidered' (Poensen 1905:278). For his part, the sultan immediately set about making preparations for resistance: 'The laxity and moderation of British conduct was mistaken for fear [...]', Crawfurd noted, 'after the signature of the treaty, an immediate start was made on the collection of troops, the manufacturing of arms and the strengthening of the defences of the cratton [*kraton*]' (Carey 2008:312). A military showdown with the British was brewing.

Preparations for War

Just as in a Greek tragedy hubris leads on inevitably to nemesis, so it was with the Yogya ruler in the early months of 1812 as he prepared to confront the emerging imperial superpower. Once again, the inability of the Yogya elite to read the runes of history would lead to disaster.

Throughout this period, Diponegoro states that he afforded his father constant support. We know from a subsequent Dutch source that the second sultan was aware of Diponegoro's actions and contemplated his murder (Carey 2008:315). Curiously, however, Crawfurd never once mentions the Crown Prince's eldest son in his dispatches. This omission is all the stranger given Diponegoro's boast that Crawfurd had discussed 'everything in person with his father and himself' (Carey 2008:109, 316), and that he himself had been charged by his father with responsibility for negotiating with the Resident (Louw 1894:36–7).

The problem for Diponegoro biographers is that a subsequent Dutch Resident and amateur historian, Frans Gerhardus Valck (1799–1842; in office 1831–41), used the Residency archive for his own researches on Yogya history (Valck 1844), and then retained many of the key documents (Carey 1978:119–20). This places professional historians in an impossible situation: they remain dependant on Valck's testimony, but have no means of verifying his sources (Carey 2008:316).

The End of the Beginning

According to Valck, Diponegoro was indeed used as a go-between between his father and Crawfurd and was 'in general very highly regarded by Europeans', a view later confirmed by senior Dutch officials at the time of his appointment as a guardian to the child sultan, Hamengkubuwono V (Carey 2008:509–10). So, until evidence appears to the contrary, Diponegoro's assertions must stand.

While these intrigues were moving towards their conclusion, the central Javanese courts came to a secret understanding against the British. One of Sumodiningrat's secret March 1812 missives to his Surakarta counterpart, the Solo *patih*, Raden Adipati Cokronegoro (in office, 1810–12), quoted the Sunan as writing 'that he wished to enter into a league and union with his 'father' [the sultan] which might descend to their latest posterity' (Carey 2008:316).

In his *babad*, Diponegoro gives a short but rather accurate description of the affair (Babad Dipanegara, II:69–70):

> XVI 23. [...]
> So His Highness the Sultan
> was certain to be the enemy of the English.
> Tumenggung Sumodiningrat
> was entrusted with the task,
>
> 24. [and] made contact with Surakarta.
> But His Highness the Sunan trusted in his younger brother
> Pangeran Mangkubumi
> and in the *patih*,
> Raden Adipati Cokronegoro.
> So there was an agreement
> that in future, if it came to battle
>
> 25. with the English, Surakarta
> undertook to fall on them from behind.
> Thus they swore together
> and exchanged documents
> with their signatures as an undertaking,
> indeed for all time.
> Thus was the agreement.

Although the Sunan assembled some 7,000 troops and appeared to 'await only on instructions from Yogya to commence hostilities', he did nothing to help his royal ally. Instead he merely placed part of his army across the British line of communications to Semarang thereby hoping to profit from any military reverse or protracted campaign (Carey 2008:321). The sultan for his part made no appeal for help from Surakarta during the British attack. Indeed, after Yogya's fall, the author of the *Babad Bedhah ing Ngayogyakarta* ('Chronicle of the Fall of Yogyakarta'), Pangeran Panular (?1772–1826), remarked that even with the Sunan's assistance, the sultanate would still not have been able to withstand the British (Carey 1992:107, 267, 433 note 167).

At the beginning of April, when evidence of the sultan's bad faith had become clear, Raffles ordered Crawfurd to open a secret channel of communication with the Crown Prince who in turn designated his *patih* (chief administrator), Raden Ngabehi Joyosentiko (?1765–1812, in office, 1810–12), as his representative. This official had been one of the junior commanders of the Yogya force sent to Batavia in October 1793 to strengthen the VOC defences at the onset of hostilities with the French Republic (Carey 2008:323; Zandvliet 1991:79–80). So he had experience of dealing with Europeans and knew of the secret correspondence between the courts. A man of unusual courage (Babad Dipanegara, II:56), he would later pay for his loyalty to the Crown Prince with his life (pp. 143–4).

When Crawfurd met Raffles in Semarang in early June ahead of the British attack, the lieutenant-governor announced his intention to depose the sultan and appoint the Crown Prince in his place. He also proposed, according to Diponegoro's autobiography, to recognise Diponegoro as the new heir apparent (*Pangeran Adipati*). But the prince refused this position (Carey 2008:324–5), taking an oath before two close friends in the Suranatan regiment as follows (Babad Dipanegara, II:75):

XV 78. [...]
    Be my witnesses

  79. if I should forget.
    I make [you] witnesses of my firmness of heart:
    let me not be made
    Pangeran Adipati [Crown Prince].
    Even if I were later to be made sultan,

>   even if it were done by my father
>   or grandfather,
>
> 80.   I myself do not wish
>   to have to repent to the Almighty.
>   No matter how long I am upon this earth,
>   I would constantly be sinful.

The whole episode as it is related in Diponegoro's *babad* is confusing. As we have seen, Diponegoro's supposed role in Crawfurd's correspondence with his father is nowhere acknowledged by the British. We only have Valck's testimony that he was known and appreciated by the British authorities. Meanwhile, Bendoro Raden Mas Sudomo had already been recognised by the Crown Prince as his lawful successor (Louw and De Klerck 1894–1909, I:115; Mandoyokusumo 1977:37; Carey 2008:326). It would have been quite out of character for Diponegoro to have coveted this position which he knew was not his by birth and which he had been specifically warned not to accept by the prophetic voice at Parangkusumo (p. 59). The only possible explanation is that either Crawfurd or Raffles misunderstood the Javanese distinction between royal sons by official (*garwa padmi*) and unofficial (*garwa ampeyan*) wives. Aware that Diponegoro was the eldest son of the Crown Prince and now an increasingly known quantity, they may have automatically assumed that the succession should be secured to him in the event that his father became sultan.

Despite Diponegoro's emphatic rejection, rumours continued to circulate concerning his ambitions. These would later poison relations between the prince and the court during the reign of his younger brother, Hamengkubuwono IV (Van der Kemp 1896:324; Louw and De Klerck 1894–1909, V:744; Carey 1976:61, 1981:269 note 134). They were even used by some Dutch officials to suggest that the real reason for Diponegoro's July 1825 rebellion was thwarted political ambition (p. 251).

As the secret negotiations with the Crown Prince continued, it became clear that action would soon have to be taken against the sultan to protect the heir apparent's life. Crawfurd pressed the Crown Prince to take refuge in the Residency House, but he refused. Instead, he continued to attend *kraton* ceremonies together with his uncle, Notokusumo, to dispel the sultan's suspicions that the two were contemplating going over to the British (Carey 2008:329).

By early June, the British expeditionary force numbering some 1,000 of their best troops, of whom half were Bengal sepoys, arrived in Semarang, Ungaran and Salatiga, advanced parties being sent down to strengthen the south-central Javanese garrisons. By 13 June, the main body was on the march to the sultan's capital. They arrived surreptitiously, entering the fort by night (Carey 2008:331).

The British Assault on the Kraton, 19–20 June 1812

According to Diponegoro, the sultan still believed the assurances of his court *haji* who assured him that the lieutenant-governor was on the march to take the Crown Prince prisoner and banish him from Java. Until the very end, the sultan apparently believed that he could persuade the British to recognise Mangkudiningrat as his successor in place of Diponegoro's father (Poensen 1905:306; Carey 1992:75, 218). Sumodiningrat was the adviser who pressed the sultan hardest to resist the British, 'steadfastly expressing his joy that [at last] it should come to battle' as Diponegoro put it (Babad Dipanagara, II:76).

On 17 June, Raffles arrived in Yogya. Two days later all the British detachments, including 500 men of Pangeran Prangwedono's legion under the prince's personal command, were in the fort. At five o'clock on the morning of 18 June, Notokusumo himself arrived with his wives and children. His followers were distributed white flashes for their left arms so that they could be recognised by the British troops during their forthcoming assault, while the prince and his sons were given British cavalry uniforms (Carey 2008:356–7, 2013:24).

Despite the Crown Prince's highly vulnerable position, both Panular's 'Chronicle of the Fall of Yogyakarta' and Valck's historical overview make it clear that he never intended treachery towards his father, but stood by in the *kadipaten* to afford the sultan assistance in the event of a British attack (Carey 1992: 67–78, 204–23). Meanwhile, small parties of pikemen, musketeers and cavalry, described as 'banditti' in the British sources, were dispatched by the sultan to mount ambushes and burn bridges (Raffles 1830:126). One of the sultan's ablest commanders, Raden Ario Sindurejo II (?1770–1814), laid a skilful ambush for an advance party of British dragoons clearing the road for the British main force in the ravine of the Kali Gajahwong at Papringan. The 25-strong squadron lost five dead and thirteen severely wounded including their British officer (Carey 2008:333).

The action proved the effectiveness of Javanese pikemen operating in disciplined formation using their long spears to dismount European cavalrymen (Thorn 1815:177–8; Carey 1992:427 note 238). But Sindurejo's action would not be repeated. If it had, the British assault on Yogya might have taken a different course, resulting in the sort of casualty levels (twenty percent of the attacking force) sustained by the British at Cornelis. Instead, the British lost just twenty-three killed and seventy-four wounded, including a single officer, out of a total attacking force of just under 1,000 men. This gives a casualty rate of just under ten percent, small if compared to the hundreds – 'dreadful' losses according to Raffles – who died on the Javanese side (Carey 1992:415 note 95).

On the day of Sindurejo's ambush (18 June), Raffles sent the Semarang Residency interpreter, C.F. Krijgsman, to deliver the sultan an ultimatum: unless he abdicated within the next two hours in favour of the Crown Prince, the British would start bombarding the *kraton*. Turning to the Crown Prince, the sultan asked if he was prepared to accede to the British demands. The Crown Prince resolutely refused, whereupon the sultan drew up a letter detailing his refusal and demanding that his brother, Notokusumo, immediately explain his recent treachery. The British artillery bombardment began that afternoon (Carey 2008:335).

According to Raffles, the lengthy cannonade had two purposes: to allow time for the main body of the British assault force to reach Yogya, and to afford the sultan space to reconsider his position. Far from being intimidated, however, the sultan appeared set on hostilities. Waving aside Mangkudiningrat's warnings about what had happened at Kartasura when the *kraton* had been stormed by the Chinese in 1742, he rejoiced one of his officials, Sumodiwiryo, succeeded in blowing the fort's powder magazine (Carey 2008:337). But his bravado soon ebbed away when the British attack proper got under way early on the morning of 20 June. His cowardly behavior at that time would undermine the fighting morale of the *kraton* defenders (Carey 2008:335).

So too would the actions of the majority of the princes of the blood, who, under withering British musket fire, cowered in the shelter of gateways or pretended they were sick (Carey 1992:67–8, 204–6, 208–9). Others slipped away over the *kraton* walls to take refuge in surrounding villages where their wives had relations, a number going with their families to Imogiri. Only a handful of princes and senior officials, amongst them Sumodiningrat and Diponegoro's future cavalry commander, Joyokusumo (post-1825, Ngabehi), led the defence with any resolution.

The Crown Prince's establishment (*kadipaten*) was especially exposed to the British bombardment positioned as it was in the northeastern part of the *kraton* closest to the fort's artillery batteries (Carey 1992:67, 69, 205, 210). Twice the Crown Prince sent word to the sultan via his uncle, Panular, that reinforcements were urgently needed to prevent his establishment falling to the besiegers. But his requests were ignored: the sultan remained in the inner *kraton* during the cannonade surrounded by members of his Amazon corps who recited prayers and incantations (*dhikr*) (Thorn 1815:293; Carey 1992:68, 70, 207–8, 211).

At nine o'clock in the evening the British guns fell silent. In the *kraton*, many of the defenders fell asleep, thinking that the fighting was over. But at three the following morning, the cannon thundered forth again with redoubled power. At daybreak, parties of British and sepoy troops along with Notokusumo's men dispersed around the walls of the *kraton* (Hageman 1857:424–5; Thorn 1815:184–7; Carey 1992:72, 214). Some bore flimsy bamboo scaling ladders prepared by the *kapitan cina*, Tan Jin Sing, whose Yogya Chinese community backed the British attack, an attitude which would later fuel powerful anti-Chinese sentiments (Carey 1984:22–4).

The *kadipaten* was the first to fall: the Poncosuro gate in the northeast bastion was blown up by Madras horse artillery and its battlements overrun by sepoys who turned the *kraton* guns on the defenders (Thorn 1815:185, Plate XIX no. F; Carey 1992:72, 214). The Crown Prince and his supporters, including Diponegoro, tried to flee into the *kraton* to join the sultan, but they were refused entry (Carey 1992:73, 215). Under continuous sepoy musketry fire from the *kraton* battlements, they approached Pasar

Ngasem near the Taman Sari, when a Bengal Light Infantry Volunteer detachment led by their C.O., Major Dennis Harman Dalton (1771–1828) (Carey 1992:512 note 543), and John Deans, the Malay-speaking Residency Secretary (in office 1811–1813), caught up with them. The Crown Prince was asked to come under armed guard to the Residency, Diponegoro receiving a light bayonet wound as Dalton's sepoys roughly disarmed him, taking his *kris*. Eventually, they reached the Residency where they were received by Raffles and Crawfurd. Notokusumo treated them icily, hardly deigning to speak with his nephew (Carey 1992:78–9, 224–5). It was half past six in the morning (Hageman 1857:425).

Meanwhile, the southern *alun-alun* had been overrun and Sumodiningrat, deserted by his troops, was soon executed in his own residence to the south of the *kraton* while trying to avoid capture, the third and last of the sultan's and Ratu Kedaton's sons-in-law to die violently within the space of just eighteen months.

With the British now poised to make a frontal assault on the *kadaton* (inner court), the sultan resolved to hoist a white flag, recall his commanders and instruct them to order a ceasefire (Carey 1992:83, 231–2). He hoped that by this voluntary submission, the *kraton* proper would be spared (Carey 1992:83, 232). On entering the *Srimenganti* pavilion, the British vanguard found the sultan and his relations dressed in white with many of the chairs also covered with torn strips of white cloth, in a scene which, if the Yogya ruler's mind had been set on death rather than surrender, might have prefigured the *prang puputan* ('final battle/ending wars') in Lombok and Bali in 1894 and 1906–8 when the rulers and their families met their deaths at the hands of the invading Dutch armies (Van der Kraan 1980:97; Creese 2006:1–38).

In the case of Yogya, the monarch and his entourage made no attempt at such a desperate stand, allowing themselves to be disarmed and their hands held at their sides by their British and sepoy guards. Even the sultan's person was secured by a British officer from a Scots regiment (Carey 1992:85, 234–5, 412 note 69a). Under these humiliating circumstances, the Yogya ruler and his relations were marched to the Residency between a row of British and sepoy soldiers with drawn swords and fixed bayonets.

As the party entered the Residency House, Panular, the author of the 'Chronicle of the fall of Yogyakarta', described how Raffles noticed with pleasure that only a couple of princes tried to get down from their chairs to pay the sultan their customary respects. He motioned these to remain seated. In tears, the sultan and his followers were now deprived of their personal *kris* and gold ornaments (Carey 1992:86, 236), the sultan's sword and stabbing dagger being sent by Raffles to Lord Minto in Calcutta as a symbol of 'the entire submission' of the Yogya court. Even the small diamond buttons of the sultan's dress jacket were subsequently cut off by his sepoy guards as he lay asleep in his place of detention (Nahuys van Burgst 1835–36, I:131). It was eight o'clock in the morning. The Parangkusumo prophecy had been fulfilled.

Conclusion

So the *kraton* of Yogyakarta fell to the British nearly fifty-seven years after it had been first occupied as Mangkubumi's capital on 6 November 1755 (Ricklefs 1974:80). In the space of just under four years, the south-central Javanese courts had been forced to accommodate themselves to a new form of centralised colonial government which stood in direct contradiction to their own political philosophy of divided sovereignty in Java. Given time, they might have been able to reshape their political conceptions to legitimize the changed realities, but they could not do it in the quick fire way demanded by Daendels and Raffles. The result was disaster.

This was particularly so for Yogya, which had entered on this period of change with ostensibly the most powerful and prosperous court, but in fact hopelessly divided against itself and ruled by a vain and inflexible man. The spread of intrigues within the *kraton* literally tore it apart just at the time when it needed its undivided energies to cope with the new challenges posed by a resurgent Europe. Mangkubumi's kingdom had been founded by the sword, in June 1812 it could be said to have perished by the sword.

For the British colonial government in Java, there was little doubt about the significance of their victory, Muntinghe hailing it as an event of similar significance to Clive's victory at Plassey on 23 June 1757 which had opened the whole of northern India to British rule (Carey 1992:60 note 102). Raffles echoed this in a dispatch to his patron, Lord Minto, when he stated that 'the European power is for the first time paramount in Java. [...] we never till this moment could call ourselves masters of the more valuable provinces in the interior, nay, our possessions on the sea coasts would always have been precarious [...]' (Carey 2008:342–3).

Although both Yogyakarta and Surakarta would continue as dismembered states after 1812, they would never again pose a threat to the position of the European government. When a new challenge did emerge under Diponegoro's Javanese-Islamic banner in July 1825, it would owe its inspiration and energies to influences outside the great court traditions. The support given to the prince by the religious communities and the Javanese peasantry, both groups who felt excluded from the new colonial order, was more important than the traditional foci of court patronage and loyalty. June 1812, rather than the end of the Java War, should perhaps be seen as the date when the new colonial era dawned in Java. Out of this collapse and the legacy of bitterness which it left, however, a new and more potent combination of elements in Javanese society would emerge. It is with these developments in the decade and more following the British attack on Yogya that the next three chapters are concerned.

Bibliography

Aukes, H.F. (1935). *Het Legioen van Mangkoe Nagoro*. Bandoeng: Nix.
Babad Dipanegara (2010). *Babad Dipanegara*, 4 vols, ed. Nindya Noegraha. Jakarta: Perpustakaan Nasional Republik Indonesia.
Bataviasche Koloniale Courant (Batavia: 's Lands Drukkerij, 1810–11) 5, 8-2-1811.
Bayly, C.A. (1989). *Imperial Meridian; The British Empire and the World, 1780–1830*. Harlow: Longman.

Carey, Peter (1974). 'Javanese Histories of Dipanagara: The Buku Kedhung Kebo, its authorship and historical importance', *Bijdragen tot de Taal-, Land- en Volkenkunde* 130:259–88.
Carey, Peter (1976). 'The Origins of the Java War (1825–30)', *English Historical Review* 91:52–78.
Carey, Peter (1978). 'The Residency Archive of Jogjakarta', *Indonesia* 25:115–50.
Carey, Peter (1980). *The Archive of Yogyakarta. Vol. I: Documents relating to Politics and Internal Court Affairs*. Oxford: Oxford University Press.
Carey, Peter (1981). *Babad Dipanagara; An Account of the Outbreak of the Java War (1825–30); The Surakarta Court Version of the Babad Dipanagara with Translations into English and Indonesian Malay*. Kuala Lumpur: Art Printers.
Carey, Peter (1984). 'Changing Javanese Perceptions of the Chinese Communities in Central Java, 1755–1825', *Indonesia* 37:1–48.
Carey, Peter (1992). *The British in Java, 1811–1816; A Javanese Account*. Oxford: Oxford University Press.
Carey, Peter (2008). *The Power of Prophecy; Prince Dipanagara and the End of an Old Order in Java, 1785–1855*. Leiden: KITLV Press.
Carey, Peter (2013). *Daendels and the Sacred Space of Java, 1808–1811; Political Relations, Uniforms and the Postweg*. Nijmegen: Vantilt.
Carey, Peter and Mason Hoadley (eds) (2000). *The Archive of Yogyakarta. Vol. II: Documents relating to Economic and Agrarian Affairs*. Oxford: Oxford University Press.
Chijs, J.A. van der (1895–97). *Nederlandsch-Indisch Plakaatboek 1602–1811*. Vol. XIV (1807–1808), XV (1808–1809), XVI (1810–1811). The Hague: Nijhoff.
Creese, Helen (2006). 'A *Puputan* tale; "The Story of a Pregnant Woman"', *Indonesia* 82:1–38.
Daendels, H.W. (1814). *Staat der Nederlandsche Oostindische Bezittingen, onder het Bestuur van den Gouverneur-Generaal Herman Willem Daendels, Ridder, Luitenant-Generaal &c. in de Jaren 1808–1811*. The Hague: Van Cleef.
Deventer, M.L. van (1891). *Het Nederlandsch Gezag over Java en Onderhoorigheden sedert 1811; Verzameling van Onuitgegeven Stukken uit de Koloniale en Andere Archieven. Vol.I: 1811–1820*. The Hague: Nijhoff.
Haan, F. de (1935). 'Personalia der Periode van het Engelsch Bestuur over Java, 1811–1816', *Bijdragen tot de Taal-, Land- en Volkenkunde* 92:477–681.
Hageman, J.Jcz. (1856). *Geschiedenis van den Oorlog op Java van 1825 tot 1830*. Batavia: Lange.
Hageman, J.Jcz. (1857). 'De Engelschen op Java', *Tijdschrift voor Indische Taal-, Landen Volkenkunde* 6:290–457.
Hannigan, Tim (2012). *Raffles and the British Invasion of Java*. Singapore: Monsoon.

Houben, Vincent (1994). *Kraton and Kumpeni; Surakarta and Yogyakarta 1830–1870*. Leiden: KITLV Press. [Verhandelingen 164.]

Kemp, P.H. van der (1896). 'Dipanegara, Eene Geschiedkundige Hamlettype', *Bijdragen tot de Taal-, Land- en Volkenkunde* 46:281–433.

Kraan, A. van der (1980). *Lombok; Conquest, Colonization and Under-Development, 1870–1940*. Singapore: Heinemann.

Louw, P.J.F. (1894). 'Crawfurd door Dipånegårå Toegelicht', in: *Feestbundel van Taal-, Letter-, Geschied- en Aardrijkskundige Bijdragen ter Gelegenheid van zijn Tachtigsten Geboortedag aan Dr. P.J. Veth*, pp. 36–7. Leiden: Brill.

Louw, P.J.F. and E.S. de Klerck (1894–1909). *De Java-Oorlog van 1825–1830*. The Hague: Nijhoff, Batavia: Landsdrukkerij. Six vols.

Mandoyokusumo, K.R.T. (1977). *Serat Raja Putra Ngayogyakarta Hadiningrat*. Yogyakarta: Bebadan Museum Karaton Ngayogyakarta Hadiningrat.

Nahuys van Burgst (1835–36). *Verzameling van Officiële Rapporten betreffende den Oorlog op Java in de Jaren 1825–1830, voorafgegaan door eenige aanmerkingen en medeelingen omtrent denzelven, benevens eene memorie over de verhuring of uitgifte van landeryen aan Europeanen*. Deventer: Ballot. Four vols.

Nahuys van Burgst (1858). *Herinneringen uit het Openbare en Bijzondere Leven (1799–1858) van Mr H.G. Baron Nahuys van Burgst*. 's-Hertogenbosch: Muller.

Peucker, P.M. and J.P.C.M. van Hoof (1991). 'Daendels, een Groot Generaal?' in F. van Aanrooy et al., *Herman Willem Daendels 1762–1818. Geldersman-Patriot-Jacobijn-Generaal-Hereboer-Maarschalk-Gouverneur, van Hattem naar St George del Mina*. Utrecht: Matrijs:47–60.

Poensen, C. (1905). 'Amăngku Buwånå II (Sĕpuh); Ngayogyåkarta's tweede sultan (naar aanleiding van een Javaansch handschrift)', *Bijdragen tot de Taal-, Land en Volkenkunde* 58:73–346.

Ricklefs, M.C. (1974). *Jogjakarta under Sultan Mangkubumi, 1749–1792; A History of the Division of Java*. Oxford: Oxford University Press.

Ricklefs, M.C. (1986). 'Some Statistical Evidence on Javanese Social, Economic and Demographic History in the later Seventeenth and Eighteenth Centuries', *Modern Asian Studies* 20–1:1–32.

Ronkel, Ph.S. van (1918). 'Daendels in de Maleische Literatuur', *Koloniaal Tijdschrift* 7:858–75.

Schoel, W.F. (ed) (1931). *Alphabetisch Register van de Administratieve-(Bestuurs) en Adatrechtelijke Indeeling van Nederlandsch-Indië. Vol. I: Java en Madoera*. Batavia: Landsdrukkerij.

Soekanto (1952). *Sekitar Jogjakarta 1755–1825 (Perjanjian Gianti-Perang Dipanagara)*. Djakarta, Amsterdam: Mahabarata.

Stockdale, J.J. (1812). *Sketches, Civil and Military of the Island of Java and its Immediate Dependencies comprising interesting details of Batavia and authentic particulars of the celebrated Poison-tree*. London: Stockdale.
Thorn, W. (1815). *Memoir of the Conquest of Java with the Subsequent Operations of the British Forces in the Oriental Archipelago*. London: Egerton.
Valck, F.G. (1844). 'Overzigt van de Voornaamste Gebeurtenissen in het Djocjocartasche rijk, sedert dezelfs Stichting (1755) tot aan het Einde van het Engelsche Tusschen-Bestuur in 1816', ed. J.C. Steyn Parvé, *Tijdschrift voor Nederlandsch Indië*, 6-3:122-57, 262-88, 6-4:25-49.
Veth, P.J. (1896–1907). *Java; Geographisch, Ethnologisch, Historisch*. Haarlem: Erven F. Bohn. Four vols.
Vink, J.A. (1892). 'Hoe Djokjakarta en Klaten nu 81 jaar geleden tot de Franschen overgingen; Procesverbaal wegens de Promulgatie van de Gewigtige en Heuchelijke Tijding der Vereeniging van het Koninkrijk Holland met de Fransch Keizerrijk te Djocjacarta en Klatten', *Indisch Militair Tijdschrift* 21:441-7.
Zaini-Lajoubert, Monique (1987). *Hikayat Mareskalk*. Bandung: Angkasa.
Zandvliet, K. (1991). 'Daendels en de Nieuwe Kaart van Java', in F. van Aanrooy et al., *Herman Willem Daendels 1762-1818. Geldersman-Patriot-Jacobijn-Generaal-Hereboer-Maarschalk-Gouverneur, van Hattem naar St George del Mina*. Utrecht: Matrijs:77-105.

PART III

Golden Years, Iron Years, 1812–1825

CHAPTER VII

Into a New Era: Diponegoro and the Post-June 1812 British Interregnum

Lineaments of a New Order

The four years following the British storming of the Yogya *kraton* marked a new era in Javanese court-colonial government relations. The balance of force had now shifted decisively in favour of the latter. Never again would a governor-general have to fear the countervailing military power of the independent rulers. The treaties imposed by Raffles in August 1812 would strip them forever of their independent military capacity.

This power shift is reflected in the Residency letters which now deal with the minutiae of colonial administration rather than the litany of threat and counter-threat of the Daendels' era (1808–11). On the economic front there were changes too. Just as the collapse of Raden Ronggo's rebellion in December 1810 swept aside the last barriers to the exploitation of the eastern *mancanagara*, so now the south-central Javanese heartlands were opened to western capital, the British period witnessing the first European land leases in the Principalities (Carey 2008:346).

The present chapter considers the impact of this power shift against the backdrop of the last four years of the British 1811–16 interregnum and Diponegoro's emerging public role.

The Plunder of the Yogya Kraton

Before the new era could dawn, Gillespie's force took the Yogya *kraton* apart. Booty was one of the major perquisites of East India Company officers. But even Raffles was shocked:

> The whole of the tangible property of Djocjocarta fell to the captors [...] but in the immediate distribution they took more upon themselves than was justifiable. [...] the mischief being once done, it was useless to object or condemn (Carey 2008:347).

Of the estimated 800,000 Spanish dollars worth of prize money, some USD20,000,000 in today's money, Gillespie helped himself to a personal reward of 74,000 Spanish dollars (present-day USD1,750,000), leaving the rest to his officers and men. Half was remitted to Bengal so that officers could draw bills of exchange to support their families in India.

The Chronicle of the Fall of Yogyakarta, describe British and sepoy troops going roughly to work: the princes and senior *kraton* officials were forced to hand over their jewel encrusted *kris* (Carey 1992:89, 240) while the court womenfolk were body searched for jewellery. Though spared the rapes which marked the fall of Plered (1677) and Kartasura (1742) (Thorn 1815:190; Carey 1992:88, 238, 415 note 84; Ricklefs 1993:41), violence was involved: the only British officer to die in the attack received a mortal wound from a court lady defending her honour (Carey 1992:414 note 78).

The plundering of the *kraton* continued for more than four whole days, the chronicle describing an unending stream of booty being carried to the Residency on ox-carts and on the backs of porters (Palmer van den Broek 1875:69; Carey 1992:94, 248, 421 note 111). Sets of shadow-play puppets, court *gamelan* (Javanese orchestras) and archives were all taken. These last included land registers (Carey and Hoadley 2000) and manuscripts, all that is except for one beautifully caligraphed *Qur'ān* which Raffles spurned as foreign to Java's *adiluhung* (high) Hindu-Buddhist culture (*Java Government Gazette*, 4–7–1812; Thorn 1815:192; Carey 1980:12–13 notes 1–5, 1992:94, 248; Tiffin 2008:341–60).

Notokusumo assisted Crawfurd and Raffles in identifying some of the manuscripts, his literary knowledge forging a lasting friendship between himself and the British officials. By the time Crawfurd left Yogya on 10 August 1816, he would describe Pakualam as 'a man of superior mind. He has a comprehensiveness of understanding to which among the natives there is no parallel' (Carey 2008:350–1).

Another such relationship of mutual literary and scholarly esteem was that of Crawfurd and Raffles for the family of the *bupati* of Semarang, Kyai Adipati Suro-Adimenggolo IV (?1760–1827, in office 1809–27, Plate 11) whose two sons, Saleh (?1801–pre-March 1856), and Sukur (?1803–pre-March 1856), would be sent for schooling in Calcutta in July 1812 'to become Englishmen' (Raffles 1817, I:273 note; Crawfurd 1820, I:48–9; Hageman 1856:412; De Graaf 1979:16–18; Carey 1992:438 note 201; Kraus and Vogelsang 2012:31).

Although such friendships were based on shared interests, they were at heart exploitative: the expertise of men such as Notokusumo/Pakualam I, Suro-Adimenggolo and the Panembahan of Sumenep, Paku-Nataningrat (reigned 1811–54) (Carey 2013:23), enabled scholar-administrators like Raffles and Crawfurd to use local sources for their histories. But the acknowledgement they received was not commensurate with their contribution.

The Appointment of Hamengkubuwono III and Kasepuhan-Karajan Rivalries

The rapid humiliation of the old ruler and the appointment of the Crown Prince as sultan did not see the end of the old sultan's party or *kasepuhan* (Carey 1992:438 note 201, 2008:352). Old hatreds lived on and would shape Java War loyalties: many more princes from the third sultan's party (*karajan*) than the *kasepuhan* would support Diponegoro in 1825.

On the night following the fall of the *kraton*, the principal supporter of the old sultan, Mangkudiningrat, ordered an amok attack on leading *karajan* officials at Tan Jin Sing's residence. The head of the *kadipaten*, Raden Ngabehi Joyosentiko, and another of the new sultan's advisers were killed, while the *Kapitan Cina* himself was gravely wounded (Carey 1992:424 note 126).

The attack was not blind. Mangkuduningrat's targets were very specific. The *Kapitan Cina* and the wider Chinese community had caused resentment as a result of their support of recent British military operations (Chapter VI), and Joyosentiko himself was slated as a future prime minister (*patih*). Had he lived, the later quarrel between Diponegoro and the man who eventually took the post in December 1813, the *bupati* of Japan (post-1838, Mojokerto), Mas Tumenggung Sumodipuro, might never have happened.

The coronation ceremony itself, however, took place without mishap on 21 June (*Java Government Gazette*, 4–7–1812:3; Carey 1992:103–4, 261–5). According to a British artillery officer, it was 'extremely impressive' (Carey 2008:355). Raffles' official proclamation was read out (Carey 1992:89, 241), ending with the warning that 'all who presume to abet the dethroned Prince in his pretensions to government will be considered as traitors to their country and dealt with accordingly' (Carey 1992:417 note 92).

Ever since Sunan Pakubuwono II's (reigned, 1726–49) formal cession of his kingdom to the VOC in December 1749, the Dutch claim to 'sovereignty' over Mataram was unenforceable. In Ricklefs' words, 'only men and gunpowder could accomplish that and of these commodities the Dutch supply was inadequate until the nineteenth century' (Ricklefs 1974:52). The British with their Indian army victorious on land and their navy unchallenged on the high seas could now announce that they were 'delegating' half the 'high lands of Java' to their client sovereign and had the power to make that delegation real. Those who opposed their new order were traitors not just to Yogya but also to the British. This was a changed world indeed.

As a nineteen-gun salute boomed forth, Javanese nobles and senior court officials came forward to pay their respects to the new ruler, led by Notokusumo and Prangwedono (Mangkunegoro II), the last greeting the newly appointed monarch with a European handshake, a further sign – along with his short-cropped hair and European uniform – that he was now a 'Company' prince (Carey 1992:105, 264, 432 note 159). When two of the older princes, who had favoured the former sultan, gave Raffles and the new ruler the two-handed Muslim greeting rather than kissing their feet, Crawfurd seized their necks and forced their heads down causing them acute embarrassment (Carey 1992:105, 264–5, 432 note 159a).

Into a New Era: Diponegoro and the Post-June 1812 British Interregnum 145

The official ceremonies over, Raffles invited the sultan and his party to inspect the British and sepoy troops arrayed in fifteen rows between the Residency and Fort Vredeburg (Carey 1992:106–8, 265–8, 429 note 146). An elaborate military display followed. This had a dual purpose: to celebrate the third sultan's appointment and to underscore the new administration's military power. Its message struck home. The author of the Chronicle remarked that it was fitting that Yogya had been conquered by such warlike enemies: even with the help of Surakarta, the Yogyanese could not have withstood them (Carey 1992:107–8, 266–8).

Creation of the Pakualaman, Exile of the Old Sultan and Disposal of Kraton Plunder

Before Raffles left Yogya on 23 June, three further ceremonies took place. The first was the formal invitation to the third sultan to 'repossess' the *kraton* – a sham 'repossession' for the plundering of the court was still proceeding. Only the cannon-pitted *kadipaten* was available as the third sultan's residence until the looted and partially burnt *kraton* could be reoccupied two weeks later (*Java Government Gazette*, 4-7-1812; Carey 1992:109, 111, 269, 272).

The second ceremony occurred on 22 June. In a still intact court pavilion, the Bangsal Kencono, Raffles gave formal notice of the annexation of Kedu and a third of the Yogya eastern *mancanagara* as repayment for recent British operations. He also announced Notokusumo's appointment as an independent prince with an independent 'Corps' consisting of a 100-strong mounted troop (Van Deventer 1891:335; Rouffaer 1905:606; Carey 1992:112, 274).

The creation of the Pakualaman marked a new political division of Yogyakarta, another sign of the sultanate's humiliation. The first Pakualam owed his allegiance exclusively to the British, a fact registered in the Javanese sources where he is referred to alternatively as the government's *miji* (directly subordinate official) and 'servant' (*rencang*) (Carey 2008:362).

The third and final ceremony was an oath-taking. This involved the public swearing of allegiance to the British government and the new Yogya ruler by the sultan's relations and senior court officials (Carey 1992:114, 281). Its solemnity altered not a whit the political realities in a deeply divided and now suddenly impoverished sultanate.

On 3 July, as the British troops departed Yogya, the old sultan, two of his sons, Mangkudiningrat and Mertosono, and Sumodiwiryo, the *bupati* who had fired the fort's powder magazine (p.131) were escorted to Semarang on the first stage of their exile journey to Pulau Pinang (Carey 1992:115, 282–3). On board the same British frigate were Suro-Adimenggolo IV's two sons, Saleh and Sukur, bound for Calcutta (Carey 1992:438 note 201). The cargo included sixty-eight chests containing 408,414 Spanish dollars in silver coin from the plundered Yogya treasury (Carey 1992:414–15 note 79). So the old sultan's wealth, extorted during the first eighteen years of his reign, travelled with him into exile. But it would not be his to enjoy. The blood and sweat of a nameless generation of south-central Javanese was now the spoil of a foreign conqueror.

As for Saleh and Sukur, they represented Java's conflicted future. As the first early-nineteenth-century Javanese to receive a European education, their prospects seemed bright. The fifteen-year-old Saleh, who won prizes in geometry, algebra and drawing, became assistant regent of Semarang on his return (May–August 1815) and went on to serve as *bupati* in Lasem and Rembang (1817–22). But both his career and that of his brother were blighted by the Java War. Sukur's decision to rally to Diponegoro and take a Muslim name implicated his whole family. Degradation, imprisonment and exile followed, Sukur and Saleh dying in exile in Ternate (pre-1856) and their respected father in Sumenep (1827) (Hageman 1856:412; De Haan 1935:641; Payen 1988:139 note 239; Carey 2008:616 note 28).

The same torn loyalties would be evident in the career of their first cousin, the pioneer of modern painting in Java, Raden Saleh Syarif Bustaman (?1811–80). After a childhood spent in Suro-Adimenggolo's household in its golden British years (1811–16), his life and artistic *oeuvre* would intersect fatefully with Diponegoro. In March 1857, he produced a painterly masterpiece depicting the prince's treacherous 28 March 1830 arrest at Magelang and would later marry the daughter of one of the Java War leader's junior commanders (Kraus 2005:278–88; Carey 2008:742; pp. 293–4; Plate 22). But bridging the cultural divide between Europe and Java proved impossible in a deeply racist and conservative Dutch East Indies.

Like his cousins, the painter Saleh would die a bitterly disappointed man (Kraus and Vogelsang 2012:121–2).

The Third Sultan's New Order

In Javanese history, a new reign offered the opportunity for re-ordering the court. Brief though it was and sadly diminished in terms of its financial resources, the third sultan's twenty-nine month rule opened with the same wholesale recasting of the *kraton*.

Two of the sultan's official wives were raised in rank. The most important was the mother of the Crown Prince, the future fourth sultan (reigned 1814–1822). A plain woman of 'great dignity', she was given the title of Ratu Kencono (circa 1780–1826; post-1816, Ratu Ibu) and would later become influential in the *kraton* during the minority of her son. Crawfurd thought highly of her (Carey 2008:367). Not so her stepson, Diponegoro, who despised her loose morals and association with two of his principal political enemies, namely the Yogya *patih*, Danurejo IV (in office 1813–1847), and her secret lover, Raden Tumenggung Major Wironegoro (?1790–pre-March 1856), commander of the sultan's bodyguard (Carey 2008:100, 367–8).

In a famous article, the Dutch historian, P.H. van der Kemp (1845–1921), compared Diponegoro to the Shakespearean tragic hero, Hamlet, basing an important strand of his argument on this enmity-filled relationship between the prince and his loose-moralled stepmother (Van der Kemp 1896:310–13).

Many of the new appointments involved those who had afforded the third sultan support as Crown Prince. Prominent here was the Danurejan family: one of Danurejo II's orphaned daughters would marry the future Hamengkubuwono IV (May 1816), a union which sealed the rehabilitation of the Danurejan family (Carey 1992:163–4, 199–201, 352, 396–8, 493 note 452, 504–5 note 509, 526 note 627; Carey 2008:762).

In July 1812, Diponegoro – then named Raden Ontowiryo – received his princely title of Bendoro Pangeran Ario Diponegoro (Carey 1992:116, 284, 442 note 211) and a 500-*cacah* apanage (Carey 2008:796). Most of his lands were situated to the south of Yogya, particularly in Bantul where the prince created a personal retreat at the cave of Secang at Selarong in the adjacent limestone hills (Van der Kemp 1896:405; Louw and De Klerck 1894–1909, I:432, V:745; Carey 1981: 6–9, 238 note 20; Chapter III).

Given the fame – or notoriety – of the name 'Diponegoro', it is worth recalling that it was not such an unusual moniker for a Javanese prince at this time: one of Sunan Pakubuwono I's (reigned 1703–19) sons, who had rebelled during the Second Javanese War of Succession (1719–23; Ricklefs 1993:87), bore this title, as did the second husband of Sultan Mangkubumi's daughter, Ratu Bendoro (?1750–86), who died in July 1787 (Padmasusastra 1902:158 no. 40; Carey 2008:370).

Only one prince at a time could bear a particular name, but since the title had long been vacant, the third sultan deemed it appropriate for his eldest son. On his exile journey, when his princely title had passed to his own son, Diponegoro II (circa 1803–circa 1870) (Carey 2008:97), Diponegoro gave an interesting etymological analysis of his name:

> 'Dipo' [from the Sanskrit '*dīpa*'] means someone who spreads enlightenment or who possesses life and force […] 'negoro' means a country […] 'Diponegoro' is thus a man who gives enlightenment, power and prosperity to a country' (Knoerle, 'Journal', 10).

The prince may have been remembering here his great-grandfather, Mangkubumi's, prophecy which had foretold that one of his descendants would rise against the Dutch, causing them even greater destruction than he had done, but only the Almighty knew the outcome (Chapter I; Carey 2008:71).

Diponegoro's Emerging Public Role: Fact and Fiction

Shortly after Raffles' departure on 23 June, Diponegoro had begged his father to be allowed to return to Tegalrejo. But his request was refused. Instead, he was lodged in the *kraton*. In mid July, he again approached the sultan stressing his deep unease (*sanget rikuh*) (Babad Dipanegara II:88).

Into a New Era: Diponegoro and the Post-June 1812 British Interregnum 149

But his father, fearing Tegalrejo was too distant, assigned him a small pavilion at Mijen on the western outskirts of Yogya (Carey 2008:373). Just how long he remained there is unclear: by late 1813, he was already back in Tegalrejo for he describes in his *babad* how Tan Jin Sing came to him with a shortlist for the new *patih* appointment (Babad Dipanegara II:90–1).

The prince's claim that he acted as his father's closest adviser during this period is fulsomely confirmed in the Chronicle of the Fall of Yogyakarta written by his great-uncle, Pangeran Panular (Carey 1992:290):

> XXIV 21. [...]
> Of the sultan's sons,
> the one who was made foremost
> was Pangeran Diponegoro,
> for he was the eldest,
> [and] his heart was at one with his father.
>
> 22. He was shrewd, generous [and] of a lively and spirited manner,
> not afraid in front of the multitudes.
> He spoke easily [and] sweetly with a friendly countenance,
> [and] took pains with all the people of the kingdom,
> for he was invested by his father.
> Great [and] small, young [and] old,
> all were under his authority.
>
> 23. He took charge of affairs with the Residency:
> on each Monday [and] Thursday the Pangeran
> visited the Residency accompanied by
> Pangeran Dipowiyono,
> the younger brother of the sultan.
> [...]

The prince's *babad* largely confirms this (Babad Dipanegara II:88), but suggests that he did not go to the Residency in person. This was the job of the acting *patih*, Mas Tumenggung Sindunegoro (Kyai Adipati Danurejo III, in office 1811–13), who reported back to the prince in the *kraton* following his twice-weekly negotiations with Crawfurd (Carey 2008:374).

Amongst the matters discussed was the British demand for the abolition of torture, in particular mutilation – the amputation of arms under Islamic law – and the pitting of criminals against tigers (Carey 1980:99;

note 101). The third sultan personally approved this clause, remarking that torture was 'certain injustice to the innocent and a double punishment even to the guilty' (Carey 2008:374). Diponegoro would later add that 'he and his father had always tried to bestow justice on the Javanese […] starting with the principle that no one should be punished who was not clearly convicted of committing a crime' (p. 41; Knoerle, 'Journal', 30).

Just how trustworthy is Diponegoro's account? We have seen (p. 126) that nowhere in Crawfurd's extant letters is there any mention of the prince. Since many of these letters were later taken by a post-war Dutch Resident, Valck, his statement that Diponegoro was used as a go-between before the British attack has been accepted. But for the subsequent treaty negotiations there is a problem: if the Java War leader did indeed enjoy such a cordial relationship with Crawfurd (Chapter II), why did the Scotsman make no mention of him to his successor, Nahuys, when he drew up a list of the key court personalities in August 1816 (Carey 2008:375)?

Since Diponegoro had returned to Tegalrejo by this time and rarely visited the court, it is just possible Crawfurd overlooked him. But on one particular detail, it can be proven beyond a shadow of doubt that the prince's pretended influence had no basis in reality. This was the matter of the appointment of the Scotsman's Dutch successor. According to Diponegoro, on learning that Java would be returned to the Dutch, he expressed his concern over the character of Crawfurd's replacement. The scholar-Resident was then supposed to have asked the prince what sort of Resident he would prefer: one who had already served in Java under the Dutch East India Company, or one more recently arrived from Europe? Diponegoro opted for the latter, whereupon Crawfurd supposedly observed that he had a good acquaintance in Batavia by the name of 'Major Nahuys', whom he would try to get as his replacement. Soon afterwards Nahuys did indeed arrive confirming Diponegoro's view of the power of the British (Carey 2008:375).

But the Dutch sources contradict this. They state that Jan Tiedeman (?1782–1840), an experienced administrator and wealthy Tanah Abang (Batavia) landowner, was initially appointed. But at the last moment he asked to be excused for family reasons: he had just remarried following the death of his first wife (Van der Kemp 1911:223; Carey 2012:437; *Indische Navorscher* 1995:140). The incoming Dutch administration had then sought a replacement, Nahuys being appointed on 22 July 1816, a choice partly dictated by his services to Pakualam and his son, Notodiningrat, in Cirebon in early May 1811 (p. 118; Louw and De Klerck 1894-1909, I:36 note 1; Van der Kemp 1913:321).

Diponegoro's unsubstantiated claim indicates that he greatly exaggerated his friendship with Crawfurd. Why? Was he influenced by his later difficulties with the post-1816 Dutch regime and his view of the British interregnum as a 'golden age'? Or was he just being inventive when he dictated his *babad* in exile in 1831-32? It is impossible to tell.

But, while not as close to Crawfurd as he later pretended, Diponegoro clearly appreciated the Scotsman's style and abilities. The 'sombre and intense' prince (Van Hogendorp 1913:146) was cut from the same cloth as the dour son-of-the-manse Scotsman (Abdullah 1970:223-4), whose character resonated well the stiff charm of the Yogyanese. Crawfurd's presence in Yogya for most of the interregnum would do much to heal the twin traumas of Daendels' December 1810 *diktat* and the subsequent British attack.

The 1 August 1812 Treaties and their Implications

The 1 August 1812 treaties legalised the political revolution wrought by the British attack. In Raffles' view, they placed the courts 'on such a footing as might no longer endanger the tranquillity of the country' (Carey 2008:377).

Article two, which required the rulers to disband their military forces, was critical. Aimed particularly at Yogya, where the second sultan had maintained a considerable (8-9,000) army (Carey 2008:5-7, 379), these troops were now dismissed. Raffles tried to send them to eastern Kalimantan (Borneo) to work on the estates of his megalomaniac friend, Alexander Hare (1775-1834) (Hannigan 2012:292-300), but most remained in the sultan's capital. Many would later rally to Diponegoro (Carey 1981:243-4 note 36, 252-3 note 72).

The third article annexed territory in the core regions and eastern *mancanagara*. The most significant region here was Kedu. 'Without doubt the finest province in Java' in Raffles' words (1817, II:266–7), it was known as the 'corn granary' of Java (Carey 2008:380). Grievances over its loss and hopes for its return would emerge as one of the key reasons for the Surakarta court's support for the sepoy conspiracy of October–November 1815, as we will see shortly (Van der Kemp 1913:324–5; Carey 1977:322 note 120).

The other provinces further to the east had extensive teak forests and access to navigable rivers, especially the Bengawan. But their distance from the courts had led to economic and administrative decay (Carey 2008:380). The population of Jipang was especially disaffected, later providing support for the rebellion of Diponegoro's brother-in-law, Raden Tumenggung Ario Sosrodilogo, in the third year of the Java War (Louw and De Klerck 1894–1909, III:360, 490; Chapter X).

Since the British only retained officials from the rank of sub-district head (*demang, mantri desa*) downwards, many *bupati* lost their positions, most returning to Yogya to eke out an impoverished existence (Carey 1992:122, 296, 454–5 note 264). The grievances of these prematurely dismissed officials, the so-called *bupati dongkol*, would cause many to join Diponegoro in 1825 (Carey 1981:240 note 28, 244–5 note 39).

The introduction of Raffles' land tax scheme in these newly annexed territories resulted in great hardship. Not only were British fiscal demands too onerous, but the cultivators had to pay in cash – preferably silver – rather than kind. This forced many into the hands of Chinese moneylenders who charged extortionate interest. The resultant ethnic tensions caused widespread discontent (Carey 1981:260 note 106).

The cession of tollgates and markets, for which the British paid an annual 100,000 Spanish dollar 'rent', was provided in the fourth article. Raffles hoped that the imposition of duties on domestically produced cloth might encourage British cotton imports (Carey 2008:384). But his plan failed when early imports of Javanese *batik* patterns were not dye-fast (Carey 2008:25, 384). Longer-term, both the British and the post-1816 returned Dutch government would raise tollgate revenues out of all proportion to economic realities, paralyzing local commerce and making the Chinese tollgate keepers (*bandar*) a target of bloody reprisals (Carey 2008:384–5; pp. 180–2).

One further clause in the treaties bore even harder on the local population. This was article eight which stipulated that all foreigners and Javanese born outside the Principalities should be tried according to government law. Designed to protect the Chinese, it caused numerous problems. After February 1814, when the Resident's courts were established, all litigation involving Chinese, foreigners and subjects born outside the territories of the south-central Javanese *kraton*, was tried under government law. Henceforth Javanese engaging in litigation with non-Javanese or those Javanese born in government territories had their cases tried in these courts.

While the Javanese rulers resented the restrictions on their judicial authority and Javanese farmers struggled with an alien judicial system, the religious communities deplored the fact that the religious court or *surambi* no longer had sole judgement in criminal cases (Carey 1987:298–9 note 67). Diponegoro, who prided himself on his knowledge of Javanese-Islamic law, later complained bitterly that:

> The [European] authority in Java was a great misfortune for the Javanese people for they had been taken away from the Holy Law of The Prophet and been subjected to European laws (Knoerle, 'Journal', 30).

He would later refer to this again during the first stage of his journey into exile, when he told his Dutch officer escort that 'people know that I long to have authority over criminal law.' 'By which he meant', the officer explained, 'that he wanted to have the right to appoint one "priest" [*pengulu*] in Djocjo [Yogya] and [one in] Solo, who could enforce the criminal law according to the Koran [*Qur'ān*] and not according to our [European] laws' (Louw and De Klerck 1894–1909, V:744; Carey 1987:300 note 72).'

Raffles' 1812 treaties, his subsequent legal reforms and the question of the sovereignty of Javanese-Islamic law in criminal cases would all prove crucial during the Java War. Diponegoro's wartime demands to be recognised as the 'regulator of religion' (*ratu paneteg panatagama*) with special competence over issues of criminal justice had widespread resonance (Carey 2008:388; p. 218, p. 298).

In Yogya, the combination of the fall of the *kraton*, the wholesale plunder of its treasury and the imposition of Raffles' treaty dealt the sultanate's a shattering blow. Early in the Java War, Diponegoro would attempt the final destruction of the Yogya *kraton* and establish a new undefiled *kraton* at another site (Carey 1981:241 note 29, 282 note 197), the Dutch lawyer, Willem van Hogendorp (1795–1838), noting:

> All Java knows this: how the Dutch allowed the *kraton* [of Yogya] to be turned into a brothel and how Diponegoro has sworn to destroy it to the last stone and expel the [European] landowners who have driven out the Javanese officials (Carey 2008:389).

The yearning for moral regeneration under the banner of Islam and the restoration of the sultanate's prestige would become significant themes in the years preceding the Java War and would explain why so many members of the Yogya court rallied to the prince in 1825.

Positive Developments during the Third Sultan's Reign

Despite the great difficulties with which the third sultan began his reign, his brief twenty-nine month rule was one of peace and modest prosperity. By the time of his death in November 1814, some 60,000 Spanish dollars had been accumulated in the *kraton* treasury and the pensions of the sultan's family were being paid regularly. The annual 100,000 Spanish dollar market and tollgate rents from the British Government were crucial here.

Plans were also made to curb the activities of the rural tax-collectors and police officials (*gunung*) (Rouffaer 1905:644–5), whom Diponegoro wanted abolished (Babad Dipanagara II:107–8). In the prince's view, they were a burden on the village administration (*parentah desa*) which should be returned to what it had been under the first sultan. His father supposedly agreed to this provided a year elapsed before the changes were implemented but he died before the year was out (Babad Dipanagara II:108).

Again, one has to wonder whether the prince was claiming rather too much influence over his father. Were these initiatives really his idea? Just three years earlier in February 1811, when his father was Prince Regent, he had already issued an order instructing that all labour services on royal apanage lands should return to what they had been under Sultan Mangkubumi (Carey 1980:21). So it is unclear what Diponegoro himself contributed.

Two other measures taken by the British government promised long-term improvements. The first was the government's decision to extend smallpox vaccination – first introduced to Java from Mauritius in 1804 – and the second was the banning of the slave trade under the terms of the 1807 abolitionist legislation (Bosma and Raben 2008:95). Neither measure had much immediate impact: the level of smallpox vaccination remained low until after the Java War (Carey 2008:43–4), and few privately-owned slaves achieved emancipation in their lifetimes (Carey 2008:393).

Nature rather than human agency was perhaps more important in improving local living conditions. The massive eruption of the Gunung Tambora stratovolcano in Sumbawa between April and July 1815, the most powerful in recorded history (four times greater than Krakatau in 1883), apparently had remarkable short-term beneficial effects on the 1815 rice harvest (Carey 2008:393–4).

Political and Administrative Changes

In the latter part of the third sultan's reign two further administrative appointments occurred which would have long-term effects.

The first was the appointment of a new *patih* to replace the near-senile Mas Tumenggung Sindunegoro (Kyai Adipati Danurejo III). Two names were considered by Diponegoro and his father: namely, a senior court official and Mas Tumenggung Sumodipuro, the erstwhile *bupati* of Japan (Mojokerto) (Carey 1992:454–5 note 264, 2008:396).

The prince chose the latter much to the astonishment of his father who stated that the *bupati* was still young and a commoner (Babad Dipanegara II:90–1), his east Javanese accent marking him out as a clodhopping provincial (Carey 1992:173, 368, 500 note 492). But Diponegoro stuck by his decision and Sumodipuro was appointed as Danurejo IV on 2 December

1813. He would remain in office for the next thirty-four years (1813–47) (Pigeaud 1931–32, II:130).

Despite his notorious subsequent reputation (Louw and De Klerck 1894–1909, III:493–4; Carey 1992:499 note 486), the new *patih* started well, the 'Chronicle of the Fall of Yogyakarta' referring to the excellent impression he made at the time of his official inauguration (Carey 1992:172–3, 368). The Dutch Java War commander, De Kock (1779–1845), would later describe him as 'a fine Javanese, who dresses well, rides magnificent horses, has beautiful women and is attached to the opium pipe'.

Longer term, these self-indulgent qualities had a corrosive effect. By the time of the fourth sultan's reign (1814–22), Yogya contemporaries were describing him as a man with 'an unclean heart'. His fondness for pleasure and personal ambition proved disastrous: cases decided in his court were always open to bribery and sexual favours (Louw and De Klerck 1894–1909, I:85–7). By the time of the Java War, corruption was rife. One contemporary Javanese text referred to him as a 'devil in human clothes' (*sétan kulambi manungsa*) who 'robbed people while sitting down' (*angècu sarwi lenggah*) (Carey 2008:398).

The second significant appointment was that of the *Kapitan Cina*, Tan Jin Sing, as a Yogya *bupati* with the title of Raden Tumenggung Secodiningrat and an apanage of 800 *cacah*, mainly in eastern Bagelen (Rouffaer 1905:594; Carey 1992:483–5 note 399). His 6 December 1813 appointment letter stated specifically that he had been given the title as a reward for his services to the British (Carey 1992:484 note 399).

But this was an appointment made under duress. For a Chinese to be given such a high position at the Yogya court was unheard of. True, there had been cases of Chinese tax-farmers administering north coast administrative districts on behalf of the Mataram rulers in the seventeenth and early eighteenth centuries (Remmelink 1994:25), but this had not been repeated in the post-Giyanti period. The first sultan in particular had forbidden Chinese from having too close a relationship with the royal family, stating that this would lead to discord (Carey 1992:462 note 304).

The former *Kapitan Cina*'s strange position suspended uneasily between three worlds was later summed up in the clever Yogya ditty 'no longer a Chinese, not yet a Dutchman, a half-baked Javanese' (*Cina wurung,*

Londo durung, Jawa tanggung), a condition akin to that of foreign-educated Javanese like the ill-fated sons of Suro-Adimenggolo (Meinsma 1876:132; Carey 1984:30–1). Diponegoro described him as having been favoured by the British 'only with the intention of keeping a better eye on the activities of the Yogya court [and] this had done much harm to the trust which [the court] placed in the Government' (Carey 2008:400).

Despite his anomalous position, Tan Jin Sing remained on good terms with Diponegoro, whose personal bodyguard he maintained in the years preceding the Java War (Carey 1981:253 note 73). He also adopted a neutral attitude to the court intrigues which so plagued the sultanate in the pre-war decade (1815–25). But his appointment was viewed by many in Yogya as yet another facet of the decline of the sultanate's post-June 1812 independence.

Diponegoro's Second Marriage and Death of the Third Sultan

Sometime before the third sultan's death in November 1814, probably on 28 September, Diponegoro married again (Carey 2008:401). This time his bride was the orphaned daughter of his hero, Raden Ronggo Prawirodirjo III, and his beloved consort, Ratu Maduretno (?1780–1809) (pp. 96–7). The description of his marriage marks a charming interlude in his *babad* and affords an insight into the very deep affection which Diponegoro felt for his second official wife.

According to the prince, his father had constantly pressed him to marry again, his first official wife having long separated from him (Chapter II). But he had always refused. Eventually, he was summoned to the *kraton* and instructed to ask for the hand of Ratu Bendoro, the childless widow of the slain Yogya army commander, Sumodiningrat. The prince made his way to the *keputren* (female quarters), a dutiful son making the next step in what seemed like a politically expedient but loveless second marriage. Then Cupid shot his arrow: as Diponegoro was passing the entrance to the religious retreat area (*panepen*) he described how he caught sight of Ratu Maduretno's daughter framed in a doorway and immediately evinced an overpowering physical attraction for her (Babad Dipanegara II:89).

This chance encounter and the prince's reaction to it, was at once reported to the sultan by his two elderly *nyai keparak* (female retainers) escorts. Once Ratu Bendoro had confirmed that she was not minded to remarry, a betrothal was speedily arranged with the *Raden Ayu*, who bore her mother's name of Maduretno. The marriage ceremony took place in the *kraton*, a feast and all-night *wayang* performance following at Tegalrejo.

We do not know the particular *wayang* plot (*lakon*), but in his *babad* Diponegoro compared his marriage with that of Wisnu and Dewi Sri, with his father as Batara Guru. We know that the figure of Arjuna, one of Wisnu's reincarnations, had a special resonance for the prince, and he drew a close parallel between himself and the handsome *wayang* hero when he received the dagger Sarutomo during his meditation at Parangkusumo on his south coast pilgrimage (p. 59, p. 61).

This comparison would be further elaborated when he was wandering almost alone in the jungles of Bagelen, Banyumas and southern Kedu in late 1829 only accompanied by his two *panakawan* (intimate retainers), Roto and Bantengwareng (?1810–58). The latter, 'a mischievous young rogue and a dwarf' according to Diponegoro, recalled the deformed servitors of Arjuna and his four Pandawa brothers who also followed their masters off into the jungles after the eldest, Yudistira, had lost their kingdom at a game of dice (Babad Dipanegara IV:106–7; Carey 2008:405).

At the practical level, Diponegoro's marriage gave him a sympathetic partner in whom to confide in the difficult years ahead, one who would endure the hardships of war and support him until her death in late November 1827 (Errembault 1825–30, 4-12-1827). Of all the prince's wives, she was the only one whom he mentioned with genuine affection in his *babad* (Carey 2012:600–1). His marriage sealed his links with the Prawirodirjan which originated in his guardian, Ratu Ageng's, sibling relationship with the third Raden Ronggo's grandfather (Carey 2008:764–5; p. 81).

In October 1814, the sultan contracted a cold which, according to Diponegoro, lasted a month (Carey 2008:406). The sultan had never enjoyed good health and the intrigues of his father's reign (1792–1810/1811–12) had taken their toll (Carey 2008:407). As November dawned, it was clear that the sultan's final sickness had begun. The 'Chronicle of the Fall of Yogyakarta' describes the deathbed scene where *dukun* (traditional medical practitioners) administered potions and *ulama* intoned *dhikr* (short repetitive phrases from the *Qur'ān*) (Carey 1992:186–7, 383).

Interestingly, the Chronicle describes how Diponegoro took exception to one of the ceremonies performed over the sultan's dying body. This involved licking the sultan's navel to facilitate the exit of the life force. Diponegoro had stepped forward at this point to replace the coverlet firmly over his father's body (Carey 1992:187–8, 383). A telling vignette this which indicates that, although a typical Javanese-Islamic mystic, the prince did not hold with some of the more arcane aspects of contemporary Javanese magico-religious lore.

At daybreak on the morning of 3 November after a reign of just 865 days, the third sultan died. Diponegoro probably spoke for many when he observed that no one in Yogya had expected the sultan to die so young (Babad Dipanegara II:105).

Accession, Regency and Marriage of the Boy Sultan, Hamengkubuwono IV

The third sultan's passing meant that Yogya was now to be ruled by a minor with all the dangers this posed. Panular, the author of the chronicle, described a dream which seemed to foretell the coming eclipse of the kingdom due to ambition amongst the sultan's leading advisers causing the state to be 'dismembered and torn to shreds' (Carey 1992: 166–7, 355, 494 note 462a; Thorn 1815:184). The British Resident, Captain Garnham (1782–1827; in office, 1814–15), meanwhile, oversaw the sealing and padlocking of the royal treasure chambers (Carey 1992:187–8, 382, 384).

But such premonitions were premature. The fourth sultan's accession took place amidst general rejoicing on 9 November with a dinner in the Residency House and the inevitable firework display arranged by the *Kapitan Cina* on the northern *alun-alun*. The regency council established by Garnham after consultation with the sultan's family found widespread approval (Carey 2008:408).

Unfortunately, Garnham's choice was not accepted by Raffles. He instructed that his friend Pakualam should be appointed sole regent, an order which caused consternation in Yogya. Garnham warned his superior that 'the Pangeran is a man of ability and acquirement, but devoid of sincerity and principle' (Carey 2008:409). Raffles replied acknowledging Garnham's reservations but stressing that 'this *Pangeran* also has claims on the Government not only for the fidelity which he showed [...] at the time of the war against the ex-sultan [...] but also on account of the promises then held out to him' (Louw and De Klerck 1894, I:43 note 1).

What were these promises? Pakualam was already an independent prince answerable directly to the British. What more did he expect: the sultanate? This was certainly the gloss put on the lieutenant-governor's decision in Yogya where it seemed that the British might even be contemplating a new division of the kingdom.

Garnham's concerns were borne out when Pakualam started to misuse his position to buy up lands on his own account and fund a more lavish life style (Carey 1992:519 note 577). It soon became clear that he should be removed from control of *kraton* finances. Shortly before August 1816, the queen mother, assisted by the *patih*, took over all his duties. Only the great seal (*cap ageng*) remained in his hands until he formally relinquished the regency on 27 January 1820 at the fourth sultan's majority. The legacy of bitterness would take years to dissipate (Carey 1992:519 note 577).

Diponegoro took an active interest in his younger brother's education, coming over often from Tegalrejo to tell him edifying stories from the *Fatāh al-Muluk* ('Victory of Kings') about the legendary rulers of Ajam (Syria) and Arabia (Carey 2008:410). The Yogya *babad* further relates that the prince recommended certain texts for his brother's reading. These included the *Serat Ambiya, Taj as-Salātīn, Hikayat Makuta Raja* ('Mirror of princes'), *Serat Menak, Babad Kraton, Arjuna Sasrabahu, Rama Badra* and *Serat Bratayuda* (Chapter II), the last a particular favourite of the prince and one which he would requested for his own children's education in Makassar (Carey 1981:lxiii note 112; p. 743; pp. 320–1). On the occasion of the fourth sultan's circumcision on 22 March 1815, it was Diponegoro who held his hands over his younger brother's eyes when the ceremonial operation took place (Carey 1992:195, 391–2, 521–2 note 597).

The fourth sultan was not a diligent student. Nine months after the appointment of his Malay language tutor, Lieutenant Abbas, he still could not string enough words together to respond to Raffles when the latter paid a brief visit to Yogya in mid January 1816 (Carey 1992:198, 394, 524 note 617). The Yogya court chronicle states that he was more interested in the martial arts, and in riding and listening to the court *gamelan* than in reading Javanese literature (Carey 2008:411). Indeed, so besotted was he with European military uniforms that his senior officials had great difficulty persuading him not to wear his Dutch major-general's uniform at that most quintessential of *kraton* ceremonies, the *Garebeg* (Van Nes 1844:164; Carey 2008:459).

On 13 May 1816, he married the eldest daughter of the murdered *patih*, Danurejo II, in a lavish celebration involving three full-length shadow plays from the Panji (*wayang gedog*), Menak (*wayang jemblung*) and Damar Wulan (*wayang krucil*) cycles, as well as masked dances (*topeng*) and Chinese masquerades (*jenggi*) (Carey 1974:9 note 25). His bride, now styled Ratu Kencono, 'an interesting pretty young woman' in Crawfurd's words (Carey 1992:504 note 509), would later suffer severe psychosis. This manifested after her husband's death in her stabbing one of his former unofficial wives, who had been instructed by Ratu Ibu to sleep with him when he was barely thirteen years old (Palmer van den Broek 1873, 20:480; Carey 1992:504–5 note 509), an action which provoked a stern letter of rebuke to the Ratu from Diponegoro (Carey 1992: 463 note 309, 505 note 509; 2008:412).

The roots of the sultanate's descent into the moral abyss, pithily described by Van Hogendorp in his reference to the Dutch transformation of the *kraton* into 'a brothel', can be traced to this period. So too can Diponegoro's implacable conviction that Yogya should be destroyed, and the Javanese apostate rulers stripped of their political power for a new moral order based on Islamic precepts and traditional Javanese values to be established.

The Sepoy Plot of 1815

As British rule drew to a close, a number of local disturbances troubled the surface calm of the Principalities. The most important of these was the Sepoy Conspiracy of October–November 1815 in Surakarta.

The plot involved the Sunan, Pakubuwono IV, and members of the Bengal Light Infantry Volunteer Battalion who had done garrison duties in south-central Java since November 1811. Its aim was the massacre of all Europeans in Java and the destruction of the court of Yogya. In return for the help afforded by the light infantry garrison forces, a sepoy *subadar* (captain) was to be appointed as the new lieutenant-governor and the administration of west Java and the north coast districts were to be entrusted to British-Indian troops. There were even reports that the Sunan was prepared to give one of his daughters in marriage to this sepoy captain (Carey 2008:415).

Raffles' later suggestion that the success of the sepoy conspiracy might have led to the immediate 'reconversion' of the Javanese to Hinduism was fanciful (Raffles 1817, II:5). But the fact that many of the temples and archaeological remains of Java's Hindu-Buddhist past were in the process of being surveyed and cleaned at this time seems to have quickened interest amongst the Javanese nobility in their Indic inheritance (De Haan 1935:492; Carey 1977:301, 316 note 54, 316–17 note 55, 1992:470–1 note 336; Carey 2008:418–19). In Yogya, for example, Diponegoro and other princes even took statuary away from nearby temples to decorate their residences (Carey 2008:421).

The paucity of British officers meant that the plot was only discovered in late October 1815, but swift action by the acting Yogya garrison commander, Lieutenant James Steel (1792–1859), proved effective. A subsequent court-martial at Serondol sentenced seventeen ringleaders to death and sent a further fifty back in irons to Bengal (Van der Kemp 1911:45; Carey 1977:321–2 note 112).

This was not, however, the last of the sepoys in Java. Many British-Indian soldiers deserted in the sultan's capital, marrying into local Javanese families. Some took service in the court as mahouts (elephant drivers) or as members of the sultan's bodyguard regiments. One of these, a man by the name of Nurngali, described as a Bengali traditional healer (*dukun Benggala*) in Diponegoro's *babad*, served as the prince's personal physician (Carey 2008:428; Babad Dipanegara IV:11-12).

During the war itself, a Calcutta bank, Palmer & Company, which had arranged a six million Sicca rupee loan (present-day USD350,000,000) to the cash-strapped Netherlands Indies government in 1824 (Tarling 1963:161-88; De Prins 2002:108), even attempted to persuade the Governor-General of India, Lord Bentinck (in office, 1828-35), to send 2,000 sepoys to help turn the tide of battle in 1827-8, a request which was dropped when it became clear that the Dutch had the upper hand (Tarling 1963:188; Van Hogendorp 1913:183; Nationaal Archief 1827).

Over a century later in 1945-6, the British would again find that using Punjabi Indian troops in Java against Indonesian nationalist forces during the battle of Surabaya in October-November 1945 would have serious drawbacks (Thorne 1988:117-18).

Conclusion

The sepoy plot of 1815 was the last important event of the British interregnum. In five short years it had effected remarkable changes in the political balance of power in south-central Java. But the benefits would not be for the British to enjoy. In May 1815, the final decision had been taken to evacuate Java under the terms of the Treaty of Vienna and the Convention of London (13 August 1814) agreeing the return of most of the former Dutch colonies in British hands,[1] part of the British policy of rebuilding Dutch strength to counter the possible threat of a resurgent France in the

---

[1] Only Ceylon (Sri Lanka), Cape Colony (South Africa), and the former VOC trading posts in Malabar and Coromandel (India) were retained by the British.

aftermath of the Napoleonic Wars. The official hand-over ceremony took place in Batavia on 19 August 1816.

By early May 1816, the Dutch commissioners-general, including the new governor-general, Van der Capellen (1778–1848; in office, 1816–26), tasked with establishing a new Dutch colonial order had arrived in Batavia. With their constitutional regulation (*regeerings-reglement*) of January 1818, the commissioners-general would preside over the birth of a new colonial entity, the Netherlands Indies (1818–1942).

But it remained to be seen whether the principles of economic liberalism referred to by the departing British would sit comfortably with a returned Dutch government fixated on securing immediate profits from their restored colony. Once again, the years ahead would prove difficult and testing ones for Dutch and Javanese alike. Far from being a gateway to a new era of industry and prosperity, the troubled period of the Dutch restoration would open a high road to war in south-central Java. This time the destruction of Java prophesied at Parangkusumo would encompass more than just the ruined sultanate of Yogya.

Bibliography

Abdullah bin Abdul Kadir (1970). *The Hikayat Abdullah*. Edited and translated by A.H. Hill. Kuala Lumpur: Oxford University Press.
Babad Dipanegara (2010). *Babad Dipanegara*, 4 vols, ed. Nindya Noegraha. Jakarta: Perpustakaan Nasional Republik Indonesia.
Bosma, U. and R. Raben (2008). *Being 'Dutch' in the Indies; A History of Creolisation and Empire, 1500–1920*. Singapore: National University of Singapore Press.
Carey, Peter (1974). *The Cultural Ecology of Early Nineteenth Century Java; Pangeran Dipanagara, A Case Study*. Singapore: Institute of Southeast Asian Studies. [Occasional Paper 24.]
Carey, Peter (1977). 'The Sepoy Conspiracy of 1815 in Java', *Bijdragen tot de Taal-, Land- en Volkenkunde* 133:294–322.
Carey, Peter (1980). *The Archive of Yogyakarta. Vol. I: Documents relating to Politics and Internal Court Affairs*. Oxford: Oxford University Press.

Carey, Peter (1981). *Babad Dipanagara; An Account of the Outbreak of the Java War (1825–30); The Surakarta Court Version of the Babad Dipanagara with Translations into English and Indonesian Malay.* Kuala Lumpur: Art Printers.
Carey, Peter (1984). 'Changing Javanese Perceptions of the Chinese Communities in Central Java, 1755–1825', *Indonesia* 37:1–48.
Carey, Peter (1992). *The British in Java, 1811–1816; A Javanese Account.* Oxford: Oxford University Press.
Carey, Peter (2008). *The Power of Prophecy; Prince Dipanagara and the End of an Old Order in Java, 1785–1855.* Leiden: KITLV Press.
Carey, Peter (2012). *Kuasa Ramalan; Pangeran Diponegoro dan Akhir Tatanan Lama di Jawa, 1785–1855.* Jakarta: KPG, second revised edition.
Carey, Peter and Mason Hoadley (eds) (2000). *The Archive of Yogyakarta. Vol. II: Documents relating to Economic and Agrarian Affairs.* Oxford: Oxford University Press.
Crawfurd, J. (1820). *History of the Indian Archipelago.* Edinburgh: Constable. Two vols.
Deventer, M.L. van (1891). *Het Nederlandsch Gezag over Java en Onderhoorigheden sedert 1811; Verzameling van Onuitgegeven Stukken uit de Koloniale en Andere Archieven. Vol.I: 1811–1820.* The Hague: Nijhoff.
Errembault (1825–30). Errembault de Dudzeele et d'Orroir, 'Journal' [Java War Campaign Diary, 22 October 1825–25 May 1830], EFEO 58653, manuscript of the École Française d'Extrême Orient, Paris.
Haan, F. de (1935). 'Personalia der Periode van het Engelsch Bestuur over Java, 1811–1816', *Bijdragen tot de Taal-, Land- en Volkenkunde* 92:477–681.
Hageman, J.Jcz. (1856). *Geschiedenis van den Oorlog op Java van 1825 tot 1830.* Batavia: Lange.
Hageman, J.Jcz. (1857). 'De Engelschen op Java', *Tijdschrift voor Indische Taal-, Land- en Volkenkunde* 6:290–457.
Hannigan, Tim (2012). *Raffles and the British Invasion of Java.* Singapore: Monsoon.
Hogendorp, H. Graaf van (1913). *Willem van Hogendorp in Nederlandsch-Indië 1825–1830.* The Hague: Nijhoff.
Houben, Vincent (1994). *Kraton and Kumpeni; Surakarta and Yogyakarta 1830–1870.* Leiden: KITLV Press. [Verhandelingen 164.]
Indische Navorscher (1995). 'J.W. Moorrees (1774–1815) / J.M. Martheze (1787/88–1843)', *De Indische Navorscher*, 8:140.
Java Government Gazette (Batavia: Government Printers), 4–7–1812.
Kemp, P.H. van der (1896). 'Dipanagara, Eene Geschiedkundige Hamlettype', *Bijdragen tot de Taal-, Land- en Volkenkunde* 46:281–433.
Kemp, P.H. van der (1911). *Oost-Indië's Herstel in 1816.* The Hague: Nijhoff.
Kemp, P.H. van der (1913). *Het Nederlandsch-Indisch Bestuur in 1817, tot het Vertrek der Engelschen.* The Hague: Nijhoff.

Knoerle 'Journal' (1830). 'Aanteekeningen Gehouden door den 2e Luit Knoerle betreffende de Dagelyksche Verkeering van dien Officier met den Prins van Djocjakarta, Diepo Negoro, gedurende eene Reis van Batavia naar Menado, het Exil van den genoemden Prins', Manado, 20-6-1830. MS 391 of the Johannes van den Bosch private collection in the Nationaal Archief, The Hague.

Kraus, W. (2005). 'Raden Saleh's Interpretation of the Arrest of Diponegoro; An Example of Indonesian "Proto-Nationalist" Modernism', *Archipel* 69:259-94.

Kraus, W. and Irina Vogelsang (2012). *Raden Saleh; The Beginning of Modern Indonesian Painting*. Jakarta: Goethe Institut.

Louw, P.J.F. and E.S. de Klerck (1894-1909). *De Java-Oorlog van 1825-1830*. The Hague: Nijhoff, Batavia: Landsdrukkerij. Six vols.

Mandoyokusumo, K.R.T. (1977). *Serat Raja Putra Ngayogyakarta Hadiningrat*. Yogyakarta: Bebadan Museum Karaton Ngayogyakarta Hadiningrat.

Meinsma, J. (1876). 'Een Anachronisme', *Tijdschrift voor Indische Taal-, Land- en Volkenkunde (TBG)* 23:126-33.

Nationaal Archief 1827. Nationaal Archief (Den Haag), Ministerie van Koloniën 2923, *Verbaal*, 6-03-1827, Litt JI [correspondence between General H.M. de Kock and Commissioner-General Du Bus de Gisignies regarding request for sepoys].

Nes, J.F.Walraven van (1844). 'Verhandelingen over de Waarschijnlijke Oorzaken, die Aanleiding tot de Onlusten van 1825 en de volgende jaren in de Vorstenlanden gegeven hebben', *Tijdschrift voor Nederlandsche Indië* 6:112-71.

Padmasusastra, K. (1902). *Sejarah-dalem Pangiwa lan Panengen*. Semarang/Surabaja: Kolff.

Palmer van den Broek, W. (1873-77) (ed. and trans.). 'Geschiedenis van het Vorstenhuis Madoera uit het Javaansch Vertaald', *Tijdschrift voor Indische Taal-, Land- en Volkenkunde* (TBG) 20:241-301, 471-563, 22:1-89, 280-310, 24:1-169.

Payen, A.A.J. (1988). *Voyage à Djocja-Karta en 1825; The Outbreak of the Java War (1825-30) as Seen by a Painter*. Edited by Peter Carey. Paris: Association Archipel.

Pigeaud, Th.G.Th. (1931-32). 'Kandjeng Pangeran Arja Adipati Danoeredja VII, Papatih Dalem ing Karaton Ngajogjakarta, Toemboek 1798/1869-1862/1931', *Djåwå* 11-4:126-32, 12-1:34-40.

Prins, Bart de (2002). *Voor Keizer en Koning; Leonard du Bus de Gisignies 1780-1849 Commissaris-Generaal van Nederlands-Indië*. Amersfoort: Balans.

Raffles, T.S. (1817). *History of Java*. London: Black, Parbury and Allen. Two vols.

Remmelink, W. (1994). *The Chinese War and the Collapse of the Javanese State, 1725-1743*. Leiden: KITLV Press.

Ricklefs, M.C. (1974). *Jogjakarta under Sultan Mangkubumi, 1749-1792; A History of the Division of Java*. Oxford: Oxford University Press.

Ricklefs, M.C. (1993). *War, Culture and Economy in Java, 1677–1726; Asian and European Imperialism in the Early Kartasura Period*. Sydney: Allen and Unwin.

Rouffaer, G.P. (1905). 'Vorstenlanden', *Encylopaedie van Nederlandsch-Indië* 4:587–653.

Tarling, Nicholas (1963). 'The Palmer Loans', *Bijdragen tot de Taal-, Land- en Volkenkunde* 119.2: 161–188.

Thorn, W. (1815). *Memoir of the Conquest of Java with the Subsequent Operations of the British Forces in the Oriental Archipelago*. London: Egerton.

Thorne, C. (1988). 'The British are Coming', in Colin Wild and Peter Carey (eds), *Born in Fire; The Indonesian Struggle for Independence; An Anthology*. Athens, Ohio: Ohio University Press.

Tiffin, Sarah (2008). 'Raffles and the Barometer of Civilisation: Images and Descriptions of Ruined Candis in *The History of Java*', *Journal of the Royal Asiatic Society*, 18:341–60.

CHAPTER VIII

Binding on the Iron Yoke: Diponegoro, the Returned Dutch Administration and the Impoverishment of the South-Central Javanese Peasantry, 1816–1822

Squaring the Circle

The 19 August 1816 British handover of Java to the returned Dutch administration led to a doomed attempt to square the circle between economic liberalism and local interests. The new governor-general, Van der Capellen (in office 1816–26), took to heart the task of protecting the local population from foreign exploitation, noting that Dutch colonialism 'could no longer go forward solely with an eye to making profit, but should secure the welfare of the people' (Nieuwenhuys 1973:82). The problem was that he was nearly a century before his time.

In the years leading up to the outbreak of the Java War the balance between businessmen-speculators and early ethici[1] like Van der Capellen, was firmly weighted in favour of the former. And the lead came from the very top as Raffles himself noted after meeting the new Dutch monarch, Willem I (reigned 1813–40), in July 1817:

---

1   The 'ethici' was the name given to those colonial officials and others who took to heart the Ethical Policy (*Ethische Politiek*) launched by the newly crowned Queen Wilhelmina (reigned 1890–1948) in her 1901 speech to the Dutch parliament stating that the Netherlands accepted an ethical responsibility for the welfare of their colonial subjects. This contrasted with the former official doctrine which stated that Indonesia was a *wingewest* (region for making profit).

The king himself and his leading minister [Falck] mean well, [but] they have too great a hankering after profit, and immediate profit, for any liberal policy to thrive under them (Raffles 1830:235).

Diponegoro's apocryphal conversation with Crawfurd about the type of Dutch Resident who should come as the Scotsman's replacement (Chapter VII) pointed to an all too present reality: the unstoppable tide of former Napoleonic War soldiers and fortune seekers who now descended on Java to 'restore [...] their dilapidated affairs in the mother country [...] so they could return home with their nests nicely feathered' (Van den Doel 1994:49, quoting Olivier 1827–30, III:425).

Baroe datang ('one who has just arrived') would soon be on the lips of all Batavia's elite *mestiço* (mixed race Portuguese-Indies-Dutch) families as they contemplated the unwelcome tide of newcomers whose arrival heralded the transformation of Indies society into a tropical *beambtenstaat* (bureaucratic state; Taylor 1983:116; Bosma and Raben 2008:185–6).

A Resident who Enjoyed Eating and Drinking and the Spreading of Dutch Ways

Although the new Yogya Resident, Nahuys van Burgst (in office 1816–22), was no stranger to Java (De Haan 1935:620; Plate 15), he belonged in his political affiliations to the post-1816 generation. Like his monarch, Nahuys had very definite views about Indies economic policy, lobbying for an increase in the number of foreign estate leasers in the Principalities. In this respect, he was a 'liberal' and stood in opposition to 'conservatives' such as Van der Capellen and his economic adviser, H.J. van de Graaff (1782–1827) (Van Hogendorp 1913:29).

Nahuys' strong views, in which his personal interests were involved (Houben 1994:104–6), were to be of great significance for his Residency. His bluff and self-confident personality also set him apart from his scholarly predecessor. He shared none of Crawfurd's intellectual interests and had little time for Javanese culture. But he made up for this by boldness and administrative zeal. His *bon vivant* lifestyle was well known (Louw and De Klerck 1894–1909, III:572), Van Hogendorp penning a vivid description of one of his Surakarta dinner parties (Van Hogendorp 1913:165–6):

> I had this opportunity to observe Nahuys in his full glory and I could perceive what a great talent he has for getting on with the natives [Javanese]. For three hours at a stretch he kept the assembled company roaring with laughter and each toast he proposed was taken up and drunk amidst enthusiastic cheers.

The contrast with his abstemious predecessor could not have been more marked: Crawfurd's Spartan Residency dinners in his Singapore years (1823–6) were the talk of the town (Singapore 1883:4–5).

When it came to ebullience and abstemiousness, the choice for Diponegoro was easily made. Comparing Nahuys unfavourably with Crawfurd, he dismissed the former in his *babad* as a man 'who [merely] enjoyed eating and drinking and the spreading of Dutch ways'. He also noticed with displeasure how many younger members of the sultan's family – heedless of the prohibitions of Islam – followed Nahuys' example by adopting his gambling and hard drinking ways (Carey 2008:437–8).

Although a taste for the bottle was nothing new in the Principalities – even Diponegoro indulged occasionally (p. 40, p. 204) – the behaviour of the post-1816 Dutch representatives was quite remarkably dissolute: both the Surakarta Resident, Rijck van Prehn (1779–1843; in office, 1818–19) and his official translator, Johannes Wilhelmus Winter (1777/8–1839; in office, 1806–20), would later be dismissed from their posts in March 1820 for accepting bribes for ensuring *kraton* appointments by illegally sitting on cases in the Sunan's court (Winter 1902:18–20; Houben 1994:104; Briët 2012:35–40).

Even when not engaging in wholesale corruption, the social behaviour of Dutch officials left much to be desired. Nahuys may have kept his Surakarta dinner guests laughing, but was this really what well-born Javanese expected of their social encounters with Dutch officials? Van Hogendorp was not so sure (Van Hogendorp 1913: 179–80):

> They have seen us drinking every day, laughing all shyness aside and asking our conversation – every word of which is utter nonsense – to be interpreted to them. [...] We have played around the *pangeran* [princes] like [so many] spoilt children.

The sexual mores of senior Dutch officials also offended. Diponegoro remarked on the curious *ménage à trois* in the post-1816 Yogya Residency in which the new Resident and his Eurasian deputy, R.C.N. d'Abo (1786–1824; in office, 1817–23), shared the same woman in common, namely D'Abo's wife, Anna Louisa, whom Nahuys would briefly later marry (Van Hogendorp 1913:149; Carey 2008:120).

Dalliances with the wives of junior officials were one thing, seducing and appropriating the womenfolk of well-born Javanese quite another. Yet this was the norm amongst Dutch officials in central Java in the pre-Java War years. In Van Hogendorp's words (1913:40): 'The hatred and contempt [which the Javanese felt for Europeans in these years] were certainly quickened by what both senior and junior officials permitted themselves with regard to [high-born] native women'.

Diponegoro's relative, the chief *pengulu* (senior religious official) of Rembang, would later single out such sexual depravity as amongst the four key issues which the Dutch needed to address before the Java War could be brought to an end (Louw and De Klerck 1894–1909, III:494). In Van Hogendorp's words:

> All Java knows this, that what happened in the Yogya [*kraton*] can never see the light of day and has rightly provoked Diponegoro's just rage' (Van Hogendorp 1913:40).

Recent work on gender, sexuality and race by feminist authors like Ann Stoler have suggested that sexual control was fundamental to the way in which colonial policies operated (Stoler 2002:78). Indeed, the Javanese elite may have perceived the sexual exploitation of their womenfolk by powerful Europeans as just another aspect of their new colonial status. But the changes which had occurred since the mid-eighteenth century were striking: one thinks here of Diponegoro's great-uncle, Panular (Carey 1992:5–6), who related in his diary-chronicle how his mother, a woman of Balambangan origin, had come to Sultan Mangkubumi's court as a present from the Javanese-speaking governor of Java's Northeast Coast, Nicolaas Hartingh (1718–66; in office, 1754–1761) (Remmelink 1994:273), in reciprocation for the first sultan's personal gift of his own favourite unofficial wife who had been given in recognition of the governor's skill in brokering the Giyanti treaty (13 February 1755) (Carey 2008:440).

Whatever one may think of the use of women as pawns in an elaborate system of exchange between powerful eighteenth-century men, a degree of respect appears to have existed between Mangkubumi and the Semarang governor. In the years preceding the Java War there were no such feelings. The relationship between Europeans and Javanese was now one of exploitation: the raiding of *kraton* treasuries and archives now had its counterpart in the raiding of the bodies of the *Raden Ayu* (court princesses) (Carey 2008:440).

The Early Challenges of Nahuys' Residency and Diponegoro's Political Alienation

Nahuys' assumption of his new post as Resident of Yogya in August 1816 was complicated by two issues: the first was the return of the exiled second sultan to Batavia from exile in Pinang. The second was an attempt by the Yogya court to dispatch a senior court official to greet the new Dutch governor-general in Batavia (Carey 2008:441).

This latter issue, which involved the sending of an emissary to convey the sultan's compliments to the incoming governor-general, went to the heart of Javanese-Dutch relations. By 1816, the Dutch assumed that the changed power relationship between Batavia and the south-central Javanese courts had made such missions redundant. They thus tried to prevent the court official from even sailing from Semarang (Carey 2008:441).

The affair showed how difficult it was for the south-central Javanese rulers to accommodate themselves to their changed political status. The long-standing Javanese concept of the political division of Java between the foreign kingdom of west Java and the Javanese heartland (*kejawen*) died hard, which was why so many members of the Yogya court rallied to Diponegoro in 1825 when his aspirations for a return to an idealized pre-Daendelian political order became apparent (Carey 1974b:285–8; 2013:13–18).

Two other events hardened the prince's attitude towards the returned Dutch administration. The first was the sudden arrest and banishment of Kyai Murmo Wijoyo, a rich and respected religious teacher from the

Pajang area. The second was a dispute over the appointment of country tax-collectors-cum-police officials (*gunung*) which set Diponegoro against the court clique around the queen mother.

Kyai Murmo was a native of the *pradikan* (tax-free) village of Mojo, home to Diponegoro's religious adviser, Kyai Mojo, who had moved at a young age to Kepundung (Delanggu), one of the richest of the Yogya *pradikan* villages and birth place of the first sultan's mother (Mandoyokusumo 1977:15; Carey 2008:443-4).

Since it is known that Murmo had close ties with Diponegoro's father, the *kyai* may have been one of the religious teachers who visited Tegalrejo during the prince's youth (Chapter I), Diponegoro later stating bitterly that Murmo had been exiled to Ambon 'only in order that [the Dutch] could make themselves masters of [his] treasure and plunder the *desa* [village] of Kepundung' (Carey 2008:447). Nahuys confirmed this view, pointing out that the seizure of Murmo's property had created a very bad impression in the Yogya *kraton*. Although allowed back to Semarang (September 1824), the *kyai*'s mental health was affected and he died shortly afterwards without ever seeing his family again (Carey 1987:294; 2008:447-8).

The treatment of Murmo was far from unusual, Nahuys even boasting of his 'strong-arm' tactics in seizing an *ulama* while giving a lesson in his *pesantren* (Carey 2008:448). Such behavior would harden following the outbreak of the Java War when the term '*santri*' – pious Muslims and students of religion – became a death sentence for those suspected of pro-Diponegoro sympathies (Payen 1988:120 note 260).

The Murmo affair marked an important stage in the deterioration of Diponegoro's relationship with the Dutch. The exile and subsequent death of such an influential *kyai* convinced the prince that the new breed of post-1816 Dutch officials and land renters were completely lacking in respect for his religion, a view widely shared. A report by a post-war Assistant-Resident of Pacitan related how a revered local official, the seventy-year old former *bupati* and mosque official, Kyai Tumenggung Jogokaryo (in office, 1812-26), had only begun to show signs of friendship towards his family when he noticed one of his sons say a Christian grace before a meal. The former *bupati* had remarked that up to that moment he had thought that all Europeans were devoid of religion (Carey 1987:291 note 48).

Binding on the Iron Yoke

Sometime after Murmo's arrest, an even more serious issue arose. This involved the appointment of rural police officials or *gunung*. The role of the *gunung* and their impact on village society had been discussed by Diponegoro and his father early in the latter's reign (p. 154). In late 1816, however, Danurejo IV appointed forty more of these officials. Salaried from the royal tax moneys, they were charged with collecting the *pacumpleng* – a door tax levied at ten to twenty cents per house entrance (Gericke and Roorda 1901, I:297). They also served as the *patih*'s thuggish law enforcers, their modus operandi being summed up by the Surakarta version of the *Babad Diponegoro* (Carey 1981:20-1, 28-9, 249 note 55):

II 15. They did exactly as they wished
Their duty was to make the rounds at night
[and] make tours inside the capital.
[…]

III 16. […]
They were puffed up with flattery and self-glorification.
Their daily task
was to strike people guilty of theft and robbery
when they lay face down and bound on a bench,
[then] they hit them time and again.

In his chronicle, Diponegoro described how the appointment had been made without his prior knowledge and how he immediately gave his younger brother, the fourth sultan, a choice: either accept his advice that the *gunung* were a burden on the local population and withdraw the letter of appointment, or allow the letter to remain in force and side openly with his two major court adversaries, Danurejo IV and bodyguard commander, Wironegoro (Carey 2008:452).

The sultan reluctantly rescinded the letter, but an angry scene occurred between Diponegoro and Wironegoro in which the latter defended his actions, arguing strongly against the annulment. When the queen mother heard that the appointment of the *gunung* had been withdrawn, she chided her son in front of the prince (Babad Dipanagara II:109; Carey 2008:452-3):

XIX 16. [...]
'Sultan, I tell you in truth
that the person who rules the state
of Yogyakarta is in reality
your elder brother Diponegoro,

17. for I was already ordered
by your father [Hamengkubuwono III] earlier
when he was still in the *kadipaten* [Crown Prince's residence].
Thus was his instruction:
"Raden Ayu, I tell you
do not hope too much for your son,
for the one my heart is fixed on
is in truth my eldest son [Diponegoro]."
I replied: "As you wish".

18. The sultan showed embarrassment
because many people knew [of this].
Thus was his speech:
'Your tale
is already known to me
[for I am aware of] my father's instructions to me.'
Pangeran [Diponegoro] smiled [and] spoke calmly:
'Ratu Ibu is like a child, My Lord,

19. in telling this secret
so that many people know of it.'
[...]

The whole incident of the *gunung*, Diponegoro's intervention and Ratu Ibu's reaction, provides a striking illustration of the growing split between the prince and the queen mother. The rivalries and suspicions which would later erupt into such poisonous and open hostility were now evident. As for the *gunung*, Diponegoro's intervention availed little: complaints were still being made about their fiscal oppression and misuse of authority on the eve of the Java War (Carey 2008:453).

Nahuys' Land Rent Policy in the Principalities and its Impact

The arrest of Kyai Murmo and the dispute over the *gunung* were soon overshadowed by the land rent question and Nahuys' proactive role in its implementation.

Before 1816, only very small plots of land had been rented out to Europeans as vegetable plots and country retreats and then only for strictly limited terms (Van der Kemp 1897:16; Louw and De Klerck 1894–1909, I:49; Carey and Hoadley 2000:317–20). Both Daendels and Raffles had continued these restrictions (Van der Chijs 1895, XIV:803; Carey 2008:454).

After mid-August 1816, however, the situation changed. First, and most important, was Nahuys' personal influence as Resident of Yogya, an office he later combined with that of Surakarta (1820–22). The second was that European planters were actively looking for land leases in the Principalities as a way of escaping restrictions on private landholdings in government territories (Day 1972:231–7).

In July 1817, Nahuys led the way by persuading the young sultan to grant him the lease of Bedoyo, a royal estate high on the flanks of Mount Merapi with four adjacent villages to provide labour for Nahuys' planned coffee estate (*Lettres de Java* 1829:100; Louw and De Klerck 1894–1909, I:602–3; Payen 1988:46). Five years later, when Nahuys retired as joint Resident, no less than 115 separate plots of lands and villages (with their inhabitants) had been rented out in the sultanate and a further 189 in the Sunan's territories (Louw and De Klerck 1894–1909, I:604–14, Veth 1896–1907, II:349 note; Carey 2008:457).

The *Angger Sepuluh*, the Javanese agrarian law code, was even modified in October 1818, seemingly under Nahuys' influence, to give European and Chinese land renters the same rights as the previous Javanese apanage holders (Winter 1902:123–8, 172; Rouffaer 1905:627–8). This meant the renters could now convert ricefields (*sawah*) to cash crops, allowing them to reap the main profits while leaving the peasant cultivators to shoulder the royal tribute payments (Louw and De Klerck 1894–1909, I:61).

Such a rapid extension of the land rent had important consequences not all as beneficial as Nahuys made out: although the princely and *priyayi* land leasers benefited from higher cash incomes, their link with their peasant cultivators (*rayat*) was broken. Smissaert, a subsequent Yogya Resident (1823–5), commented that the peasant cultivators on the estates regarded the Europeans as 'domineering foreigners', a sentiment echoed by Javanese contemporaries (Carey 2008:458). This caused difficulties for the local population and put the renters at odds with their tenants, a situation exacerbated by the fact that few European land renters spoke Javanese despite the figment of their adopted Javanese names (Carey 2008:459).

Even the higher cash incomes were problematic: all too often, the cash acquired from land leases was used by the leasers not for capital improvements but for the purchase of luxury imported goods. This led not just to an increase in alcohol consumption at the courts, but also the use of European dress, furniture, carriages and card games (Carey 1981:269 note 137; 2008:459). More traditional in its tastes than Surakarta (Van Hogendorp 1913:91; Carey and Houben 1987:30 note 26), Yogya also witnessed changes. Here European military uniforms became the rage with the fourth sultan using them to equip new companies of *kraton* troops and donning his Dutch major-general's outfit on his sorties outside the court (Van Nes 1844:164; Carey 2013:24).

Predictably, Diponegoro's reaction to the land rent issue was hostile. He did not himself rent out any of his apanage holdings and was renowned for his careful administration: his close ties with his peasant cultivators and extensive land improvements, which all made him one of the richest landowners in the sultanate (Van der Kemp 1896:331; Louw and De Klerck 1894–1909, V:743; Van Hogendorp 1913:160; Carey 1981:282).

But it is clear that he was disturbed by Nahuys' initiatives. Valck referred to him 'often remonstrating' with his younger brother, the fourth sultan, about the issue (Valck, 'Overzigt', 153; Carey 2008:461). The *Buku Kedung Kebo* (Chronicle of the Buffaloes' Watering Hole) even relates how, at the *Garebeg Puwasa* of 12 July 1820, Diponegoro publicly rebuked Danurejo IV for allowing the rental of royal *sawah* (ricefields). When the *patih* answered him frivolously, the prince took off his slipper and struck him hard across the face (Hageman 1856:45; Van der Kemp 1896:308, 313–14, 362; Carey 2008:461 citing KITLV Or 13, 52–56:IV.69–75; Plate 16).

As a guardian (*wakil-Dalem*) of the child sultan, Hamengkubuwono V (1822–6, 1828–55), Diponegoro would later attack the whole policy: 'Must we continue to burden our people, who suffer so much', he stated in a

January 1823 Yogya regency council meeting, 'with the renting out of their lands [while we] acquiesce with those who rent them?' (Van Nes 1844:147).

Diponegoro's concerns won him much popular support: in the words of his first cousin, Mangkudiningrat II (born circa 1800):

> Amongst the village people who gave assistance to Diponegoro, there were those who had nothing to eat, and those whose means of livelihood were crime, robbery and theft. [...] As for the village officials and village tax-collectors [most followed him] because of their grievances against the Chinese whose behaviour was very different from [before]. They now expected people to make a *sembah* of humble greeting to them and they sat high up [on chairs] while the village officials [were forced to] sit cross-legged on the floor in front of them (Carey 2008:462).

As conditions deteriorated in south-central Java in the pre-war decade so popular resentment of the land rent deepened. This resulted in a growing number of attacks on isolated estates in which local estate workers, vagrants and professional bandits (*wong durjono*) took part (Carey 2008:463–4).

Raffles' Land Tax, Coffee Plantations and the Situation in Kedu

The problems associated with the land rent had their counterpart in the newly annexed districts. Here the issue was the land tax introduced by Raffles in 1812–13 (Bastin 1954:93–112). In theory, this was designed to benefit the local population by relieving them of forced dues and labour services in return for the payment of a single land tax. Indeed, Raffles' aim was to give Javanese farmers freedom of cultivation and production (Van Deventer 1891, I:cxvi; Burger 1939:62; Day 1972:172–6).

But the tax was raised unfairly. Detailed cadastral surveys and trained revenue collectors were lacking (p. 152). Raffles' hope that it could be paid in cash was also ill-judged: the Javanese peasant economy was barter-based at this time and his initiative drove the Javanese peasantry into the clutches of local Chinese money-lenders (Bastin 1954:101).

Meanwhile, the abuses of the old Javanese fiscal system remained. How could it be otherwise? The land tax itself was nearly always collected by Javanese officials, many of whom were former members of the royal administrations. They insisted on traditional services and forced deliveries (Levyssohn Norman 1857:192; Bastin 1954:179).

Nowhere were these problems more acute than in Kedu, once one of the most prosperous of the courts' central apanage areas (p. 152). After 1816, coffee plantations were introduced over a wide area and a decade later they covered nearly three-fifths of all high altitude land in the district. The extreme hatred evinced by peasant cultivators for the heavy labour services on the coffee estates resulted in widespread local support for Diponegoro (Carey 2008:466–7).

In 1822, the distressing situation was described in a report by Raden Mas Sukur, the youngest son of the Semarang *bupati*, Suro-Adimenggolo IV, who told of peasant cultivators being reduced to eating leaves and weeds following the destruction of the 1819 and 1822 rice crops by mice and rats, and the failure of the 1823 tobacco harvest (*Residentie Kadoe* 1871:89; Soekanto 1951:29; De Graaf 1979:17–18; Carey 2008:466). Warning that a popular uprising was imminent (Soekanto 1951:29), he was vindicated in July 1825 when the 35,000 inhabitants of the southern district of Probolinggo rose *en masse* after the failure of the tobacco harvest and news of Diponegoro's rebellion (Carey 1981:266 note 123). They targeted the houses and offices of European land tax agents and estate overseers, and forced the resident Chinese to flee for their lives to the provincial capital, Magelang (Carey 1981:260 note 106).

The Working of the Tollgates and their Impact on Internal Trade and Sino-Javanese Relations

The plight of the Chinese in southern Kedu in July 1825 was made more acute by another aspect of the post-1816 European government, namely the tollgates (*bandar*). In the space of just twelve years (1812–24) following the British takeover (p. 152), the revenue from the *bandar* in the Yogya territories almost quadrupled (Carey 2008:467). By 1824, according to the Dutch commissioners charged with enquiring into the tollgate administration, there was a tollgate 'at the entrance of nearly every village and hamlet' (Carey 2008:468).

One of the commissioners, Van Sevenhoven (1782–1841), considered the *bandar* along with the porters' guilds as the two greatest evils of prewar Javanese peasant society. He described how a Javanese on the way to market would be forced to wait for hours in a queue before his load was inspected. If his buffaloes grazed on the tollgate keeper's land he would be fined. If the fine was not paid his buffaloes would be impounded so that at harvest the farmer would have to surrender the bulk of his profits to cover the rent of his own animals from the local *bandar* (Carey 2008:470-1).

In the event of an overnight stay at the tollgate, there would be the added attraction of *ronggeng* (dancing girls, prostitutes), gambling parties and opium, which would further eat into the farmer's meagre savings. If he had serious ill-luck at cards, the farmer would often be forced to part with his clothes and money which many Javanese traders and peasant cultivators borrowed from their village heads (*lurah*) to cover toll dues. In such a situation, it was not uncommon for a peasant cultivator to take to a roving life as a bandit or porter on the roads rather than face the ignominy of returning empty-handed to his village (Carey 2008:471).

The only way a 'little man' (*wong cilik*) could revenge himself on a tollgate keeper was by enlisting the help of local bandits and inciting them to plunder and burn the *bandar*. Such cases of burglary were frequent in the years before the Java War as can be seen from the value of stolen tollgate goods which rose tenfold between 1817 and 1824 (Carey 2008:471). The situation became critical following the outbreak of the Java War when all the tollgates in the vicinity of Yogya were burnt and the local Chinese massacred (Payen 1988:62, 116 note 141; Carey 1984:1-2; 2008:473, 617).

Faced with the threat of constant attack, tollgate keepers began to organize their own 'private armies' of bodyguards and thugs, some of them recruited from former Bengal sepoys. This added another twist to the spiral of violence in country areas as the Java War loomed (Carey 1981:243 note 36).

The European government was well aware of the effects of the tollgates and attempted reform: the British abolished the *bandar* along the Solo River in February 1814 and the Dutch followed suit in Kedu in 1824, the same year in which Van der Capellen appointed the three-man team of commissioners to enquire into the working of the tollgates (Carey 2008:474).

Reporting back in October 1824, the commissioners recommended the immediate abolition of all internal customs posts, suggesting that the government indemnify itself for the lost revenue by annexing the western outlying provinces of Bagelen and Banyumas. They also urged that all Chinese residents in country areas be ordered to move to the royal capitals, no new Chinese immigration being allowed (Carey 2008:474).

MacGillivray, one of the commissioners, summed it up:

> The Chinese are our work tools and although each year we may rejoice in the increased [revenues] […], we bind the iron yoke more firmly onto the shoulders [of the Javanese]. For a million guilders a year worth of taxes we sacrifice the welfare and happiness of almost two million inhabitants who are not immediately under our protection but whose interests are so clearly linked to our own (Carey 2008:474–5).

Only the local population's 'good nature and peacefulness' – a self-deluding Dutch trope this (Carey and Houben 1987:13; Carey 2008:475) – had enabled the oppression of the tollgate system to continue for so long in the commissioners' view. But they ended with a fearful prophecy:

> We hope they [the Javanese] will not be awoken out of their slumbering state, for we reckon it as a certainty that if the tollgates are permitted to continue, the time is not far distant when the Javanese will be aroused in a terrible fashion (Carey 2008:475).

Their warning went unheeded (Van der Kemp 1896:44–5); the near threefold rise in profits from the Yogya tollgate farms between 1816 and 1824 had made the government deaf. Writing in November 1824, a mere two months after leasing the once profitable tollgates of Bantul and Jatinom to the south of Yogya, the local Chinese tollgate keeper reported that he had gone bankrupt. A prolonged and severe drought had destroyed the local cotton crop and basic foodstuffs were scarce. Rice prices were soaring, but trade was at a standstill because local markets had collapsed (Carey 2008:475).

In these terrible months before the Java War, the south-central Javanese countryside became a place of suspicion and terror. Armed gangs operated with impunity, murders were rife and the daily activities of the local peasant cultivators took place under the ever-watchful eyes of the tollgate keepers' spies positioned on every country road (Carey 2008:473). The Chinese were now viewed both by the Dutch and the Javanese as a 'race of customs agents' (*bangsa bandar*). But they were not by nature oppressors. Before the post-1816 Dutch administration had ratcheted its fiscal demands to intolerable levels, some Chinese, such as the principal land renter in Wirosobo in east Java, had been singled out as 'kind and indulgent master' under whom the Javanese common man (*wong cilik*) liked to take service because his 'lands and villages were better looked after than elsewhere' (Carey 2008:478).

What had changed in the post-1816 period was not the character of the Chinese but the character of the fiscal regime they served. And for this the post-1816 Dutch colonial government must take full responsibility.

The Effects of the Opium Monopoly

Yet not all the social evils which befell the Javanese in the pre-Java War period can be laid at the door of the Dutch. Their predecessors, the British, were midwives to an equally disastrous development: the rapid extension of the opium retail trade.

The greater ease of opium imports from Bengal following the lifting of the British blockade of Java in August–September 1811 was mainly responsible for this (Hasselman 1858:18–37), revenue from the Yogya opium farm increasing fivefold between 1814 and 1824.

Once again, the Chinese were cast in an invidious role, opium retail and tollgate farming going hand in hand: by 1820 there were 372 separate places licensed to retail opium in the sultan's territories, namely, one for every major tollgate, sub-tollgate and market (Carey 2008:479).

Late nineteenth-century consumption figures suggest that sixteen percent, or just over three million of the twenty-million Javanese population in the mid-1880s, took opium (Wiselius 1886:6). But if one counts all those who inhaled and digested 'poor men's' varieties of the drug, such as opium-soaked cigarettes, opium-seasoned coffee, and opium-laced betelnut, the incidence of narcotic consumption was certainly much higher (Rush 1977:20).

All too often opium offered the only release from a life of hardship and drudgery. In Pacitan, a huge religious feast would be held every year to celebrate the end of the coffee harvest, government crop payments going on 'opium eating' (Kern 1908:163). During the Java War itself, there were reports that Diponegoro's troops were 'falling sick' for want of the drug, Chinese opium peddlers doing a brisk trade behind the prince's lines when the violent sinophobe sentiments of the initial months had abated (Louw and De Klerck 1897–1909, II:215–16; Payen 1988:68, 123–4 note 179).

A pastime for the rich, opium addiction was a disaster for the poor. Even the slightest predilection for the drug could tip a Javanese peasant cultivator into a life of crime. The road to social degradation lay wide open. Nahuys later urged the rounding up of the thousands of landless labourers and footloose vagrants, 'whose [thin] shoulders and smooth hands bear no marks of labour and whose eyes, lips and colour betray the habitual use of narcotics' (Carey 2008:480).

Millenarian Movements and Prophecies in South-Central Java

Between 1817 and 1822, the gathering socio-economic crisis gave rise to a number of millenarian movements and an elite-led revolt in Kedu. All were portents for the future.

In January 1817, the so-called 'Umar Mahdi' affair occurred in eastern Bagelen. Named after a Yogya inhabitant of the village of Sambiroto (Nanggulan, Kulon Progo) (Dumont 1931:321), its protagonist claimed to be a 'soldier' (*prajurit*) of the Ottoman sultan ('Sultan Rum'). Declaring that Sunan Bonang, a previous apostle of Islam (*wali*) in Java, and the sultan's follower, Umar Moyo, would assist him in the 'purification' of Java, he urged the expulsion of both Chinese and Europeans, instructing his followers to make for the weaving centre of Jono in eastern Bagelen where there was a sizeable Chinese community. But before this could happen, Umar Mahdi was arrested with thirty-six of his followers. Under cross-questioning, he was found not to speak a word of Arabic, only Javanese with a strong Yogya accent (Carey 2008:482–3).

Mahdi's movement has interesting resonances with Diponegoro's great rebellion of 1825–30. First, there is the juxtaposition of Javanese traditions and messianic expectations, the names Umar Mahdi and Umar Moyo being taken from the great Javanese-Islamic epic, *Menak Amir Hamza*, relating the legends of the uncle of The Prophet Muhammad, in which the hero's *panakawan* bear the same monikers (Pigeaud 1950:235–40, 1967–80, I:212–16, III:420; Carey 1992:487 note 414).

The reference to Sultan Rum arriving in Java with sheikh (*seh*) from Arab lands can also be traced back to the traditions of the Aji Soko tales and Joyoboyo prophecies which held that the Ottoman sultan had organised the peopling and civilizing of Java (p. 60). Finally, the use of Sunan Bonang's name was a direct allusion to the famous Sino-Javanese apostle of Islam or *wali* of the Demak period in the late fifteenth and early sixteenth centuries who spread Islam to central and east Java (Solichin Salam 1963:35–8; De Graaf and Pigeaud 1974:48–50). Traditions concerning the *wali* had close links with the 'Just King' (Ratu Adil) traditions: in one version of the Joyoboyo prophecies the latter is described as 'a descendant of the *wali*' who would be 'raised as a priest-king', and in another as a *waliyullah*, a messenger of Allah (Brandes 1889:386–7; Wiselius 1892:188).

In both the Umar Mahdi affair and Diponegoro's rebellion, an attack on Chinese merchants and tollgate keepers was regarded as a preliminary to the 'purification' of Java before the rule of the Just King or Ratu Adil could be established. Moreover, the white tabards and multi-coloured turbans adopted by Diponegoro and his troops during the Java War (Carey 1981:276–7 note 169) were also evident in the earlier movement, as was the use of Javanese titles such as *Raden Mas* alongside Arabic 'holy war' monikers (Carey 2008:484).

Other millenarian movements occurred in Java in 1817. In July, Nahuys received news from his colleague, the acting Resident of Semarang, that 4,000 Javanese had gathered at the Yogya village of Ketonggo in the Madiun area, a place renowned in Javanese literature as the site where the Just King would establish himself (Carey 2008:484). Hailing from Madiun and other eastern outlying districts, the participants brought unhusked rice (*padi*) from the recent harvest and congregated at the village 'because of an old prophecy that a new and mighty ruler would establish himself there', a clear reference to the Ratu Adil (Carey 2008:251, 484).

Two years' later (1819), a similar gathering was reported by the Resident of Pasuruan, Malang and Bangil, J.C. Ellinghuijsen (1782–1825; in office 1818–1825) (Hageman 1864:253). This time it was in the 'forest of Ketonggo'. It involved people from adjacent outlying districts such as Japan (Mojokerto), Rowo (Tulung Agung) and Malang, who were said to have been summoned 'to undertake a great work' (*pekerjaan besar*), namely the establishment of a new ruler in Malang, and an attack on the adjacent north coast districts of Surabaya, Bangil and Pasuruan, where the local Chinese and European communities were to be destroyed (Carey 2008:484–5).

One of the most disturbing prophecies at this time was that of a wandering sage in Blitar, east Java, Iman Sampurno (the 'Sage of Perfect Faith'), who foretold in graphic detail – albeit a year out – the coming Asiatic cholera epidemic of May 1821 (Carey 2008:485–9).

> In the coming Javanese year Alip (AD 21 October 1819–8 October 1820), there will be a very great epidemic from the western part. The army of the spirit Taragnyono will be like a mist; the forms will be various, some in the shape of poisonous millipedes, scorpions, snakes and tigers, all of whom will be venomous. The plague from the east will be brought by Nyai Roro Kidul and her army, Sunan Lawu and his army and all the spirits of Java. [...] They will deal with everyone according to his kind, just as the heathen struck by the *tahlil* [confession of faith], arrogant people [will be] speared by pikes, for gamblers dice will be thrown by the spirits, arrogant people will be clawed by the spirits, greedy people will be destroyed by the spirits. After the epidemic has come, Java will become a sea of blood with drifting corpses.

The sage suggested ways whereby those who practiced the true faith as Muslims could ward this off, his proclamation containing much that would have resonated with members of the Javanese religious communities. One thinks here of the *kyai*'s reference to the need for religious ceremonies at which food would be distributed (*sedhekah*) and *dhikr* (litanies) recited, as well as his stress on the prophetic beliefs associated with the *Kitab Musarar* text ascribed to Prabu Joyoboyo (Carey 2008:490).

The same amalgam can be seen in Diponegoro's own writings, especially his reference to the 'perfect man' (*insan kamil*) (Babad Dipanegara IV:99; pp. 33–4). We also know from a Dutch report written just a year after the outbreak of the Java War that belief in the Joyoboyo prophecies was widespread both at the courts and amongst the religious communities (Carey 1981:lxiv note 122):

> At the courts a prophecy exists [...] from a certain ruler Joyoboyo that [...] a Javanese *kraton* cannot stand for longer than a hundred years. The rulers, courtiers, scholars and men of religion all have a deep respect and belief in this prophecy and are of the firm opinion that the term of the Yogyakarta court has been fulfilled and that of Surakarta will soon be ended. They are all confirmed in this conviction because, so they say, the prophecies have never failed (Carey 2008:490).

Sampurno made a connection between the coming of the Just King with the establishment of a monarch who would be a [*Ratu*] *Paneteg Panatagama*, a '[Royal] Maintainer and Regulator of Religion', a person who would be a 'most winning personality, a true Mataram man' (Carey 2008:490). Both suggest that Sampurno might have had someone very much like Diponegoro in mind. Not only was he a Mataram prince by virtue of his birth as the eldest son of the third sultan, but he also saw himself as a 'Maintainer and Regulator of Religion', a central aspect of his calling as a Just King (Carey 1974a:29; Chapter IX). He also had charisma – 'winning ways' – as his uncle, Panular, pointed out when he described his impact as a public speaker (p. 149).

The Crisis in the Javanese Countryside, the Cholera Epidemic of 1821 and Pangeran Diposono's Revolt

During the four years which elapsed between the Umar Mahdi affair of January 1817 and the cholera epidemic of April 1821, conditions in the south-central Javanese countryside deteriorated. A run of poor rice harvests and a crisis in the indigenous sugar industry all contributed. In early 1821, the situation was exacerbated when the harvest failed in many areas due to an unusually long drought. The situation in Pacitan was especially bad, the local Dutch plantation overseer (*opziener*) reporting that it was 'a very dismal sight' with many ricefields unworkable for lack of water and those that had been planted drying out quickly under the parching wind from the sea (Kern 1908:162, 173–4; Carey 1986:123 note 237).

In June 1821, the first Asiatic cholera epidemic struck causing many fatalities amongst the already weakened Pacitan population: every day farmers had to be pulled from the pepper and coffee plantations dead from exhaustion and fever (Carey 1986:123 note 238). By November, the overseer was writing of the 'total demoralization' of his local work force (Carey 1986:123 note 239), many of whom now moved to adjacent areas to escape the forced labour. In the space of just two years (1819–21), Pacitan lost ten percent of its population (Kern 1908:166, 173; Carey 1981:293 note 243, 1986:124 note 240).

In Java, the epidemic struck a 'virgin population' with no inbuilt immunity to the disease (Boomgaard 1983:13). Brought by sailors from Pulau Pinang and Melaka, it first manifested in Semarang (Muller 1832:2–3) and by early May had spread along the north coast, the worst outbreaks occurring in the colonial capital, Batavia (156 reported deaths a day), Surabaya (76 deaths a day) (Muller 1832:3), and eastern salient (Oosthoek), where seven percent of the 110,000-strong population succumbed (Carey 1986:133 note 288). The scarcity and expense of foodstuffs, and the fact that the epidemic occurred during the fasting month (*Puwasa*), when resistance to disease was lower, may have contributed to the high mortality (Carey 1986:133 note 290).

For the lucky ones who survived, the memory of those terrible months must have been profoundly disturbing. The virulence of the disease and its manifestation at one of the holiest times of the year indicated for many an upheaval in the natural order. Such a *goro-goro* (commotion in nature) or 'time of wrath' (*jaman kala-bendu*) traditionally preceded the coming of the Just King whose arrival is heralded by natural portents and disasters (Brandes 1889:374; Carey 1986:131 note 279).

In late January and early February 1822, a revolt occurred in south-central Java involving a son of the first sultan, Pangeran Diposono (born circa 1778), whom Diponegoro described as a small man with a disability, who had suffered from a form of mental sickness since his youth (Babad Dipanegara II:110). Skilled at augury and well versed in *primbon* (divination manual) literature (Pigeaud 1975:212–13; Ricklefs and Voorhoeve

Binding on the Iron Yoke 189

1977:63; Carey 2008:496), he tried to use his contacts with the spirit world to expel the Dutch and Chinese, and replace the fourth sultan (Nahuys van Burgst 1852:180). After recruiting the help of various robber chiefs in Kedu and a wandering female *dukun* (magic practitioner), two uprisings were planned: one in southern Kedu and another to the south of Yogya at Gading Temahan and Lipuro (Carey 2008:496), the latter a significant place for Mataram royal pretenders (p. 62).

Diposono's plan was to draw troops away from Yogya by the initial uprising in Kedu, and then fall on the sultan's capital (Nahuys van Burgst 1852:134). But his strategy failed. Support from local officials was fitful and the Dutch overcame the 27–28 January 1822 movement in Kedu without Yogya reinforcements. Diposono's own uprising in Yogya then collapsed quickly around Lipuro in early February. The disabled prince was brought to trial in Yogya, his sentence of death by garroting being commuted to lifetime exile in Ambon (Carey 2008:497–8).

A Poisoned Legacy: Hamengkubuwono IV's Final Year

In Yogya, the period following Diposono's abortive revolt witnessed a revival of the old intrigues which had so poisoned relations between Diponegoro and the court.

One incident in particular raised tensions to breaking point. This involved a document, written by Diponegoro's father, the third sultan, which may have recognised his eldest son's rights to the Yogya throne (Carey 2008:502). This had already been the subject of an altercation between the prince and his stepmother at the time of the dispute over the appointment of new police officials (*gunung*) referred to earlier.

The fourth sultan apparently came out to Tegalrejo in late 1822 to ask for this document which Diponegoro had kept in his personal archive. The prince gave it reluctantly under the strict injunction that it should be kept safely. But the young ruler immediately burnt it to destroy evidence which might compromise his own position (Carey 2008:502). The prince did not find out until nine months after the sultan's death in December 1822 when he wrote to the queen mother to ask for the document as a guideline for the recently appointed guardians of the child sultan, Hamengkubuwono V, of whom he was one (Van der Kemp 1896:335–7).

The prince's reaction to the queen mother's acknowledgement that the document had been lost was said to have been one of extreme anger (Carey 2008:502). It would later precipitate his refusal to continue to perform his guardianship duties and led to his complete break with the *kraton*. One of the last acts of the fourth sultan's reign thus had disastrous consequences for the future (p. 210).

Shortly afterwards, on 6 December 1822 at half past three o'clock in the afternoon the young monarch died after returning to the *kraton* from a tour of one of his country estates (*pesanggrahan*). The manner of his death was extremely violent: he succumbed to a sudden fit while eating and his body immediately swelled up, an indication, some contemporaries thought, that he had been poisoned (*Kronijk van Nederlandsch-Indië* 1842, I:206–7; Louw and De Klerck 1894–1909, V:744).

But the sources do not confirm this. In fact, the teenage sultan's corpulence, love of highly spiced food and excessive exertions in the saddle seem to have precipitated a heart attack at the remarkably young age of eighteen (Carey 2008:503). His indulgent lifestyle – encouraged by the likes of Nahuys – had brought him to an early grave, the first royal victim of the westernising tide which swept the south-central Javanese courts after 1816. And he would not be alone. The fourth sultan's own son, who reigned for two decades as Hamengkubuwono V (1822–6, 1828–55), was a syphilitic wreck in his twenties due to over-indulgence in alcohol and women encouraged by unscrupulous European suppliers (Houben 1994:154, 200–2).

Conclusion

So ended the reign of Diponegoro's younger brother. It closed a lamentable chapter in Yogya's history. Within the *kraton*, the incipient rivalry between Diponegoro and the court clique around the queen mother was rapidly hardening into open warfare. A complete rift was only months away.

The return of the profit-hungry Dutch in August 1816 had accelerated processes begun by the British, the most important of which was the integration of Java into the global economy and the opening of the island's interior to western capital. Meanwhile, the arguments over the land rent exposed the deep rifts in Van der Capellen's administration. His subsequent decision to prohibit the leasing of land to private investors in May 1823 created more problems than it solved (Chapter IX). His insatiable revenue needs, coupled with what Raffles had correctly surmised as a 'hankering after immediate profit' on the part of the royal government, meant that those in charge of colonial policy were increasingly oblivious to the plight of the Javanese peasantry.

In July 1825, Van der Capellen would report that the news of Diponegoro's rebellion had reached him 'completely unexpectedly' (Van der Capellen 1860:363; Carey 1981:283 note 201). Yet only an inveterate optimist could have written thus. The ever more urgent reports of Dutch officials regarding the crisis in the Javanese countryside all pointed to one conclusion – a major popular uprising was imminent. Only the timing and leadership were unclear. The combination of the land tax, poor harvests, the 1821 cholera epidemic, the tollgates and the renting of estates to Europeans had turned south-central Java into a powder keg. The popular disturbances of 1817–22 with their quirky millenarian hopes were a symptom of this deepening despair.

In Yogya, the desire for regeneration and the re-establishment of the pre-Daendelian political order now fused with messianic expectations of a coming golden age of justice and plenty. All that was now needed was for a leader of sufficient stature to proclaim himself and bind the discontented to his cause.

Bibliography

Babad Dipanegara (2010). *Babad Dipanegara*, 4 vols, ed. Nindya Noegraha. Jakarta: Perpustakaan Nasional Republik Indonesia.
Bastin, J. (1954). *Raffles' Ideas on the Land Rent System in Java and the Mackenzie Land Tenure Commission*. The Hague: Nijhoff. [KITLV, Verhandelingen 14.]

Boomgaard, Peter (1983). 'Disease, Death and Disasters in Java, 1820–1880; A Preliminary Survey and Analysis of Changing Patterns of Morbidity and Mortality'. Paper, Conference 'Disease, Death and Drugs in Modern Southeast Asia', Australian National University (Canberra), May.

Bosma, U. and R. Raben (2008). *Being 'Dutch' in the Indies; A History of Creolisation and Empire, 1500–1920*. Singapore: National University of Singapore Press.

Brandes, J. (1889). 'Iets over een Ouderen Dipanagara in Verband met een Prototype van een Voorspelling van Jayabaya', *Tijdschrift van het Bataviaasch Genootschap van Kunsten en Wetenschappen (TBG)* 32:368–430.

Briët, Kees (2012). *Het Proces van Rijck van Prehn en Johannes Wilhelmus Winter; Een Bijzondere Zaak voor het Hooggerechtshof van Nederlands-Indië in 1820*. Hilversum: Verloren (Extra Nummer *Pro Memorie* 14.2).

Burger, D.H. (1939). *De Ontsluiting van Java's Binnenland voor het Wereld Verkeer*. Wageningen: Veenman.

Capellen, G.A.G.Ph. van der (1860). 'Aanteekeningen van den Gouverneur-Generaal Baron Van der Capellen over den Opstand van Dipo Negoro in 1825', *Tijdschrift voor Nederlandsch-Indië (TNI)* 22:360–87.

Carey, Peter (1974a). *The Cultural Ecology of Early Nineteenth Century Java; Pangeran Dipanagara, A Case Study*. Singapore: Institute of Southeast Asian Studies. [Occasional Paper 24.]

Carey, Peter (1974b). 'Javanese Histories of Dipanagara; The Buku Kĕdhuŋ Kĕbo, its Authorship and Historical Importance', *Bijdragen tot de Taal-, Land- en Volkenkunde* 130:259–88.

Carey, Peter (1980). *The Archive of Yogyakarta. Vol. I: Documents relating to Politics and Internal Court Affairs*. Oxford: Oxford University Press.

Carey, Peter (1981). *Babad Dipanagara; An Account of the Outbreak of the Java War (1825–30); The Surakarta Court Version of the Babad Dipanagara with Translations into English and Indonesian Malay*. Kuala Lumpur: Art Printers.

Carey, Peter (1984). 'Changing Javanese Perceptions of the Chinese Communities in Central Java, 1755–1825', *Indonesia* 37:1–48.

Carey, Peter (1987). 'Satria and Santri; Some Notes on the Relationship between Dipanagara's Kraton and Religious Supporters during the Java War (1825–30)', in: T. Ibrahim Alfian, H.J. Koesoemanto, Dharmono Hardjowidjono and Djoko Suryo (eds), *Dari Babad dan Hikayat sampai Sejarah Kritis; Kumpulan karangan dipersembahkan kepada Prof. Dr. Sartono Kartodirdjo*, pp. 271–318. Yogyakarta: Gadjah Mada University Press.

Carey, Peter (1992). *The British in Java, 1811–1816; A Javanese Account*. Oxford: Oxford University Press.

Carey, Peter (2008). *The Power of Prophecy; Prince Dipanagara and the End of an Old Order in Java, 1785-1855*. Leiden: KITLV Press.
Carey, Peter (2012). *Kuasa Ramalan; Pangeran Diponegoro dan Akhir Tatanan Lama di Jawa, 1785-1855*. Jakarta: KPG, second revised edition.
Carey, Peter (2013). *Daendels and the Sacred Space of Java, 1808-1811. Political Relations, Uniforms and the Postweg*. Nijmegen: Van Tilt.
Carey, Peter and Mason Hoadley (eds) (2000). *The Archive of Yogyakarta. Vol. II: Documents relating to Economic and Agrarian Affairs*. Oxford: Oxford University Press.
Chijs, J.A. van der (1895). *Nederlandsch-Indisch Plakaatboek 1602-1811*. Vol. XIV (1807-1808). The Hague: Nijhoff.
Day, C. (1972). *The Policy and Administration of the Dutch in Java*. Kuala Lumpur: Oxford University Press.
Deventer, M.L. van (1891). *Het Nederlandsch Gezag over Java en Onderhoorigheden sedert 1811; Verzameling van Onuitgegeven Stukken uit de Koloniale en Andere Archieven. Vol.I: 1811-1820*. The Hague: Nijhoff.
Doel, H.W. van den (1994). *De Stille Macht; Het Europese Binnenlands Bestuur op Java en Madoera, 1808-1942*. Amsterdam: Bert Bakker.
Dumont, C.F.H. (1931). *Aardrijkskundig Woordenboek van Nederlandsch Oost-Indië*. Rotterdam: Nijgh & Van Ditmar.
Gericke, J.F.C. and Roorda, T. (1901). *Javaansch-Nederlandsch Handwoordenboek*. Amsterdam: Muller, Leiden: Brill. Two vols.
Graaf, H.J. de (1979). 'Het Semarangsche Geslacht Bustam in de 18e en 19e Eeuw; Afkomst en Jeugd van Radèn Salèh', *Bijdragen tot de Taal-, Land- en Volkenkunde*, 135.2/3:252-81.
Graaf, H.J. de and Th.G.Th. Pigeaud (1974). *De Eerste Moslimse Vorstendommen op Java; Studiën over de Staatkundige Geschiedenis van de 15de en 16de Eeuw*. The Hague: Nijhoff. [KITLV, Verhandelingen 69].
Haan, F. de (1935). 'Personalia der Periode van het Engelsch Bestuur over Java, 1811-1816', *Bijdragen tot de Taal-, Land- en Volkenkunde* 92:477-681.
Hageman, J.Jcz. (1856). *Geschiedenis van den Oorlog op Java van 1825 tot 1830*. Batavia: Lange.
Hageman, J.Jcz. (1864). 'Namen der Gewestelijke Europesche Gezaghebbers, enz, op Java en Madoera', *Tijdschrift voor Indische Taal-, Land- en Volkenkunde (TBG)* 13:227-65, 557-64.
Hardouin, G. and W.L. Ritter (1853-55). *Java; Toonelen uit het Leven, Karakterschetsen en Kleederdragten van Java's Bewoners*. The Hague: Fuhri.
Hasselman, J.J. (1858). 'Nota omtrent de Opium-Pacht op Java en Madoera', *Handelingen en Geschriften van het Indisch Genootschap* 5:18-37, 107-80.

Hogendorp, H. Graaf van (1913). *Willem van Hogendorp in Nederlandsch-Indië 1825–1830*. The Hague: Nijhoff.

Houben, Vincent (1994). *Kraton and Kumpeni; Surakarta and Yogyakarta 1830–1870*. Leiden: KITLV Press. [Verhandelingen 164].

Kemp, P.H. van der (1896). 'Dipanegara, Eene Geschiedkundige Hamlettype', *Bijdragen tot de Taal-, Land- en Volkenkunde* 46:281–433.

Kemp. P.H. van der (1897). 'De Economische Oorzaken van den Java-Oorlog van 1825–1830', *Bijdragen tot de Taal-, Land- en Volkenkunde* 47:1–48.

Kern, R.A. (1908). 'Uit Oude Bescheiden (Geschiedenis van de Afdeeling Patjitan in de Eerste Helft der 19e eeuw) met Bijlage', *Tijdschrift van het Binnenlands Bestuur (TBB)* 34:157–90.

Kronijk van Nederlandsch-Indië (1842). 'Kronijk van Nederlandsch-Indië, loopende vanaf het Jaar 1816; De Jaren 1822 en 1823', *Tijdschrift voor Nederlandsch-Indië* 4–1:129–228.

Lettres de Java (1829). *Lettres de Java ou Journal d'un Voyage en cette Île, en 1822*. Paris: n.p. [J. van Schoor pseudonymous author.]

Levyssohn Norman, H.D. (1857). *De Britsche Heerschappij over Java en Onderhoorigheden (1811–1816)*. The Hague: Belinfante.

Louw, P.J.F. and E.S. de Klerck (1894–1909). *De Java-Oorlog van 1825–1830*. The Hague: Nijhoff, Batavia: Landsdrukkerij. Six vols.

Mandoyokusumo, K.R.T. (1977). *Serat Raja Putra Ngayogyakarta Hadiningrat*. Yogyakarta: Bebadan Museum Karaton Ngayogyakarta Hadiningrat.

Muller, M.J.E. (1832). 'Kort Verslag aangaande de Cholera-morbus op Java', *Verhandelingen van het Bataviaasch Genootschap* 13–1:1–111.

Nahuys van Burgst, H.G. (1852). *Reminiscences of the Public and Private Life of H.G. Baron Nahuys van Burgst (1799–1849)*. Arnhem: [privately printed].

Nes, J.F.Walraven van (1844). 'Verhandelingen over de Waarschijnlijke Oorzaken, die Aanleiding tot de Onlusten van 1825 en de volgende jaren in de Vorstenlanden gegeven hebben', *Tijdschrift voor Nederlandsche Indië* 6:112–71.

Nieuwenhuys, Rob (1973). *Oost-Indische Spiegel; Wat Nederlandse Schrijvers en Dichters over Indonesië hebben Geschreven, vanaf de Eerste Jaren der Compagnie tot op Heden*. Amsterdam: Querido.

Olivier, J. (1827–30). *Land- en Zeetogten in Nederland's Indië, en Eenige Britsche Establisementen gedaan in de Jaren 1817 to 1826*. Amsterdam: Sulpke. Three vols.

Payen, A.A.J. (1988). *Voyage à Djocja-Karta en 1825; The Outbreak of the Java War (1825–30) as Seen by a Painter*. Edited by Peter Carey. Paris: Association Archipel.

Pigeaud, Th.G.Th. (1950). 'The Romance of Amir Hamza in Java', in: *Bingkisan Budi; Een Bundel Opstellen aan Dr. Philippus Samuel van Ronkel door Vrienden en*

Leerlingen Aangeboden op zijn 80e Verjaardag 1 Augustus 1950, pp. 235–40. Leiden: Sijthoff.

Pigeaud, Th.G.Th. (1967–80). *Literature of Java; Catalogue Raisonné of Javanese Manuscripts in the Library of the University of Leiden and Other Public Collections in the Netherlands*. The Hague, Leiden: Nijhoff. Four vols.

Pigeaud, Th.G.Th. (1975) *Javanese and Balinese Manuscripts and Some Codices Written in Related Idioms Spoken in Java and Bali*. Wiesbaden: Steiner. [Verzeichnis der orientalischen Handschriften in Deutschland 31].

Raffles, Lady Sophia (1830). *Memoir of the Life and Public Services of Sir Thomas Stamford Raffles*. London: Murray.

Remmelink, W. (1994). *The Chinese War and the Collapse of the Javanese State, 1725–1743*. Leiden: KITLV Press.

Residentie Kadoe (1871). *De Residentie Kadoe naar de Uitkomsten der Statistieke Opname en andere Officiele Bescheiden bewerkt door de Afdeling Statistieken ter Algemeene Secretarie*. Batavia: Landsdrukkerij.

Ricklefs, M.C. and P. Voorhoeve (1977). *Indonesian Manuscripts in Great Britain; A Catalogue of Indonesian Manuscripts in British Public Collections*. London: Oxford University Press.

Rouffaer, G.P. (1905). 'Vorstenlanden', *Encylopaedie van Nederlandsch-Indië* 4:587–653.

Rush, J.R. (1977). *Opium Farms in Nineteenth Century Java; Institutional Change and Continuity in a Colonial Society, 1860–1910*. PhD thesis, Department of History, Yale University.

Singapore (1883). *Singapore Sixty Years Ago; Including a Journal by Mr Walter Scott Duncan, February to June 1824*. Singapore: Straits Times Press.

Soekanto (1951). *Dua Raden Saleh, Dua Nasionalis dalam Abad ke-19; Suatu Halaman dari Sejarah Nasional Indonesia*. Djakarta: Poesaka Aseli.

Soeripto (1929). *Ontwikkelingsgang der Vorstenlandsche Wetboeken*. Leiden: IJdo.

Solichin Salam (1963). *Sekitar Wali Sanga*. Kudus: Menara.

Stoler, A.L. (2002). *Carnal Knowledge and Imperial Power; Race and the Intimate in Colonial Rule*. Berkeley: University of California Press.

Taylor, J.G. (1983). *The Social World of Batavia; European and Eurasian in Dutch Asia*. Madison: University of Wisconsin Press.

Valck, 'Overzigt': F.G. Valck, 'Overzigt der Voornaamste Gebeurtenissen in het Djokjocartasche Rijk sedert dezelfs Stichting in den Jare 1755 tot aan het Einde van den door de Opstand van den Pangeran Ario Dhipo-Negoro Verwekten Oorlog in den Jaren 1825 tot en met 1830', 1-8-1833. Bundel Djokjo Brieven 9A (and 19[1]) of Arsip Nasional Republik Indonesia (ANRI), Jakarta.

Veth, P.J. (1896–1907). *Java; Geographisch, Ethnologisch, Historisch*. Haarlem: Erven F. Bohn. Four vols.

Winter, J.W. (1902). 'Beknopte Beschrijving van het Hof Soerakarta in 1824', *Bijdragen tot de Taal-, Land- en Volkenkunde* 54:15–172.

Wiselius, J.A.B. (1886). *De Opium in Nederlandsch- en Britsch-Indië, Economisch, Critisch, Historisch*. The Hague: Nijhoff.

Wiselius, J.A.B. (1892). 'Djåjå Båjå, Zijn Leven en Profetieën', *Bijdragen tot de Taal-, Land- en Volkenkunde* 42:172–217.

CHAPTER IX

Waiting for the 'Just King': Diponegoro's Final Visions and the Road to War in South-Central Java, 1822–1825

The Man of Destiny

In the two and a half years which elapsed between the death of the fourth sultan and the outbreak of the Java War the crisis in the Javanese countryside deepened.

As we have just seen (Chapter VIII), several revolts had occurred in the previous five years (1817–22), some of a pronounced millenarian character. None, however, had involved figures of stature and authority. Apart from the quirky Diposono, whom Diponegoro mentions specifically in his *babad*, the other leaders were all commoners. They lacked the influence to turn their movements into major uprisings.

Most likely unaware of these self-appointed prophets in the Javanese countryside, the time was coming when, summoned by prophecy, the prince would himself step forward from the obscurity of Tegalrejo and stand centre stage as the longed for Ratu Adil (Just King). The period foretold by the Parangkusumo prophecy – 'you alone are the means, but that not for long only to be counted amongst the ancestors' (p. 59) – was at hand. The next two chapters will describe how the prince's destiny was fulfilled.

Aftermath of the Fourth Sultan's Death and Diponegoro's Guardianship

The fourth sultan's unexpected fit on returning from his riding tour shocked the court. Diponegoro was hastily summoned from Tegalrejo. But when he arrived his younger brother was already dead.

The Residency surgeon suggested an incision be made in the sultan's thigh to ascertain blood circulation, but Diponegoro intervened, stating that it was against Javanese-Islamic practice for a body to be mutilated after death. One recalls here the prince's refusal to accept the arcane magico-religious practices for releasing the life force at his father's November 1814 deathbed (p. 159).

Raden Mas Alip, one of Diponegoro's sons, would later recall that his father had shown pleasure at his sibling's death stating:

> 'Thank God! How could it be otherwise than that he should die in such a fashion? Since he could not bring himself to make war to regain his kingdom or even to rule it properly, it is good that he no longer remains in this world. Now everything will go better' (Nahuys van Burgst 1835–6, I:12; Van Nes 1844:145).

But this is not corroborated in other sources.

Early the following day, 7 December, Acting Resident De Salis arrived from Surakarta and the sultan's body was buried near the grave of his father at Imogiri. The queen mother, Ratu Ageng, and the late sultan's official consort, Ratu Kencono (circa 1802–circa 1827), then 'beseeched' the Dutch authorities to confirm the two-year-old Crown Prince on the throne. They also urged that Pakualam I not be re-appointed regent, Ratu Ageng even suggesting that the European government might itself assume the regency (Carey 2008:507).

To all these requests, the cautious De Salis replied that he would await Van der Capellen's instructions. But he had already consulted the Residency archives (p. 160) and concluded that Pakualam should not act again as regent. On 14 December, in a secret resolution, Van der Capellen endorsed De Salis' recommendations. The guardianship and education of the young sultan, together with *kraton* finances and governance, were to devolve on four guardians: Ratu Ageng, Ratu Kencono, Mangkubumi and Diponegoro, the first two being charged with the child sultan's upbringing, the last with the management of the sultanate during the minority (1822–36).

The tollgate and market rents worth 100,000 Spanish dollars annually were to be paid directly to these two princely guardians without Danurejo IV's intervention, the last only being permitted to interfere in internal *kraton* administration if Diponegoro and Mangkubumi were found to be delinquent.

The day after the receipt of Van der Capellen's resolution, the toddler Crown Prince was appointed sultan (19 December 1822). In the intimacy of the sultan's private apartments (*Proboyekso*), the Resident's proclamation was read out and the oaths of the child sultan's guardians registered. All this occurred 'with the general approval of the Ratu and the most important courtiers in Yogya [...] Diponegoro also seemed outwardly pleased about it' (Carey 2008:509), according to De Salis, a judgement confirmed by General de Kock who reflected on the esteem in which the prince was held at this time:

> Earlier one heard nothing but good about him. He was on cordial terms with Nahuys and did not seem to have a bitter heart against the government. That this [happened] was entirely due to the disdain heaped on him by Resident Smissaert and [Assistant-Resident] Chevallier.

Describing Diponegoro and his fellow guardian as men 'who on all former occasions of misunderstanding [between the Yogya court and the European government] had stood quite neutral', Nahuys endorsed De Kock's view stating that the princely guardians were 'universally considered as good quiet persons without the least ambition' (Van der Kemp 1896a:415).

'[I] always followed the straight path without deviousness in [my] dealings with the European Residents' (Carey 2008:510) was Diponegoro's later reflection, and he added:

> I was on especially good terms with De Salis, with him affairs went well. But, as soon as the others came – he meant Smissaert [and Chevallier] – everything was plunged into disorder (Louw and De Klerck 1894–1909, I:743).

Despite the antagonism between Diponegoro and his stepmother, the prince appears to have discharged his guardianship duties diligently for nearly a year after his appointment. It was only after Smissaert's arrival in mid-February 1823, and that of his disastrous assistant, Chevallier, six months later that personal antagonisms made such cooperation impossible. By then the issue of the land rent abolition and the indemnification of the European planters had soured relations between the guardians and the Dutch authorities.

But the prince was clearly conflicted: recalling his own intense disappointment at being appointed a guardian of his young nephew, Diponegoro states that, while present at the coronation ceremony, he experienced such mortification at being sworn in as a guardian that he accidentally tore his state clothes (*kampuh*) and was unable to sign his name or affix his seal to the guardianship document (Babad Dipanegara II:114–15).

Returning to Tegalrejo, he even contemplated suicide so great was his distress, but was restrained by his wife, Raden Ayu Maduretno (Babad Dipanegara II:115–17). Afterwards, in his account, he returned his seal to Mangkubumi, refusing to take any further part in his guardianship duties and giving out that he would henceforth only be called by his religious name, 'Ngabdulkamit' (Babad Dipanegara II:117–18; p. 60).

None of this accords with the available historical evidence, even being contradicted in the prince's own *babad* where he appears once again to have renounced any rights he may have had to the Yogya throne (Babad Dipanegara II:114; Van der Kemp 1896a:315, 325–7, 350, 353–6; Kumar 1972:90–9).

Diponegoro's disappointment was understandable. Rouffaer, the ever insightful historian of the Principalities, would later put it succinctly: why place a child of barely three years on the Yogya throne just because he was born from an official consort when in neighbouring Surakarta just a year later the son of an unofficial wife was elevated as Susuhunan Pakubuwono VI (reigned 1823–1830)? And why fail to respect Diponegoro's own rights as the eldest son of a ruler, rights which he should have been allowed to assert with due honour as the child sultan's eldest uncle and guardian? The reason for the Java War lay there, Rouffaer asserted, in the crass mishandling of the prince by incompetent Dutch officials (Rouffaer 1905:600).

The December 1822 Eruption of Mount Merapi and the Joyoboyo Prophecies

Shortly after the fifth sultan's coronation, a significant event occurred in the natural world affecting all the inhabitants of Yogyakarta. This was the violent eruption of Mount Merapi, the volcano overlooking the city, on 28–30 December 1822.

In his *babad*, Diponegoro related how on Friday, 26 December he had been to the house of his younger brother, Suryobrongto, for his son's circumcision (*supitan*). After supervising the ceremony, he had remained overnight playing chess with his old friend, Raden Ayu Danukusumo (Chapter II). Returning in the early hours to Tegalrejo, he had slept right through the day and well into the following night (Babad Dipanegara II:118–19).

Then, early on Sunday morning, 28 December 1822 after a series of heavy earth tremors, Merapi began to erupt. By morning, streams of glowing lava could be seen pouring down the mountain with rains of ash and sand, and a massive column of smoke rising into the night sky, a scene vividly captured by Diponegoro (Babad Dipanegara II:119):

> XIX 98. Mount Merapi caught fire
> as though its peak reached to the heavens.
> Yogyakarta seemed filled with it.
> The sky became fire
> [and] the noise of it was terrifying;
> it thundered and roared,
> the fires radiating everywhere.
> In great commotion, together,
> everywhere people desperately sought refuge.

The prince went into the front courtyard of Tegalrejo with his wife, Raden Ayu Maduretno, and looked up into the sky. Seeing the burning mountain and the heaving earth, he described how he smiled inwardly to himself knowing that this was a sign of God's wrath (Babad Dipanegara II:119–20).

Dutch reports confirm that the eruption was just as violent as Diponegoro had made out. On the flanks of the mountain, people fled their homes, three Kedu villages being destroyed (*Residentie Kadoe* 1871:15; Carey 2008:513). It was the worst eruption in living memory (the last had been in 1772).

Besides the physical damage, the event almost certainly heightened millenarian expectations. Occupying a special place in local Javanese mythology, the mountain's protector spirit, Kyai Sapu Jagad ('Honourable Sir Sweeper of the World'), is regarded, along with Ratu Kidul (Chapter III), as one of the two guardian spirits of the sultanate (Ricklefs 1974b:233 note 21). Any volcanic activity on Mount Merapi, not least a violent eruption, would have been viewed by the local population as a portent of coming change.

Diponegoro's reflections on divine wrath were widely shared. In the Joyoboyo prophecies, the coming of the Javanese Just King (Ratu Adil) is described as being preceded by rains of ash, earthquakes, flashes of lightning, thunderbolts, heavy rain, gusts of wind, and eclipses of the sun and moon (Wiselius 1892:186). The 1821 cholera epidemic, soaring rice prices (Carey 2008:812) and the breakdown of society would have been easily connected in the popular mind with the time of madness or *jaman edan* before the coming of the Just King.

In this final age of disorder – the *kaliyuga* – before the establishment of the Ratu Adil, the world would be turned upside down: fathers would forget their children, children their parents, masters would neglect their servants and servants their masters, and the Javanese would become like 'winnowed rice' (*lir ngabah dinginteri*) (Carey 2008:517).

A Small, Fat and Shy Man: Yogyakarta's New Resident

Just as these events were taking place in Yogya and popular millenarian expectations rising, new Dutch officials were appointed whose impact would be equally catastrophic.

On 1 November 1822, Nahuys resigned as Yogya Resident to return to the Netherlands to argue his economic plans with the Dutch king (Nahuys van Burgst 1858:129; Louw and De Klerck 1894–1909, I:51 note 2, 52–3,

74). His post remained vacant until 3 January 1823 when Van der Capellen nominated the forty-five-year old Resident of Rembang, Jonkheer Anthonië Hendrik Smissaert (1777–1832) (De Haan 1935:648-9).

An official with no experience of the Javanese courts, Smissaert was appointed to enhance his pension before his retirement. The governor-general also hoped he would act more obediently than Nahuys over the land rent and survey the Yogya territories to facilitate territorial annexations (Van der Kemp 1896a: 377 note 1, 379-80; Carey 2008:520).

D'Abo, Nahuy's cuckolded assistant, was dismissed, Van der Capellen promising to find Smissaert a 'capable official' to act as his deputy (Van der Kemp 1896a:379). This man was soon identified in the governor-general's inner circle. The son of Van der Capellen's children's tutor, Pierre Frederic Henri Chevallier's (1795–1825) personal impact on the sultanate's fortunes would be almost as disastrous as that of his witless superior (Louw and De Klerck 1894–1909, I:306; Carey 2008:520).

As for Smissaert, what Van der Capellen expected and what the former Rembang Resident had in mind were hopelessly at odds. Whereas the latter dreamt of a quiet but lucrative appointment to feather his retirement nest, the governor-general thought of his imminent land rent abolition and planned territorial annexations. For such tasks, Smissaert was manifestly unsuited. A person of distinctly mediocre talents, his physical appearance was unprepossessing: a fat, balding, middle-aged man of stocky build, Smissaert was desperately shy (Van Hogendorp 1913:146; Carey 1981:255 note 87, 273 note 152) – a fatal combination for the Javanese who were shrewd judges of men and valued bearing and physiognomy (Ricklefs 1974a:27-31; Plate 17).

Smissaert began with the collection of statistics on Yogya's lands, population and administration, but encountered uncooperative royal officials whom he found reserved and dour: 'it makes one too despondent to ask them anything', he wrote, '[...] none of the *bupati* seem to know their areas well [and] the *patih* himself has visited many places near Yogya for the first time with me' (Carey 2008:521).

He also formed a poor opinion of the child sultan's two princely guardians, Mangkubumi and Diponegoro: 'good people but lazy who know very little about the administration for no registers have been kept since the

[British] sack of the court' (Chapter VI). For his part, the prince considered Smissaert 'a good man but weak' (Louw and De Klerck 1894–1909, V:743), but appreciated his wife, Clara Elisabet, the daughter of a former Surakarta Resident,[1] whose hospitality he frequently enjoyed:

> I used to go now and then to Bedoyo [and whenever] I went, Mrs Smissaert out of the goodness of her heart used to come to me offering a bottle of sweet [Constantia] wine which she knew I liked at the time (Knoerle, 'Journal', 35–6).

Smissaert's judgement of Danurejo was severe: '[too] much taken up with women on whom he spends all his money' (Carey 2008:522). Yet it was precisely this man on whom he relied for help and advice. Out of his depth, he gave the *patih* too many responsibilities, while the latter took advantage of the new Resident's weakness to further his own interests. That these included a love of the opium pipe, fine clothes and nubile girls hardly honed his administrative zeal (Louw and De Klerck 1894–1909, I:450).

Smissaert was also at odds with his two Dutch colleagues, the Residency Translator and Assistant-Resident (Louw and De Klerck 1894–1909, I:280; Van der Kemp 1896a:377). Yet he still delegated key duties to them (Kielstra 1885:410). How could it be otherwise? For Smissaert was to all intents and purposes an absentee Resident. Arriving in Yogya in February 1823, he found the Residency House in disrepair – it had suffered earthquake damage – and a complete renovation was required (Payen 1988:8 note 6). Work did not commence until November 1824 under the direction of the Belgian artist-architect AAJ Payen (1792–1853), but the rainy season intervened, work only resuming at the end of June 1825 (Carey 2008:523).

This situation proved fateful for Dutch interests. Between August 1823 and September 1824, Smissaert and his family stayed in the house of the former *Kapitan Cina*, Tan Jin Sing, before moving to temporary lodgings in the Dutch fort. During this time, they frequently went up to Bedoyo, Nahuys' former estate on the flanks of Mount Merapi, where Smissaert stayed 'for months on end' in De Kock's words, leaving Residency office

---

1   Bogislaus Frederich von Liebeherr (1756–1821; in office, 1806–8), see *De Wapenheraut*, 2 (1898):149.

affairs in the hands of a clerk (Carey 2008:523–4). The Resident's absence during the critical weekend before the war (20 July 1825) would stymy negotiations with Diponegoro (Carey 2008:600).

Smissaert was also politically naïve, his first major blunder was his 'agreement' in his words to represent the young sultan at the *Garebeg Puwasa* of 9 June 1823 by sitting on the vacant Yogya throne (*dampar*). Given the heartache this royal perch had caused during the second sultan's reign (p. 72, p. 125), Smissaert should have left well alone. He blamed the guardians who told him that by right one of their number should represent the child ruler. But, as this choice would give rise to jealousy and suspicion – neither Ratu Ageng nor Ratu Kencono would have wanted to see Diponegoro sit on the throne – Smissaert had been invited to 'represent' them (Carey 2008:525).

Whether this was just the pro-Dutch Ratu Ageng's idea is unclear. What is certain is that Smissaert's action pained Diponegoro deeply (Carey 2008:526). The presence of an ungainly Dutchman seated on the Yogya throne receiving the homage of the court *bupati* during the five *Garebeg* ceremonies of his thirty-one-month Residency was seen by the prince and his contemporaries as an affront to Javanese dignity (Louw and De Klerck 1894–1909, I:449–50, 453).

The Abolition of the Land Rent and its Consequences

Well before Smissaert's arrival in Yogya, the government had been contemplating a decision of great importance: the ending of all land rent contracts to non-Javanese in the Principalities.

Both Van der Capellen and his principal adviser, Inspector-General of Finances, Hendrik Jan van de Graaff (1782–1827; in office, 1820–26), had long been concerned by this issue. In their view, such land leases conflicted with government policy and the protection of the Javanese (Chapter VIII).

In late August and September 1819, they journeyed to south-central Java and discovered that Nahuys had arranged land leases in Yogya and Surakarta for his friends. Their extent was not yet so striking (p. 177), but both Nahuys and his Surakarta colleague, Van Prehn (in office, 1818–19), were instructed to make a report, an order they both ignored (Hageman 1856:21; Louw and De Klerck 1894–1909, I:49 note 7, 53–5; Van der Kemp 1901–2, I:193, 199).

In 1821, Van de Graaff made his second journey to the Principalities and 'saw the evil [of the land rent] grow to enormous proportions; British, German, French and Dutch planters had taken over extensive lands right in the middle of the princely territories' (Van der Kemp 1901–2, I:149; Rouffaer 1905:628). Castigating the 'highly illiberal nature' of the land rent, Van de Graaff compiled a report (March 1823) describing the Javanese peasant as 'deprived of his property rights [...] his status debased to that of a coolie' (Van der Kemp 1890:148–94).

Aware that the Dutch monarch, Willem I, was preparing to back the planters and raise the coffee price, Van der Capellen decided to act (Day 1972:234–5). On 6 May 1823, he promulgated his fateful decree ordering that all land rented by Europeans and Chinese in the Principalities should be returned to their original owners by 31 January 1824.

This decision caused mixed feelings at the courts. In Surakarta, Pakubuwono V (reigned, 1820–23), was 'greatly dismayed [...] pointing out that the rent contracts from the leased lands bore the authorisation of his royal seal and that, by breaking the contracts, his seal would be much degraded and it would be very difficult to come to terms with the lessees' (Van der Kemp 1897:26). In Yogyakarta, however, it was initially applauded: 'everyone was pleased about it', Mangkubumi observed, 'It was as though we had been showered with water. We had been hot, now we were refreshed' (Van Nes 1844:147; Carey 2008:532).

Such euphoria was soon dashed, however, by the financial realities of the planters' compensations (Van der Kemp 1897:32–5; Louw and De Klerck 1894–1909, I:75–6; Carey 2008:532). Yogyakarta was more heavily burdened than Surakarta. In the latter, the estates were to be reimbursed according to their annual produce, the payments being spread over many months. In Yogyakarta, indemnities had to be made directly from the sultan's treasury, the estates being immediately taken back by the ruler (Van der Kemp 1897:32–4; Van Hogendorp 1913:147).

Why this distinction was made is not clear. It may be that Europeans, who had leased lands from the Sunan's family, realised that they had no prospect of getting immediate compensation from their impecunious landlords. They thus petitioned the government to be allowed to hold on to their estates until they could be reimbursed through the sale of cash crops such as coffee (Van der Kemp 1901–2, I:197–8; Carey 2008:532–3).

In Yogyakarta, where the land rent was more bitterly resented (Van Hogendorp 1913:147), the decision was taken to adopt a system of immediate compensation (Van der Kemp 1901–2, I:198). Pressure from Ratu Ageng and Danurejo IV may have forced this policy, the Ratu feeling it better to obey the government's instructions in view of her grandson's tender age (Valck, 'Overzigt', 175; Van der Kemp 1901–2, I:197–8).

Whatever the case, it soon became clear that the Yogya treasury could not meet the payments. The indemnity for one royal estate alone, Rojowinangun (p. 77), was nearly half the total annual income received by the sultanate from the government (Van Enk 1990:27, 1999:210). The *kraton* faced bankruptcy: moveable goods and family heirlooms (*pusaka*) had to be sold to meet day-to-day expenses and Diponegoro forced to sanction a *f* 37,000 loan from the Yogya *Kapitan Cina* (Carey 2008:533).

Given the scale of the indemnities, many Yogya princes and court officials suspected fraud (Louw and De Klerck 1894–1909, I:59). Given their dependence on land rent payments for their daily sustenance and their use of their cash incomes to finance imported European luxuries (Chapter VIII), they were soon in debt. Given prevailing interest rates – as high as three percent monthly – many faced ruin (*Kronijk van Nederlandsch-Indië* 1845:37; Van der Kemp 1896b:569; Louw and De Klerck 1894–1909, I:600).

At the village level, lawlessness increased. Encouraged by estate workers itching to square accounts with their detested foreign masters, bandits and criminal elements began attacking European properties (Carey 2008:535–6) which would later become focal points for wartime guerilla activities – what the Dutch termed 'bandit' centres (Carey 2008:536) – while the original plantations were razed (Payen 1988:74; Carey 2008:536–7).

Diponegoro's Role as Guardian and the Land rent Indemnities

As a guardian of the young sultan with responsibilities for *kraton* finances, Diponegoro played a key role in the early indemnity negotiations. The first case involved Bedoyo, for which Nahuys requested a hefty *f* 50,000 (present-day USD1,250,000). Smissaert informed Diponegoro and Mangkubumi that this sum covered the house, the warehouses, coffee trees, pepper bushes and the six years' annual rent paid to the deceased fourth sultan. As Nahuys was departing for Europe, immediate compensation was demanded (Van der Kemp 1896a:341–3; Louw and De Klerck 1894–1909, I:55).

The guardians visited Bedoyo on 29 July. After inspecting the house and its environs, they concluded that Nahuys' price was far too high (Carey 2008:540). Instead, they proposed just 800 Spanish dollars (present-day USD20,000), Diponegoro observing (Van Nes 1844:150):

> 'How can Smissaert order us to take over all the land and coffee plantations from Nahuys? The house itself is perhaps an exception because that can be of use to the sultan, but what possible profit can we expect from the coffee and other plantations? The arrangement would amount to nothing more than debts for us [because] we cannot make the same profits from the plantations as the Europeans' (Van Nes 1844:148–50; Carey 2008:540).

Danurejo was then asked to provide details of Nahuys' labour costs (Carey 2008:463):

> 'Yes', answered Mangkubumi, leaning his head back on his chair, 'if you want to reckon everything together, but what possible value does it have for the young sultan?' Diponegoro stared straight ahead [...] and eventually spoke in a surly way: 'If my father hadn't died, he would still be alive. If Nahuys hadn't spent so much money, he would still have it in his pocket.' Afterwards he spoke not a word and just shook his head (Van Nes 1844:149).

But Smissaert held out for the original figure, observing:

> 'You should be content with that sum. If it was my own property, I would not relinquish it for such a small price' (Van Nes 1844:150).

When Mangkubumi proposed that the property be leased for two more years so that Nahuys could make the necessary profits from his cash crop sales, Smissaert refused, suggesting a compromise sum of 26,000 Spanish dollars (present-day USD800,000). When the guardians again demurred, Smissaert cited the former Resident's friendship with the fourth sultan, whereupon Diponegoro burst out:

> 'My God! Nahuys may well have been a friend of the sultan, but he never did him a favour. Now does he want his friendship paid for in money? *He* never put the sultan on the throne! Mr [John] Deans [Secretary of the Yogya Residency, 1811–1813] was a good friend of [my father, Hamengkubuwono III]; he even facilitated his accession [...] but he never received any repayment for his efforts other than that the sultan bought him a horse for 700 Spanish dollars' (Carey 2008:541).

The meeting broke up in acrimony, the guardians going straight to Ratu Ageng to stress the dire financial consequences if Smissaert's compromise was accepted. The Ratu, however, desperate to keep in with the Dutch, instructed Danurejo to accept the Resident's offer (Carey 2008:541). The guardians were summoned to the Residency with their seals to authorize a 26,000 Spanish dollar pledge, whose contents were withheld from them (Van Nes 1844:151 note 1; Louw and De Klerck 1894–1909, I:602–3).

On their return to the *kraton*, the guardians realised they had been duped. Soon afterwards, the Rojowinangun reimbursement came up, but Diponegoro refused further involvement (Van Nes 1844:151–3) and stopped coming to the *kraton*. Mangkubumi also withdrew. Affairs of state were decided in their absence by Smissaert and his Assistant-Resident, Chevallier, in consultation with Ratu Ageng, the *patih*, the sultan's bodyguard commander, Wironegoro, and Residency Interpreter, Johannes Godlieb Dietrée (1782–1826; in office, 1796–1825) (Carey 2008:542).

'As a guardian, I always had nothing to do', Diponegoro would later reflect, adding:

> 'We were informed about the payments into the sultan's treasury because I had to give my seal for that, but we never had any knowledge about the money paid out [...] When I was outside [at Tegalrejo post-February 1824], I heard there was no longer any money in the treasury, although everyone knew there must be still much left. [But] the *patih* [...] needed money, first with this, then with that excuse [and] things were always being built [...]. Everything of importance was decided without us' (Louw and De Klerck 1894–1909, V:743).

Diponegoro's Break with the Court

Although Smissaert refused to read the signs, by February 1824 the prince's break with the court was complete.

Late the previous year, two of his close friends – Mas Tumenggung Kertodirjo II (born 1779, in office 1812–1821), the *bupati* of Kerjo (Sukowati), and the Yogya *pengulu* (chief religious official) Kyai Rahmanudin (in office, 1812–23) (Carey 1992:442 note 210) – had both been dismissed from their offices on Danurejo and Ratu Ageng's instruction.

Rahmanudin was replaced by his religious assistant (*ketib*), an inexperienced cleric. The prince immediately wrote to Ratu Ageng pointing out that the appointment of the new *pengulu* was ultra vires because of his deficiencies in scriptural knowledge (Carey 2008:545). In the same letter, he also asked the Ratu to return the British contract which he had earlier lent to the fourth sultan and which had been burnt (p. 190). Ratu Ageng replied, declaring the contract 'mislaid', an admission which so incensed Diponegoro that he broke off further relations.

> 'As for the matters of the *Qur'ān* and *Hadīth* [Prophetic traditions]', the Ratu continued, 'I don't know. Therefore, he [Kyai Rahmanudin] has been replaced by [Ketib] Abuyamin because this has the permission of Resident Smissaert, for it is now the Dutch who exercise authority here [in Yogya]. Now stop constantly making trouble. If you want to change this you could hardly do it; if you could, you would scarcely dare; if you dared you could barely carry it out. In the end, it is best just to accept it' (Carey 2008:545).

Ratu Ageng's letter with its barely concealed impatience with her stepson – 'now stop constantly making trouble' – reveals the chasm which had now opened between Diponegoro and the court. On the one side, were Ratu Ageng and her clique, determined to keep in with the Dutch. On the other, Yogya's very own stormy petrel, Diponegoro, convinced that the dowager queen and her allies were ruining the sultanate.

The erstwhile *pengulu*, Kyai Rahmanudin, meanwhile, took up residence at Tegalrejo now fast becoming a refuge for all those who had fallen foul of the new regime. He would stay for nearly a year until late May 1825 when he departed on *haj*, thus enabling him to give Diponegoro advice during the crucial period when the prince was experiencing his pre-war visions (Carey 2008:546).

The Moral Rot: Danurejo IV's Rule and the Conduct of Senior Dutch Officials in Yogya

'Uncle, I left Yogyakarta because I was repudiated by the Europeans and by Danurejo [IV]' (Carey 2008:546). Diponegoro's words to Kyai Mojo when he arrived at Selarong in August 1825 were a classic Javanese understatement. Crass humiliation might be a better term.

The dismissal in quick succession of Kertodirjo and Rahmanudin was a sign of the times. 'Wilful and corrupt' was how one wartime Yogya Resident would later put it. The sale of offices, dismissal of officials and embezzlement of *kraton* revenues – the guardians' payments were made in devalued paper while the *patih* received the tollgate and market rents in good silver coin – were all of a piece (Valck, 'Overzigt', 166; Carey 2008:547).

His conduct with the *kraton* ladies was also 'improper'. According to Mangkubumi, he took 'women from the court to the villages to "debauch" them' (Van Nes 1844:154–5). Such behaviour was not unique: the Residency interpreter, Dietrée, a convert to Islam and ostensibly pious, also maintained clandestine relations with various court women, one of whom was Mangkubumi's sister (Van Nes 1844:154 note 1, Dwidjosoegondo and Adisoetrisno 1941:99; Van der Kemp 1896a:313; Houben 1994:124).

Informed by Ratu Ageng about these affairs, Diponegoro replied, 'I wish to know nothing about them, I leave them all to your ordering!' (Carey 2008:549). The prince's unwillingness to intervene, understandable given that Ratu and the child sultan's mother, Ratu Kencono, were charged with *kraton* domestic affairs, opened the way for yet more scandalous behaviour on the part of Dutch officials. With Danurejo and Dietrée's encouragement, Chevallier now joined the Bacchanal. Driven by an erotic energy bordering on the manic, his behavior was further debased by his racist contempt for the *inlander* (natives) (Carey 2008:549). A typical product of post-Revolutionary Europe and ignorant of Javanese culture – like so many who made their way to the post-1816 Indies – this unscrupulous and amoral man could perhaps be seen as a classic illustration of Ann Stoler's argument about colonial authority and sexual control (Stoler 2002:78; pp. 172–3). Only in this case, unbridled lust not control characterised Chevallier's dealings with the *Raden Ayu*.

Amongst Chevallier's conquests was a sister of Diponegoro and one his *selir* (unofficial wives) with whom he lived for several months (Van Hogendorp 1913:143; Van Praag 1947:266). When the discarded *selir* attempted to return to Tegalrejo, Diponegoro refused her entry, provoking Chevallier's personal intervention. In the ensuing confrontation, the prince pointed out that he did not maintain his wives for the pleasure of the Assistant-Resident at which Chevallier became angry declaring that 'he would do what he liked with native women' and had hit the prince over the head (Carey 2008:551).

This report, relayed by a Yogya contemporary, Pangeran Blitar (?1784–1828), is so outrageous that it would be hard to credit, but for separate evidence that Diponegoro's treatment by Dutch officials was quite unbelievably awful. A key witness here was Kyai Gajali, one of Kyai Mojo's inner circle, who related an incident at a Residency reception when both Smissaert and Chevallier had ridiculed Diponegoro, scoffing that he was a 'madman', 'priest' and 'wierd cove' (*grove vent*) (Carey 2008:551). Seeing the prince's rage, Wironegoro had quickly brought him home to Tegalrejo (Carey 2008:551).

The date of this reception is not clear, but it may have been just after the *Garebeg Puwasa* (21 May 1825), when we know from other sources that the contempt was mutual with Diponegoro insulting his Dutch hosts in Low Javanese (*ngoko*) and calling the Resident 'the bald-headed one' (*si buthak-ngelathak*) (Louw and De Klerck 1894–1909, I:47 note 1; Schoemaker 1893:414–16; Carey 1981:273 note 152; Payen 1988:49). But even if Diponegoro did trade insult for insult, the picture this gives of Dutch relations with the *kraton* elite on the eve of the Java War is deeply unedifying.

Diponegoro's anger against the pre-war Dutch officials and their inability to speak anything but market Malay (*pasar Maleisch*) was later summed

Waiting for the 'Just King' 213

up in his pithy observation that 'Chevallier and other Dutchmen had trotted into our *kraton* as though it was a stable and had shouted and called as though it had become a *pasar*' (Knoerle, 'Journal', 41; Van der Kemp 1896a:313–14), recalling Van Hogendorp's remarks about the Dutch turning the Yogya *kraton* into a 'brothel' and Diponegoro vowing to 'destroy it to the last stone' (p. 154).

Diponegoro's Pre-war Visions (1): Meeting with the Ratu Adil (19 May 1824)

Throughout this period, the prince had continued to lead an active spiritual life engaging in silent retreats in his cave of Secang at Selarong (Carey 1981:246 note 43), returning at least once to meditate on the south coast (Carey 2008:564). The fifteen months from May 1824 to July 1825, were a crucial time for him. During this period, a number of dreams and visions occurred which would clarify the role he would be called upon to play in the coming war (Carey 2008:564–83).

The first vision took place during the fasting month (*Puwasa*) of 1824 on 21 Ramelan AJ 1751 (19 May 1824), when the prince was at Selarong. The following is his account (Babad Dipanegara II:120–2):

> XX 7. [...]
>   Now we tell
>   how in the year Dal
>   in the month of Ramelan
>   on the date, the twenty-first,
>
>   8. the prince was in a cave
>   the name of which was Secang.
>   Every month of Ramelan
>   thus was the inclination
>   of the prince: to associate with the Almighty in prayer
>   inside the cave
>   without returning home [to Tegalrejo].
>   Such was his goal.

He was sitting on a *sela gilang* [a stone which radiated light called] Ambarmoyo.

9. These were his pleasures.
The interior of the cave he regarded as his residence;
[there was] a bathing pool in a trough
[and] next to it a pond [formed by] water oozing [from the rock]
designed like a well.
There was a fenced *widoro* tree.
Now the audience place
had a great doorway and steps made of *gebang* palm trunks.
The prince's eyes were half-closed as though asleep,
then there was

10. a man who appeared before him
accompanied by a wind.
He stood in front of him
[and] his clothes were like those of a *haji* [returned Mecca pilgrim].
The prince was amazed
and spoke softly:
'I do not know you,
where are you from?' The one asked made a gesture of respect
[and] said:
'I have no home.

11. I have come because I have been ordered to summon you Noble Sir.'
The prince said:
'What is the name of the one who sent you
and where is his dwelling?'
The man said calmly:
'Indeed, he has no home;
all the land of Java
is regarded as his home.
He it is who bears the title of Ratu Adil,
he is the one who sent me

12. in truth to call your honourable self.
At present he stands
at the top of a mountain,
which from here

lies in a southeasterly direction.
Mount Rasamuni is its name.
But, my lord,
you are not permitted to take any retainers.'
The prince set out immediately, accompanied
by the man,

13. as was the wish of God,
which the prince merely followed.
In a short time they arrived
at the foot of the mountain.
The one who had summoned him disappeared from sight.
Now we tell
of the Ratu Adil who
stood at the mountain top,
competing in brilliance with the lordly sun
which for long glowed but palely.

14. The prince had not the strength to know
or to look upon the countenance
of the Ratu Adil, whose brilliance
indeed eclipsed the sun.
Only his clothing was closely observed
by the prince in its entirety.
His turban was green
[and] he wore a white *jubah* (tabard),
white trousers [and] a red shawl.
He faced to the northwest

15. standing at the summit of the mountain
on top of a smooth stone.
There were no shadows
and the grass could not be seen.
It was as clean as if it had been swept.
The prince from below
looked upwards
facing to the southeast.
Then the Ratu Adil spoke in a friendly way:
'Ah, you Ngabdulkamid,

16. the reason I have summoned you
    is for you to set my army fighting.
    Let Java be conquered immediately!
    If anyone
    should ask you
    for your mandate, it is the *Qur'ān*.
    Order them to seek it [there]!'
    Ngabdulkamid said:
    'I beg leave [for] I am unable to fight
    and I cannot

17. bear to see death.
    And, moreover, earlier I
    in truth have already carried out
    tasks which were exceedingly [heavy]
    amongst my fellow men.'
    The Ratu Adil said:
    'That may not be.
    It is already the wish of the Almighty,
    [for] the fate of Java has been determined by Him;
    he who will perform this role is you

18. for there is no-one else.'
    Afterwards there was a shattering sound
    as though
    a dish had been struck by a stone.
    Then he disappeared.
    Thus it was impossible to
    describe this [further].
    So thus were
    the feelings of the prince
    as he stood upon the mountain;

19. his stance was no different [from that of the Ratu Adil]
    facing to the northwest then did he stand.
    Great was the prince's astonishment
    and his chest felt
    as if fireflies were flickering everywhere,
    and he was shaken to the core. Then
    Bocah-Becik

and Pututlowo
screamed, the sea flamed,
the noise thundered

20. and roared like Mount Merapi.[2]
The prince descended and departed from there
looking around him immediately.
But we say no more of this.
[...]

Such is Diponegoro's remarkable description of his encounter with Java's mythic Ratu Adil. It is without doubt the most crucial vision of his life and the one that had the most influence on his subsequent actions. Its mixture of Javanese-Islamic traditions and beliefs is striking.

Amongst the specifically 'Islamic' elements was the Ratu Adil's call to arms. Thus Diponegoro was summoned by someone wearing the clothes of a Mecca pilgrim (*haji*) and the vision occurred on the night of the twenty-first (*malem slikur*) of the fasting month, which is celebrated in Java, along with the twenty-seventh (*malem pitulikur*), as the night of the heavenly dispensation (*lailat al-ḳadar*) when the Holy *Qur'ān* was imparted to The Prophet Muhammad (Juynboll 1930:106–8; Carey 1974a:34–5). Significantly Diponegoro's second major vision – that of the eight *wali wudhar* (prophets who held two divine offices) – would also occur on a *ḳadar* night.

Then, when the Ratu Adil appeared, the Islamic aspects become even clearer. The Just King is described as having his face turned towards the northwest, the direction which forms the *qiblah*, the position in which Javanese Muslims today set their faces when they perform the five daily prayers (*ṣalat*) (Juynboll 1930:59, 67). This was not the traditional orientation of most mosques in south-central Java: the Great Mosque

---

2 There seems to be some confusion here because earlier in his vision he was instructed to take no followers with him for his Ratu Adil meeting. The description here may refer to Diponegoro's earlier experience during the eruption of Mount Merapi on the night of 27–28 December 1822 when he had been awakened by the screams of his servants, Babad Dipanegara II, 119; p. 201.

(Mesjid Ageng) in Yogya, for example, faced due west and it was only in the early twentieth century that the *qiblah* was changed under the influence of the Modernist Muslim *Muhammadiyah* (Way of Muhammad) (Noer 1973:74). One can only surmise that Diponegoro's vision of the Ratu Adil facing in the right direction may have reflected his stricter religious practise.

Finally, the order given by the Ratu Adil is described as having been 'authorised' by the *Qur'ān*, thus underscoring Diponegoro's mission as a Javanese Muslim to raise up the high state of the Islamic religion in Java and carry out his duties as royal regulator of religion (*ratu paneteg panatagama*) (Carey 1981:241 note 30).

Besides these Islamic aspects, there are others, not necessarily in conflict with the first, which reflect Javanese beliefs. Thus the clothes worn by the Ratu Adil identified him with Sultan Ngrum, the mythical ruler of Turkey who organized the peopling and civilising of Java, and from whose territories the Javanese Just King was thought to originate (p. 60). The Ratu Adil's supernatural appearance standing on a mountain top – Rasamuni – also suggests a Javanese mountain god such as Sunan Lawu or Merapi's guardian spirit, Kyai Sapu Jagad ('Sir Sweeper of the World'), Rasamuni itself having interesting links with Sultan Agung, the great seventeenth-century Mataram ruler of the whose spiritual and temporal achievements Diponegoro so much admired (Gandhajoewana 1940:215–17; De Graaf and Pigeaud 1974:142, 260 note 76; Chapter III).

The theme of Arjuna, discussed earlier in connection with Diponegoro's 1805 pilgrimage (Chapter III) and September 1814 marriage (pp. 157–8), can be discerned here too, his summons from his cave retreat recalling Arjuna's encounter in the *Arjuna Wiwāha* with the god Indra dressed in the clothes of a wandering mendicant. At the same time, his initial refusal to lead the Ratu Adil's army in battle on account of his revulsion at the sight of death reflects Arjuna's own unwillingness in the *Mahabhārata* to consent to Kresna before his fight with his kinsman Karna in the *Bratayuda*, the great 'brothers' war' (Carey 1974a:13; pp. 123–4).

Diponegoro's Pre-war Visions (2): The Prince as Ninth Wali Wudhar (16 May 1825)

There remains the question of just how Diponegoro saw himself fulfilling his Ratu Adil role. This is best answered by considering his remaining pre-war visions.

In June 1824, after the prince returned to Tegalrejo, he described how his stepmother, Ratu Ageng, had the same dream three times. In it, she heard a voice telling her (Babad Dipanegara II:122):

> XX 24. 'Ratu Ageng, Ratu Kencono
> must marry a *wali wudhar*
> whose residence is to the northwest.
> If this does not take place,
> it is certain that Java will be devastated
> and I will take your life.'
> [...]

Terrified, Ratu Ageng summoned Mangkubumi. Both concluded that the residence to the northwest must refer to Diponegoro's estate at Tegalrejo (Carey 2008:572).

Mangkubumi then sent his senior wife, Raden Ayu Sepuh, one of the few bold enough to crack jokes with the prince, to persuade him to marry the recently widowed Ratu Kencono (?1802–?1827) (Babad Dipanegara II:123; Carey 2008:572–3; p. 161). But her mission failed: Diponegoro ridiculed her attempts to make him take another wife, telling her there was no woman in Java equal to his beloved Maduretno (Babad Dipanegara II:123; Chapter VIII). Given Ratu Kencono's disturbed mental state, he probably needed no persuading that she was deeply unsuitable (Hageman 1856:40; Van den Broek 1873–77, 20:480; Carey 1992:504 note 509; pp. 157–8).

Later, when Diponegoro asked his uncle the meaning of *wali wudhar*, Mangkubumi suggested it meant an apostle of Islam who had failed as a *wali* (Babad Dipanegara II:124; Van der Kemp 1896a:418). Diponegoro felt ashamed. Returning to Tegalrejo, he shut himself away at his Selorejo retreat for three days where Rahmanudin sought him out (Babad Dipanegara II:124). On hearing Mangkubumi's explanation, the former *pengulu* replied that the meaning of *wali wudhar* was quite different. In his view, it meant a *wali* who had two offices, the Almighty having given him power to administer temporal justice and exercise spiritual authority (Babad Dipanegara II:124-5).

What Rahmanudin understood by the term *wali wudhar* were apparently prophets (*nabi*) rather than *wali* in the usual sense of 'friends of God' (saints) such as are found in Sufi teachings grudgingly accepted in orthodox Islam (Hitti 1974:438-9). Amongst the 124,000 prophets, there were only six, in his view, who merited the *wali wudhar* title, namely, Adam, Noah, Abraham, Moses, Jesus and Muhammad, the final one being the last of the great prophets (*nabi pungkasan*) (Babad Dipanegara II:24-5; Knoerle, 'Journal', 14-15).

To these six great prophets, Rahmanudin added two from Java – Sunan Giri and Sultan Agung – explaining that these had also held the double office characteristic of a *wali wudhar*. The former *pengulu* then suggested that Diponegoro might be the ninth but 'God alone knows the outcome' (*inggih Walahu Alam*) (Babad Dipanegara II:125). Whereupon the prince, remembering his recent Ratu Adil vision, reflected inwardly and then out loud (Babad Dipanegara II:125):

> XX 45. [...]
>   'So it is not possible
>   that I can escape it.'
>   But he did not speak this out,
>   [but] kept it hidden and smiling said calmly:
>   'Thanks be to God!
>
>   46. What do men in this life wait for
>   if, grandfather, they are not awaiting
>   some exceptionally important task?'
>   The Kyai Pengulu said:
>   'Indeed, lord, if they are strong enough [for it]
>   then even more excellent
>   is the true grace [they receive].'
>   The prince said:
>   'Grandfather, let us render up thanks to God,
>   may it prove successful.'

Waiting for the 'Just King'

The Rahmanudin's explanation holds the key to Diponegoro's pre-war visions and suggests a unique Javanese historical tradition. It also constituted a major heresy for, although the *Qur'ān* allows that some prophets are more important than others (Arberry 1955, I:308, XVII.57), the idea that there were major prophets after Muhammad is not permitted. Thus one of the most fundamental tenets of Islam had apparently escaped the former Yogya *pengulu*.

The following year, during the fasting month (18 April–18 May 1825), Diponegoro went again to Selarong. Wandering through the garden outside his cave, he sat down under a banyan tree. It was just after the midday prayer when he heard a remote but clear voice (Babad Dipanegara II:125):

> XX 48. [...]
>> 'Ah, you, Ngabdulkamid,
>
>> 49. you have been given the title
>> by the Almighty
>> of Sultan Ngabdulkamid
>> Erucokro Sayidin
>> Panatagama of Java
>> Kalifat Rasulullah.
>> Blessings be upon you!'
>> Following which the voice vanished.

The prince returned to Secang. It was the night of the 27 Ramelan AJ 1752 (AD 16 May 1825). After eating his post-fast meal, he fell asleep on top of his meditation stone (Babad Dipanegara II:125–6):

> XX 51. [...]
>> Now the prince
>> dreamt in his sleep in the cave [of Secang]
>> as though he were [back] at Selorejo.
>
>> 52. He was sitting on the *selo gilang* there
>> in the Pulo Waringin [banyan tree island].
>> Then suddenly
>> eight men arrived,
>> the ends of their head-dress all hung down.

The one in front bore a letter
which he carried in both hands.
The prince stared [at them]
[and] came forward intending to greet them,
looking fearful of the eight, whose radiance
was like the full moon.

53. The prince stood before them in respectful greeting,
[but] the arrivals paid no heed to [him]
and went straight to the pond.
The prince followed them.
Then all [eight] stood at the edge,
Five to the east
and three to the south.
The prince joined those
to the south, making four
who all faced north.

54. Those to the east faced westwards:
the one who bore the letter was in front,
the others flanking him on both sides.
Then the letter was read out
[and] its meaning was the same
as the voice at [the garden of] Modang.
It read: 'His Highness
Sultan
Ngabdulkamid Erucokro Sayidin
Panatagama

55. Kalifat Rasulullah
of the land of Java.'
Then together [the others] responded:
'*alaihi 's-salām* [peace be upon him]!'
The one who had read [the letter] corrected them sharply with a
calm speech:
'That is the wrong response!'
Those he had reprimanded said:
'How so, Panembahan?'
The reply of the reprimanding one was delivered quietly:
'This is a matter which exists:

56. young friends, the response *'alaihi 's-salām*
is for what shall be. But for what already exists
only the *takbīr* is the response.'
Then all
eight recited the *takbīr* together,
with the prince as the ninth
who joined in [the recital of] the *takbīr*[3]
After this, the letter
was dropped into the pond, sank into the water
and was seen no more.

57. The eight men [then] vanished from view.
From where they had been standing
[they had evaporated] like smoke
The prince
was left standing alone.
[...]

This dream brought to a close a period of testing and preparation which had begun when Diponegoro had withdrawn from the world as a young man to engage in ascetiscism (*tirakat*) (Carey 1981:236–7 note 14; Chapters II and III). He had been tested and proven: in the Ratu Adil's words, his fate had been fixed by the Almighty, reflecting what Soemarsaid Moertono (1976:16) has characterized as the quintessentially Javanese acceptance that everything in eternity has been fixed by the Almighty. It was in this context that the prince accepted the former *pengulu*'s explanation of the term *wali wudhar*, his dream of the eight prophets confirming his new-found favour.

Like the earlier vision of the Ratu Adil, the northern and westerly directions in which the *wali wudhar* face once again make up the *qiblah* of Java to Mecca. Even the *wali*'s turbans seemed to be associated with famous apostles of Islam in Java such as Sunan Kalijogo (p. 51) and great Javanese-Islamic rulers like Sultan Agung (De Graaf 1958:138; Louw and De Klerck 1894–1909, VI:247–52; Houben 1994:241–2). Particularly interesting too is the gesture of casting the letter into the pond seemingly

---

3   The *takbīr* is the glorification of God by the repetitive recital of the phrase *Allahu Akbar* ('Allah is Great!'), Gericke and Roorda 1901, I:644.

confirming Diponegoro's new position by contact between the living water and the eternal underworld.

Finally, the titles which Diponegoro received prefigured those he would later assume on 1 Sura AJ 1753 (15 August 1825) after the outbreak of the Java War (Carey 1981:261 note 108, 287 note 218), namely 'Sultan Ngabdulkamid, the Just King (*Erucokro*), Lord of the Faith (*Sayidin*), Regulator of Religion (*Panatagama*) and Caliph of The Prophet of Allah (*Kalifat Rasulullah*)' (Carey 2008:581). The assumption of such titles was part of his attempt to create a new *kraton* (Carey 1981:241 note 29), an important aspect of every major Javanese rebellion (Chapter V). Traditional hopes for status and office were essential for Diponegoro and his elite supporters, concerned as they were with rank and relationships, especially good marriages for their children (Van den Broek 1873–77, 22:69; Knoerle, 'Journal', 34; Louw and De Klerck 1894–1909, III:370, 488, 493). Such priorities dismayed his *santri* supporters and would later lead to a fatal split between the prince and Kyai Mojo (pp. 249–56).

The prince's use of the Yogya sultan's titles did not mean, however, that he wished to succeed them. He had made this clear when he refused the title of Crown Prince in place of his younger brother during the British interregnum (pp. 128–9), remarking that 'he had never aimed at the title of Sultan of Yogyakarta [for] there was already a lawful ruler on hand for this throne and that it had never occurred to him to act against the institutions of The Prophet and expel the young sultan' (Knoerle, 'Journal', 18; Van der Kemp 1896a:304).

Diponegoro's Understanding of his Role as Ratu Adil and his Attitude towards the Dutch

Diponegoro's Ratu Adil aspirations can best be understood in his statement that 'he had always felt the calling to become a "supreme priest" of Java' (Knoerle, 'Journal', 18), a position which the English land renter William Stavers (1789–1862) would later translate as *raja Islam* ('ruler of Islam')

(Louw and De Klerck 1894–1909, III:249). What this entailed has been discussed in the context of Raffles' legal reforms, and the prince's claim to adjudicate in cases between Europeans and Javanese on the basis of Javanese-Islamic law (p. 153).

The prince's assumption of the titles of Sultan Ngabdulkamid Erucokro and his reference to himself as *sang murtining ngajurit* ('the embodiment of the fight') (Babad Dipanegara II:149; Carey 2008:585) indicate that he saw himself fulfilling the role of the Javanese messianic Ratu Adil. His Erucokro epithet also recalled the Hindu god Wisnu in his seventh incarnation as world ruler bearing the *cakra* (solar discus) weapon (Cohen Stuart 1872:285–8; Pigeaud 1947:270–3; Carey 1974a:32 note 106), the prince's key wartime task being the waging of a purging campaign to establish a new moral order.

The prince's lyrical description of Selarong after he had set up his first wartime headquarters there in late July 1825 echoed the passage in the Joyoboyo prophecies regarding the Ratu Adil's reign of justice and plenty (Carey 1974a:28 note 95, 1981:241 note 29; Babad Dipanegara II:145):

> XXII 36. So [Selarong] had become a capital.
> Yogyakarta had moved there.
> Its market was very large.
> Everything to be bought was cheap and readily available there;
> [quickly] sold were the goods of the traders,
> thus all were greatly pleased.
> They were no lies or deceit.

For this benign priest-king role Diponegoro's meditative and charismatic character was supremely well suited. Often withdrawing from day-to-day leadership tasks to meditate by himself, usually at the junction of rivers, or close to waterfalls and ponds, once sites of Hindu antiquity, he sent his gold state umbrella (*payung*) out to villages to raise support while he himself resided in places far removed from the conflict (Louw and De Klerck 1894–1909, II:244; Carey 1974a:26; p. 15).

Besides this ascetic side, the awe-inspiring nature of the Erucokro ruler was projected by Diponegoro's widely believed powers of invulnerability (p. 39) and his mastery of the science of physiognomy (*ngelmu firasat*) (p. 32, p. 250).

Diponegoro himself did not think the Dutch should be expelled from Java completely, although Kyai Mojo and other *ulama* undoubtedly held this view. Thus, during the disastrous Battle of Gawok on 15 October 1826, when Diponegoro suffered his first major defeat just to the west of Surakarta, the prince remarked that 'it was as though something within me told me to spare the Europeans because we could not be in Java without them' (Louw and De Klerck 1894–1909, V:745).

If the Dutch had allowed the prince a free hand in south-central Java with authority over Javanese-Islamic law courts and Islamic religious practice, there seems no reason to doubt his confidant, Basah Kerto Pengalasan's, assertion that all Diponegoro asked of the Dutch was that (Carey 1974b:288):

> He would not be appointed nor take orders from the government, except that they [Diponegoro and the European government] would be as good friends, neighbours and brothers, just like children who have not been on speaking terms and who now talk with one another again.

Such co-existence would have been short-lived, however, given that Diponegoro, at Sentot's urging, was contemplating conquests beyond Java and the establishment a latter-day Majapahit empire[4] (Knoerle, 'Journal', 39–40; Gomperts, Haag and Carey 2010:13). Indeed, the times were long past when the European government could have contemplated a return to a pre-Daendels era when the European presence in Java had been largely confined to the 'foreign kingdom' of west Java and contacts with the south-central Javanese *kraton* maintained as though through embassies between sovereign states.

The prince's awareness of historical precedents and Qur'ānic example suggests that he would have sought to exercise a form of theocratic authority akin to the sixteenth and seventeenth-century priest-kings of Giri (De Graaf and Pigeaud 1974:137–55; Ricklefs 1993:76). But, as with Giri, Diponegoro

---

4 Majapahit (1293–circa 1510s) was the great east Javanese empire which had reached its apogee in the fourteenth century when its influence had been felt throughout the present-day Indonesian archipelago and beyond.

presented the Dutch with a formidable challenge: a Javanese leader of great personal charisma and an ability to bind disparate social elements to his cause. If successful, he would have spelt the downfall not only of the Dutch colonial order but also the authority of their *kraton* allies.

Preparations for Rebellion

Even before Diponegoro's last vision on 16 May 1825, he had begun discussions with Yogya *pangeran* and officials disturbed by recent events. The first meeting seems to have taken place at Tegalrejo on 29 October 1824, but not all attending were in favour of rebellion (Jayadiningrat 1855–7:16; Kielstra 1885:412; Carey 1981:240 note 28). Rumours about unpleasant incidents between Diponegoro and the Dutch made many fear for the prince's life (Jayadiningrat 1855–7:16).

According to Diponegoro's son, Raden Mas Alip, serious wartime preparations had begun at least two months before his father's planned rebellion with the prince remitting the May *Puwasa* taxes to allow his tenants to purchase arms and food (Carey 1981:262 note 112, 290 note 229). This process escaped the notice of the Dutch officials in Yogya whose profound ignorance can be seen in Smissaert's bemused letter to Van der Capellen written just a day before the prince's flight (20 July 1825):

> Prince Diponegoro appears for some time now to have given himself over to fanaticism [...]. He is known as someone who from time to time is tormented by madness [...] in which state he had previously, more than once, embarked upon stupid steps and forced religious duties [...]. All the princes and *bupati* [...] strongly disapprove of his actions and ascribe them to zealotry (Van der Kemp 1896a:382; Carey 2008:594).

On 19 May 1825, at the end of the fasting month, Diponegoro described how he had returned to Tegalrejo to be greeted by the news that the Dutch were seeking ways to arrest him. The former *pengulu* warned him that large numbers of Dutch troops had recently arrived in Semarang (Babad

Dipanegara II:126). False intelligence this, for the soldiers were being assembled not to attack the prince but to reinforce General Joseph van Geen's Bone expedition (1824–5) whose fortuitous return in early August would turn the tide of battle on the north coast (Valck, 'Nota', 22-03-1830; Louw and De Klerck 1894, I:367–9; Van der Kemp 1901–2, II:226 note 5). Indeed, it was not until the very eve of the Dutch attack on Tegalrejo on 20 July that Diponegoro's arrest was even suggested (Carey 1981:256–7 note 92).

It is clear, however, that Diponegoro was already mentally preparing himself for war, telling Rahmanudin that it was his duty to ready himself for a martyr's (*shahid*) death in battle (Babad Dipanegara II:127):

> XX 64. 'Grandfather, I will take pleasure in war:
>   death [in battle] is good, so they say.'
>   [...]

When the former *pengulu* stated that he himself was too old to participate, but would make the *haj* (pilgrimage) to Mecca instead, Diponegoro told him to spend the rest of his days in Arabia, urging his friend to seek the intercessions of The Prophet as he bowed before the holy *Ka'bah* or Sacred House (*Baytu al-Harām*) in Mecca. He also asked him to solicit the prayers of the heads (*imām*) of the four *fiqh* law schools for the success of his efforts (Babad Dipanegara II:127–8).

The Outbreak of the Java War

The *pengulu's* departure to take ship in Semarang occurred shortly after Smissaert took the decision to repair the side roads around Yogya. One of these skirted the eastern fence of Tegalrejo (Carey 1981:245–6 note 42). On 17 June 1825, this was staked out by the *patih's* men. The blocking off of the road caused considerable inconvenience for Diponegoro and his tenants (Carey 1981:251 note 64).

Danurejo had not informed the prince of Smissaert's order, the planting of the marker stakes being the first indication of the proposed road improvement (Carey 1981:246 note 43). A deliberate slight, it sparked skirmishes between Diponegoro's followers and the *patih*'s men which soon involved local villagers (Carey 1981:247 note 47). By early July, when Diponegoro's tenants from his more distant lands began to arrive to defend him, the skirmishes took on a more serious character. Plans for a mid-August uprising were now brought forward, the dispute ending any lingering doubts about the necessity for military action (Van der Kemp 1896a:389–90; Carey 1981:247 note 47, 262–3 note 112).

Ordering that the stakes marking the road be replaced by pikes as a sign that he considered the road work a *casus belli*, Diponegoro prepared to send his wives, children and older retainers to Selarong with money to pay his troops (Carey 1981:277 note 170; Payen 1988:50, 93 note 36). He also began wearing his favourite *kris*, Kyai Abijoyo, which he seldom carried (Van Nes 1844:156, 158; Carey 1981:277 note 169).

These developments were reported to the Yogya authorities, but no action could be taken because of the *patih*'s absence overseeing road construction work near Klaten (Carey 1981:57, 268 note 130), and Smissaert's inevitable recess at Bedoyo (Hageman 1856:65; Van der Kemp 1896a:383–4, 389–90; Carey 1981:256 note 90). So a crucial weekend (15–17 July) was lost and when the harassed Dutch and Javanese officials came together again in Yogya on Monday, 18 July, the time for negotiations had passed.

Even if such talks had started, however, Diponegoro's demand that Danurejo be dismissed was unacceptable to Smissaert, whose handling of the situation, in particular his insistence that the prince should come in person to Yogya, left him with no room to manoeuvre. The prince was now a prisoner of his own supporters, who included his uncle, Mangkubumi. They refused to allow him to go to Yogya to meet the Resident (Van der Kemp 1896a:394; Carey 1981:272 note 146).

As for Smissaert himself, he clearly feared for his life (Carey 2008:601):

> I felt I must stay in Yogya to confer with the military commander and to keep the peace. [...] If I had gone [to Tegalrejo] and been killed, my death would have put the whole European community in Yogyakarta in danger [...] [It] would have worked the Javanese up into a murderous frenzy.

Thus the age-old European bogey of the Javanese in an *amok* state was cited as the problem. After describing Diponegoro as a fanatic, Smissaert was now suggesting that he was about to run amok as well, although he acknowledged his political importance (Carey 2008:601):

> This was not a question of [arresting] a common Javanese or even a robber leader, but a man of extreme importance in the Yogyakarta kingdom – a prince who had been appointed as a guardian of the young sultan by the Netherlands Indies government itself.

Given this situation, the missions dispatched by the Resident, Danurejo and others between 18 and 20 July failed. The last of these, led by two senior court *bupati*, departed for Tegalrejo in the early afternoon of Wednesday 20 July. Backed by a mixed Javanese-Dutch force (Carey 1981:271 note 145, 278 note 186, 280 note 185), it aimed to take Diponegoro and Mangkubumi prisoner thus nipping any incipient rebellion in the bud. But the prince had been alerted by the Yogya blacksmiths who had shoed the expedition's cavalry horses (Carey 1981:257 note 92, 274 note 156).

The arrival of this force precipitated an open conflict with Diponegoro's supporters. After a hard-fought skirmish, the prince's residence fell to the Dutch-led force and was immediately put to the torch. The princes, however, made good their escape with the majority of their followers through the western gate. Making their way across small paths over the unseasonally inundated ricefields, they swiftly outrode their pursuers (Carey 1981:280 note 186, 188).

Payen, who received a full report of the failed military operation from his friend, Lieutenant Jean Nicolaas de Thierry (1783–1825), commander of the hussar detachment, gave a vivid description of the princes' flight:

> With the cavalry on one side and the infantry on the other, the [Dutch-led force] went round the village which enclosed the estate. They could see the rebels withdrawing slowly across the ricefields. Pangeran Diponegoro was not very far away mounted on a beautiful black horse [Kyai Gitayu] with a superb harness. He was clad entirely in white in the Arab style. The end of his turban flapped in the wind as he made his horse prance. The reins attached to his belt, he [seemed] to be dancing (*tandak*) in the midst of his lance-bearing bodyguard (Payen 1988:51).

The following day, Thursday 21 July 1825, Diponegoro and his uncle arrived at Selarong and there near the cave where the prince had so often meditated they set up the standard of revolt. The Java War had begun (Büchler 1888, II:25–9; Van der Kemp 1896a:400; Carey 1981:282 note 197).

Conclusion

Who can fail to be moved by the poignancy of this moment? Diponegoro dressed for the holy war fleeing across the ricefields while the flames engulfed his beloved Tegalrejo. As he unfurled his battle standard as Java's long awaited Ratu Adil, he could have had no illusions what this meant. A Rubicon had been crossed. Ahead lay nearly five years of war which would cost the lives of perhaps as many as 200,000 Javanese and disrupt the existence of two million more. During this time the last remnants of Java's old order would be consumed. Just over a century would have to pass before Java would again know freedom as part of an independent Indonesia.

The vicissitudes of war and the loneliness of exile lay before him. During this time, he would revise his views about his destiny. Instead of seeing himself as the promised Ratu Adil who would drive the Dutch from Java, by the war's end he indicated that he would be content with the restoration of a pre-Daendelian status quo in which the Dutch would remain on the island as traders and settlers along the north coast. By this time his break with the *santri* communities was complete and his hopes of gaining recognition from the Dutch as a regulator of religion were fast receding. Just how Diponegoro experienced the bitterness of these years will be the subject of the final three chapters.

Bibliography

Babad Dipanegara (2010). *Babad Dipanegara*, 4 vols, ed. Nindya Noegraha. Jakarta: Perpustakaan Nasional Republik Indonesia.

Broek, W. Palmer van den (1873–77) (ed. and trans.). 'Geschiedenis van het Vorstenhuis Madoera uit het Javaansch Vertaald', *Tijdschrift voor Indische Taal-, Land- en Volkenkunde (TBG)* 20:241–301, 471–563, 22:1–89, 280–310, 24:1–169.

Büchler, A.P. (1888). 'Soerakarta vóór 63 Jaren', *Tijdschrift van Nederlandsch-Indië*, 17–1:401–31, 17–2:1–38.

Carey, Peter (1974a). *The Cultural Ecology of Early Nineteenth Century Java; Pangeran Dipanagara, A Case Study*. Singapore: Institute of Southeast Asian Studies. [Occasional Paper 24.]

Carey, Peter (1974b). 'Javanese Histories of Dipanagara; The Buku Kĕdhuŋ Kĕbo, its Authorship and Historical Importance', *Bijdragen tot de Taal-, Land- en Volkenkunde* 130:259–88.

Carey, Peter (1981). *Babad Dipanagara; An Account of the Outbreak of the Java War (1825–30); The Surakarta Court Version of the Babad Dipanagara with Translations into English and Indonesian Malay*. Kuala Lumpur: Art Printers.

Carey, Peter (1992). *The British in Java, 1811–1816; A Javanese Account*. Oxford: Oxford University Press.

Carey, Peter (2008). *The Power of Prophecy; Prince Dipanagara and the End of an Old Order in Java, 1785–1855*. Leiden: KITLV Press.

Cohen Stuart, A.B. (1872). 'Eroe Tjakra', *Bijdragen tot de Taal-, Land- en Volkenkunde* 19:285–8.

Day, C. (1972). *The Policy and Administration of the Dutch in Java*. Kuala Lumpur: Oxford University Press.

Dwidjosoegondo, R.W. and R.S. Adisoetrisno (1941). *Serat Dharah inggih 'seseboetan Radèn' mawi ngèwrat Sujarahipun para Nata Jawi sawatawis sarta para Wali*. Kediri: Tan Khoen Swie.

Enk, E.M.C. van (1990). *Pionieren in de Cultures. Harvey Thomson (1790–1837) op Java temidden van andere Buitenlandse Ondernemers*. Zutphen: Van Enk.

Enk, E.M.C. van (1999). *Britse Kooplieden en de Cultures op Java; Harvey Thomson (1790–1837) en zijn Financiers*. Leiden: Grafaria.

Gandhajoewana, R.M. (1940). 'Overblijfselen van Kerta en Plèrèd', *Djåwå* 20–3:217.

Gericke, J.F.C. and Roorda, T. (1901). *Javaansch-Nederlandsch Handwoordenboek*. Amsterdam: Muller, Leiden: Brill. Two vols.

Gomperts, Amrit, Arnoud Haag and Peter Carey (2010), 'Rediscovering the Royal Capital of Majapahit', *IIAS Newsletter* No.53 Spring (Leiden), pp. 12–13.

Graaf, H.J. de (1958). *De Regering van Sultan Agung, Vorst van Mataram, 1613–1645, en die van zijn Voorganger Panembahan Séda-ing-Krapyak, 1601–1613*. The Hague: Nijhoff. [KITLV, Verhandelingen 23].

Graaf, H.J. de and Th.G.Th. Pigeaud (1974). *De Eerste Moslimse Vorstendommen op Java; Studiën over de Staatkundige Geschiedenis van de 15de en 16de Eeuw*. The Hague: Nijhoff. [KITLV, Verhandelingen 69].

Haan, F. de (1935). 'Personalia der Periode van het Engelsch Bestuur over Java, 1811–1816', *Bijdragen tot de Taal-, Land- en Volkenkunde* 92:477–681.

Hageman, J.Jcz. (1856). *Geschiedenis van den Oorlog op Java van 1825 tot 1830*. Batavia: Lange.

Hitti, Philip K. (1974). *History of the Arabs; From the Earliest Times to the Present*. London: Macmillan.

Hogendorp, H. Graaf van (1913). *Willem van Hogendorp in Nederlandsch-Indië 1825–1830*. The Hague: Nijhoff.

Houben, Vincent (1994). *Kraton and Kumpeni; Surakarta and Yogyakarta 1830–1870*. Leiden: KITLV Press. [Verhandelingen 164.]

Jayadiningrat (1855–1857). 'Schetsen over den Oorlog van Java, 1825–30, Opgesteld door den Bopati [sic] van Karang Anjar Raden Adipatti Aria Djaja Diningrat, 1855–1857'. Ed. J. Hageman Jcz. Perpustakaan Nasional (Jakarta) MS ML 97.

Juynboll, Th.W. (1930). *Handleiding tot de Kennis van de Mohammedaansche Wet volgens de Leer der Sjâfi'itische School*. Leiden: Brill.

Kemp, P.H. van der (1890). 'Rapport van den Waarnemend Hoofdinspecteur van Financiën H.J. van de Graaff, dd. Batavia 23 Maart 1822 aan Gouverneur-Generaal Van der Capellen, over de Landverhuringen aan Europeanen in de Vorstenlanden', *Tijdschrift voor Nijverheid en Landbouw in Nederlandsch-Indië* 41:143–95.

Kemp, P.H. van der (1896a). 'Dipanegara, Eene Geschiedkundige Hamlettype', *Bijdragen tot de Taal-, Land- en Volkenkunde* 46:281–433.

Kemp. P.H. van der (1897). 'De Economische Oorzaken van den Java-Oorlog van 1825–1830', *Bijdragen tot de Taal-, Land- en Volkenkunde* 47:1–48.

Kemp, P.H. van der (1901–2), *Brieven van en aan Mr H.J. van de Graaff (1816–26); Een Bijdrage tot de Kennis der Oost-Indische Bestuurstoestanden onder de Regeering van G.A.G.Ph. Baron van der Capellen*. Batavia: Albrecht, The Hague: Nijhoff. Three vols. [Verhandelingen van het Bataviaasch Genootschap van Kunsten en Wetenschappen 52.]

Kielstra, E.B. (1885). 'Een en ander omtrent Dipo Negoro', *De Gids* 2:407–35.

Knoerle 'Journal' (1830). 'Aanteekeningen Gehouden door den 2e Luit Knoerle betreffende de Dagelyksche Verkeering van dien Officier met den Prins van Djocjakarta, Diepo Negoro, gedurende eene Reis van Batavia naar Menado, het Exil van den genoemden Prins', Manado, 20-6-1830. MS 391 of the Johannes van den Bosch private collection in the Nationaal Archief, The Hague.

Kronijk van Nederlandsch-Indië (1845). 'Kronijk van Nederlandsch-Indië, loopende vanaf het jaar 1816; De jaren 1824 en 1825', *Tijdschrift voor Nederlandsch-Indië* 7-3:43-109.

Kumar, Ann (1972). 'Dipanegara (?1787-1855)', *Indonesia* (April) 13:69-118.

Lettres de Java (1829). *Lettres de Java ou Journal d'un Voyage en cette Île, en 1822*. Paris: n.p. [J. van Schoor pseudonymous author.]

Louw, P.J.F. and E.S. de Klerck (1894-1909). *De Java-Oorlog van 1825-1830*. The Hague: Nijhoff, Batavia: Landsdrukkerij. Six vols.

Nahuys van Burgst, H.G. (1835-6). *Verzameling van Officiële Rapporten betreffende den Oorlog op Java in de jaren 1825-1830, voorafgegaan door eenige aanmerkingen en medeelingen omtrent denzelven, benevens eene memorie over de verhuring of uitgifte van landeryen aan Europeanen*. Deventer: Ballot. Four vols.

Nahuys van Burgst, H.G. (1858). *Herinneringen uit het Openbare en Bijzondere Leven (1799-1858) van Mr H.G. Baron Nahuys van Burgst*. 's-Hertogenbosch: Muller.

Nes, J.F. Walraven van (1844). 'Verhandelingen over de Waarschijnlijke Oorzaken, die Aanleiding tot de Onlusten van 1825 en de volgende jaren in de Vorstenlanden gegeven hebben', *Tijdschrift voor Nederlandsche Indië* 6:112-71.

Noer, Deliar (1973). *The Modernist Muslim Movement in Indonesia, 1900-1942*. Singapore: Oxford University Press.

Payen, A.A.J. (1988). *Voyage à Djocja-Karta en 1825; The Outbreak of the Java War (1825-30) as Seen by a Painter*. Edited by Peter Carey. Paris: Association Archipel.

Pigeaud, Th.G.Th. (1947). 'Erucakra-Vairocana', in: *India Antiqua; A Volume of Oriental Studies presented by his Friends and Pupils to Jean Philippe Vogel C.I.E. on the Occasion of the Fiftieth Anniversary of his Doctorate*, pp. 270-3. Leiden: Brill.

Praag, S. van (1947). *Onrust op Java; De Jeugd van Dipanĕgara; Een Historisch-Literaire Studie*. Amsterdam: Nederlandsche Keurboekerij.

Residentie Kadoe (1871). *De Residentie Kadoe naar de Uitkomsten der Statistieke Opname en andere Officiele Bescheiden bewerkte door de Afdeling Statistieken ter Algemeene Secretarie*. Batavia: Landsdrukkerij.

Ricklefs, M.C. (1974a). *Jogjakarta under Sultan Mangkubumi, 1749-1792; A History of the Division of Java*. Oxford: Oxford University Press.

Ricklefs, M.C. (1974b). 'Dipanagara's Early Inspirational Experience', *Bijdragen tot de Taal-, Land- en Volkenkunde* 130:227-58.

Ricklefs, M.C. (1993). *A History of Modern Indonesia since c. 1300*. Basingstoke: Macmillan.

Rouffaer, G.P. (1905). 'Vorstenlanden', *Encylopaedie van Nederlandsch-Indië* 4:587-653.

Schoemaker, J.P. (1893). 'De Onderwerping en Gevangenneming van Dipo Negoro Hoofd der Opstandelingen in den Java Oorlog 1825-1830', *Indisch Militair Tijdschrift* 1-6:407-91.

Stoler, A.L. (2002). *Carnal Knowledge and Imperial Power; Race and the Intimate in Colonial Rule*. Berkeley: University of California Press.

Valck, 'Overzigt': F.G. Valck, 'Overzigt der Voornaamste Gebeurtenissen in het Djokjokartasche Rijk sedert dezelfs Stichting in den Jare 1755 tot aan het Einde van den door de Opstand van den Pangeran Ario Dhipo-Negoro Verwekten Oorlog in den Jaren 1825 tot en met 1830', 1–8–1833. Bundel Djokjo Brieven 9A (and 19[1]) of Arsip Nasional Republik Indonesia (ANRI), Jakarta.

Wiselius, J.A.B. (1892). 'Djåjå Båjå, Zijn Leven en Profetieën', *Bijdragen tot de Taal-, Land- en Volkenkunde* 42:172–217.

Plate 1. Sketch of Diponegoro as a young man, circa 1807.

Plate 2. Diponegoro giving instructions to two followers, Kyai Joyomustopo and Kyai Mopid, for their Nusa Kambangan pilgrimage.

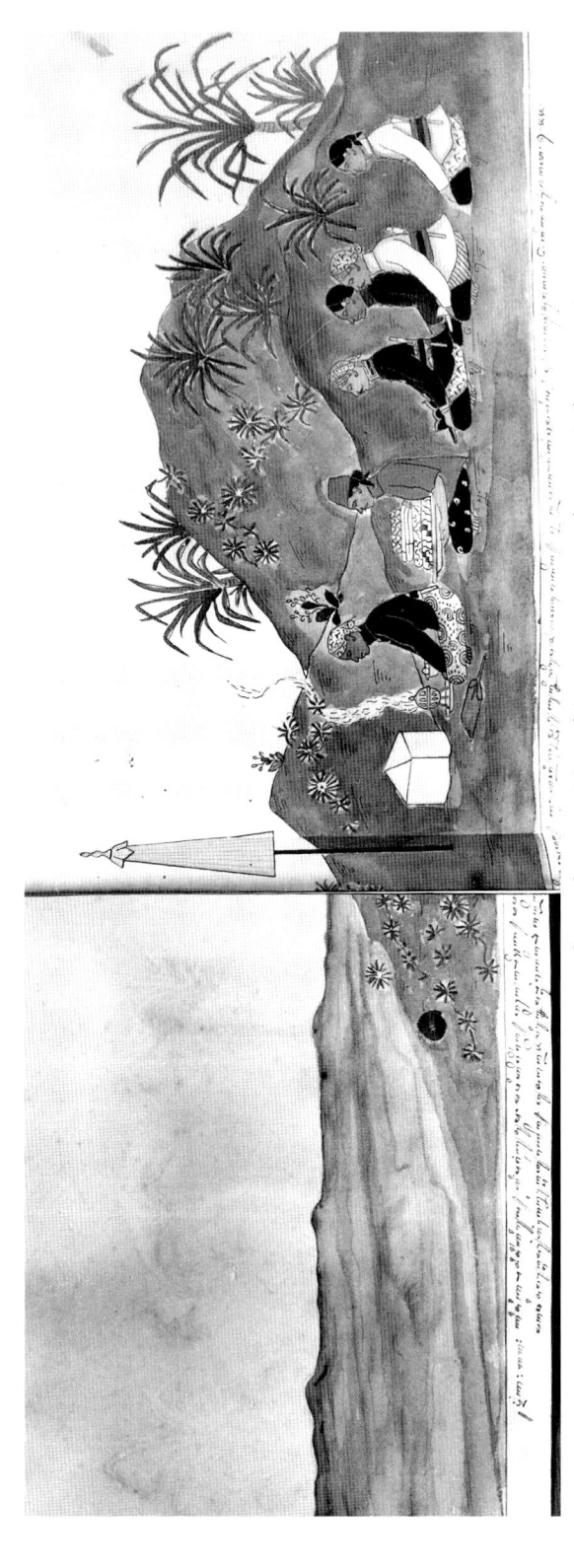

Plate 3. Yogya court delegation with offerings for the goddess of the Southern Ocean (Ratu Kidul) at Parangkusumo.

Plate 4. Kyai Mojo (circa 1790–1849).

Plate 5. Herman Willem Daendels (1762–1818) by Raden Saleh.

Plate 6. Painting of the governor-general's carriage being drawn up Daendels' *postweg* by a yoke of buffalo in the Priangan highlands by Payen.

Plate 7. Ali Basah Abdul Mustopo Prawirodirjo (Sentot) (circa 1808–55).

Plate 8. A Javanese chief in war dress.

Plate 9. Boats of HM Sloop Procris attacking and capturing six French gunboats off Indramayu, 31 July 1811.

Plate 10. Light Infantry Battalion sepoy (right) and grenadier sepoy (left)

Plate 11. Javanese grandee and servant, 1811–12.

Plate 12. Javanese grandee and a European, 1811–12.

Plate 13. Equestrian portrait of Sultan Hamengkubuwono IV (reigned 1814–22).

Plate 14. Chinese inhabitants of Java in the early nineteenth century.

Plate 15. Huibert Gerard baron Nahuys van Burgst (1782–1858).

Plate 16. Raden Adipati Danurejo IV (in office, 1813–1847) being hit with a slipper by Diponegoro.

Plate 17. Jonkheer Anthonië Hendrik Smissaert (1777–1832), Resident of Yogyakarta, 1823–5.

Plate 18. Sketch of Diponegoro and his pikemen entering the prepared encampment at Metesih, Magelang, on 8 March 1830.

Plate 19. Charcoal sketch of Diponegoro by A.J. Bik (1790–1872) in Batavia, April 1830.

Plate 20. Letter of Diponegoro to Colonel Jan-Baptist Cleerens and Major Hendrik Frederik Buschkens, 14 February 1830.

Plate 21. 'The Submission of Diponegoro to Lieutenant-General De Kock, 28 March 1830' by Nicolaas Pieneman.

Plate 22. 'An Historical Tableau, the Arrest of the Javanese Chief Diponegoro' by Raden Saleh.

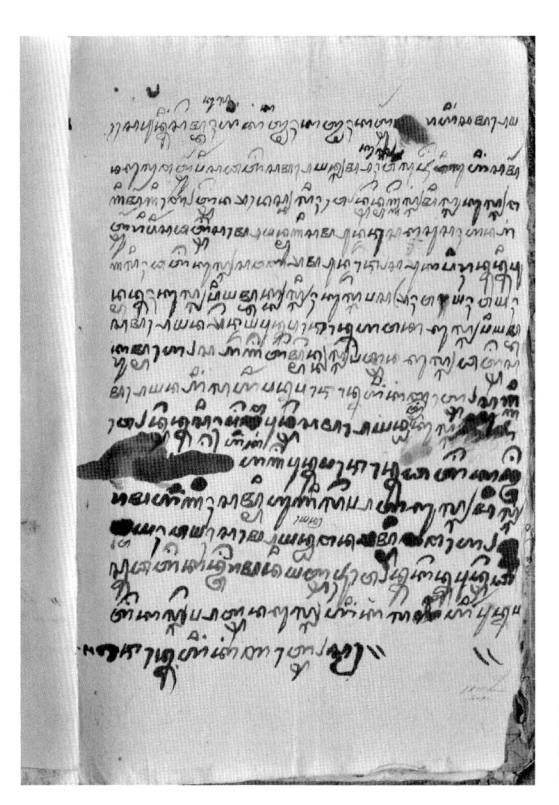

Plate 23. Diponegoro's personal letter to his mother, Raden Ayu Mangkorowati, written from Batavia in late April 1830.

Plate 24. Diponegoro in Fort Rotterdam (Makassar) reading an Islamic mystical text accompanied by his family.

PART IV
War and Exile, 1825–1855

CHAPTER X

The Last Stand of the Old Order: Diponegoro and the Java War, 1825–1830

Introduction

The past nine chapters have described Diponegoro's life from his birth in 1785 through his upbringing at Tegalrejo to the outbreak of the Java War. The main sources for these years are the Residency archives and the Javanese *babad*, in particular the prince's own remarkable autobiography (Babad Dipanegara I–IV).

With the outbreak of the Java War, we enter new territory. The Javanese chronicles remain, but instead of the Residents' reports, the wartime years are dominated by the dispatches of General De Kock and his field commanders. These military archives have been the subject of close study by a number of Dutch historians of whom P.J.F. Louw (1856–1924) and E.S. de Klerck (1869–1939), both officers of the Netherlands East Indies Army, are the recognised authorities here. Their magisterial six-volume history (Louw and De Klerck 1894–1909) covers the Java War from both the Dutch and Javanese sides.

Such a benchmark work needs no repeating. Instead, this chapter adopts a thematic approach, looking in turn at Diponegoro's methods of mobilization, armaments and taxation (Section 1); the role of women in the conflict (Section 2); Javanese cultural and linguistic issues, in particular the prince's attitudes towards the Dutch and the Chinese (Sections 3 and 4); and leadership and regional loyalties, especially the prince's links with the *santri* (Sections 5 and 6). The breakdown of his relationship with two of his key supporters, Kyai Mojo and Sentot, both of whom cut their own deals with the Dutch in 1828–9, forms the core of this chapter (Sections

7 and 9). A brief synopsis of the principal wartime events can be found in the penultimate section, which also analyses Dutch military and political tactics (Section 8).

The present chapter is part of a trilogy. The two other chapters give an account of the war's tragic ending and deal in turn with the prince's decision to meet with General de Kock, his capture at Magelang on 28 March 1830, subsequent journey to Batavia (Chapter XI), exile voyage to Manado (28 March–12 June 1830) and banishment, first in Manado (13 June 1830–20 June 1833) and then Makassar (11 July 1833–8 January 1855) where he died (Chapter XII).

Mobilization for War: Finance, Tactics, Peasant Manpower and Armaments

By the time Diponegoro and Mangkubumi reached Selarong, the prince's tenants had already been mobilized (Louw and De Klerck 1894–1909, I:208). Three months before the Dutch attack on Tegalrejo, the prince had already begun to remit the End-of-Fast (*Puwasa*) taxes and gather funds for his campaign (p. 227).

The early financing of the war relied on traditional sources: jewellery, cash and valuables were carried into the war zone by the wives and daughters of Diponegoro's elite supporters, a time honoured system repeated during the Indonesian Revolution (1945–9) (Simatupang 1972:52, 152; Carey 1981a:xl, 2008:607). Dutch treasure convoys were also attacked (Carey 1981a:255 note 83, 290 note 230), the captured specie financing some of Diponegoro's early campaigns.

The prince's village levies prepared for battle by arming themselves with traditional armaments such as slings, cudgels, catapults, and lances made of sharpened bamboo (Payen 1988:53; Carey 1981a:275 note 166). Arriving in Selarong in late July and early August, they left immediately for their designated posts after receiving Diponegoro's orders (Louw and

De Klerck 1894–1909, I:262. 400; Aukes 1935:79–81; Carey 1981a:285 note 208).

The prince's style of warfare made full use of these levies. Their first task was to prevent the arrival of Dutch reinforcements, so trees were felled, wooden bridges burnt and roads dug up and planted with bamboo stakes (Payen 1988:53, 55, 102 note 79). Disruption of communications was as critical for Diponegoro as it had been at the time of Raden Ronggo's November 1810 rebellion (Chapter V).

The prince kept his own communications open by appointing one of his uncle, Mangkudiningrat I's, sons as captain of his Progo River ferryboats (Carey 1981a:243 note 36, 267 note 124) and using professional bandits, the scourge of the pre-war countryside as local specialists in gunpowder manufacture and weapons procurement (Carey 1981a:243–4 note 36; Chapter II).

His forces mounted skilful ambushes (Louw and De Klerck 1894–1909, II:486, III:442; *Javasche Courant* 1, 1-1-1828): their favoured tactic was to hide in the long grass at the roadside and deploy in semi-circular fire attack formation (De Stuers 1833:6–7; Louw and De Klerck 1894–1909, III:98). The encircling stone walls of villages, built earlier to prevent pillaging, were used to great effect, as were fortified places such as Sunan Amangkurat I's former *kraton* of Plered (De Stuers 1833:2; Louw and De Klerck 1894–1909, III:126.5). Neighbouring villagers were involved in such ambushes. Taking up their farm implements, they impeded the retreat of Dutch columns which were sometimes overwhelmed. The construction of Dutch military stockades (*benteng*) was a partial response to this situation as we will see (De Stuers 1833:7; p. 260).

Diponegoro's regular troops had firearms and Dutch sources mention the prince's purchase of rifles (Carey 2008:609). Captured Dutch weaponry, including cannon, were also used (Djamhari 2003:80). European artillery techniques were carefully studied: one of the prince's Yogya siege commanders noted that Dutch cannon fired too high because their artillerymen used too much gunpowder (Portier, 'Verklaring', n.y. [? 9–1826]). Captured supplies were supplemented by gunpowder and munitions of local manufacture: Samen near Bantul (Carey 1981a:243 note 36, 275 note 166; pp. 49, 101–2), Into-Into on the Progo River (*Javasche Courant* 111,

16-9-1828; Lagordt Dillié 1863:32), and Dekso, the prince's first Kulon Progo headquarters (Carey 2008:609), were all places where high quality propellants were prepared by village women (Lagordt-Dillié 1863:32).

The main armaments centre was Kota Gede (Carey 2008:8). The presence of the *kalang*, a local community of artificers and metalworkers (Carey 1992:473 note 348), provided the skills needed for the manufacture of munitions. Kota Gede's status as a neutral city – inviolate due to its joint Yogya-Solo administration and ancient royal graveyard (burial site of Panembahan Senopati) – encouraged many to move there during the war (Babad Dipanegara III:127; Van Mook 1972:23–4; Carey 1981a:275 note 266; 2008:610).

The Javanese stabbing dagger (*kris*) was the weapon most often used against Dutch troops (Louw and De Klerck 1894–1909, I:401; V:630–1; Carey 2008:610). Mounted at the end of a length of thick bamboo, this made a serviceable pike which could be used to dismount Dutch cavalry (Louw and De Klerck 1894–1909, II:380). De Stuers, a Java War veteran, described how Javanese peasants could move easily from their agricultural duties to participating in ambushes by keeping their *kris* blades always with them. Following a successful action, they would break the haft of their weapon, remove the *kris* blade and melt back into the countryside resuming their previous peasant cultivator identities.

The conflict was thus a classic agrarian insurgency, part *jacquerie* (peasant uprising), part guerrilla war, part regular military campaign (De Stuers 1833:4–10; Tilly 1964:331–9). This in turn required the Dutch to revise their battlefield tactics, a subject to which we will return in the penultimate section.

Women as Combatants

In February 1831, when the Dutch authorities were deciding what to do with Kyai Mojo's part-Balinese wife, Raden Ayu Mojo, Valck, then serving as Yogya Resident (in office 1831–8/1838–41), commented (Carey 2008:613):

When one calls to mind the scenes of the recently ended war and takes a moment to dwell on the harm and mischief wrought by various wives of prominent Javanese chiefs, one can list here [certain] women who excelled in [...] acts of cruelty.

Who were these women? Valck had two particularly in mind: Raden Ayu Serang (circa 1769–1855), the mother of Pangeran Serang II (circa 1794–1852) and wife of the heir to the Kalijogo apostle of Islam (*wali*) line (Chapter III; Mashoed Haka 1976); and Raden Ayu Yudokusumo, a daughter of the first sultan (Mangkubumi), who was married to a Yogya outlying district regent (*bupati*) (Carey 1992:456 note 272).

The first led a 500-strong force in the Serang-Demak area during her son's attack on Dutch positions on the north coast in August–September 1825 (Louw and De Klerck 1894–1909, I:369–91; Ricklefs 1974:241–4; Carey and Houben 1987:21, 35 note 14), and was renowned for her spiritual power (*kasekten*) (Carey 1981a:284 note 205; 2008:614; Carey and Houben 1987:21, 35 note 15; p. 52).

The second, Raden Ayu Yudokusumo, 'a lady of shrewd intelligence, outstanding ability and manly ingenuity' (Carey 1992:122, 297, 456 note 272; Louw and De Klerck 1894–1909, III:510), masterminded the attack on the Chinese community in Ngawi on 17 September 1825 (Louw and De Klerck 1894–1909, I:525; Carey 1984:1–2; 1992:456 note 271) and later joined forces with Raden Sosrodilogo during his November 1827–March 1828 campaign (Louw and De Klerck 1894–1909, III:510). At the time of her surrender in October 1828, it was noted that, along with the rest of her family, she had shaved off her hair as a sign of her commitment to the holy war (Louw and De Klerck 1894–1909, III:514–15).

Nor was it only well-born Javanese women who made their mark. At the customs post of Ngawi on the Bengawan Solo, a *peranakan* (mixed race Javanese-Chinese) woman established a local police force following Raden Ayu Yudokusumo's attack (Carey 2008:616). In fact, the reports of women preparing gunpowder in Yogya villages (Lagordt Dillié 1863:32), bringing valuables into the war zones, and wearing full male battle dress (*prajuritan*) (Carey 1981a:xliii), are consistent with what we know of their pre-war role in Javanese society (Carey and Houben 1987:12–42). These were definitely not the simpering *Raden Ayu* of Dutch colonial fiction and their role would not be forgotten when Indonesia fought for its independence in the mid-twentieth century (Carey and Houben 1987:21).

Xenophobia and Identity (1): Changing Attitudes towards the Chinese Community

The attack on the Chinese community in Ngawi underscored the intense xenophobia which gripped many who rallied to Diponegoro in July-August 1825, an attitude most tellingly displayed in Diponegoro's view of the Chinese and his treatment of Dutch prisoners.

Given the invidious role which the inhabitants of the Middle Kingdom had been called upon to play in the pre-Java War period (Chapter VIII), it is understandable that they should have been singled out once hostilities had commenced. Some 25,000 mainly mixed blood (*peranakan*) Chinese were thought to be at risk (Carey 1981a:260 note 106). Besieged in Yogya, the Belgian artist-architect, Payen, observed in his diary on 10 August that 'everywhere the Chinese are massacred, they spare neither women nor children' (Payen 1988:62, 116 note 141).

The fate of the Chinese communities in Bagelen is instructive here. The great *peranakan* weaving centres of Jono and Wedi on the Lereng River held out for a time. Their locally raised police force and *benteng* (redoubt) helped here (Payen 1988:74, 131-2 note 215). But, in 1827, the entire community of 147 men, 138 women and 185 children were evacuated to Wonosobo (Louw and De Klerck 1894-1909, III:86, 108-9). The local Javanese soon begged for their return, stating that they needed their business skills to market their cottons (Louw and De Klerck 1894-1909, V:433), but the community was never re-established.

The fate of the Bagelen Chinese was replicated in many areas of central and east Java. But, although there were some diehard xenophobes like Kyai Mojo (De Stuers 1833:15; Carey 1979:73, 1981a:260 note 106), the prince's *prang sabil* was not just an anti-Chinese *battue*. As the war progressed a more varied picture emerged. Not only did Chinese merchants supply Diponegoro with arms, opium and money (Van den Broek 1873–77, 20:561), some even fought on his side. This was the case in Tuban and Lasem on the north coast where the local Chinese community, nearly all converts to Islam and descended from long-established mixed-race (*peranakan*) families, collaborated closely with Sosrodilogo's forces and faced reprisals after his January 1828 defeat (Louw and De Klerck 1894–1909, III:444–5; Carey 1984:2 note 5). Away from the north coast, however, such instances of Sino-Javanese cooperation were rarer. The bloody events of July–September 1825 had traumatized the Chinese community and a deep suspicion of Javanese intentions remained.

Such attitudes were reciprocated by the Javanese: Diponegoro led the way by forbidding his commanders to have political relations with the Chinese. This repeated his great-grandfather, Sultan Mangkubumi's, warning against allowing the Chinese too close a relationship with the Yogya court for fear of sowing discord (Carey 1992:462 note 304; 2008:399), a warning reiterated by Pakualam following Tan Jin Sing's elevation as a court *bupati* (Carey 2008:618).

But Diponegoro went further. He instructed his commanders to desist from all forms of sexual relationship with *peranakan* women, arguing that it would bring misfortune (Carey 1984:2). This was definitely not something insisted on in pre-war *kraton* circles where liaisons between Javanese rulers and attractive Chinese mixed-blood women were the norm (Carey 1984:14–15). One example was the prince's own grandfather, Hamengkubuwono II, whose favourite unofficial wife, Mas Ayu Sumarsonowati, was of partly Chinese descent (Van den Broek 1873–77, 24:87; Mandoyokusumo 1977:21 no. 30; Carey 1984:20–1). Her son, Pangeran Joyokusumo (circa 1785–1829; post-August 1825, Pangeran Ngabehi), would become one of the prince's top commanders (Carey 2008:79).

Why this change? Much can be explained by the war's antecedents, especially the fiscal oppression of the Chinese (pp. 180–3). But the prince may also have had personal reasons: in his *babad*, he relates that he himself had succumbed to the charms of a captured Chinese woman (*nyonyah*), who had been brought to him as a masseuse just before the disastrous mid-October 1826 battle of Gawok (Louw and De Klerck 1894–1909, II:517 note 1; Carey 1981a:260 note 106; 2008:619; Babad Dipanegara III:104):

XXXVIII 13. In Kedaren
at night, the one who was ordered to provide a massage
was a female prisoner, a Chinese woman [*nyonyah*].
His Highness the sultan behaved wrongly.
Because of his feelings for his wife [Raden Ayu Maduretno]
confused was the [sexual] solace.

Diponegoro blamed this dalliance for his subsequent defeat, his two battlefield wounds, an indication that his spritual powers of invulnerability had been temporarily neutralized (Carey 2008:121). He would revert to this theme later in his *babad* when he blamed his brother-in-law, Sosrodilogo's, successive defeats in January 1828 on the neglect of his prohibitions regarding Chinese women, his relative having ravished (*anjamahi*) one of the *peranakan* ladies of Lasem following his capture of the north coast town on 31 December 1827 (Babad Dipanegara III:6; Carey 2008:619).

Xenophobia and Identity (2): Issues of Javanese Language, Fashion and Culture

Underlying these cross-racial sexual insecurities, another theme may be discerned: what shrewd Dutch observers termed a 'feeling of [Javanese] nationality' (Preface). This can be seen most clearly in Diponegoro's treatment of Dutch prisoners whom he insisted should speak High Javanese (*kromo*) rather than Malay, that 'language of chickens which no ruler in Java wished to hear' (p. 32), dress in Javanese not European dress, and consider conversion to Islam (Portier, 'Verklaring', n.y. [? 9–1826]; Carey 1974b:285, 287).

This last was something which the prince also expected of the Chinese, the process of 'becoming a Muslim' being quite simple: namely, having their pigtails cut off, undergoing circumcision and uttering the declaration of The Faith (*sahadat*) 'there is no God but God and Muhammad is His Prophet' (Louw and De Klerck 1894–1909, III:465; Carey 1981a:259 note 106). In the early seventeenth century, Sultan Agung, whom Diponegoro took as a model in so many things, made efforts to have Dutch prisoners circumcised (De Graaf 1958:102). But the prince's insistence on Javanese sartorial and linguistic codes went further and were probably a reaction to the Europeanising influences in south-central Java in the pre-war decade (Carey 2008:459).

The report of a Dutch-Javanese inspector of birds' nest rocks on the south coast following his August–September 1826 captivity (Portier, 'Verklaring', n.y. [? 9–1826]) gives an insight into the pressures placed on Dutch prisoners to adopt Javanese cultural and religious norms. Told that he must convert to Islam to save his life, the inspector was assured that if he did so he would be given a military command with appropriate pay and privileges. Already circumcised, his 'conversion' was not so difficult. Given the new Muslim name of Nur Samidin, he was immediately invested with his 'symbols of office', namely a horse, a *kris* with a gold sheath and a Javanese striped cotton (*lurik*) jacket. Contemplating his changed appearance, the inspector noted that 'he had [now] become just like a Javanese even down to my dress' (Carey 2008:589).

We would need more accounts like this to build up a picture of how Dutch prisoners were treated. Javanese sartorial codes, for example, were not always insisted on. After his surrender in mid-October 1829, Sentot forbade his soldiers from wearing Javanese dress demanding that they maintain their holy war apparel (Van den Broek 1873–77, 24:93). A 'fashion war' even developed with senior Dutch commanders attempting to persuade him to re-adopt his 'national dress' – in particular the *blangkon* (Javanese head-dress) – and give up the turban which they argued had 'long gone out of fashion' (Carey 2008:621).

Leadership and Regional Loyalties

Although many local officials supported Diponegoro's war effort, the main leadership was provided by the Yogya princes and senior officials (Carey 2008:795–806). Having set fire to their residences to prevent them falling into enemy hands (Payen 1988:56, 105 note 95; Van Hogendorp 1913:173–4), they came to the prince's headquarters at Selarong to receive their commands in late July.

Even before his flight from Tegalrejo, Diponegoro distributed letters of authority (*piagem*) mandating various princes and senior *priyayi* to act as his local commanders. These carried his princely seal and were intended as 'declarations of the holy war'. According to a Javanese source, Diponegoro proclaimed himself as the head (*imam*) of the Islamic religion in Java at this time (*Buku Kedung Kebo*:89, IX.7–8; Carey 2008:622), announcing his intention of waging a *prang sabil*.

These letters of authority were so popular that local elites from as far afield as the north coast and the eastern *mancanagara*, begged for them. One of these, Pangeran Serang II (Carey 2008:132–3), the son of the famed female commander (p. 243), was invested by Diponegoro, while he was at Selarong, as a commander in the holy war in his native Serang-Demak and given the title of 'he who fixes firm the Islamic religion' (*Senopatining Prang Sabilollah ingkang anetepaken Agami Islam*, Carey 1981a:241 note 30).

This pattern would continue throughout the war with the prince investing his commanders with titles such as *Basah* ('Pasha'; Carey 2008:153) or *Dullah* (Carey 1982:5 note 22; 2008:623) and new Muslim names. He also used members of the religious communities to maintain contacts with his far-flung supporters and encourage others to join the *prang sabil*.

The war had strong regional aspects. Although its main base remained south-central Java, in particular the Mataram heartland around Yogya, campaigns took place in other areas such as Demak (August–September 1825), Madiun (November 1825–January 1826), Rembang, and Jipang-Rajegwesi (November 1827–March 1828). This regional dimension compromised the prince's war effort, as we will see in the tensions between Kyai Mojo's Pajang troops and Diponegoro's Mataram levies during his August–October 1826 advance on Surakarta (Louw and De Klerck 1894–1909, II:499, 520).

In Diponegoro's view, the fighting quality of his troops varied considerably from region to region (Louw and De Klerck 1894–1909, V:743), and he echoed his eldest son, Pangeran Diponegoro II's, views about the character of Mataram men, namely, that they could keep secrets, had a generous heart, and were strict in their religious observance (Carey 2008:71):

The people of Madiun are good at resisting a first attack and they acquit themselves well, but afterwards they are not much use. The people of Pajang are also brave, but likewise for a short space of time. The people from Bagelen are better, but they must fight in their own area; if they are outside they collapse quickly. But the people of Mataram are the best of all; they fight well, they persevere and they know how to withstand the hardships of war.

Similar observations would be made during the Indonesian Revolution (1945–9) when military commanders from Kedu and Bagelen were singled out for praise, along with those from Banyumas, such as Panglima Besar Sudirman (?1915–50), dubbed the 'Prussians' of Java (Simatupang 1972:76).

The Role of the Santri Communities

The second group which rallied to Diponegoro at Selarong were the 'men of religion' (*santri*). Some two hundred men and women are named in the Dutch reports and Javanese *babad* (Carey 2008:786–94). Amongst these were some Arabs and mixed blood Chinese (*peranakan*). Others were court *santri*, who were members of the official Islamic hierarchy, religious regiments like the Suranatan and Suryogomo, as well as inhabitants of the Yogya-administered tax-free villages (*pradikan*) and religious schools. Another large group was brought over by Kyai Mojo when he joined the prince at Selarong in early August. These included members of his extensive family and students from his two *pesantren* at Mojo and Baderan near Delanggu (Carey 2008:91–2).

Of those whose titles can be identified, twenty-two were returned Mecca pilgrims (*haji*) and seventeen listed as *Seh* (Syeikh) or *Sarif* (Sherif), an epithet usually given to Arabs of good birth or those claiming kinship with The Prophet's family (Carey 2008:786–94). Only three were Arabs – namely, the Jeddah-born Seh Abdul Ahmad bin Abdullah al-Ansari, his son-in-law, also known as Seh Ahmad (p. 27), and Sarif Samparwedi (Hasan Munadi), Diponegoro's Barjumungah religious bodyguard commander (Carey 2008:787, 793).

There were some eighteen religious and mosque officials as well as ten listed as religious teachers (*kyai guru*). These included the heads of *pesantren* from Bagelen, Kedu, Mataram, Pajang, Ponorogo and Madiun. The remaining 121 were referred to as '*kyai*', a term used loosely in Java as a title for revered country gentlemen as well as teachers of religious and spiritual disciplines.

Not all those listed as *kyai* were 'men of religion' in the strict sense: several were adepts in the mystical 'sciences' (*ngelmu*), who taught their followers esoteric arts such as the inculcation of warlike virtues (*ngelmu kadigdayan*), the art of striking fear (*ngelmu kawedukan*) and invulnerability to bullets and sharp weapons (*ngelmu kaslametan*; Carey 1981a:253 note 75). Their charms and amulets (*jimat*) were believed to turn Dutch gunpowder and lead into water (Louw and De Klerck 1894–1909, I:208; Aukes 1935:74; Carey 1981a:276 note 168; Payen 1988:72, 129 note 200).

The prince himself was seen as a living *jimat* with magical powers enabling him to fly and influence the weather (Carey 1981a:276 note 168). Others trusted in his invulnerability and capacity to read character through facial expression (*ngelmu firasat*; Carey 1981a:276 note 168; p. 32). Many desired to develop closer links with him. Kyai Banjarsari, the head of the well-known religious school near Madiun, begged for a '*jimat* of his blood' in the person of his sister, Raden Ayu Sosrodiwiryo, to establish family ties (Louw and De Klerck 1894–1909, II:568; Carey 1981a:276 note 168).

Diponegoro's status in the eyes of his *santri* supporters was enhanced by the religious character of the war (Carey 2008: 583–91; p. 218). The Dutch Colonial Minister, C.Th. Elout (in office 1824–1829), described how in nearly every engagement religious scholars (*ulama*), clad in their distinctive white or green tabards and turbans, stiffened the resolve of the prince's troops by their chanting of phrases from the *Qur'ān* (*dhikr*) (Carey 2008:629). His description was confirmed in other Dutch sources, which mention that both Diponegoro's male and female followers shaved their heads, wore 'priestly' dress and went into battle chanting *dhikr* (Carey 1987:277 note 17), a change from the early stages of the war when the body of at least one female fighter was found during the August 1825 Yogya siege attired in male Javanese fighting dress (*prajuritan*) (Carey 1981a:xliii).

The war's religious character convinced Elout that hostilities could not be ended by giving Diponegoro an independent kingdom like Mangkubumi (Hamengkubuwono I), Raden Mas Said (Mangkunegoro I) and Notokusumo (Pakualam I). In Elout's view, Diponegoro's claim to be recognised as a protector and regulator of religion, and his *santri* links made such concessions impossible. The war's religious character threatened the foundations of the Christian West's authority in Java, distinguishing it from the dynastic struggles of previous centuries (Carey 2008:629).

Satria and Santri: The Breakdown in Relations between Diponegoro and Kyai Mojo

Why did the *santri* rally to Diponegoro? The question is worth asking because historically relations between the Mataram court and the religious communities had been hostile. One thinks here of the bloody events of Sunan Amangkurat I's reign (1646–77) when thousands of 'men of religion' and their relatives had been massacred on the Plered *kraton*'s great square (*alun-alun*) in circa 1650. The so-called Javanese 'Succession Wars' of the late seventeenth and early eighteenth centuries also witnessed *kraton* and *kauman* (firm religious community) tensions: religious scholars and revered 'saints' like the Kajoran religious head, Panembahan Rama (circa 1620–80), participated anti-Mataram rebellions such as that led by the pious Madurese nobleman, Raden Trunojoyo (circa 1649–80) in 1676–80 (De Graaf 1940:273–328; Ricklefs 1993:30–57).

Why should the Java War have been different? The uniqueness of Diponegoro's upbringing by his formidable great-grandmother at Tegalrejo counted for much here (Chapter I), as did his personal commitment to Islam and extensive contacts with the south-central Javanese *santri*. These marked him out as a very unusual Javanese nobleman (Carey 2008:98–101; Chapter II). But this was problematic. Just where did his loyalties lie? Did he remain at heart a Yogya prince with an unusual *santri* childhood? Or had he entirely forsaken the respect due to him as a *satria* (warrior prince) and joined the men of religion? For the author of the Surakarta version of the *Babad Diponegoro* the answer was clear (Carey 1981a: xvii–xix, 19):

> II. 8. [...]
> 'It is a sham his giving himself over to religion,
>
> 9. and often going away to perform asceticism.
> He is hand in glove with the *santri*.
> He has given up the sense of honour of the *satria*,
> for he has accepted the sense of honour of the *santri*.
> [...]
>
> 10. [...]
> He mixes with the scum of the nation
> [and] is arrogant enough to invite battle.
> But these *santri*, what do they amount to?
> [...]

Another Javanese source, the *Buku Kedung Kebo*, went a stage further, going beyond the questioning of Diponegoro's religious commitment and looking at the appropriateness of his decision to vest political power in the *santri*. Again the reply was negative (Carey 1974b:259–84; 1981a:248–9 note 54):

> XIV 35. The *santri* cannot govern the state
> for that is the character of the *santri*.
> They seek themselves.
> They cannot wield political authority
> for their minds are narrow.
> Very different is the charisma of a king.

The problem for Diponegoro was that he was waging a holy war. For this, he needed *santri* support to interpret his Qur'ānic mandate (p. 216, p. 218). But he was also a Javanese aristocrat, quintessentially so according to some Dutch observers (p. 9). As a scion of the Yogya royal house, he naturally thought in terms of setting up a *kraton* with all the trappings of monarchy, albeit one with a distinctive Javanese-Islamic hue.

This image of royalty was reinforced by conferring titles on his close family (Carey 2008:765–8), marrying key supporters to his relatives, and presiding over *Garebeg* ceremonies where traditional royal largesse was distributed

(*Bataviasche Courant* 44, 2–11–1825; *Javasche Courant* 53, 1–5–1828). He had one of his *santri* advisers act the court jester (Carey 2008:676) and bestowed yellow *payung* (state umbrellas) on his princely followers (Carey 1981a:285 note 209, 286 note 215; Louw and De Klerck 1894–1909, II:244). The fact that these quintessential *kraton* symbols were described in the Javanese sources as 'signs of the holy war' (*pratandha prang sabil*) reflected the confusion about what Diponegoro was doing. Was he establishing a *kraton* or fighting for a new moral order in which the high state of the Islamic religion would be restored as his *santri* advisers claimed (Carey 1987:279–81)?

When Kyai Mojo surrendered to the Dutch on 12 November 1828, it became apparent that his relationship with the prince had broken down. And precisely this issue of war aims was the cause. As Mojo confided to his captors (Carey 1987:282):

> The first proposal which won me over to waging war was that Diponegoro promised me the restoration of our Faith. Believing this, I joined him wholeheartedly. But later I discovered this was not his real aim as he speedily began setting up and organising a *kraton*. I made representations to him which he took very much amiss, so much so that we exchanged bitter words. Since that time I was in disagreement with him, which led him to order me to bring the war to an end in one way or another.

Such clear evidence of the rift between the two principal Java War leaders raises questions about the nature of Diponegoro's leadership. What was the problem?

One element relates to the regional rivalries discussed earlier. Diponegoro's base was Mataram, whereas Mojo's loyalties lay in Pajang. After Mojo had rallied to the prince at Selarong in August 1825, many of his *ulama* joined the prince's elite bodyguard units or were appointed to positions in his civil administration (Carey 1987:287). In late August 1826, with much of his native Pajang under the prince's control, Mojo began to press for an all-out attack on Surakarta (Louw and De Klerck 1894–1909, II:469–70). The *kyai* saw this as his natural sphere of influence, boasting that the previous generation of Surakarta princes had studied under his father, Kyai Baderan, and now their sons were his pupils. He also belittled the prince's standing in Surakarta, suggesting that the court was no longer in sympathy with him (Babad Dipanegara III:84).

Diponegoro was irked by this attitude (Babad Dipanegara III:84), the dispute undermining the momentum of his campaign. Precious weeks were lost and when at last the prince's army took up its attack positions to launch an assault on Surakarta, it was comprehensively defeated at Gawok on the city's western outskirts (15 October 1826). Bitter recriminations followed: The prince's *kraton* and *santri* supporters blamed each other for the disaster, the former accusing Mojo and his family of having recklessly pressed the Surakarta campaign to further their own interests (Louw and De Klerck 1894-1909, II:496-520; Carey 1987:287). What had been a festering rivalry was now an open conflict.

Besides regionalism, another issue was the distribution of political authority. In August 1827, at the time of the Salatiga peace negotiations (Louw and De Klerck 1894-1909, III:264-76), a major dispute arose between Diponegoro and his chief religious adviser over this issue. Mojo, according to Diponegoro's account, challenged the prince's position as Sultan Erucokro by asking him to divide his sovereignty into four parts, that of *ratu* (king), *wali* (apostle of religion), *pandita* (one learned in the law) and *mukmin* (the believers), suggesting that Diponegoro should choose one of these four functions. If he chose that of *ratu*, Mojo implied that he himself would take that of *wali* and enjoy undisputed religious authority.

Diponegoro refused stating that Mojo – whom he addressed as 'uncle' (*paman*) thereby acknowledging his seniority despite his younger age (he was seven years his junior) – clearly wished to exercise authority over him. He even drew a comparison between the kyai and the spiritual lords of Giri in the sixteenth and seventeenth centuries, who, in Diponegoro's view, had exercised power over the sultans of Demak (Babad Dipanegara III:151-2).

Later, the prince proposed that Mojo should take over as his *pengulu* (Carey 2008:789), citing the example of the early sixteenth-century Sunan Kudus, a *wali* whom Diponegoro suggested had acted more like the *pengulu* of the sultan of Demak, and had shown himself more amenable to carrying out the orders of the Demak rulers (Babad Dipanegara IV:23). This time Mojo refused stating that he was not from a *pengulu* family and could not accept such a position. Instead, he demanded recognition as *imam* or head of the Islamic religious community (Babad Dipanegara IV:23; Carey 2008:635), a suggestion Diponegoro dismissed, pointing out that the argument over the delineation of functions was specious because God had chosen him – and him alone – as the Caliph of The Prophet of God in the Holy War in Java. Only the Almighty knew when that commission would be withdrawn (Babad Dipanegara IV:29).

Diponegoro's argument with his chief religious adviser, which drew on the historical example of the *wali*, proved impossible of resolution. The fact that Mojo was the principal ideological driving force behind the war and perhaps Diponegoro's intellectual superior only made things worse (Somer 1938, II:447–8).

And what was Mojo's view? A Javanese manuscript originating in the Kampung Jawa Tondano, Minahasa (North Sulawesi), where Kyai Mojo and his followers were exiled in May 1830, gives an insight into how he may have seen things (Babcock 1981a:281–92. Knoerle, 'Journal', 49). This states that Diponegoro still sought worldly goals gives (*nedi 'aradl dunya*) and violated the *syariah* (Islamic religious law) (Babcock 1981a:302). The prince's attempt to establish a *kraton* was evidence of such worldly ambitions, as was his fascination with *pusaka* (heirloom) daggers, some of which he had obtained through ascetic practices and encounters with the Javanese spirit world, actions deemed inappropriate for a strict follower of Islam (Babcock 1981a:302 note 8; Carey 2008:636, 813–15).

A self-opinionated and intractable character, Mojo also had large personal ambitions (Babcock 1981a:301; Carey 1981a:262 note 110). This can be seen from the manner of his surrender in mid-November 1828 when he took 500 of Diponegoro's best Bulkio troops and tried to cut a separate deal with the Dutch involving the return of his family to Pajang with special privileges, his recognition as a regulator of religion at the courts, and the privilege of a personal *barisan* (troop) (Louw and De Klerck 1894–1909, IV:590–1). Such *barisan* had been permitted to certain noble supporters of Diponegoro,[1] but the Dutch treated members of the nobility who came

---

1   After his surrender (16-10-1829), Sentot was allowed his own 500-strong *barisan* (troop), which subsequently saw service in west Sumatra against the Padri (1832–3) (Soekanto 1951:60 note 18). Accused of collusion with pro-Padri leaders, he was exiled to Bengkulu (1833–55) where he died (17 April 1855).

over to their side much more leniently than prominent *santri* like Mojo whom they deemed primarily responsible for stoking the fires of religious zealotry (Somer 1938, II:447; Babcock 1981b:77 note 9).

After the war, Diponegoro and Kyai Mojo initially found themselves sharing the same Minahasan exile (Knoerle, 'Journal', 49; Babcock 1981a:284; Chapter XII). Their behavior at that time was a study in incompatibility: whereas the prince showed continuing solicitude for his erstwhile religious adviser, complaining that the *kyai* had not been allowed to bring his part Balinese wife into exile with him (Knoerle, 'Journal', 23), and sending him a cash gift of ƒ50, Mojo spurned his gift stating that his Dutch government monthly allowance was more than sufficient for his needs (Carey 2008:639). The Dutch authorities seized on the breach, informing Diponegoro that no further communications with Mojo would be allowed.

The Java War protagonists would never meet again. Mojo died in his fifty-ninth year in Tondano on 20 December 1849 (Babcock 1981a:307), while Diponegoro, who outlived him by six years, expired just three months before his much younger army commander, Sentot (Soekanto 1951). So the Java War leaders passed from the world, divided in death just as they had been in life by the vicissitudes of war and the polarities of personal ambition. The temporary alliance of *satria* and *santri* had imbued the five-year conflict with a unique social breadth and religious fervor. But it was a deeply unstable relationship which even a *santri* prince of Diponegoro's stature could not bridge.

Dutch Military and Political Tactics

If the prince's side was so riven with internal rivalries, why did it take two years (1825–7) for the Dutch to hit on a winning strategy, namely the combined use of battlefield fortifications – the so-called *benteng* system – and a greatly increased number of mobile columns (Djamhari 2003:88–201; Louw and De Klerck 1894–1909, V:644)?

From the start, the Dutch officers misunderstood the nature of the war they were fighting. Their European military training had not prepared them for the fast-moving counter-insurgency conflict which they were forced to fight in south-central Java. Subsisting on minimal rations, the Javanese guerrilla fighters wore them down, allowing them few chances for pitched battles (Louw and De Klerck 1894–1909, V:632).

Dutch attrition rates were also very high, many soldiers succumbing to disease: of the 6,000 European infantry on active service in south-central Java between July 1825 and April 1827, twenty-seven percent (1,603) were dead by the war's second year (Djamhari 2003:81). The small number of European troops made it difficult for Dutch commanders to take offensive action and locally raised Indies auxiliaries were of limited value. Apart from the Madurese and those from Minahasa and South Sulawesi (Carey 2008:358–9, 2012:7), most were addicted to opium. Their insistence on bringing their families on campaign complicated the movement of the Dutch mobile columns turning them into baggage trains (Louw and De Klerck 1894–1909, I:206; Hooyer 1895–97, I:62; Djamhari 2003: 80–1, 88; Carey 2008:641).

Throughout the rainy season of November 1825 to April 1826, Diponegoro's forces moved with impunity through the Mataram countryside. They also held key strongpoints like Amangkurat I's old *kraton* at Plered, which had to be besieged by De Kock's chief engineer officer, Colonel Frans David Cochius (1787–1876), for close on three months before the 400 defenders could be dislodged in a bloodbath which left all but a handful dead (9 June 1826) (Louw and De Klerck 1894–1909, II:297–9; Portier, 'Verklaring', n.y. [?9–1826]).

In late July, Diponegoro's forces under Sentot's command struck out from his Dekso headquarters in Kulon Progo, winning a string of victories at Kasuran (28 July), Lengkong (31 July), where the flower of the Yogyakarta nobility perished, Bantul (4 August), Kejiwan (9 August), and Delanggu (28 August), which brought them to the outskirts of Surakarta. Dutch officers spoke of the prince's troops charging the Dutch lines in a 'seeming frenzy with blood-curdling shrieks and lowered heads' (Louw and De Klerck 1894–1909, II:378).

In desperation, the Dutch began stripping their outer island garrisons of troops and throwing in soldiers newly arrived from Europe (Louw and De Klerck 1894–1909, II:501 note 2; Carey 2008:642). Their position seemed hopeless (Louw and De Klerck 1894–1909, II:509). Only Kyai Mojo and Diponegoro's dispute over tactics allowed them to concentrate sufficient troops to gain a victory over the prince at Gawok on 15 October 1826. Even then Diponegoro's forces remained present in much of Pajang and Mataram for most of the following year.

By the end of 1827, a new front had opened in Rembang and Jipang-Rajegwesi when Diponegoro's brother-in-law, Sosrodilogo, went into revolt. For some anxious weeks between early December 1827 and mid-January 1828 the government's overland communications between Semarang and Surabaya were cut (Louw and De Klerck 1894–1909, III:490). De Kock cancelled plans to return to the Netherlands and vest operational command with Van Geen (Louw and De Klerck 1894–1909, III:391–400), a serendipitous decision given the hatred aroused by the latter's scorched earth tactics and widespread use of torture (Knoerle 'Journal', 32; Chambert-Loir 2000:284; Djamhari 2003:68–9).

A year before Sosrodilogo's Rembang revolt, Dutch military and civilian officials began to look for ways to end the war (Louw and De Klerck 1894–1909, II:573–8). The financial situation was dire. With the south-central Javanese economy at a standstill and military costs mounting, the colonial state was facing bankruptcy (Van der Kemp 1901–2, II:271–2; Louw and De Klerck 1894–1909, II:573–7; De Prins 2002:137; Djamhari 2003:69). Even supposedly loyal rulers like Sunan Pakubuwono VI were wavering (Carey 2008:559). Two-faced at best, the mercurial Sunan protested his loyalty to the Dutch while preparing to throw in his lot with the prince in the event of his victory (Carey 1981a:292–3 note 241; Djamhari 2003:69).

Disputes between Du Bus and De Kock over battlefield tactics made the search for a political resolution more difficult. The commissioner-general fancied himself a military tactician. He had no time for the expense and patience involved in De Kock's fortification system. Fixated on the tactics of the French Revolutionary, he thought of *levée en masse* (mass mobilization of the population) and diplomatic breakthroughs with the enemy. He tried both in September 1827 at Salatiga, coming in person to central Java to participate in the talks initiated by William Stavers and Kyai Mojo, and then issuing a grandiloquent appeal for a general popular uprising against Diponegoro (De Prins 2002:148–9). Both fell flat. In the words of Du Bus' biographer, Bart de Prins, 'the princely states and Yogyakarta were not France or Paris, [and] to the great annoyance of De Kock and his generals, Du Bus completely failed to see it' (De Prins 2002:149).

Other political strategies canvassed in this 1826–7 period, were rejected as impractical. These included the dismemberment of Yogya and its division between the government, the Susuhunan and the Mangkunegaran (Louw and De Klerck 1894–1909, II:411–16). So too was the idea of dividing the sultanate and offering Diponegoro an independent principality which, as we have seen, was dismissed out of hand by Colonial Minister Elout (Louw and De Klerck 1894–1909, V:724–5; Weitzel 1852–53, II:530–32; Kielstra 1896:86).

The only political expedient tried was the restoration of the exiled second sultan of Yogya in August 1826 (Louw and De Klerck 1894–1909, II:433–43). But this had little impact. The seventy-six year old second sultan was in his dotage. Dominated by his rapacious, low-born and obese last official consort, Ratu Sultan (Carey 1992:413 note 73), an erstwhile Amazon corps commander, the sixteen months of his third and last reign were deeply demoralizing for the Yogya court (Knoerle 1835:151).

Undaunted by this failure, De Kock studied the military situation and came up with a five-point strategy. The key socio-military elements were a commitment to take back those areas of Mataram still under Diponegoro's control and restore an effective system of government so the local economy could be revived. He also planned to contain the prince's forces within a narrow strip of mountainous land between the Progo and Bogowonto rivers to isolate them and wear them down. This would create what in modern military parlance is called a 'killing area' (Djamhari 2003:78–9). He also resolved to capture Diponegoro and the other Java War leaders by putting prices on their heads: the reward offered for Diponegoro was set at 10,000 Spanish dollars (present-day USD250,000) – dead or alive, the price for the dead prince to be paid on receipt of his severed head at

De Kock's Magelang headquarters (Djamhari 2003:78–9; Louw and De Klerck 1894–1909, V:377–8; Sagimun 1965:401). There were no takers.

The key to De Kock's success was the system of temporary battlefield fortifications (*benteng stelsel*) pioneered by Cochius (Louw and De Klerck 1894–1909, I:260 note 1; Djamhari 2003:87; Carey 2008:646). Early in the conflict (October 1825), the engineer officer had established his first *benteng* at Kalijengking in southern Kedu on the Magelang-Yogya road to protect military convoys and provide overnight shelter for his troops. Other mobile column commanders followed suit (Djamhari 2003:83). Cochius' original design was very simple. After choosing a suitable strategic location, usually on a hill top or some other natural defence, he built a rectangular barrack-like structure sufficient to house a platoon (25–30) of soldiers. He then defended it by erecting a stout coconut palm-tree trunk stockade roughly 1.7 metres high with one or possibly two elevated gun-emplacements at the corners. Given their temporary nature, such fortifications could be easily abandoned and new *benteng* built in other locations where there was need for troop support (Weitzel 1852–53, I:39; Louw and De Klerck 1894–1909, II:578–80; Djamhari 2003:84–5, 231–2, 305–8).

Introduced on a systematic basis from May 1827 as part of De Kock's new integrated battlefield strategy, the *benteng*, along with the eleven mobile columns operational in south-central Java by the end of the war, were the key to Dutch military success (Djamhari 2003:78–215). By March 1830, no fewer than 258 such temporary fortifications had been constructed, the largest number (ninety) being built in 1828 (Djamhari 2003:319). Covering a vast area from the district capital of Banyumas in the west to Ponorogo in the east, sixteen of these structures were large enough to house over 100 troops with numerous cannon (Djamhari 2003:315).

Cochius' own contribution would be set in stone with the construction of one of the largest of these fortresses – the post-war Fort Cochius at Gombong in Kebumen Residency, western Bagelen (Houben 1994:111), which would later serve as the first posting of an obscure Javanese corporal of the Netherlands Indies Army by the name of Suharto (1921–2008), the future second president of Indonesia (1967–98). In this fashion, the *benteng stelsel* would resonate in modern Indonesian history.

Diponegoro's Fiscal Regime; Sentot and the Problems of Dwifungsi

How did this strategy impact on Diponegoro? The answer lies in part in the prince's wartime fiscal administration. After the initial ad hoc financing, Diponegoro began to organize his own tax regime. This included land tribute and levies on local markets. *Bupati* and other officials in places designated as armaments centres, such as Kota Gede, were tasked with channeling taxes, food and war matériel to his forces (Carey 1981a:275 note 166, 288 note 221, 2008:582).

Military and administrative duties were strictly separated. Occasionally, the prince's *bupati* would participate in fighting, but they restricted themselves mostly to local administration. Chosen largely from the ranks of the senior court *priyayi*, they had ample experience serving the sultanate. One such family was the Danurejan who had supplied all the chief ministers (*patih*) in Yogya up to Sumodipuro's disastrous December 1813 appointment (Carey 2008:395–7; Chapter VII).

For military commands, Diponegoro adopted different criteria. Here the yardstick was personal bravery and military flair. In the prince's view, courage was essentially a youthful quality. Many of his senior commanders (*basah*) were very young, either in their late teens or early twenties, and for the Javanese the war was a '*pemuda*' (youth) revolution which anticipated that of 1945–6 (Carey 2008:648; Anderson 1967). The most important of Diponegoro's teenage commanders was Sentot (1808–55).[2] Styled Ali Basah (the 'High Pasha') Abdul Mustopo Prawirodirjo, this illiterate young nobleman, a son of Raden Ronggo Prawirodirjo III by an unofficial wife (Carey 2008:79), had joined the prince at Selarong when he was just seventeen. Described by De Stuers as 'young, fiery and in every respect a brilliant Javanese' (De Stuers 1833; Soekanto 1951:42; Carey 2008:648), he would carve a name for himself for his courage and skill on the battlefield.

---

2   A name derived from the Javanese *mak sentot* meaning 'to fly' or 'to dash', see Gericke and Roorda 1901, I:753; Knoerle, 'Journal', 40.

By late 1828, when he was in his twentieth year, he had already emerged as Diponegoro's leading strategist and military commander (Knoerle, 'Journal', 15–16). Despite some brilliant victories, which included the destruction of Major H.F. Buschkens' 8th mobile column at Kroya in eastern Bagelen at the beginning of October 1828 (Louw and De Klerck 1894–1909, IV:492–502), the tide of war was starting to turn against the prince.

As we have seen (p. 255), in mid-November 1828, Kyai Mojo had allowed himself to be taken prisoner with 500 seasoned troops. The prince and his remaining forces were now confined into the narrow strip of territory between the Progo and Bogowonto rivers. In this area, the Dutch strategy of establishing temporary battlefield fortifications (*benteng*) to protect the villages recently 'pacified' by their troops denied both Diponegoro and his commanders vital supplies. Difficulties were experienced in the collection of taxes and Diponegoro's *patih*, Raden Adipati Abdullah Danurejo (in office, 1828–30), was blamed by the prince's military commanders for his ineffective administration.

In December 1828, Sentot demanded that he be placed in overall command of the prince's forces, and allowed to levy taxes directly, thus bypassing the *patih*'s administration (Louw and De Klerck 1894–1909, IV:673). This troubled Diponegoro, who was conscious of his role as a Ratu Adil (Just King) who would ensure a regime of light taxation, and the provision of cheap food and clothing (Carey 1981a:xxxix–xl; p. 225). He feared that the common people would be oppressed if the spendthrift Sentot, was allowed to combine administrative and military responsibilities (Carey 1981b:56 note 8). He canvassed the views of his other commanders, asking his uncle, Pangeran Ngabehi (Babad Dipanegara IV:54):

> XXXV 47. 'If he who holds the sword
> is also given the holding of money, how [then]?
> Might that not lead to a mess?'

In these three short lines Diponegoro seemed to anticipate late twentieth-century debates about the appropriateness of the dual function (*dwifungsi*) of the Indonesian army (*Tentara Nasional Indonesia*) as a military and socio-political force during Sukarno's 'Guided Democracy' (1957–65) (Crouch 1978:25; Carey 1981b:51). But this is to get ahead of our tale.

Eventually a reluctant Diponegoro agreed, ordering that the monthly market taxes be divided between Sentot and himself, with two-thirds going to his army commander and the last third being retained for his own use (Louw and De Klerck 1894–1909, IV:674). He immediately regretted his decision. In his *babad*, he related that the Dutch immediately started building a large new *benteng* at Nanggulan guarding the Sentolo-Dekso highway (Louw and De Klerck 1894–1909, IV:675; Djamhari 2003:315). But Sentot did not react quickly enough because he was preoccupied with financial administration (Babad Dipanegara IV:56). When the youthful commander did eventually order a full-scale attack, he found the Dutch too firmly entrenched and his troops were repulsed (8 January 1829) (Louw and De Klerck 1894–1909, IV:678–82).

In June 1829, the month in which the Dutch captured part of Diponegoro's administrative archive in an engagement on the south coast (Louw and De Klerck 1894–1909, V:207), Ngabehi wrote to Sentot informing him that one of his tax officials had been punished with a public beating for levying more taxes than was permitted (Carey 1981a:xl). Food supplies were also getting scarce. Local officials, who had once supported the prince, were now turning against him. Many moved to areas under the control of Dutch *benteng* where the security and economy were better (Carey 2008:651–2).

There were even cases in the last year of the war (1829–30) of local people turning against unpopular officials in areas controlled by the prince and assassinating them so great was their craving for peace (Louw and De Klerck 1894–1909, V:516, 519–20). The Dutch *benteng* commanders also had a role here. They promised the local population free ploughs, draught animals and seeds – as well as lower tax rates, diminished corvée demands and higher day labour wages – if they moved to areas under their control (Carey 1981a:lxviii note 185; 2008:44; Houben 1994:20).

By the end of September 1829, the fourth year of the war, organized resistance to the Dutch in the fertile rice plains of south-central Java was at an end (Djamhari 2003:217). The crucial bonds of trust and cooperation between Diponegoro's forces and the local population had been sundered. Without them, there could be no successful prosecution of the war (Carey 2008:652).

The same period witnessed the nadir of Diponegoro's personal fortunes. On 21 September 1829, his last remaining senior commander, Pangeran Ngabehi, and his two sons, were killed in a bloody encounter in the Kelir Mountains on the Bagelen-Mataram border. Sentot negotiated his own surrender shortly thereafter (16 October). On 11 November 1829, following his near capture by Major A.V. Michiels' 11th mobile column, Diponegoro decided to wander off into the jungles of western Bagelen, accompanied only by his two *panakawan* (intimate retainers), Bantengwareng and Roto (Louw and De Klerck 1894–1909, V:423; Carey 1974a:25). These wanderings, which would take him to the remote Remo area between Bagelen and Banyumas, would continue until early February 1830 when his first direct negotiations with Colonel Jan Baptist Cleerens (1785–1850) began (pp. 273–8).

Diponegoro's privations during this period are poignantly described Dutch military historian, George Nypels:

> Constantly harried and pursued, Diponegoro was able to keep [four] flying columns [...] as well as various locally raised *barisan* (troops) busy from October 1829 to February 1830. Over mountains and through forests, into wildernesses and caves, seeking help wherever he could in the driving rains of the west monsoon, he often escaped when people thought he was nearby. The numbers of his close followers had almost completely melted away. He suffered from every kind of want: often without a roof over his head and frequently without sufficient food, he found the local population reluctant to help him. In January 1830, even his loyal *patih* [Raden Adipati Abdullah Danurejo] left his side. Although suffering from a wound in his leg and sick from all his physical privations and exhaustion he bore resolutely with these conditions until 9 February 1830 [when his negotiations with Colonel Cleerens commenced]. (Nypels 1895:153)

As he dragged his weary and malaria-ridden body along the rhinoceros' paths to the peasant huts in which he hid for over three months (Louw and De Klerck 1894–1909, V:525–6; Carey 1981b:56 note 10; Chapter XI), the prince may have reflected that although his defeat was probably inevitable – witness the Parangkusumo prophecy (p.59) – it had undoubtedly been hastened by his disastrous concession to Sentot a year earlier.

Conclusion

The Java War constituted a huge upheaval in Javanese society. It affected two million people – one third of Java's population – and claimed the lives of 200,000 more. One fourth of Java's cultivated area sustained damage. In securing their pyrrhic victory, the Dutch lost 8,000 European troops as well as 7,000 local auxiliaries (Preface). The twenty-five million guilder (present-day USD2.2 billion) cost to their exchequer (De Graaf 1949:399) would only be recouped through Van den Bosch's Cultivation System, which brought an estimated 832 million guilders (present-day USD75 billion) profit to the home government between 1831 and 1877 (Ricklefs 1993:123; Preface).

The last stand of Java's 'old order', the Java War witnessed the dismemberment of the south-central Javanese courts as their remaining outlying territories were annexed (1830–31) (Houben 1994:17–72). As such it was was the last in a long line of military disasters beginning with the Trunojoyo Rebellion (1676–9), which had destroyed the power of Sultan Agung's Mataram. By the end of the conflict, the Dutch remained in undisputed control of the island. Their rule would last for the next 112 years (1830–1942).

In retrospect, it seems strange that the Dutch took as long as they did to address the military challenge posed by Diponegoro's rebellion given the inherent tensions between the prince's *santri* and *kraton* supporters, as well as intense regional rivalries. Too much time was spent thinking that Diponegoro might be bought off with a quasi independent principality. It did not help that Dutch army was so ill-suited to the challenges of fighting a guerrilla war, nor that the relationship between the Dutch civilian and military authorities – represented by Du Bus and De Kock – was so poor.

Perhaps the greatest deficiency lay in the Dutch analysis of the Islamic community. Here they were fighting blind. There was no Christiaan Snouck Hurgronje (1857–1936)[3] to advise them. Had there been, De Kock and

---

3   A famous nineteenth-century Dutch scholar of oriental cultures and languages, who had served the colonial government as Adviser on Arab and Native Affairs

his military commanders might have exploited the tensions between Diponegoro's *santri* and *kraton* supporters much earlier, thus avoiding Van Geen's scorched earth strategy and the alienation of local civilian populations. A policy of attraction based on the honouring of Islamic institutions and practices, in particular a restoration of the competence of the Islamic law courts (*surambi*) (Carey 2008:386–7, 706; p. 153, p. 298), would have gone far to satisfying the religious grievances of Diponegoro's *santri* supporters.

One non-negotiable area was probably Javanese identity. Diponegoro had lived through a period when Javanese society had been turned upside down. His own experiences of the 20 June British attack on the Yogya *kraton*, his treatment at the hands of the post-1816 Dutch representatives and the seemingly irreversible tide of Europeanisation, had convinced him that the restoration of specifically Javanese values was a key priority and integral to his goal of 'raising up of the high state of the Islamic religion'. This explains his attitude to non-Javanese during the war, especially the Dutch and Chinese.

The Java War was the last attempt by the Javanese *ancien régime* to turn back the colonial tide. As such it was a magnificent failure. But it would inspire future generations of Indonesian nationalists (pp. 325–6). Transported on the first stage of his journey into exile on that most quintessential of products of the new industrial age – the first steamship in Netherlands Indies service – Diponegoro would have ample opportunity to reflect on the bitterness of defeat and the fate of those born to live in changed times.

(1889–1906) and had used his knowledge of Islamic cultures to crush resistance in Aceh while acting as political adviser to the local Dutch military commander and governor, General J.B. van Heutsz (1851–1924; in post, 1898–1904). Professor of Arabic at Leiden University (1906–36).

Bibliography

Anderson, B.R.O'G. (1967). *The Pemuda Revolution: Indonesian Politics, 1945–1946*. 2 vols. Ann Arbor: Michigan University Microfilms.

Aukes, H.F. (1935). *Het Legioen van Mangkoe Nagoro*. Bandoeng: Nix.

Babad Dipanegara (2010). *Babad Dipanegara*, 4 vols, ed. Nindya Noegraha. Jakarta: Perpustakaan Nasional Republik Indonesia.

Babcock, T.G. (1981a). *Religion and Cultural Identity in Kampung Jawa Tondano, Sulawesi Utara, Indonesia*. PhD thesis, Department of Anthropology, Cornell University [subsequently published as *Kampung Jawa Tondano; Religion and Cultural Identity*. Yogyakarta: Gajah Mada University Press, 1989].

Babcock, T.G. (1981b). 'Muslim Minahasans with Roots in Java; The People of Kampung Jawa Tondano', *Indonesia* 32:74–92.

Bataviasche Courant 44, 2–11–1825. Batavia: Landsdrukkerij.

Buku Kedung Kebo. Koninklijk Instituut (Leiden) manuscript. KITLV Or 13 (7–11–1866).

Broek, W. Palmer van den (1873–77) (ed. and trans.). 'Geschiedenis van het Vorstenhuis Madoera uit het Javaansch Vertaald', *Tijdschrift voor Indische Taal-, Land- en Volkenkunde (TBG)* 20:241–301, 471–563, 22:1–89, 280–310, 24:1–169.

Carey, Peter (1974a). *The Cultural Ecology of Early Nineteenth Century Java; Pangeran Dipanagara, A Case Study*. Singapore: Institute of Southeast Asian Studies. [Occasional Paper 24].

Carey, Peter (1974b). 'Javanese Histories of Dipanagara; The Buku Kĕdhuŋ Kĕbo, its Authorship and Historical Importance', *Bijdragen tot de Taal-, Land- en Volkenkunde* 130:259–88.

Carey, Peter (1981a). *Babad Dipanagara; An Account of the Outbreak of the Java War (1825–30); The Surakarta Court Version of the Babad Dipanagara with Translations into English and Indonesian Malay*. Kuala Lumpur: Art Printers.

Carey, Peter (1981b). 'The Indonesian Army and the State; Problems of Dwi Fungsi in Early Nineteenth-century Perspective', *Indonesia Circle* 26:51–8.

Carey, Peter (1984). 'Changing Javanese Perceptions of the Chinese Communities in Central Java, 1755–1825', *Indonesia* 37:1–48.

Carey, Peter (1987). 'Satria and Santri; Some Notes on the Relationship between Dipanagara's Kraton and Religious Supporters during the Java War (1825–30)', in: T. Ibrahim Alfian, H.J. Koesoemanto, Dharmono Hardjowidjono and Djoko Suryo (eds), *Dari Babad dan Hikayat sampai Sejarah Kritis; Kumpulan karangan dipersembahkan kepada Prof. Dr. Sartono Kartodirdjo*, pp. 271–318. Yogyakarta: Gadjah Mada University Press.

Carey, Peter (1992). *The British in Java, 1811–1816; A Javanese Account*. Oxford: Oxford University Press.
Carey, Peter (2008). *The Power of Prophecy; Prince Dipanagara and the End of an Old Order in Java, 1785–1855*. Leiden: KITLV Press.
Carey, Peter (2012). *Kuasa Ramalan; Pangeran Diponegoro dan Akhir Tatanan Lama di Jawa, 1785–1855*. Jakarta: KPG.
Carey, Peter and Vincent Houben (1987). 'Spirited Srikandhis and Sly Sumbadras; The Social, Political and Economic Role of Women in the Central Javanese Courts in the 18th and Early 19th Centuries', in: E. Locher-Scholten and A. Niehof (eds), *Indonesian Women in Focus; Past and Present Notions*, pp. 12–42. Dordrecht, Providence: Foris. [KITLV, Verhandelingen 127].
Chambert-Loir, Henri (2000). 'Le Chagrin d'un Belge; Le Journal de Campagne du Comte Édouard Errembault de Dudzeele durant la Guerre de Java', *Archipel* 60:267–300.
Crouch, H. (1978). *The Army and Politics in Indonesia*. Ithaca, London: Cornell University Press.
Djamhari, Saleh As'ad (2003). *Strategi Menjinakkan Diponegoro; Stelsel Benteng 1827–1830*. Jakarta: Yayasan Komunitas Bambu.
Gericke, J.F.C. and Roorda, T. (1901). *Javaansch-Nederlandsch Handwoordenboek*. Amsterdam: Muller, Leiden: Brill. Two vols.
Graaf, H.J. de (1940). 'Het Kadjoran-Vraagstuk', *Djåwå* 20:273–328.
Graaf, H.J. de (1958). *De Regering van Sultan Agung, Vorst van Mataram, 1613–1645, en die van zijn Voorganger Panembahan Séda-ing-Krapyak, 1601–1613*. The Hague: Nijhoff. [KITLV, Verhandelingen 23.]
Hogendorp, H. Graaf van (1913). *Willem van Hogendorp in Nederlandsch-Indië 1825–1830*. The Hague: Nijhoff.
Hooyer, G.B. (1895–97). *De Krijgsgeschiedenis van Nederlandsch-Indië van 1811 tot 1894*. Den Haag: Van Cleef, Batavia: Kolff. Two vols.
Houben, Vincent (1994). *Kraton and Kumpeni; Surakarta and Yogyakarta 1830–1870*. Leiden: KITLV Press. [Verhandelingen 164.]
Javasche Courant 1, 1–1–1828; 53, 1–5–1828; 111, 16–9–1828. Batavia: Landsdrukkerij.
Kemp, P.H. van der (1901–2), *Brieven van en aan Mr H.J. van de Graaff (1816–26); Een Bijdrage tot de Kennis der Oost-Indische Bestuurstoestanden onder de Regeering van G.A.G.Ph. Baron van der Capellen*. Batavia: Albrecht, The Hague: Nijhoff. Three vols. [Verhandelingen van het Bataviaasch Genootschap van Kunsten en Wetenschappen 52.]
Kielstra, E.B. (1896). 'De Gevangenneming van Dipa Negara', *Tijdspiegel* 53:84–92.
Knoerle 'Journal' (1830). 'Aanteekeningen Gehouden door den 2e Luit Knoerle betreffende de Dagelyksche Verkeering van dien Officier met den Prins van Djocjakarta,

Diepo Negoro, gedurende eene Reis van Batavia naar Menado, het Exil van den genoemden Prins', Manado, 20-6-1830. MS 391 of the Johannes van den Bosch private collection in the Nationaal Archief, The Hague.

Lagordt Dillié, P.M. (1863). *Bijdrage tot de Kennis der Oorlogvoering in de Nederlandsche Oost-Indische Gewesten*. Semarang: De Groot, Kolff.

Louw, P.J.F. and E.S. de Klerck (1894-1909). *De Java-Oorlog van 1825-1830*. The Hague: Nijhoff, Batavia: Landsdrukkerij. Six vols.

Mashoed Haka (1976). *Dunia Nyi Ageng Serang; Sejarah Wanita Pejuang Bangsa*. Jakarta: Kinta.

Mook, H.J. van (1972). *Kuta Gedé*. Jakarta: Bhratara [Reprint from 'Koeta Gedé', *Koloniaal Tijdschrift*, 1926, 15-4:353-400.]

Nypels, George (1895). *De Oorlog in Midden-Java van 1825 tot 1830*. Breda: Koninklijke Militaire Akademie.

Payen, A.A.J. (1988). *Voyage à Djocja-Karta en 1825; The Outbreak of the Java War (1825-30) as Seen by a Painter*. Edited by Peter Carey. Paris: Association Archipel.

Portier, P.D. (1826). 'Verklaring van Paulus Daniel Portier houdende een Verhaal van Zijn Gevangenschap bij de Muitelingen', Koninklijk Instituut (Leiden) manuscript, KITLV H 263, n.d. [? September 1826].

Prins, Bart de (2002). *Voor Keizer en Koning; Leonard du Bus de Gisignies 1780-1849 Commissaris-Generaal van Nederlands-Indië*. Amersfoort: Balans.

Ricklefs, M.C. (1974). *Jogjakarta under Sultan Mangkubumi, 1749-1792; A History of the Division of Java*. Oxford: Oxford University Press.

Ricklefs, M.C. (1993). *A History of Modern Indonesia since c. 1300*. Basingstoke: Macmillan.

Simatupang, T.B. (1972). *Report from Banaran; Experiences during the People's War*. Translated by Benedict Anderson and Elizabeth Graves. Ithaca: Modern Indonesia Project. [Cornell University Southeast Asia Program, Translation series 55.]

Soekanto, R. (1951). *Sentot alias Alibasah Abdulmustopo Prawirodirdjo Senopati Diponegoro (Seorang Terkemuka dalam Abad ke-19 dari Sedjarah Nasional Indonesia)*. Djakarta: Poesaka Aseli.

Sagimun, M.D. (1965). *Pahlawan Dipanegara berjuang; (Bara api Kemerdekaan nan tak kundjung padam)*. Djakarta: Gunung Agung.

Somer, J.M. (1938). *Drie Figuren uit den Java-oorlog; Dipa Negara, Kjahi Madja, Sentot*. Bandoeng: Visser.

Stuers, F.V.H.A. de (1833). *Mémoires sur la Guerre de l'Île de Java*. Leiden: Luchtmans.

Tilly, C. (1964). *The Vendée*. London: Arnold.

Valck, 'Overzigt' [F.G. Valck, 'Overzigt der Voornaamste Gebeurtenissen in het Djokjokartasche Rijk sedert dezelfs Stichting in den Jare 1755 tot aan het Einde van den door de Opstand van den Pangeran Ario Dhipo-Negoro Verwekten Oorlog in den Jaren 1825 tot en met 1830', 1–8–1833. Bundel Djokjo Brieven 9A (and 19[1]) of Arsip Nasional Republik Indonesia (ANRI), Jakarta].

Weitzel, A.W.P. (1852–53). *De Oorlog op Java van 1825 tot 1830; Hoofdzakelijk bewerkt naar de Nagelatene Papieren van Zijne Excellentie den Luitenant-Generaal Baron Merkus de Kock.* Breda: Broese.

CHAPTER XI

Betrayal or Honourable Submission? Diponegoro's Capture at Magelang and Journey Through Batavia, February–May 1830

Introduction

By the end of September 1829, it was clear that the Dutch had won the war. Earlier that month, Diponegoro had confided to Mangkubumi that he had received a divine instruction (*wangsit*) that his efforts would come to nought (17 September). Nothing remained for him in this world but to die a martyr's death in battle.

This conviction was confirmed four days later by the gruesome deaths of his uncle, Pangeran Ngabehi, and two sons in the Kelir mountains (21 September). When news of this terrible loss reached Diponegoro, he confided in his *babad* that he realised that he now remained alone in this world (Babad Dipanegara IV:87):

> XXXVII 97. [...]
> Tears welled up [and] the Sultan
> felt he was left alone
> in the Land of Java.
> He felt he could not control,
> even if he strove all the time,
> those that remained behind.
> [...]

The combination of strategic forts (*benteng*) and the doubling of Dutch mobile columns had hemmed Diponegoro into a narrow strip between the Progo and Bogowonto rivers. If September 1829 had been a black month,

October was no better: Sentot, who negotiated his own surrender (Carey 2008:652), and Diponegoro's mother, Raden Ayu Mangkorowati, and the prince's daughter, Raden Ayu Gusti (Carey 2008:73), were all in Dutch hands by the month's end.

Following his near capture on 11 November (Carey 2008:652-3), Diponegoro struggled on almost alone for three months assailed by acute tropical malaria and hiding out in the jungles of western Bagelen (p. 264). But with Dutch military strength at its peak, a f20,000 price on his head, and four mobile columns searching for him, his days as a fugitive were numbered. He would soon be forced to negotiate his surrender.

The present chapter describes the process whereby Diponegoro came to the negotiating table, starting with his initial contacts with Colonel Cleerens in mid-February 1830 through to his arrest at Magelang on 28 March and subsequent journey through Batavia (8 April–3 May) in preparation for his Sulawesi exile.

The Colonel's Promise: Diponegoro's Negotiations with Cleerens and the Question of Safe Conduct, 9–16 February 1830

After his defeat at Siluk (17 September 1829) (Louw and De Klerck 1894–1909, V:385–9), Diponegoro escaped across the Progo River. Then, following Ngabehi's death, he moved further west, fording the upper reaches of the Bogowonto River and travelling into central Bagelen (Louw and De Klerck 1894–1909, V:425–6). In Saleh Djamhari's words (2003:217), these events marked the end of the war: 'the majority of his troop commanders now gave themselves up out of frustration and sheer exhaustion'.

Hasan Munadi, his priestly Barjumungah regimental commander, counseled the prince to make for the mountain region of Remo between Bagelen and Banyumas, home of the Danurejan family, where his young commander, Basah Ngabdulmahmud Gondokusumo, was still holding out (Carey 2008:661).

Betrayal or Honourable Submission?

Munadi asked him whether he would ever surrender or settle for Yogyakarta as a consolation prize? No, the prince answered, he would never give himself up. He would feel too ashamed. As for being appointed sultan of Yogya 'then I should have only half succeeded [...] and all our troubles would have been in vain' (Carey 2008:661).

Regarding the Europeans, Munadi thought the prince would let them all remain in Java, but only as traders and then only in specially designated port towns on the north coast such as Batavia and Semarang (Carey 2008:661). The administration of the interior would be his and his alone. Despite the price on his head, Diponegoro would never be betrayed by his supporters. The only way he would be brought to submission would be by Dutch capture.

Munadi saw Diponegoro's plans to 'raise up the high state of the Islamic religion' as a ploy. This was not, however, the view of his other commanders. They saw him acting for the 'welfare of Java' because the sultan (Hamengkubuwono V) was not able to act as 'protector of the Islamic religion' (Carey 1974:287-8).

Munadi's refusal to give credence to the prince's aim of securing recognition as a 'regulator of religion' overlooked a central plank of his war effort. This issue alone would make a negotiated peace impossible at Magelang in March 1830. Munadi also missed something else: the possibility that Diponegoro might have a secret strategy to exhaust the Dutch treasury. As Pangeran Blitar II put it when Cleerens assured him that the Dutch would fight for as long as it took to bring Diponegoro to submission:

> Yes, that is what you say colonel, but people outside believe differently. Diponegoro says that the government cannot sustain its present-day expenditure and if he can remain hidden for one or two more years it will be unable to pay its troops (Carey 2008:662).

If this was his strategy, it was working. For three weeks following his near capture by Michiels' mobile column on 11 November 1829 (Carey 2008:652; p. 264), the prince disappeared. Then the Dutch had a breakthrough. Basah Kerto Pengalasan, the battle-scarred opium addict who had commanded the prince's forces in eastern Bagelen (Carey 1974:281), promised to open peace negotiations. He wrote to the prince's *patih*, Raden

Adipati Abdullah Danurejo, who was then hiding in western Bagelen (Carey 1974:281–2).

On 2 December, he received a reply: his messengers had been well treated. Danurejo requested a fourteen-day ceasefire. De Kock refused: there would be no ceasefire until Diponegoro wrote confirming his willingness to negotiate. Pengalasan then drafted another letter (Carey 1974:285) purporting to summarize 'His Highness the Sultan of Java's conditions for a peace settlement' (Carey 1974:285–8).

Unlike Munadi, Pengalasan gave due prominence to the prince's wish 'to restore the high state of the Islamic religion throughout the whole of Java', stating that 'if the Sultan of Java does not succeed in his determination to raise up [the Islamic] religion [...] he would rather depart this earth.' As we have seen (p. 226), he suggested that the prince and the Netherlands Indies government would be:

> as good friends, neighbours, and brothers [...] they should not order each other, neither should they be ordered by each other (Carey 1974:287–8).

Echoing Munadi, he thought the Dutch would be offered four choices: first, if they wished to remain in Java as soldiers in the pay of the Javanese, they would be allowed to keep their ranks and stipends provided they became 'the sword of religion', a reference to the VOC troops who had been used by seventeenth-century Mataram rulers against seditious movements like the Kajoran faction (De Graaf 1940:273–328).

Second, if they 'felt at home in Java' and stayed in a private trading capacity, they would only be permitted if they remained in specially designated north coast towns. Third, if they wished to return home to the Netherlands, 'we will continue to be forever as brothers with each other'. Fourth, if the Dutch 'entered the True Faith' and became Muslims then their livelihood and positions would be improved (Carey 1974:287–8).

But there were conditions: if the Dutch wanted Javanese produce they would have to pay the right market price for it and if they wanted 'to cultivate ricefields in Java' – namely lease land – they would have to pay the going rent (Carey 1974:287–8). If accepted, they would have prevented the subsequent excesses of the Cultivation System (1830–70) (p. 265, p. 326).

Betrayal or Honourable Submission? 275

And what of the Dutch: what were they prepared to offer now that the war was ending in their favour? The answer was not long in coming: on 4 January 1830, His Dutch Majesty's frigate *Rupel* anchored in Batavia road (Louw and De Klerck 1894–1909, V:529). On board was the new governor-general, Johannes van den Bosch (in office, 1830–4), bringing King Willem I's personal instructions that 'there should be no further negotiations, only an unconditional surrender will be permitted' (Kielstra 1896b:299):

> Do not enter into any agreement with him [...] only on the understanding of life imprisonment can his surrender or capture be sanctioned. No other understanding whatsoever [is allowed] (Carey 2008:666).

Diponegoro might even be killed Van den Bosch suggested (6 January 1830). This negated Pengalasan's promise that no harm would come to Diponegoro once negotiations began (Carey 2008:666). It was also not De Kock's style. A humane man, who had experienced the bitterness of wartime detention in Bengal and England (1811–13) (p. 121), he had some sympathy for the Javanese, preferring them to the 'infinitely worse' Belgians (Carey 2008:666–7; pp. 315–6). Even Diponegoro got a favourable press (Van der Kemp 1896:416; Kielstra 1896a:92; Carey 1981:lxix note 194). In Van den Bosch's words:

> Our officers, who have associated much with him [in Magelang, 8–28 March] over the past days, speak with praise about his intelligence and frank character, and General de Kock completely shares that opinion' (Van der Kemp 1896:416).

How could De Kock possibly accomplish Diponegoro's surrender if no negotiations were allowed? On 29 January, after handing command to Cochius (Louw and De Klerck 1894–1909, V:510), he hurried to Batavia to reason with the new governor-general (Louw and De Klerck 1894–1909, V:531; Kielstra 1896a:90), informing Cochius on 8 February:

> General Van den Bosch is no longer so completely set against negotiations, he only says that in Europe people are very much against (Kielstra 1896a:90).

The following day, he assured Diponegoro that 'he would be well received', a condition which Sentot had indicated he would insist on given the way he had been treated by previous pre-war Dutch officials (Kielstra 1896a:90; Chapter IX). De Kock's flexibility was not backed by Van den Bosch: after Diponegoro's arrival in Magelang, he wrote:

> Despite his capabilities [...] [Diponegoro] remains a criminal who inspires contempt [...]. To show favour to such a man would certainly be regarded as unpardonable weakness [...]. How would it appear if we favoured a man who has been so badly beaten as to be reduced to wandering in the forests with only two followers? (Carey 1982:7, 2008:668)

Temporary exile in Bandung with a vague promise that he might be allowed to undertake the *haj* (pilgrimage to Mecca) or return to the princely states when the political situation settled was the most he could hope for: 'In any event, once he has come to Magelang, he should not be allowed to slip through our fingers' (Louw and De Klerck 1894–1909, V:570).

Far away in western Bagelen, Cleerens had the delicate task of convincing the prince's intermediaries that it was in Diponegoro's interests to meet De Kock and open peace talks. What bait could he offer?

Diponegoro devotes almost a tenth of his chronicle to the process of these so-called 'peace negotiations' (Babad Dipanegara IV:118–87). Initially he refused even to receive Cleerens' letters (Babad Dipanegara IV:123). But eventually (9 February), he agreed to open talks with the Colonel, 'a man whose heart could be trusted' (Babad Dipanegara IV:133). Privately, however, he acknowledged that it was God's Will that he should experience 'suffering and shame in this world', predicting his later betrayal (Babad Dipanegara IV:126).

The prince's *pengulu*, Kyai Pekih Ibrahim, and confidante, Haji Badarudin, met Cleerens and invited him to confer with Diponegoro at Remokamal on the upper reaches of the Cingcinguling River on Tuesday, 16 February (Babad Dipanegara IV:126–8). Enough black cloth for 400 troops, ƒ200 in cash, one gold state umbrella (*payung*) to mark the prince's royal status and two pairs of scissors to cut his own and his troops' hair were requested (Carey 2008:670).

Cleerens asked the prince put his demands in writing. The resultant letter, however, caused consternation: Diponegoro had placed his *pegon* seal in the middle and used coarse Low Javanese (*ngoko*) of the sort employed by the sultan to junior court officials (Plate 20). In Yogya, the Resident, Van Nes, had never seen the like. The seal's position indicated, he thought, that Diponegoro 'stood in the centre of Java, and with his arms [outstretched], [...] wished to draw everything to him' (Carey 2008:672).

Diponegoro had a different take: he had only placed his seal at the centre because that was the position of The Prophet's city, Mecca, the centre of the world: 'You may not wish to pay your respects to The Prophet, who is most excellent', he told Cleerens, 'but it is my duty because in truth I am a believer in the The Prophet's religion' (Babad Dipanegara IV:137). As for the tone of the letter and the language used, he was just giving instructions to subordinates for the preparation of temporary bamboo pavilions (*pesanggrahan*). As a sultan, it was right for him to use Low Javanese to his juniors even if, in this case, the latter were Dutch officers (Carey 2008:671).

On 16 February, a 'polite and familiar' meeting took place at Remokamal. No conditions were agreed but friendly relations were established (Louw and De Klerck 1894–1909, V:554, 721). Diponegoro arrived with his mounted bodyguard, his commander, Mertonegoro, carrying the prince's heirloom *kris*, Kyai Ageng Bondoyudo, to ward off danger (Babad Dipanegara IV:135). Cleerens came late but treated the prince with great respect. Dismounting far from the pavilion, he doffed his cavalry *kepi* and walked the last distance under the midday sun (Babad Dipanegara IV:136). Pleasantries and jokes were exchanged, the prince observing sardonically that he required no further cannon salutes from the Dutch given that over 100,000 had been fired in his honour during the war (Babad Dipanegara IV:137)!

With De Kock absent in Batavia, the prince suggested he await his return in western Bagelen, but Cleerens persuaded him to journey on to Menoreh, a Dutch-held town on the Bagelen-Kedu mountain border (Louw and De Klerck 1894–1909, V:723). Greeted everywhere by an adoring population, his entourage had more than doubled to 700 by the time he reached Menoreh on 21 February.

The prince would spend just over a fortnight in the garrison town before setting off for Magelang on 8 March. During this time, despite his contempt for western medicine (p. 37), he allowed himself to be treated by a Dutch military doctor for his malaria and commenced preparations for the start of the fasting month on 25 February (Louw and De Klerck 1894–1909, V:723). Despite his robust constitution (Carey 2008:116; p. 36), it was clear that the privations of his fugitive months in western Bagelen had taken their toll. Cleerens reported that 'more than anyone else, [he] needs rest, his whole body is tired out' (Kielstra 1896b:299), his physical condition a reason for his willingness to enter negotiations.

At Menoreh, an issue came up with long-term consequences for both the prince and his Flemish host. This concerned the undertaking which Diponegoro thought Cleerens had given him regarding the forthcoming Magelang negotiations: namely, that if they proved not to his liking he would be allowed to return to Bagelen (Carey 2008:825–6). After his capture, he discussed this issue at length with his Javanese-speaking Dutch officer escort, Captain Roeps, stating that he had been under the impression that if no agreement could be reached, people should have 'let him return without hindrance to the mountains' (Louw and De Klerck 1894–1909, V:741).

The prince never forgot this betrayal. Five years after the war, when Cleerens had returned to Java loaded with honours as a titular major-general, Diponegoro wrote secretly to him from Makassar reminding him of his previous 'statements', a fateful communication which led immediately to tighter restrictions on the prince's life in Fort Rotterdam (Chapter XII), and possibly hastened the Flemish officer's replacement as military commander of Sumatra's West Coast (31 May 1837) (Louw and De Klerck 1894–1909, I:326 note 1; Carey 2008:676).

While none of the colonel's letters suggest that he gave any written promises to the prince, he certainly tried to reassure him, stating that he held himself personally responsible for his interests (Carey 2008:825–6). Repeating De Kock's promises that no harm would come to him, he treated Diponegoro like royalty, addressing him as 'sultan' and speaking to him directly in Malay. Privately, however, he took a critical view describing him as 'either a very stupid or a very dissembling person' and belittling his understanding of Islam (Carey 2008:676).

Strange Fast: Diponegoro at Magelang, 8–27 March 1830

On his return to central Java in early March, De Kock ordered Cleerens to bring the prince immediately to Magelang, but no sooner had Diponegoro begun his journey than he asked to return to Menoreh. There was no point in going to Magelang, he told Cleerens, because all he could do would be to pay De Kock a polite visit. No serious discussions could take place until after the end of the fasting month (27 March).

Eventually a compromise was reached; Diponegoro would meet De Kock initially for a courtesy visit. He would then observe the fast with his entourage in a specially prepared encampment on a promontory in the Progo River known locally as Metesih just to the northwest of the Magelang Residency House. Only when the fast was over would proper talks begin.

On 8 March at around noon, Diponegoro with his young commanders and an entourage now swollen to 800 entered Magelang (Louw and De Klerck 1894–1909, V:598; Carey 2008:678).[1] With so many Javanese troops in the heart of the garrison town and more expected, the Dutch feared they might have a fight on their hands should the prince have to be seized *manu militari* (Babad Dipanegara IV:173; Carey 2008:678). As a precaution, advance units of two Dutch mobile columns were brought up to Magelang to supplement the forces already at military headquarters (Louw and De Klerck 1894–1909, V:562, 644, 758).

De Kock's detailed report of the events of Diponegoro's time at Magelang up to his discretely termed 'coming over' (*overkomst*) is a major source for this three-week period (De Kock, 'Verslag', 1830; Louw and De Klerck 1894–1909, V:560–75, 588–90). Its self-reflective tone makes it especially interesting. De Kock was clearly troubled by the manner of the Java War leader's arrest as the juxtaposition of his description of the prince's formal reception on 8 March and his evening diary entry show.

---

1 Some impression of the number of Diponegoro's armed followers can be seen from the list of weapons taken from the prince's *prajurit* when they were disarmed during his arrest. These included 832 pikes, 87 rifles and a large number of *kris*, Carey 2008:678.

In a formal meeting attended by all senior Dutch officers and officials, but with no local Javanese *bupati* and princes of the blood present at Diponegoro's express request, De Kock received the prince, his commanders and religious advisers in the Residency House. Welcoming him as 'Pangeran [Prince] Diponegoro', he let him sit directly to his left, his entourage being placed on a row of chairs on both sides of the principle guest (Carey 2008:679).

The meeting was short. The commander-in-chief opened by saying that out of respect for 'different ways of thinking and the stipulations of other religious persuasions', the prince would be left in peace during the fasting month. But he hoped that after it was over, 'matters between them would be speedily settled'. Now that they had been enemies for five years, he trusted their friendship would endure much longer, the Netherlands Indies government being 'just and mild' (Carey 2008:679).

After conversing in a friendly fashion with the Dutch officers, Diponegoro was escorted to his prepared encampment at Metesih, De Kock's son-in-law, De Stuers, immortalizing the scene in a deftly executed sketch depicting a sombre prince, surrounded by his pikemen, riding up to the large bamboo and palm-leaf roofed pavilions (*pesanggrahan*) in the late afternoon sun (Carey 2008:684–5; Plate 18).

That evening, De Kock confided his doubts to his diary, doubts which would later be echoed by the Dutch king, Willem II's, son, Prince Hendrik 'De Zeevaarder' (1820–79) (Wassing-Visser 1995:246; p. 741; p. 319). 'According to some people' the Dutch commander wrote (Louw and De Klerck 1894–1909, V:566–7):

> I should have placed Diponegoro under immediate arrest because he is a rebel who had waged an insurrection against his ward and legal sovereign [Sultan Hamengkubuwono V] and against the Netherlands-Indies government. As a subject of one of the Javanese rulers, he had no right to any special consideration. [But] had he perceived [...] that his wishes would not be met, it is possible that he would have silently departed and recommenced hostilities. I realised that such a way of acting on my part was ignoble and dishonest [*onedel en oneerlijk*] since Diponegoro had come to Magelang in good faith to meet me. Indeed, [...] for anyone with even the slightest knowledge of the Javanese, the high degree of trust evinced by Diponegoro was striking.
>
> [...] I [thus decided] to win his trust in all ways possible so that if need be I could act forcibly at the end of the fasting month. [In this way] both Europeans and Javanese

Betrayal or Honourable Submission?

would be convinced that Diponegoro had only his own rash behaviour to blame for forcing me to take such drastic measures.

De Kock's behaviour towards Diponegoro was thus political: to ensure the submission of his remaining commanders and lull him into a false sense of security. His subsequent arrest would not appear an act of treachery, but an outcome of his intransigence. It was neither open nor honourable to proceed in this fashion, but in De Kock's view the end justified the means. Indeed, after the 8 March reception, he informed Van den Bosch that the prince's arrival in Magelang constituted a de facto submission (Louw and De Klerck 1894–1909, V:569).

De Kock's gestures of friendliness and consideration towards the prince continued: he allowed members of his family[2] to join him (Babad Dipanegara IV:165), and met him twice for pre-dawn walks in the Resident's garden as well as coming once to see him in person at Metesih before the start of the daily fast (Carey 1982:9 note 36). These encounters took place in 'a pleasant and unrestrained atmosphere', the two men exchanging jokes and taking pleasure in each other's company: the fact that both were mourning the deaths of their wives, who had died in the same year (1827–8), made their personal bond all the stronger (Babad Dipanegara IV:176–7; Louw and De Klerck 1894–1909, V:576; Carey 2008:683).

De Kock soon realised that Diponegoro would never surrender unconditionally. A spy, Tumenggung Mangunkusumo, whom the Kedu Resident, Valck, had placed in his entourage, reported that the prince was steadfast in his intention of obtaining recognition as sultan over the southern part of Java. Other senior officials stressed that Diponegoro wanted nothing less than the position as 'royal maintainer and regulator of religion in Java' or 'head of the Islamic religion' (Louw and De Klerck 1894–1909, V:573, 585; Carey 1982:10).

---

2   Those brought to Magelang included his mother, two daughters and two youngest sons, Raden Mas Joned and Raden Mas Raib (Louw and De Klerck 1894–1909, V:591). His second and third sons, Diponingrat and Dipokusumo, may also have joined him from Semarang (Carey 2008:682). His eldest son, Diponegoro II, arrived separately with the prince's northern Kedu commander, Basah Imam Musbah, from Gunung Sundoro.

Realising that such demands could not be considered without compromising the south-central Javanese rulers, De Kock decided to act decisively at the end of Ramadan. On 25 March, just two days before the end of the fast, he gave secret orders to two of his infantry commanders, Lieutenant-Colonel Louis du Perron (1793–1855) and Major A.V. Michiels (1797–1849) (Carey 2008:678), that when Diponegoro came to him to discuss his peace terms, all the necessary military preparations should be in place to secure his arrest (De Kock, 'Verslag', 1830).

On the day that Diponegoro was expected – 28 March 1830 – the usual guard at the Residency House was to be doubled, a move not expected to arouse suspicion because it was a Sunday when all troops paraded in full dress uniforms. On De Kock's instructions a detachment of hussars was dispatched to Bedono on the Kedu-Semarang border to escort the prince to Semarang (De Kock, 'Verslag', 1830). Meanwhile, the carriage of the Resident of Kedu was to be held in readiness to take Diponegoro immediately away from Magelang, Valck himself having penned a memo for Van den Bosch three days earlier urging Diponegoro's immediate exile from Java (Valck, 'Nota', 22–03–1830).

The senior infantry officers were enjoined to go about their task with the greatest possible composure and ensure that no one was harmed unnecessarily. Any resistance, however, was to be met by overwhelming force (Louw and De Klerck 1894–1909, V:589; Carey 1982:10 note 39). In this fashion everything was in place to secure Diponegoro's capture, disarm his 800 armed followers, and scotch last-minute opposition.

Betrayal or Honourable Submission? Diponegoro's End-of-Fast Meeting with De Kock, Sunday, 28 March 1830

Was it possible that Diponegoro was oblivious to these preparations? Did his sudden arrest during a courtesy visit to De Kock at the end of the fasting month really take him by surprise? Given his supposed skills in the

Betrayal or Honourable Submission?

science of physiognomy (*ilmu firasat*) why did he not immediately discern the proposed treachery on the faces of De Kock and his senior officers on his arrival in Magelang?

Gondokusumo, his young Remo-based commander, who accompanied him throughout, would later remark that Diponegoro always knew that he would be arrested. Decades later, at the end of a distinguished career as *patih* of Yogyakarta (in office, 1847–79), he had been asked by the Yogya Resident, A.J.B. Wattendorff (1827–1903; in office 1873–1878), what had really happened (Kielstra 1896a:85–6; Louw and De Klerck 1894–1909, V:573–4):

> [When Wattendorff] expressed the opinion that the capture of Diponegoro could not be reconciled with the highest standards of justice, the *patih* [Gondokusumo] showed himself considerably surprised.
> 'But Diponegoro already knew beforehand that it would turn out thus!' According to the *patih*, Diponegoro's pride prevented him from taking any other solution. He always put forward his demands to be recognised as sultan and head of the Islamic religion in Java, knowing full well that General De Kock would never permit them. He was *malu* [ashamed and embarrassed] to drop them, but he saw no ignominy in submitting to superior force. In this way his prestige in the eyes of the people would remain undiminished'.

By the time of his conversation with the Resident, Gondokusumo had been a senior official of the Yogyakarta sultanate for nearly fifty years. He would not have wanted to cause the Dutch offence (Carey 2008:168). But there is more than diplomatic deception in his explanation of the way in which Diponegoro met his fate.

In the prince's own *babad*, there are many indications that, although De Kock's volte-face pained him deeply, the arrest itself was not totally unexpected. In the view of Muslims, there is no dishonour in submitting to superior force. The way Diponegoro described the event and its antecedents indicates that he had long since given himself up to his destiny: 'we talk of the sultan [how] on the morning [of 28 March 1830] he was like gold being carried along by water' (Babad Dipanegara IV:279; Carey 1982:12).

This accepting attitude was later confirmed by De Stuers (Louw and De Klerck 1894–1909, V:746):

> If a trait in Diponegoro struck Captain Roeps and myself in particular then it was his unchanging indifference, resignedness or submission – I do not quite know how to describe this feeling [...] – concerning the dispositions which would be pronounced regarding his future life in exile [...].

The prince felt himself swept along by forces outside his control, an impression strengthened by a brief exchange with Gondokusumo on the morning of his arrest. When the latter suggested that all the prince's armed followers should accompany him to the Residency, Diponegoro realised that such was not God's Will. Telling Gondokusumo that such a move would cause 'unpleasant surprise', he ordered that everything should happen 'as normal' (*lir adat kewala*). On hearing this, the young *Basah* had kept silent despite his deep forebodings (Babad Dipanegara IV:179–80).

If such an incident did indeed occur – and in fact we know from other sources that Diponegoro brought over one hundred armed men with him to the Residency (De Kock, 'Verslag', 1830; Louw and De Klerck 1894–1909, V:590) – then it may have reinforced Gondokusumo's own premonition (*firasat*).

At eight in the morning of 28 March, Diponegoro described how he departed for the Residency 'suspecting nothing' (De Kock, 'Verslag', 1830; Louw and De Klerck 1894–1909, V:590). He did not even bother to wear his official clothes, but dressed 'as though for a pleasure trip' (Babad Dipanegara IV:180), a garb later depicted in Raden Saleh's famous arrest painting (March 1857) and a Madurese source (Van den Broek 1873–77, 24:99) as a green turban with a red-and-white pompom, long white *jubah* (tabard) worn over pantaloons, long-sleeved jacket, broad gold batik cloth belt with a string of prayer beads (*tasbeh*) attached and light batik shawl flung over his shoulders.

On his arrival, he was greeted by Valck and shown into De Kock's study. His three sons, Pangeran Diponegoro the Younger, Raden Mas Joned and Raden Mas Raib, along with his religious advisers, two *panakawan*, along with his bodyguard commander, Mertonegoro, accompanied him, others sitting on stools just outside the room where Diponegoro could see them. Lieutenant-Colonel Roest (1796–1875), one of De Kock's senior staff officers, Major-Adjutant De Stuers, and the military interpreter for Javanese, Captain Roeps, sat with the prince's entourage inside the study. The other Dutch officers present, including the artillery and cavalry commanders, Lieutenant-Colonel Aart de Kock van Leeuwen (1792–1840) and Major

Johan Jacob Perié (1788–1853), remained outside in the inner gallery to keep an eye on Diponegoro's followers and engage them in 'friendly conversation' (De Kock, 'Verslag', 1830; Louw and De Klerck 1894–1909, V:590-1).

The number of men fully equipped and armed in the vicinity of the Residency House aroused no suspicions amongst the prince's party. None considered that anything untoward was afoot (Louw and De Klerck 1894–1909, V:590). Indeed, Diponegoro remarked that everyone in his group felt fully at ease because De Kock behaved no differently than before (Babad Dipanegara IV:180). But no sooner had De Kock begun speaking than the mood changed. Remarking that the prince should not return to Metesih but should remain in the Residency House with him, Diponegoro immediately replied:

> Why should I not be allowed to return [general]? What should I do here? I have only come for a short time to pay you a friendly visit such as is the Javanese custom after the fasting month. At this time, those who are younger go to the homes of those who are older to nullify all the faults which have been committed [during the previous year]. In this case you, general, are the older party (Babad Dipanegara IV:181).

At this De Kock replied: 'the reason I [want to] detain [you] is that I wish to clear up all the matters between us this very day'.

With the conversation now taking an unexpected turn, Diponegoro remarked with great surprise: 'What matters, general? Indeed, I have neither matters on my mind nor do I harbour any [in need of discussion between us]' (Babad Dipanegara IV:181; Carey 2008:689). Valck then explained that for as long as Diponegoro had been at Magelang, the general and his officers had thought of nothing else but the issues to be settled between them. To which Diponegoro's commander, Mertonegoro, immediately interjected that political affairs (*prakawis*) were far from the prince's heart and that another day should be set to discuss them (Babad Dipanegara IV:180-1; Carey 1982:13-14).

> 'No!' answered De Kock, 'that cannot be allowed. Whether he wants it or not I wish to finish everything now!' (Babad Dipanegara IV:181).

De Kock's own testimony confirms this (De Kock, 'Verslag', 1830; Louw and De Klerck 1894–1909, V:14):

> I told him that I was responsible to the governor-general [Van den Bosch] and that I would be blamed if I did not make a speedy end to all outstanding matters [...] the costs of the war were rising and the time for repatriating the Dutch troops and Indonesian auxiliaries had almost passed. Again Diponegoro answered me that he could not discuss any matters with me today because he was not prepared for it. He asked me [to allow him] to return home so that he could think things over [and] would tell me later when he wished to come to speak with me. I told him a second time that matters must be ended now [and] that he had had enough time to think everything over during the fasting month. Whereupon Diponegoro observed that during that time he had not thought at all about political matters. I replied that I had thought about little else and that the welfare of my troops and that of the Javanese people had caused me to be continually mindful about ways in which the war could be brought to an end. Since God had now given me the opportunity, I should make good use of it [and] I would not be put off by any further delays or promises. In the name of the governor-general I now ordered Diponegoro to tell me what his intention had been when he requested to meet me, what he had to say to me and in what way he desired that the war should be brought completely and utterly to a close.

When this was translated, the prince complained bitterly about the way he was being treated, saying that he had come to Magelang of his own free will and that, according to Cleerens' undertaking, he should be at complete liberty to depart if he could not come to an agreement (Carey 2008:690). De Kock noted that 'much conversation occurred between Diponegoro and the people with him. But when he saw that I could not be moved to change my previous decision [insisting on immediate negotiations], the big words came out: Diponegoro said that he wanted nothing else than to be the head of the Islamic religion in Java and to retain his title of sultan. He left all the other arrangements entirely up to the discretion of the government' (De Kock, 'Verslag', 1830; Louw and De Klerck 1894–1909, V:595; Carey 2008:690).

On hearing this, De Kock instructed his chief-of-staff, Roest, to order Du Perron to march his troops out of the Magelang barracks and bring them to the Residency. Meanwhile, the Residency guard entered the front gallery where Diponegoro's other followers were seated (De Kock, 'Verslag', 1830; Louw and De Klerck 1894–1909, V:597). The prince's arrest was just minutes away.

Diponegoro also referred to De Kock's orders to the awaiting Dutch troops, but before doing so he reported a more emotional conversation

Betrayal or Honourable Submission?

between himself and the Dutch commander-in-chief (Babad Dipanegara IV:183–4):

> 'You ask who is the chief man [*panggedhé*] of the war in Java, he is none other than I, General De Kock! Muslims do not leave their own kind. If people engage in war there must be an opposing party. People do not quarrel with their own friends. It is you, general, who out of your own wishes, want to dispense justice. [But] whoever heard of such a case in which one of the quarrelling parties acts as magistrate [*jeksa*]? If such is the situation, it only occurs because of your wickedness. I am not afraid of death. In all the fighting I escaped it. [As for my followers] they merely carried out my orders during the war [...] and thus cannot be held responsible. Now indeed nothing else remains [for me] except to be killed [and] I am not intending to avoid it. But I charge you, when I am dead, to bring my body back to Jimatan [Imogiri] so that I can be together with my wife [Raden Ayu Maduretno].' General De Kock could not raise his eyes, as though exceedingly ashamed, so he just [sat] with bowed head and said softly: 'Indeed, Tuwan, I have no intention of killing you. But [...] it would not be fitting to follow your desires here for if they were followed, the Sunan [of Surakarta] would be deeply ashamed.'

In his report, De Kock also mentioned Diponegoro's request to be killed on the spot rather than be sent away into exile (Louw and De Klerck 1894–1909, V:597–8; De Kock, 'Verslag', 1830):

> I told Diponegoro that his conduct up to that time had made me fear that he would come up with such rash demands [and] that he could have easily concluded that the government could not now permit what had not even been discussed in 1827 [during the Salatiga negotiations, p. 259]. He knew well that the government had promised and given protection to the Sunan of Surakarta and the Sultan of Yogyakarta for the past five years, and that these rulers were, according to eastern custom, themselves the heads of religion in their own lands. Diponegoro then said that if what he wanted was not accorded him, the government could do with him what it chose, but that he himself was not going to give up his demands. To which De Kock replied that in his view Diponegoro had forfeited all further trust and that he could detain him as a prisoner, and send him to Ungaran or Salatiga, leaving subsequent decisions as to his fate to the governor-general (De Kock, 'Verslag', 1830; Louw and De Klerck 1894–1909, V:597).

De Kock was less than honest here given that arrangements had already been made with De Kock's adjutant and son-in-law, De Stuers, and his military interpreter for Javanese, Roeps, to escort Diponegoro first to Semarang and then to Batavia. Perhaps he just wanted to pretend that Diponegoro would be kept initially at Ungaran or Salatiga in order to reassure him that he would not be required to leave the Javanese heartland or *kejawèn* (Carey 2008:693). 'Hereupon', noted De Kock ('Verslag', 1830; Louw and De Klerck 1894–1909, V:597–8):

> Diponegoro protested strongly asking about what in fact the government would permit. I answered that it was at present too late to return to that again because he was now entitled to neither trust nor consideration. If he had wanted to live as a simple *pangeran* [prince] with his family and a good income in the territories of the government, or if he wanted to make the journey [*haj*] to Mecca, the governor-general might well have allowed him his more modest requests. But after the obstinate pride he had shown, there was nothing more to be done with him, and moreover the peace of Java, and the protection which the government had promised the Javanese rulers, urgently demanded that he should be removed from the princely territories.

During the time when this conversation was taking place, Major Michiels with his mobile column troops and Du Perron's Magelang garrison force were nearing the Residency. Michiels went straight to Diponegoro's encampment at Metesih to disarm the prince's armed followers then on their morning exercises. This occurred peacefully. Once De Kock had been informed, he immediately ordered the disarming of the hundred or so troops who had accompanied Diponegoro to the Residency House. Their commanders, who were sitting in the front gallery, were asked to surrender their *kris*[3] (Carey 2008:693).

De Kock then told the prince that he must leave at once under the escort of the two designated officers. Any of his wives and children who wished to follow him had permission to do so. To which Diponegoro replied, 'very simply that he did not wish to depart and that I could have

---

[3] According to Dutch sources, Diponegoro later surrendered one of his heirloom daggers, Kangjeng Kyai Nogo Siluman (His Highness the Magician King of the Snakes), to De Kock following his arrest. Subsequently given to King Willem I (reigned 1813–40), and kept in the Royal Curio Collection (*Koninklijk Kabinet van Zeldzaamheden*), it was seen by Raden Saleh in January 1831, see *De Indische Courant* (Surabaya), 23-12-1931; Kraus 2005:280; Carey 2008:813; Hari Atmoko, 25-11-2013.

him killed on the spot for he did not want to be sent away. [Moreover,] the treatment he was receiving was wholly contrary to what had been promised him [by Cleerens]' (De Kock, 'Verslag', 1830; Louw and De Klerck 1894–1909, V:598).

> 'I told him', reported De Kock, 'that he must not forget that he had been the guardian of the young sultan of Yogyakarta, and that instead of protecting him he had betrayed and hurt his pupil, [acting entirely] contrary to the prohibitions of the *Qur'ān*. That notwithstanding all the misfortunes he had brought to Java and which he himself had experienced, he could not be dissuaded from his detestable plans for which reason he could count on no compassion [from me]. That [any such treatment] would betray great weakness on my part and that I had not waited so patiently until the end of the fasting month [to behave so] (De Kock, 'Verslag', 1830; Louw and De Klerck 1894–1909, V:598).'

Diponegoro then asked his chiefs and children whether they would allow him to be carried off in this manner, but they all cast their eyes to the ground and did not answer. Soldiers encircled the Residency House. At this point, according to De Kock ('Verslag' 1830; Louw and De Klerck 1894–1909, V:598-9):

> Diponegoro wanted absolutely to talk with his *pengulu*, Kyai Pekih Ibrahim, who was brought into the room. 'Did you not ask Colonel Cleerens on my behalf', Diponegoro said, 'that I would be free to return if I did not reach an agreement with the government?' 'Yes!' answered the *pengulu*. After which Diponegoro spoke again with his chiefs and took a cup of tea. When I saw it was nearly ten o'clock and that he must depart, I let the [Resident's] carriage drive up and ordered Major-Adjutant De Stuers and Captain Roeps to take the prisoner on the first day to Ungaran and the following one to Semarang, and from there to depart by the first shipping opportunity to Batavia. I gave these officers a written order and it was just striking ten o'clock when the disturber of the peace of Java, stripped of all his greatness, was taken away as a prisoner. *Gelukkig* [Thank goodness]! Praise be to God! All is concluded.

News of the event was immediately sent to the governor-general, the Residents of Java, and senior officers and officials in the Principalities. On 1 April, the government newspaper, *Javasche Courant*, published a special 'arrest' supplement and soon all the European community in Java were apprised.

On the same day as this publication, De Kock finished his report and made three concluding observations: first, that throughout the proceedings Diponegoro had shown not the slightest fear; second, that De Kock regarded the report as a way of defending his actions against the censure of future critics one of whom would be no less a person that the eldest son of the Dutch king (Wassing-Visser 1995:246; Kattendijke-Frank 2004:121; Chapter XII); and third, that had Diponegoro not come to the Residency House, he would have gone to Metesih to 'carry him off' (*oplichten*). But such a course would have been fraught with danger, and it was likely that the prince would have left everything and escaped (Louw and De Klerck 1894–1909 note 1).

Paintings and Perceptions; Dutch and Javanese Views of Diponegoro's Arrest

The general's tactics of feigned friendship and accommodation had paid off. Diponegoro was arrested without bloodshed and De Kock could boast that after five years of bitter warfare he had obtained victory. On returning to a hero's welcome in the Netherlands in late October 1830, he would commission the most celebrated Dutch history painter of his age, Nicolaas Pieneman (1809–60), to execute a tableau of the moment when he had come out on the steps of the Residency House to point Diponegoro into the Resident's waiting carriage (Carey 2008:695–6; Plate 21).

Entitled 'The Submission of Diponegoro to Lieutenant-General De Kock, 28 March 1830', it is a paean to De Kock's victory. As Raden Saleh's biographer, Werner Kraus (2005:282), points out, Pieneman made Diponegoro and his retainers look duly submissive. All seemed to understand that De Kock's stern action was for the best for the Javanese and that he had no choice but to send the prince away 'just like a loving father sending a misguided son away to teach him a valuable lesson'. Here was no 'monstrous colonizer' but 'an educated and civilized gentleman, respected

Betrayal or Honourable Submission?

leader of the [Indies] freemasons' (Kraus 2005:282). All those depicted in the painting are relaxed, even those in tears. 'There is no resistance, no commotion and high above the pageant flies merrily the Dutch tricolor [...] Pieneman's painting is a tribute to the glory of the Dutch. The pain of the Javanese is nowhere to be seen' (Kraus 2005:282–5; Carey 2008:695–6).[4]

But this was not how Diponegoro or most of his followers saw it. After De Kock had pointed out that any change in the supervision of religion in south-central Java would cause shame and embarrassment to the Sunan, the prince replied disdainfully in Low Javanese (Babad Dipanegara IV:184–5):

> 'Heh, general, I think a man with such ideas will have a lot of trouble with my religion! Moreover, general, why are you, who do not [even] follow [my] religion talking thus? In truth, I am not asking about [my] religion [...]. Even if you should leave [the regulation of] your [Christian] religion in my hands, I certainly would not be willing, [for] what should I do with it? But as for Muslims who misrepresent their religion, I desire to put them in order. [Now] there's a difficult business! They do not side with you, but it is not sure that they will side with me [either]. What should one call people who act thus, general? All the same, have them choose between my religion and yours [and see] which they choose. Only then will it be apparent what they have set their hearts on.'
>
> The general answered: 'That would be to my liking!'
>
> His Highness the sultan replied: 'If, general, this is what you are content with, I cannot parley with you [...] The only purpose of my coming here was to press you to make good what you had earlier written in [your previous] letters, [namely] your promised undertaking that I should become head of the Islamic religion in Java. Now you have broken [your promise] and I stand as a witness to all your treachery. For earlier, Colonel Cleerens gave me an undertaking that if the discussions came to nought, I would be invited to return to Kecawang.'
>
> The general spoke thus: 'If, Tuwan, you return war will not fail to break out again.'

---

4   Pieneman's painting (oils on canvas, 77 × 100 cms) was completed sometime between 1832–35 and hung in De Kock's study in The Hague. It was presented by De Kock's grandson to the Rijksmuseum in Amsterdam in January 1907 and can be viewed on the Rijksmuseum website – https://www.rijksmuseum.nl/ (SK-A-2238), persistent URL http://hdl.handle.net/10934/RM0001.COLLECT.7679. Raden Saleh appears to have seen the painting in Pieneman's studio during his artistic apprenticeship in The Netherlands (1830–9), inspiring him to paint his Javanese 'nationalist' interpretation of the arrest scene in 1856–7, see Plate 22.

His Highness the sultan replied: 'Why are you fearful of war if you are soldiers and real men?'

General De Kock said, 'If it is thus, [...] I cannot settle the question, because I am no longer in a position to do so [a reference to De Kock's subordinate position to Van den Bosch]. But at Salatiga there is someone [Van den Bosch] with a further mandate. He can settle it. So you had better go to Salatiga.'

His Highness the sultan said in a friendly voice: 'Why should I go to Salatiga? What would I seek there, general? I have not the slightest intention of seeking justice in Salatiga! Moreover, if you, De Kock, want [to finish things] here now, I am not willing.'

General De Kock then went out and with a thunderous voice ordered all the troops to enter the Residency.

At this point, according to a Dutch source, one of the prince's followers drew his *kris* and placed himself in front of Diponegoro as though to protect him, a detail confirmed in the prince's *babad* where his eldest son, Pangeran Diponegoro [the Younger] is described as '[getting] up from his seat [...] and coming close to the Resident [Valck]' (Babad Dipanegara IV:185–7):

> Whereupon the sultan winked to Raden Basah Mertonegoro and said: 'General, you are bringing everything into a difficult pass!' [...] Then De Kock took His Highness by the hand and brought him to sit on the sofa. The general also sat. Time and again, the sultan debated in his heart: 'If I kill the general, the end will be trouble for it is beneath the dignity of a prince to fight as one who runs amok. It would bring me into disrepute. [The Dutch are perpetrating] an unheard of treachery, but I have no companion [*kanthi*] [and] it is better that I give myself up to my fate. Those who remain can decide whether they wish to follow my orders in life and death as so many have already done. I had better share their lot!'
>
> The sultan then instructed that Mas Pengulu [Pekih Ibrahim] should be summoned. Once he had come [...] the sultan said, 'How comes it *pengulu* that things have turned out thus?' Mas Pengulu replied: 'It is best, Highness, that you just follow the instructions of your brother [De Kock].' The sultan smiled [and] said in a companionable way: 'Come on, Major [De Stuers] let us depart!' The general then said: 'Will you not [take] your sons, army commanders and soldiers?'
>
> The sultan replied: '[No], that would [only] give more trouble!' His Highness then got into the coach, only one intimate retainer followed him, Roto by name, who bore the sultan's betelbox. [They sat] together with Captain Roeps [and] Major de Stuers [...]. The sultan was greatly ashamed at heart and was prepared to die. It was on a Sunday, the second of the [Javanese] month Sawal in the [Javanese] year Jimawal [28 March 1830] that His Highness departed from the land of Java. The

Betrayal or Honourable Submission? 293

wish of His Highness was to go on the pilgrimage [to Mecca] because of his great shame. He was not attached to all his high dignity nor to his loved ones, to his mother [and] his children. As regards his followers, nothing remained for them but to await the sultan's yielding to superior power and resigning himself to God's dispensation [...].

Thus Diponegoro closed his account of his dramatic and – in his view – treacherous – meeting with De Kock in Magelang. Whether he came to Magelang under the impression that his demands to be appointed as 'regulator of religion' in Java would be honoured or whether, as Gondokusumo has it, he came in the full knowledge that he would be taken prisoner, must remain an open question. The latter is more likely. Not only would it demonstrate that he had been forced to bow to superior force, but it would also salve his pride and guarantee his place in history (Carey 2008:697–8).

Twenty-seven years after Pieneman painted the heroic scene of the prince' 'submission', another artist, Arab-Javanese this time, Raden Saleh Syarif Bustaman (circa 1811–1880), would produce a very different tableau (March 1857). Entitled in German *'Ein Historisches Tableau, die Gefangennahme des Javanischen Häuptlings Diepo Negoro'* ('An Historic Tableau, The Arrest of the Javanese Chief Diponegoro') (Carey 1982:1, 1988:139 note 239), the composition has an extraordinary emotional quality. A clearly furious Diponegoro stands at the centre of the painting having just emerged onto the steps of the Residency House. Struggling to keep his feelings under control, his look is charged with a fiery determination. His left hand clenched across his waist, he stretches out his right to console a weeping Javanese woman – perhaps his wife[5] – who is clutching distraughtly at his leg. As Kraus (2005:285–6) describes, the faces of De Kock and the other Dutch officers are frozen as though staring into the middle distance (Plate 22).

Whereas in Pieneman's version, the prince is placed a step lower than the general, Saleh sets Diponegoro on the same level, but to the right thus

---

5   Raden Ayu Retnoningsih: this was a piece of artistic licence on Saleh's part because were no women in Diponegoro's entourage at the Residency.

placing the Dutchman on the weaker female side in the Javanese spatial order. Instead of pointing the prince out of his country, the Java War leader is being 'invited' by a somewhat hapless De Kock to enter the waiting coach. Most significantly, the heads of De Kock and his fellow officers are out of proportion, too big for their bodies, a feature immediately noticed by a Dutch reviewer at Saleh's *vernissage* (unveiling) of his painting in Batavia in March 1857 (*Java Bode*, 1857). By contrast, the heads of the grieving Javanese witnesses are of the right size. No error this, but a message: the heads of the Dutch officers are those of *raksasa* (monsters), that of De Kock being depicted as a female *raksasa*, a particularly revolting form of ogre (Kraus 2005:286).

The major difference, Kraus argues, is in the perspective with which Pieneman and Saleh chose to depict the drama. Whereas the Dutch artist constructed his painting from the northwest, Saleh took the northeast as his point of departure. In Kraus' words (2005:286):

> The Dutchman Pieneman introduced a sharp wind from the west – common in Holland – that gives the Dutch flag a very dynamic appearance. In Raden Saleh's work the atmosphere is absolutely quiet. The universe holds its breath, no leaf and certainly no flag is moving. [In fact,] Raden Saleh has 'forgotten' the Dutch tricolor altogether.

In Saleh's painting it is morning, the dawn of a new day: not only the dawn of a new colonial era, but also one which would herald the collapse of that order. The memory of Diponegoro – his genius and his suffering – would one day, Saleh seems to tell us, redeem the nation from the shackles of colonialism (Kraus 2005:278).

As if in response, nature itself would put on its own awesome display of power as a counterpoint to the drama of that historic morning in Magelang, the garrison town whose High Javanese name means 'stubborn' (Gericke and Roorda 1901, II:521). As the Dutch mobile column commanders returned to their respective posts in Bagelen and Kulon Progo, the heavens opened and sheets of torrential rain lashed the south-central Javanese countryside sweeping away the horse of Colonel Cleerens' deputy as he tried to ford a swollen river. So the Java War ended as it had begun under the watery sluice of the west monsoon (p. 230).

Steamboat to Batavia: How Diponegoro received the Governor-General's Life Sentence

'How have I come to this? How did I come to this?' Diponegoro's exclamations broke the silence in the carriage which bore him on the first leg of his journey under cavalry escort to Bedono (Louw and De Klerck 1894–1909, V:741). Still suffering from malarial fevers, he did not speak another word throughout the remainder of his journey (Carey 2008:699).

Reaching Ungaran fort[6] in the late afternoon, Diponegoro asked to be excused to go up to pray on the battlements, his first *ṣalāt al-maghrib* (evening prayer) as an exile. De Stuers and Roeps watched him. He then dined with the commandant and his officer escorts, De Stuers observing that he 'had a very good understanding of European customs. I had [...] never seen a prince [...] sit and eat so decently at table' (Louw and De Klerck 1894–1909:741; Carey 2008:699).

Arriving in Semarang on the evening of 29 March, Diponegoro spent a week in the Residency House in Bojong, Van den Bosch having decided not to hold him in the town jail. Eating every day at the Resident's table, he refused wine, but developed a liking for freshly baked white bread and Dutch potatoes (*kentang Welondo*) or 'exile's potatoes' (*kentang sabrang*) in the punning words of his *panakawan*, Roto (Knoerle, 'Journal', 4, 11–13, 34, 47; Carey 2008:700; p. 308). Although watched by a strong guard and never allowed out of his escorts' sight, the prince 'gradually got into a good mood and was pleased with the considerate treatment at the Residency' (Carey 2008:701).

On 3 April, when informed that he would board the steamship SS *Van der Capellen* for Batavia, the prince 'expressed immediate readiness, only requesting that [on arrival in Batavia] long negotiations would not be held with him again, 'People know that I long to have my legal rights

---

6   Fort De Ontmoeting, a name derived from Governor-General Van Imhoff's (in office, 1743–50) meeting with Sunan Pakubuwono II (reigned, 1726–49) at Ungaran on 11 May 1746.

or be sent to Mecca or to [some] other place." De Stuers explained that these 'legal rights' meant that 'he [would have] the authority to appoint one priest at Yogya and one in Solo, who would exercise the law according to the *Qur'ān* and not according to our [European] laws' (Louw and De Klerck 1894–1909, V:744).

That this 'other place' might mean exile in eastern Indonesia was clearly on the prince's mind. He asked De Stuers whether Ambon was a large island, but the major suggested that he would decide his own fate, only breaking the news that he would be placed at the governor-general's disposal once they had boarded the steamer (Louw and De Klerck 1894–1909, V:742, 744; Carey 2008:701).

On the morning of 5 April, Diponegoro's nineteen-strong party went down to the harbour, De Stuers reporting that (Louw and de Klerck 1908, V:746),

> Diponegoro was in good heart but silent, perceiving many people on the wharf [...] [he] covered his face with an end of his turban, which excited the multitude even more, but caused at the same time a great disappointment [...] I saw no emotion in him. On board everything suited him very well: 'Here I am', he said, 'entirely at my ease, so I could quite remain thus. I am perfectly content provided people treat me in a polite and friendly manner (looking at us), but my present situation is the consequence of the surly and contemptuous treatment which I had to experience before [at the hands of Smissaert, Chevallier and Dietrée].'

To strengthen his spirits, he drank a bottle of zemzem water from Mecca given him in Magelang by a recently returned *haji* (Knoerle, 'Journal', 42). So fortified, he prepared to learn what the governor-general had in store for him on his 8 April arrival in Batavia.

Although news of the prince's arrival had not been gazetted (De Haan 1935, II:222 note 1), crowds of curious European onlookers chartered small boats or gathered at the wharf to watch him disembark. One of these was a young Scotsman, George Frank Davidson, brother of the SS *Van der Capellen* captain (Campbell 1915, II:780):

> I saw him landed at Batavia [...] from the steamer which had brought him from Semarang. The governor[-general's] carriage and aide-de-camps were at the wharf to receive him. In that carriage he was driven to gaol, whence he was banished, no

Betrayal or Honourable Submission?

one knows whither [...] Poor fellow! How his countenance fell [...] when he saw where the carriage drew up! He stopped short on putting his foot on the pavement, evidently unwilling to enter the gloomy looking pile. [He] cast an eager eye around and, seeing there was no chance of escape, walked in. Several gentlemen followed. Before the authorities had the door closed, I saw the fallen chief, with his two wives[7] confined to two miserable looking rooms (Davidson 1846:9).

'The gloomy looking pile' was the Batavia *Stadhuis* (Town Hall) where Diponegoro was held from 8 April–3 May 1830 (Van Doren 1851, II:54; De Haan 1935, II:222) and the 'two miserable looking rooms' the jail warder's quarters situated above the city prison in the *Stadhuis'* cellars, where Kyai Mojo and his party had recently been held (January 1829–February 1830) in terrible conditions (Carey 2008:703, 789). The two high-ceilinged rooms on the upper storey of the west wing of the Town Hall was a place used for detaining prominent local chiefs and Europeans (De Haan 1935, II:222).

During his time in the fetid colonial capital, the prince was met by members of the Batavian city administration led by the president of the *landraad* (town court) – Jan van der Vinne (1793–1870; in office, 1829–31) – a man of great vision and energy, who served as vice-president of the Bataviaasch Genootschap van Kunsten en Wetenschappen (Batavian Society of Arts and Sciences), a learned society which would later copy his *babad* (Nieuwenhuys 1973:82; Chapter XII note 1). They included the Batavia chief magistrate (*hoofdbaljuw*), Adrianus Johannes Bik (1790–1872; in office, 1828–30) (Bervoets 1977:2), who served as Diponegoro's guardian during his sojourn in the *Stadhuis*. A gifted draughtsman, Bik sketched a vivid likeness of the prince,[8] showing him with very high cheek bones and sunken cheeks, a result of his recurrent malaria (Plate 19).

Diponegoro clearly found his twenty-eight-day stay in the Stadhuis a trial, later telling Knoerle during his Manado journey that 'his health did

---

7   These were in fact Diponegoro's wife, Raden Ayu Retnoningsih, and his younger sister, Raden Ayu Dipowiyono, who accompanied him into exile, pp. 311–2.
8   This once hung in the Musium Kota (post-2006, Museum Sejarah Jakarta) where I photographed it in February 1977. It has since been taken off the walls because of damp and apparently placed in store. But all subsequent requests to trace it have failed.

not permit him to remain in Batavia where he was exposed to the frightful heat prevailing in the place' (Knoerle, 'Journal', 47).

The prince was not the only dignitary in the colonial capital suffering from poor health. Sixty kilometres away in the cooler mountain air of Bogor, the prince's nemesis, Johannes van den Bosch, was also indisposed (Carey 2008:703). Captain Roeps, who had remained in Batavia with the prince, was summoned to give him a personal report on his recent talks with Diponegoro during their journey to Batavia, Roeps dwelling particularly on the religious aspects of the war and the influence of the *ulama* (Carey 2008:706).

Van den Bosch immediately confided to the Councillor of the Indies (*Raad van Indië*), Pieter Merkus (1787–1844; in office, 1829–35), that 'the perturbation of priests', in particular their discontent over the abolition of penalties of the *Qur'ān* (p. 153), was the key reason the widening of the war. He asked Merkus to enquire into ways of 'pacifying the priestly class', suggesting that the government might be more accommodating over the issue of Islamic law (Carey 2008:706).

With regard to Diponegoro, he showed himself much less flexible. His initial suggestions that the prince might remain in Java were now replaced by lifetime banishment. He was thus to be held as a state prisoner (*staatsgevangene*) in Manado, 'the most suitable place outside Java', whither Kyai Mojo and his party had recently been dispatched (February 1830) (Carey 2008:706).

Given Van den Bosch's illness, the terms of the prince's banishment were worked out by two other Indies councillors, J.C. Goldman and Isaac Bousquet, who sent their draft *besluit* (government order) and instructions to Bogor for his signature. On 30 April 1830, both were officially approved, the order stipulating that 'a suitable residence' be found 'in accord with Diponegoro's rank', if possible on a river with a piece of adjacent ground where he could 'wander' and where a garden could be laid out for him (Carey 2008:706–7).

In his *babad* and shipboard conversations with Knoerle, Diponegoro also mentions these stipulations, suggesting that they were part of a promise made him by Van den Bosch. In Knoerle's words ('Journal', 47):

Betrayal or Honourable Submission?

> Diponegoro made it appear as if his removal to Manado was due to his own wishes. [...] People had promised [him] gardens, carriages, and as it were unconstrained use of his personal liberty. [...] [He] always seeks every available [opportunity] to persuade me that his freedom may not be hampered in Manado.

As De Kock had done in Magelang, the officers dealing with Diponegoro in Batavia were perhaps being economical with the truth, encouraging him in the notion that his Manado exile constituted a form of temporary 'retirement' until the Dutch monarch could approve his long-desired Mecca pilgrimage (Babad Dipanegara IV:196).

That this was far from the spirit of Van den Bosch's order can be seen from the stipulations regarding the prince's state prisoner status. These speak of Manado more as part of a Dutch eastern Indonesian 'gulag' (concentration camp area) than a place of honourable retirement. As many as fifty soldiers were to accompany Diponegoro on his Manado voyage. On their arrival, the Resident was to retain a sufficient number to guard the prince and ensure that he could not escape (Carey 2008:707–10).

Despite this close surveillance, Diponegoro was to be treated 'in a friendly fashion' and due account taken of his birth and rank. The same 600-guilder monthly stipend accorded the second sultan in Ambon (1817–25) was to be paid, and he was permitted to choose two 'priests' from Kyai Mojo's following in Tonsea Lama (Tondano) to assist him in his religious duties (Carey 2008:710).

The governor-general's order likewise made arrangements for Diponegoro's family. Since none of the prince's children wished to follow him to Manado, it was proposed that his eldest son, Pangeran Diponegoro II, and other family members should be allowed to return to Tegalrejo[9] (Babad Dipanegara IV:197), a request Van den Bosch approved providing 'they did not constitute a danger for Java'. Others, such as the prince's second eldest son, Pangeran Dipokusumo, and third son, Pangeran Diponingrat, were to be given quarters in the Yogya *kraton* (Van den Broek 1873–77, 24:105). Finally, the draft decree made provision for the division

---

9 Tegalrejo had been so badly destroyed at the start of the Java War (20 July 1825) that it proved uninhabitable for Diponegoro's relatives, Carey 2008:711.

of Diponegoro's heirloom *kris* and pikes, Captain Roeps being tasked with their distribution to family members (Carey 2008:813–15). The only exception was Diponegoro's personal *kris*, Kyai Ageng Bondoyudo, which remained with him until his death (Carey 2008:813; p. 323).

On 27 April, Knoerle received his secret orders direct from Van den Bosch. These tasked him as officer escort during Diponegoro's Manado voyage (Knoerle, 'Journal', 1). He was chosen because of his supposed knowledge of Javanese, Roeps being unavailable[10] and Diponegoro having insisted on being accompanied by an officer who could converse with him in his mother tongue rather than the detested language of the colonial state – market Malay (Babad Dipanegara IV:198).

With the governor-general's 30 April order in hand, Knoerle called on Diponegoro at the Stadhuis (Knoerle, 'Journal', 2; 1835:166) before boarding the Dutch naval corvette, the *Pollux*, then lying at anchor in Batavia road (Carey 2012:845). Recently arrived from Europe, it was deemed the most suitable available transport for the prince equipped as it was with a deck battery of sixteen small calibre naval guns sufficient to deter attack by Bugis pirates (Gresham 2002:12–17, 87).

Although Diponegoro and his party were originally intended to embark on 1 May, there was a delay due to the need for the corvette to take on six-weeks' supply of fresh water and food, no stopovers being envisaged because of the political sensitivities of the voyage. Eventually, at eight o'clock on the morning of Monday, 3 May, Diponegoro and his nineteen followers (eleven men and eight women) came on board, accompanied by Roeps and the same Batavian city administration officials who had originally greeted him (Carey 2008:712).

Kapitein-ter-zee (naval captain) Christiaan Eeg (1774–1832), the Pollux commander, and his officers gave them a formal welcome. The ship's doctor, Surgeon Major Hermanus Schillet (1794–1861) (Schillet 1832), made an immediate impression given that his face reminded Diponegoro of his

---

10 Roeps went on two-year furlough to Holland (23–07–1830–30–05–32) before being posted to the Dutch army in Zeeland (31–05–1832–5–06–1835) during the Belgian crisis (pp. 315–6). He returned to Java on 29–01–1836.

Betrayal or Honourable Submission?

'friend', former British Resident, John Crawfurd (Knoerle, 'Journal', 40–1; Carey 2008:713; p. 32). Once the prince's luggage had been stowed, the city officials took their leave, Van der Vinne, stressing that Diponegoro should address himself immediately to the Manado Resident for all personal requests (Babad Dipanegara IV:200).

There being no wind the corvette rode at anchor for almost a day and a night, much to Diponegoro's annoyance. The prince was anxious to put Java behind him. 'He was ashamed ever to see Java again', Knoerle reported, 'and longed for his arrival in Manado [where] he would ask the governor-general for money and a vessel for a journey to Mecca as soon as he was strong and his heart was calm and at rest again' (Knoerle, 'Journal', 14).

At five o'clock the following morning (4 May), a light breeze began to blow off the land and the corvette set sail as the first streaks of dawn stole over Batavia Bay. A new chapter in the prince's life had begun. He would never set foot on the island of his birth again. A quarter of a century of exile and imprisonment lay before him.

Conclusion

Diponegoro's departure from Batavia marked the end of the third and last great 'tsunami' in his life. The first had been in 1793, when, as a pre-pubescent child, he had been adopted by his formidable great-grandmother and taken to live with her at Tegalrejo (Chapter I). The second had occurred on 20 July 1825 when the Dutch had attacked and burnt Tegalrejo, precipitating the Java War (Chapter IX). The final one had been at Magelang on 28 March 1830 – his arrest and exile. Each marked a Rubicon, a point of no return. Before and after were two different worlds.

To experience three such events in a single lifetime is rare. Yet Diponegoro used each as an opportunity. Drawing on his inner creativity, he now began to withdraw from the physical and enter the spiritual, his life as an exile witnessing the flowering of a remarkable literary talent as witnessed by his *Babad Diponegoro* (1831–2) and Makassar Notebooks

(1838). In this third and final phase of his life he would prepare for eternity by opening 'the gateway to death' and in so doing develop a rich inner world (Chapter XII).

In a destined life, such as that lived by Diponegoro, the spirit of patient endurance – what the Buddha once described as 'the supreme austerity' – is essential. Whether he was genuinely surprised by De Kock's actions or had long since prepared himself to endure the unendurable we may never know. What is certain is that he would travel into exile with his creative powers undimmed, his eyes still 'afire' in the words of Prince Hendrik (p. 318). It is to this final phase in the prince's life that we must now turn.

Bibliography

Babad Dipanegara (2010). *Babad Dipanegara*, 4 vols, ed. Nindya Noegraha. Jakarta: Perpustakaan Nasional Republik Indonesia.

Bervoets, J.A.A. (1977). *Inventaris van Papieren Afkomstig van Leden van het Geslacht Bik en Aanverwante Geslachten*. Den Haag: Algemeen Rijksarchief, Tweede Afdeling.

Campbell, D.M. (1915). *Java; Past and Present; A Description of the Most Beautiful Country in the World; Its Ancient History, People, Antiquities and Products*. London: Heinemann. Two vols.

Carey, Peter (1974). 'Javanese Histories of Dipanagara; The Buku Kĕdhuŋ Kĕbo, its Authorship and Historical Importance', *Bijdragen tot de Taal-, Land- en Volkenkunde* 130:259–88.

Carey, Peter (1981). *Babad Dipanagara; An Account of the Outbreak of the Java War (1825–30); The Surakarta Court Version of the Babad Dipanagara with Translations into English and Indonesian Malay*. Kuala Lumpur: Art.

Carey, Peter (1982). 'Raden Saleh, Dipanagara and the Painting of the Capture of Dipanagara at Magelang", *Journal of the Malaysian Branch of the Royal Asiatic Society* 55–1:1–26.

Carey, Peter (2008). *The Power of Prophecy; Prince Dipanagara and the End of an Old Order in Java, 1785–1855*. Leiden: KITLV Press, second revised edition.

Carey, Peter (2012). *Kuasa Ramalan; Pangeran Diponegoro dan Akhir Tatanan Lama di Jawa, 1785–1855*. Jakarta: KPG.

Davidson, G.F. (1846). *Trade and Travel in the Far East or Recollections of Twenty-one Years passed in Java, Singapore, Australia and China*. London: Madden and Malcolm.

Djamhari, Saleh As'ad (2003). *Strategi Menjinakkan Diponegoro; Stelsel Benteng 1827–1830*. Jakarta: Yayasan Komunitas Bambu.

Doren, J.B.J. van (1851). *Reis naar Nederlands Oost-Indië of Land- en Zeetogten gedurende de Twee Eerste Jaren Mijns Verblijfs op Java*. The Hague: Van Langenhuysen. Two vols.

Gericke, J.F.C. and Roorda, T. (1901). *Javaansch-Nederlandsch Handwoordenboek*. Amsterdam: Muller, Leiden: Brill. Two vols.

Graaf, H.J. de (1940). 'Het Kadjoran-Vraagstuk', *Djåwå* 20:273–328.

Gresham, J.D. (2002). 'The British Rating System', *Military Heritage* 3–4:12–17, 87.

Haan, F. de (1935). *Oud Batavia; Gedenkboek uitgegeven door het Bataviaasch Genootschap van Kunsten en Wetenschappen naar Aanleiding van het Driehonderd Jarig Bestaan der Stad in 1919*. Bandoeng: Nix. Two vols.

Hari Atmoko, M. (2013). '"Sang Pangeran" Keluar dari "Warangka"', *Antara Jateng. com*, 25 November.

Huyssen van Kattendijke-Frank, Katrientje (2004). *Met Prins Hendrik naar de Oost: De Reis van W.J.C. Huyssen van Kattendijke naar Nederlands-Indië, 1836–1838*. Zutphen: Walburg.

Indische Courant (Surabaya) (1931). 'Een Kris van Diponegoro', 23 December.

Java Bode (1857). 'Radhen Saleh [...] Vervaardigde Schilderij Voorstellende het Vertrek van Diepo Negoro van Magelang naar Samarang', 18 March.

Kemp, P.H. van der (1896). 'Dipanegara, Eene Geschiedkundige Hamlettype', *Bijdragen tot de Taal-, Land- en Volkenkunde* 46:281–433.

Kielstra, E.B. (1896a). 'De Gevangenneming van Dipa Negara', *Tijdspiegel* 53:84–92.

Kielstra, E.B. (1896b). 'Eenige Personen uit den Java-Oorlog', *Tijdspiegel* 53:290–301.

Knoerle 'Journal' (1830). 'Aanteekeningen gehouden door den 2e Luit Knoerle betreffende de Dagelyksche Verkeering van dien Officier met den Prins van Djocjakarta, Diepo Negoro, gedurende eene Reis van Batavia naar Menado, het Exil van den genoemden Prins', Manado, 20-6-1830. MS 391 of the Johannes van den Bosch private collection in the Nationaal Archief, The Hague.

Kock, H.M. de (1830). 'Verslag van het Voorgevallene met den Pangeran Dipo-Nagoro kort Vóór, Bij en Na Zijne Overkomst', Magelang, 1 April 1830. Manuscript in the Koninklijk Instituut, Leiden: KITLV H 340.

Kraus, W. (2005). 'Raden Saleh's Interpretation of the Arrest of Diponegoro; An Example of Indonesian "Proto-Nationalist" Modernism', *Archipel* 69:259–94.

Louw, P.J.F. and E.S. de Klerck (1894–1909). *De Java-Oorlog van 1825–1830*. The Hague: Nijhoff, Batavia: Landsdrukkerij. Six vols.

Nieuwenhuys, Rob (1973). *Oost-Indische Spiegel; Wat Nederlandse Schrijvers en Dichters over Indonesië hebben Geschreven, vanaf de Eerste Jaren der Compagnie tot op Heden*. Amsterdam: Querido.

Palmer van den Broek, W. (ed. and trans.) (1873–77). 'Geschiedenis van het Vorstenhuis Madoera uit het Javaansch Vertaald', *Tijdschrift voor Indische Taal-, Land- en Volkenkunde (TBG)* 20:241–301, 471–563, 22:1–89, 280–310, 24:1–169.

Schillet, H. (1832). 'Eenige Waarneming omtrent de Cholera Orientalis', *Verhandelingen van het Bataviaasch Genootschap* 13–2:113–82.

Valck, F.G. (1830). 'Nota [over] [...] het Lot van den Hoodfmuiteling Dipo Negoro, nu hij tot ons overgekomen, behoord te worden', 22 March 1830. Manuscript in the Koninklijk Instituut, Leiden: KITLV H 452a.

Wassing-Visser, Rita (1995). *Royal Gifts from Indonesia; Historical Bonds with the House of Orange-Nassau (1600–1938)*. Zwolle: Waanders.

CHAPTER XII

Surviving the Dutch Gulag: Diponegoro's Years of Exile and Death, 1830–1855

Introduction

For a Javanese for whom the nearest encounters with the ocean had been brief visits to the south coast in circa 1805 and 1824 (Chapter III, p. 213), Diponegoro's nearly six weeks at sea – much of it becalmed – would not be a pleasant experience. Vividly memorialized in the diary of the German officer tasked with escorting the prince, it would turn into an epic (Knoerle, 'Journal' 1830; 1835:135–80) (Section 1).

Following his 12 June arrival, the prince's initial three-year exile in North Sulawesi began (Section 2). Here his experiences with the local population were less than happy. But he started a new family with Raden Ayu Retnoningsih (4 January 1832), and completed his 43-canto autobiographical chronicle (*Babad Diponegoro*) (3 February 1832).

On 20 June 1833, the exigencies of international politics forced his transfer to Makassar. A more constrained period now began in the confines of Fort Rotterdam where the prince spent his last twenty-two years (Section 3). During this time, he prepared for eternity by 'opening the gateway to death' through his Shaṭṭārīyya-inspired mystical writings, oversaw his children's education and attempted to take leave of his surviving family (Section 4).

On 8 January 1855, he died and his surviving family moved into the town of Makassar. Their fate and Diponegoro's legacy as a 'national hero' are briefly described (Section 5). A final conclusion sets the prince's life in the wider sweep of Javanese history and assesses his significance as an historical figure in the context of contemporary Indonesia (Section 6).

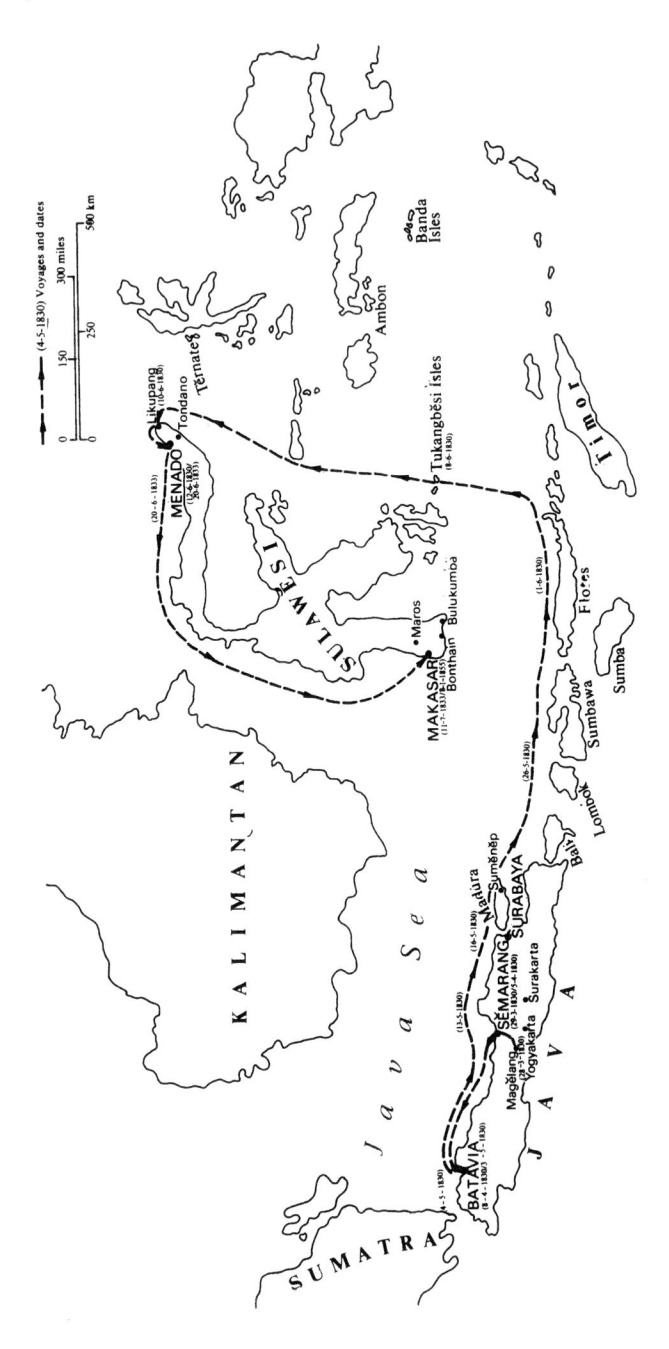

Map 6. Diponegoro's journey into exile in Manado (May–June 1830) and subsequent voyage to Makassar (June–July 1833).

The Raft of Medusa: Surviving the Corvette Pollux, 4 May–12 June 1830

> XLIII 308. The sails were set and [we] left
> Batavia for Manado,
> but there was no wind
> and the boat was exceedingly slow.
>
> 309. [...] many of the accursed [Dutch crew and soldiers] were sick
> and died
> on board ship.
> The sultan was troubled at heart.
>
> 310. Maybe we will all be damned [to die] and not reach
> Manado.
> We speak no further of this.
> They arrived in Manado.
>
> 311. Two and a half months long [sic]
> was the sultan's journey
> from Batavia to Manado
> because there was no wind (Babad Dipanegara IV:200).

The prince's laconic reference to his purgatorial odyssey echoes Knoerle's diary. In the first five days of the voyage, four of the fifty-strong military detachment sent to guard the exile died, the ceremonies for their burials – the slow march of the honour guard and muffled drums – distinctly audible in the prince's cabin below the quarter deck (Knoerle, 'Journal', 12).

Laid low by his malarial fevers and afflicted by sea sickness, the prince grew steadily weaker (Knoerle, 'Journal', 8–9, 11–12). But he was not yet at death's door. In the periods when his fever lifted, he showed an intense interest in his surroundings. The geography of eastern Indonesia fascinated him. How far was Ambon from Manado? Was Manado a long way from Makassar? Could he see the map of 'Makassar', which he had noticed on the foredeck, so that he could acquaint himself with the island of Sulawesi (Knoerle, 'Journal', 44)?

When Knoerle told him the ship's chart was the only one available for navigational purposes, the prince persisted with his line of questioning. What was the sea route to Jeddah? Were the coasts of Sulawesi navigable? And what sort of inhabitants lived there, Christians or Muslims (Knoerle, 'Journal', 45)?

At turns fascinating and difficult, the prince was a trial for the German officer. Yet, here was the same prince who insisted on sending Knoerle rice cakes every day, inviting him to breakfast off potatoes, *sambal* (spiced chilli condiment), black tea and ship's biscuits while they sat together on his large straw mattress. The same man who delighted in the pictures in the books and almanacs which Knoerle lent him (p. 33), and in the Rhenish and Cape wines which the officer escort procured from the reluctant officers of the corvette as 'medicine' for his impromptu wine tastings (Knoerle, 'Journal', 36–7).

During these encounters – 'conversations on a straw mattress' in Knoerle's words ('Journal', 14) – the prince ranged over a huge range of topics, including Javanese history, mythology, and recent European history. Was it the custom he asked, to exile a defeated leader to a far off island and cut him off from all his relatives? Knoerle cited the example of Napoleon, like the prince just forty-four when exiled to Elba (March 1814), but did so 'in a gentle way omitting all painful reminiscences' (Knoerle, 'Journal', 8). At Knoerle's prompting, Diponegoro also reminisced about his life and times, in particular his wartime experiences, the German officer seeking political intelligence for the governor-general (Knoerle 1835:135–80).

The prince's character perplexed Knoerle: on the one hand, he was full of praise for the Java War leader's 'strong and enterprising character', 'shrewdness', and 'acute judgement' (Knoerle 1835:171–2). On the other, he disdained his religious convictions: 'a zealot, who considered his religious principles the highest and most elevated on earth, and wished to erect his religious order on the ruins of all other systems' (Knoerle 1835:171). Here he betrayed the prejudices of his age: even the great colonial author, Multatuli (Eduard Douwes Dekker, 1820–87), would later dismiss the prince as a 'poor fanatic' (Multatuli 1862–77, IV:286; Carey 2008:719).

On 12 June 1830, the *Pollux* finally dropped anchor in Manado bay. Disembarking the following day, the prince and his party were escorted to the Dutch redoubt, Fort New Amsterdam, later destroyed by earthquake (14 May 1932) and American bombing (7 December 1944). It would be their home for the next three years.

A Minahasan Interlude: Diponegoro's Manado Years, 1830–1833

Van den Bosch had promised the prince 'seclusion and quiet' in a large house with an extensive view close to mountains and sea in a place with large gardens, fine houses, and places to wander undisturbed (Carey 2008:707). So what did he find? 'One of the prettiest towns in the East' with magnificent volcanic peaks 'forming grand and picturesque backgrounds' noted British naturalist, Alfred Russel Wallace (1823–1913), four years after Diponegoro's death (Wallace 1890:185).

Although the scenery lived up to the governor-general's promise (Knoerle, 'Journal', 50), Van den Bosch's intention that the Java War leader be lodged in a secure location in the interior was impractical. When Knoerle met with the Manado Resident, D.F.W. Pietermaat (in office, 1827–31), they decided that he should be detained initially in a four-room apartment in Fort New Amsterdam (Knoerle, 'Journal', 49–50).

To furnish this space, suitably 'elegant' furniture was acquired, including a book shelf, writing desk with drawers, and large standard lamp with the latest patent oil light (Knoerle 1835:173; Carey 2008:722): Diponegoro clearly intended some writing during his Minahasan exile. Two horses were also bought so he could ride out into the surrounding countryside (Carey 2008:722).

By the time Knoerle departed on 20 June, the decision had been taken that the prince would stay in Manado. In the intervening days (14–17 June 1830) the German officer had toured the interior, noting that the only exile spot was Tondano. But he immediately saw a problem: Kyai Mojo and his 62-strong following had been settled in this selfsame district just a month previously (Knoerle 1835:173–5; Carey 2008:638–9). Both Knoerle and the Manado Resident were adamant that the Java War leaders should not share the same exile location (Knoerle 1835:173–4). The chill of the high Tondano plateau also made the prince prefer the Minahasan capital (Knoerle, 'Journal', 51; Atlas 1990:26; Wallace 2002: paragraph 179).

On 19 June, Knoerle took his final leave of the prince, a meeting attended by the *Pollux* commander and Pietermaat. After confirming his ƒ600 monthly stipend, Captain Eeg suggested that the prince might have a personal message or a letter for the governor-general. 'No', Diponegoro replied, 'I have no desire to send a letter for I cannot write [...] just send my regards to General Van den Bosch!' (Babad Dipanegara IV:201).

The prince was being disingenuous: he could write Javanese albeit ungrammatically (Carey 2008:822–4; pp. 30–1; Plate 23). He could even dictate major literary works such as his 43-canto autobiographical *babad*. So his plea of illiteracy was perhaps his way of indicating that the governor-general's absence during his Batavia sojourn had been noted.

Privately, however, Diponegoro did seek to get messages through to 'his exalted friend': asking that his remaining wives (Carey 2008:766–8), and those of Kyai Mojo and his followers, should be brought to Manado. He also requested that Haji Badarudin and Haji Ngiso, two of his closest confidantes, should join him, and that Van Den Bosch should remain the 'protector' of his children in south-central Java (Babad Dipanegara IV:201; Carey 2008:725).

Although Kyai Mojo's wife was indeed brought to Minahasa – though not on compassionate grounds (Carey 2008:638; pp. 242–3) – none of Diponegoro's other requests were taken up. Neither his remaining official wives nor his two *haji* advisers wished to share his exile (Carey 2008:725). Their refusal underscored just how difficult his exile life would be.

The sudden contraction of the prince's world to four small rooms in Fort New Amsterdam after the solitude of his last fugitive months was a purgatory. Scarcely a month after his arrival, he decided he no longer wished to go out riding, the environs of Manado not being suitable for horseback excursions (Carey 2008:726). He also asked that he should be henceforth addressed as 'Pangeran Ngabdulkamit', a title he later altered to the more ascetic '*fakir* (mendicant) Ngabdulkamit' after arriving in Makassar (Carey 2008:151–2).

In keeping with his mendicant aspirations and to save money for his Mecca pilgrimage, Diponegoro became very tight fisted: by late August 1830, Pietermaat became alarmed that he was building up a 'war chest' so substantial were his savings (Carey 2008:726). The prince's stipend was cut by two thirds. This was too drastic. The exile needed at least half this ƒ200 monthly allowance just to maintain his table and servants. But he kept silent, reflecting: 'It is well. The government fixed my income at ƒ600 without consulting me. [It] can [now] act as it thinks fit!' (Carey 2008:726). Raised to ƒ500 by 1850, it was still not sufficient – given the prince's growing family – to prevent him from ending his days in 'near poverty' (Carey 2008:727).

Such Dutch penny-pinching, the same mean-mindedness which made Tuanku Imam Bonjol's (1772–1864) Minahasan exile life (1840–64) such a misery (Dobbin 1972:19), took its toll. Like Bonjol after him, Diponegoro was not well received in the Minahasan capital: popular tradition has it that he became so incensed at the abuse he received in the local market that he had flung his heirloom walking staff on the ground causing the *pasar* to rock as though in an earthquake (Carey 2008:116).

He was also rebuffed when it came to seeking a local bride, his eye having fallen on the daughter of one of Manado's leading Muslim citizens, Lieutenant Hasan Latif, who remarked that the union would bring his child 'ill fortune' (p. 37), a sentiment echoed by Resident J.P.C. Cambier (in office, 1831–42) (Carey 2008:727).

The rebuff did not prevent Diponegoro leading an active sexual life: Pietermaat had already reported that Diponegoro's 'greatest conversation is about women of whom he seems to have been a great lover' (p. 37) and he would go on to have no less than seven children in exile, most by Javanese women other than his official consort (Carey 2008:769).

In the enclosed confines of Fort New Amsterdam a family crisis was brewing. 'Resolute, free [...] and of a very vivacious disposition' (Knoerle, 'Journal', 9), the prince's younger sister, Raden Ayu Dipowiyono, went head-to-head with her elder brother in numerous family tiffs. Just ten months into his exile, Cambier was reporting, the prince [...] leads a very unpleasant life and his own intolerant humour is the cause of it [...] most of the time he is quarrelling with his sister, or his wife and brother-in-law [Raden Tumenggung Dipowiyono], [who] have pressed to buy [him] a garden (Carey 2008:728).

In his *babad*, Diponegoro mentions these developments (Babad Dipanegara IV:202),

> XLIII 329. Many trials
> came to test the sultan.
> Often his own
> younger sister,
> Raden Ayu Dipowiyono,
> caused him feelings of shame
> together with the *tumenggung* [her husband].
> But the sultan paid the two no attention.
> Night and day
> only the Almighty
> afforded the sultan protection,
> [along with] the grace of [His] Holy Prophet.

Such tensions took their toll. Soon the Resident was reporting that, given the choice, all Diponegoro's family would elect to return to Java (Carey 2008:729). Only the prince's younger sister, brother-in-law and dependants, however, made the homeward journey in August 1832. Retnoningsih, who had just been delivered of her first child, Raden Mas Kindar (4 January 1832), elected to stay with her husband (Carey 2008:729, 769).

The departure of his feisty sibling and her equally troublesome husband was a relief: the four rooms in Fort New Amsterdam were now left free for the prince and his wife to care for their eight-month-old son, whose birth, according to Cambier, had given him much pleasure (Carey 2008:729–31). His child would grow into a strikingly handsome and energetic young man – a 'warm and zealous Muslim' in the words of a Dutch official report – whom Diponegoro would educate – along with his younger brothers, Raden Mas Sarkumo (1834–49) and Raden Mas Dulkabli (born circa 1835) (Carey 2008:731, 769) – 'as a priest', namely in the *pesantren* (religious boarding school) tradition.

Surviving the Dutch Gulag: Diponegoro's Years of Exile and Death 313

Kindar would retain a deep hatred of all things Dutch (Sagimun 1965:359–60; Carey 2008:731), an attitude encouraged by his father, who, according to the last Celebes Governor of the prince's exile, Colonel Alexander van der Hart (in office, 1853–5), had educated his children in the iniquities of Dutch rule, regaling them with his experiences:

> an embittered father, he considered us his [sworn] religious enemies and the cause of all his misfortunes [...] He thus imprinted little love for [the Dutch] on his children's [minds] (Sagimun 1965:360).

The principal vehicle for Diponegoro's instruction was his autobiography whose inception the prince described as follows (Babad Dipanegara IV:201–2; Carey 1981:lx note 78):

XLIII 322. [...]
Resident Pietermaat

323. enquired of the sultan [Diponegoro]:
'What is the reason
Your Highness came here?'
Smiling the sultan replied:

324. 'Ah, Resident, if you ask me, promise me
can you
deliver this letter [requesting permission to depart on the *haj*]
to the King of the Netherlands [William I, reigned 1813–40]?

325. If you promise it, I will indeed tell you the reason
why I came
to Manado.
If you cannot promise, then it is in vain

326. that I tell you the real facts.'
The Resident gave his pledge.
Then he was given
the chronicle from the very beginning

327. until the final arrival in Manado.
Resident Pietermaat,
when he heard the truth,
became deeply ashamed

328. because of the perfidy of his countrymen,
how they had been able
to end the war in this treacherous fashion.
We talk no more of this.

By the time the prince began his *babad* (20 May 1831), Pietermaat had long since left Manado (January 1831), so his role in its inception seems dubious (Carey 2008:732).

Completed in just under nine months (20 May 1831–2 February 1832), the *pegon* script original ran to over 1,000 folio-sized pages. Kept by his family following his death and copied on the orders of the Batavian Society of Arts and Sciences in 1866–7 (Notulen 1877:91, 94, 1878:13, 35; Carey 1981:lix note 73),[1] it is divided into two parts. The first, roughly a third of the entire work, gives the history of Java from the fall of Majapahit (circa 1510s) to the peace of Giyanti (1755), while the second deals with the prince's own life and times from his birth in 1785 to his exile in Manado.

Written when tensions between Diponegoro and his family were at their height, it is little wonder that he became so cantankerous (Carey 2008:733). What author, cooped up in four rooms in a hot fortress town, whose inhabitants were hostile and with argumentative relatives, would not have felt as he did? The pains of authorship and exile hardly come more purgatorial than this. But what a manuscript would result. The source of Diponegoro's anti-Dutch teachings for his growing exile family and the first autobiography in any Indonesian language, it would prove to be one of the great literary productions of modern Java. Accepted on 22 June 2013 by UNESCO for inclusion in its coveted International Register of the Memory of the World (Preface), it remains to this day a forgotten national treasure.[2]

Here is how this magnificent work begins (Babad Dipanegara I:6):

---

[1] The original was lost after it was returned by the Batavian Society to Diponegoro's family in Makassar in 1867. The *pegon* copy, made by the Batavian Society in circa 1865–6, was accepted by UNESCO for inscription in their International Register of the Memory of the World on 22 June 2013.

[2] The last Javanese script edition of the prince's *babad* was published by Albert Rusche & Co in 1908–9 in Surakarta (reprinted 1917). It has never been republished. None of the texts are available online.

I 1. 'I lay out the feelings of my heart
in the [sad] Mijil metre.
Created to bring solace to my heartfelt desires,
it was done in the town of Manado
without being seen by anyone,
but the grace of The All-Knowing One.

2. Much does my heart feel
of [past] discordant actions.
So now my heart is fixed.
How would it be with my actions
if there was not also
the forgiveness of The Almighty?

3. I have experienced shame and suffering,
but my request
is that all former things should be set aside,
[and] that my family should truly observe
the Religion of The Prophet
thereby gaining succour.

Closing the Circle: The State Prisoner of Fort Rotterdam, Makassar, 1833–1855

Even as Diponegoro was dictating these lines, half a world away in the ill-fated Kingdom of the United Netherlands (1815–30), events were taking place which would transform the conditions under which both he and his family were held.

Exasperated by the same Dutch quest for immediate profit which had led to such suffering in south-central Java before the Java War (Chapter VIII), the inhabitants of the Southern Netherlands (post-1830, Belgium) revolted (24 August 1830) and declared their independence (4 October 1830). A new monarch, Leopold of Saxe-Coburg-Gotha (reigned 1831–65), was installed by the European powers. But the Dutch king, Willem I, refused to recognize the *fait accompli*. A French army under Marshal Gérard

(1773–1852) then entered Belgium (August 1831) and invested Antwerp, which surrendered after a heroic two-year siege (December 1832).

In early 1833, it seemed that Gérard's army might cross the Dutch-Belgian border. With a European war looming, Van den Bosch became alarmed that 'an unscrupulous enemy' – namely the British – would seek to use the large numbers of exiles in the Dutch 'outer possessions' for political purposes. In particular, he was concerned that Diponegoro might escape and return to Java to lead a new rebellion. Given Britain's naval strength, the prince's place of exile was too exposed. He thus ordered the trusted Pietermaat to return to Manado and arrange for Diponegoro's transfer to a newly constructed strongpoint deep in the Minahasan interior (Carey 2008:735).

Once in Manado, Pietermaat realised that Van den Bosch's proposals were impractical. The Netherlands Indies Government had no legal sovereignty in the interior and without the local authorities' permission no fort could be built. Besides, none of the chiefs would believe that such a strongpoint was being constructed only to house an 'unimportant person' like Diponegoro. Instead, they would suspect an annexationist move and they would resist. An alternative strategy would have to be found.

Van den Bosch's first plan was to send Diponegoro to the Netherlands for detention in a royal fortress such as Loevestein (Gelderland) or Woerden (Utrecht). Fortunately, King Willem I rejected this proposal: he had enough problems on his hands without a Javanese Ratu Adil expiring in one of his castles (Carey 2008:736): if Diponegoro had rejected Tondano with its sixty-nine degree Fahrenheit temperature as too chilly (Atlas 1990:26; Wallace 2002: paragraph 179), little imagination is required to contemplate how many Dutch winters he would have survived in the damp fortresses of the New Dutch 'water line' (*Nieuwe Hollandse waterlinie*).

Instead, Van den Bosch was ordered to find an Indies alternative. His decision was swift: the prince would be moved south in deepest secrecy to Makassar where he would be held until his dying breath in Admiral Speelman's (1628–84) great redoubt, Fort Rotterdam. Instead of Manado's puny forty-strong garrison, the south Sulawesi fortress boasted a complement of 200 soldiers and powerful gun batteries covering all sea and land approaches. It was altogether a more formidable structure.

Surviving the Dutch Gulag: Diponegoro's Years of Exile and Death

And so in a clandestine twenty-one day (20 June–11 July 1833) odyssey, Diponegoro, his wife, two sons and twenty-three followers were transported the length of the Dutch 'gulag' archipelago from Fort New Amsterdam to Fort Rotterdam, a secret journey made all the more poignant by the name of the vessel tasked with their transport: the naval yacht *Circe* (Carey 2008:738), styled after the silver-tongued queen goddess in Homer's epic who could transform men into animals.

The yacht's native sailors apparently reacted badly to the former Java War leader's presence in their midst prompting a debate in the Council of the Indies (*Raad van* Indië) with one counsellor advising that Diponegoro should never again be transported on a Dutch naval vessel given the possibility of mutiny amongst the ship's native crew (Carey 2008:738–9).

The conditions under which the prince and his family were held in Makassar were much tighter than in Manado: neither the prince nor his followers were allowed outside the fort's walls and they were kept in an officer's billet close to the main guardhouse with an attic view over Makassar harbour and the high inner curtain wall of the fort blocking their landward perspective (Eerdmans 1922: I.2:355–6; Map 6). It would be their home for the next twenty-two years (Carey 2008:739).

Despite their restricted existence, Diponegoro and his followers found ways of smuggling letters. This can be seen in the episode of the prince's correspondence with the recently promoted Major-General Cleerens (p. 278). Not only was Diponegoro informed of the Flemish officer's return to Java within weeks of his 13 October 1835 arrival in Batavia, but he was also able to dictate and send a formal letter to him complete with yellow silk cover and seal a month later (Carey 2008:826–7). So much for Van den Bosch's security!

How could it be otherwise? Diponegoro's family and followers could not be insulated from contacts with Makassar society. His followers lived in the servants' quarters in the fort where they mixed freely with the locally born members of the garrison, giving them ample opportunity to smuggle news out of the prince's fortress prison. Besides, Makassar was not Manado. Unlike Christian Minahasa – the so-called 'thirteenth province of Holland' (Carey 2008:740), where a majority Christian population looked askance at pious inner island Muslim exiles – the Makassarese and Bugis had no love for the Dutch. The prince's devotion to Islam, albeit one tinctured by his Javanese beliefs, commanded their respect.

And the feeling was mutual: in April 1844, after Dutch de facto recognition of Belgian independence (1840) had removed any lingering threat of war, the Governor of the Celebes, P.J.B. de Perez (in office, 1841–8), had asked Diponegoro whether he might like to be transferred to another part of the Netherlands Indies where he and his family could enjoy more living space. No, answered the prince, he wished to spend his dying days in Makassar, a decision reinforced five years later by his request to be buried close to the grave of his second son rather than have his body sent for interment at Imogiri beside the tomb of his beloved Raden Ayu Maduretno (Carey 2008:740–1).

Through a Glass Darkly; Diponegoro's Exile Life, Family, and Literary World

In early March 1837, just before the colonial government imposed new restrictions on Diponegoro's movements, the prince received a highly placed Dutch visitor. This was Prince Hendrik 'De Zeevaarder' ('The Seafarer') (1820–79), the sixteen-year-old son of the Dutch king, Willem II (reigned, 1840–9), then on a sea voyage to the Indies on the frigate *Bellona* in the company of his tutor, Pieter Arriëns (1791–1860), the warship's captain. On 10 March, the teenage prince wrote to his father (Wassing-Visser 1995:246):

> The first day [in Makassar] on going to see the Fort here, I saw our unhappy prisoner Diepo Negoro who [...] fell into our hands by treachery. He came to me immediately, taking my hand and having conducted me to his [first-floor] chamber, [...] said to the governor [Reinier de Fillietaz Bousquet, in office, 1834–41] that it gave him great pleasure that one had come to visit him in his miserable dwelling. [...] He laughed, but it is said that this gaiety is forced or [...] not natural. [...] He is very aloof: earlier, he did not even wish to speak Malay. He has a pleasant appearance and one sees that he is still full of fire.

Surviving the Dutch Gulag: Diponegoro's Years of Exile and Death

Prince Hendrik also noted in his diary that the former Java War leader's treatment would drive all the other local chiefs to join the enemy camp in any future conflict with the Dutch (Taylor 2003:235; Huyssen van Kattendijke-Frank 2004:121), a warning tragically fulfilled in the mid-twentieth century during the Indonesian Revolution (1945–9):

> [...] Everyone knows that Diponegoro rose in rebellion against us but his arrest will always, in my view, be a slur on our age-old Dutch word of honour. It is true he was a rebel, but he came to put an end to a war which had cost both him and us so many lives. [...] Then he was captured on the orders of General de Kock. I believe that this matter, which has been so useful to us (in relation to our possession of the whole of Java), will do us the greatest harm in moral terms because if we ever have the misfortune of fighting another war in Java one or other of us will go under – either ourselves or the Javanese – because there will be no local chief who will ever want to have anything to do with us [again]. And this [...] will happen not just in Java but everywhere [in the Indies].

News of the prince's situation continued to get out and Diponegoro continued to correspond with his Yogya relatives: in late 1839 he tried to get a letter through to his mother. But the Dutch authorities refused to deliver it because he used his Java War titles. Just under a decade later, in January 1848, an article fiercely critical of the way he was being treated appeared in the French press (Carey 1982:3):

> Enclosed between the four walls of a little fort, separated from his family, closely watched, denied the means of writing either to the governor-general or to whoever else, treated over the past eighteen years with a harshness and a cruel severity little worthy of the government of this country [the Netherlands].

How did such news leak? The decision to open Makassar as a free port in 1847 attracted more local and Arab vessels to the harbour town (Van Marle 1971:37; Dick et al. 2002:20; Bosma and Raben 2008:145). This in turn created new opportunities for contact with the outside world. Through such informal channels, the Semarang-based family of the Javanese-Arab painter, Raden Saleh Syarif Bustaman (circa 1811–80), may have been informed of Diponegoro's plight (Carey 1982:5 note 22, 2009:139). Saleh himself might have even been the source of the press report given his frequent sojourns in the French capital in the late 1840s (Carey 1982:3–4; Scalliet 2005:253).

The Dutch Minister of the Colonies, J.C. Baud (in office 1840–48), immediately wrote to reassure King Willem II: the prince was not being held in a small fort but in the 'spacious surroundings' of Fort Rotterdam where he occupied one of the officer's quarters. Far from being deprived of his family, he had his wife and seven exile-born children with him, one of whom was now of marriageable age. Indeed, so extensive had his family become that an adjacent officer's dwelling had had to be converted for his use (April 1844) (Carey 2008:743).

True, as a state prisoner (*staatsgevangene*) he could not write letters but he could write for his own 'amusement' and had with him books and Javanese manuscripts copied for him at government expense (Chapter II). In March 1837, the king's son, Prince Hendrik, had noticed that Diponegoro spent much of his time copying verses (*ayat*) from the *Qur'ān* and 'drawing', a possible reference to his interest in mystical diagrams (*daerah*) (Wassing-Visser 1995:246; pp. 33–4).

In 1838, the prince had begun the composition of two substantial *pegon* script prose manuscripts entitled *Sejarah Ratu Tanah Jawa* ('The History of the Kings of Java'), and the *Hikayat Tanah Jawa* ('Chronicle of the Land of Java') respectively (Carey 2008:745). Written in a curious Javanese with many Arabic words and phrases, they recall the style of Diponegoro's personal letters rather than the polished cadences of his *babad* (Carey 2008:733, 822–4). The first deals with the history of Java and Javanese historical legends from Adam to the fall of Majapahit in circa 1510s and the coming of Islam. Written anecdotally with many digressions on diverse topics such as the *wayang*, legendary heroes and holy sites, the prince was seemingly recalling his conversations with his family and setting down various discourses for their subsequent instruction and entertainment.

The second, *Hikayat Tanah Jawa*, specifically states that it was composed by Diponegoro, who referred to himself by his Java War titles. Dealing with the prince's understanding of Islam, religious experiences, Sufi prayers, and various meditation techniques, it also contains diagrams (*daerah*) for the use of Arabic words and breathing exercises during prayer (Chapter II). The whole composition recalls a Javanese divination manual or *primbon* (Carey 1981:xxx–xxxi).

In January 1844, Diponegoro asked the governor for a number of Javanese texts for the education of his sons, three of whom were reaching puberty (Carey 1981:lxiii note 112; p. 30). Two of these texts, the *Serat Menak* and the *Asmara Supi*, a romance related to the *Menak* cycle, had strongly Islamic themes describing the life of The Prophet, the exploits of his uncle, Amir Hamza, and of the latter's fictive descendant, Asmara Supi (Pigeaud 1967–80, I:132–3, 212–14, 223). Such texts were popular in religious boarding schools in Java, but they caused the government concern: why should they be helping Diponegoro bring up his children as pious Muslims? So the *Serat Menak* was dropped from the texts copied for the prince in the Surakarta *kraton* (Carey 2008:744–5).

Opening the Gateway to Death, 1845–55

In the last decade of his life, the prince began preparing for his own death – what in the Shaṭṭārīyya mystical tradition to which he belonged is known as *plawanganing pati* ('[opening] the gateway to death') (Harianto 2013:16). In late 1848, he asked the governor if he might be allowed to see two of his sons, Pangeran Dipokusumo (?1805–died pre-March 1856) and Raden Mas Raib (?1815–?), who had been banished to Ambon in 1840 along with their insane sibling, Pangeran Diponingrat (?1807–died post-March 1856). He also enquired anxiously after his eldest son, Pangeran Diponegoro II (?1803–died post-March 1856), whose whereabouts as an exile in Sumenep were still unknown to him (Houben 1994:238–9; Carey 2008:746).

Although the Dutch authorities had accommodated the prince by raising his stipend and enlarging his living quarters (Carey 2008:743, 746–7), their compassion did not extend to bringing him together with his exiled offspring. They may also not have wanted him to learn the full scale of the tragedy which had befallen his family: the death of his second youngest son, Raden Mas Joned, in a brawl in Yogya with a Dutch officer (1837) (Hageman 1856:412), the banishment of his other sons, at least one of whom had gone mad (Houben 1994:243), the sexual exploitation of two of his daughters by his erstwhile army commander Basah Mertonegoro, and the spinsterhood of a third whom no Yogyanese dared marry (Carey

2008:768, 823). As for his Tegalrejo residence, it had become grazing land for the Yogya Resident's horses (Carey 2008:85).

As late as June 1849, when one might have expected that Diponegoro's name would no longer hold terrors for the government, one of his brothers, Pangeran Ario Ronggo, was exiled to Ternate for no greater a crime than having contact with 'priests', and referring to his elder sibling as 'Sultan Erucokro' for whom he was prepared to sacrifice his life (Houben 1994:243-4) – so much for Van den Bosch's promise to look after the prince's family. As the last vestiges of the Dipanegaran were expunged from the *kraton*, even the Java War leader's princely moniker became anathema never again to be bestowed on any post-1830 member of the south central Javanese elite (Carey 2008: 369, 747).

In these months when Diponegoro was trying to take his leave of his children, a letter arrived out of the blue. It was from his aged mother in Yogya, Raden Ayu Mangkorowati (pp. 6–7). In 'high excitement', the prince sought an immediate interview with the Governor. Stating that his dearest wish was to live out his days with his parent at his side, he asked De Perez that she be given permission to join him in Makassar? As for the practicalities, she could travel by steamship in just five days from Semarang thus avoiding the purgatory of his sailing odysseys on the *Pollux* and *Circe*. One intimate retainer (*panakawan*), his erstwhile Bagelen commander then resident in Semarang, Pengalasan, could accompany her (Hageman 1856:412–13; Carey 1974:282).

In a heart-rending image of an exile's unrequited longing, he told his mother that whenever a ship steamed into Makassar harbour, he and his grandchildren would now be climbing the stairs to the attic to look out over the port to see if she had arrived. Come quickly was the message, but if you cannot come 'no matter since we are both friends' (Carey 2008:751). Mangkorowati, now approaching eighty and suffering from dropsy, declined to make the journey (Carey 2008:74). Instead, she wrote to her son stating that her dearest wish was they should both enjoy health and prosperity (*wilujeng*) until they returned together to eternity (Carey 2008:752). Mother and son would die just over two years apart on 7 October 1852 and 8 January 1855 respectively (Hageman 1856:412).

In early March 1849, tragedy struck when Diponegoro's second son, the fourteen-year-old Raden Mas Sarkumo, died after a short illness. Buried in a small plot of government land in the Malay Quarter (Kampung Melayu) of Makassar, this sudden bereavement set the prince thinking. Now well into his sixties, his body weakened by wartime privations, his days were numbered. He thus told De Perez's successor, Pieter Vreede Bik (in office, 1849–52), that arrangements should be made for himself and family. These included encircling his son's grave with a low stone wall, setting aside an adjacent burial plot for himself, building a dwelling and outhouses for his wife, family and retainers, and a small mosque so that he could enjoy more freedom in his remaining years. Even if he remained confined to Fort Rotterdam, a residence should still be prepared for his wife and surviving family where they could move after his death (Carey 2008:749).

In the same dispatch in which the Yogya Resident, Baron A.H.W. de Kock (in office, 1848–51), forwarded Mangkorowati's letter, he advised Governor-General J.J. Rochussen (in office, 1845–51) against allowing Diponegoro outside Fort Rotterdam: the political situation in the Yogya *kraton* was still too delicate and there were fears that the prince might escape now that Makassar had become a free port (Carey 2008:752).

And so it was decided. On 11 May 1849, the governor-general passed a secret decree ordering that Diponegoro spend his remaining days within the walls of Speelman's great fortress. Apart from the issue of the prince's finances, a subject of obsessive Dutch correspondence, the former Java War leader rates no further mention in the colonial records. None that is until the morning of Monday, 8 January 1855, when the Dutch authorities were roused early from their beds: the prince had died just after sunrise at 6.30, almost the same time as the moment seventy years earlier when he had uttered his first cries after coming into the world before the pre-dawn fasting month meal (Chapter I).

Diponegoro's death certificate stated the cause of death as 'diminished physical strength due to advanced years' (Sagimun 1965:358). The family was given a burial allowance and on the same afternoon the prince was laid to rest in Kampung Melayu, his heirloom *kris*, Kangjeng Kyai Bondoyudo (Carey 2008:813), being buried with him. According to the notice, which appeared a month later in the *Javasche Courant* (10, 3-2-1855) and carried in the Dutch press (*NRC* 92, 2-4-1855), the burial ceremony had occurred 'with full Islamic rights and with respect for his high birth [...] in accordance with the wishes of the dead man, he was interred [...] near the grave of his son [Sarkumo]'.

The Aftermath: Diponegoro's Family and the Making of a National Hero

Seven days later, his widow and children met with Governor Van der Hart, and stated that they wanted to remain in Makassar to be near the grave of their recently departed relative. Relieved that they were so minded, the government ruled that under no circumstances be permitted to return to Java, Van der Hart fearing that the prince's male offspring, especially his 'highly capable' eldest son, Raden Mas Kindar, could become the 'centres of rebellion' if allowed back to Yogya. In Makassar, despite their 'religious connections', they had no sway over the local population (Carey 2008:754).

On 10 May 1855, Governor-General Duymaer van Twist (in office, 1851-6), passed a secret decree in council ordering that Diponegoro's widow and children be treated as exiles and confined to Makassar, but that they would be allowed to retain the prince's former *f* 6,000 stipend which would continue to be paid annually by the Yogya court. He also permitted them to live freely in the town where a residence would be found (Carey 2008:754).

Van der Hart had recommended that the family be given a sufficiently large plot to plant fruit trees and develop some ricefields, arguing that if the prince's children were able to find useful employment they would find a better 'direction for their energies' and make good marriages (whether to local Makassarese or Makassar-domiciled Javanese he did not say) thus dissuading them from involvement in anti-Dutch activities (Carey 2008:754).

Subsequently, a one hectare block of land was acquired adjacent to Diponegoro and his son's graves with sufficient space for orchards, a market garden and *sawah* as well as a modest Dutch colonial style house.[3] This was very much in line with what the prince had asked for at the time of his early March 1849 audience with the acting governor, and this is where his family and household retainers moved to in the year following his death (Carey 2008:754–5).

After the death of Raden Ayu Retnoningsih in 1885, Diponegoro's grave and that of his son were moved to the recently opened Kampung Melayu public graveyard between present-day Jalan Andalas and Jalan Irian a short distance from the family house. A private burial ground, demarcated by a low brick wall, was set apart in the innermost part for Diponegoro's family and two imposing white stuccoed tombs erected for the prince and his consort (Rouveroy van Nieuwaal 1928:208). Known as the 'grave of the Sultan of Java' (*kuburan Sultan Jawa*), the area around the twin tombs would become the final resting place for the prince's Makassar-born descendants (Kalff 1927–28:523).

While Diponegoro's memory was revered in Makassar and more widely in the Netherlands Indies in nationalist and communist circles,[4] his family found the upkeep of their estate beyond their very limited means. During the course of the century following the prince's death, most of the orchards and ricefields were sold. A report from the late 1920s speaks of the gravesite as a collection of 'dirty moss-covered stones, a broken down limestone-leached little wall and the rotting remains of vegetation' (Kalff 1927–28:523).

Following independence in 1945, it would become a place of national reverence. The hundredth anniversary of Diponegoro's death in January 1955 was celebrated at his now restored gravesite with great pomp (Sagimun 1965:455) and memorial addresses given by President Sukarno and two

---

3   This stood until 2000 when a local Chinese entrepreneur bought it and knocked it down to make way for shops.
4   These included inter-war youth groups like Jong Celebes ('Young Celebes') and Jong Java ('Young Java'), and the Indonesian Communist Party (Partai Kommunis Indonesia / PKI) whose Madiun headquarters had Diponegoro's portrait on the wall, Ricklefs 2007:233.

cabinet ministers[5] at the State Palace in Jakarta (*Nieuwsblad van Soematra*; *De Nieuwsgier*, 10-1-1855). Finally, on 10 November 1973, during Suharto's New Order (1966-98), the prince was made a *pahlawan nasional* (national hero).

So the wheel of history turned full circle. The much feared exile of Fort Rotterdam had become the hero *par excellence* of the modern Indonesian state. This pious and complex man, whom the Parangkusumo prophecy would warn would only be 'counted amongst the ancestors' for a brief moment, was now vested with immortality in the national pantheon of a country he had never dreamt of in his lifetime. Historical transformations rarely come stranger than this.

Conclusion

It is a truism that men and women are shaped by their age. Diponegoro was no exception. Born into the seemingly immutable 'old order' of the late eighteenth-century Principalities, he died in the high colonial era when steamboats had begun to ply the inter-island shipping routes (à Campo 1992:579-612) and free ports replace the closed monopoly of the Netherlands Trading Company (NHM) (Dick et al. 2002:92). This was the age when the Dutch were reaping fabulous profits from the Cultivation System (1830-70) on the backs of Javanese peasant cultivators who suffered famines and disease (Elson 1994:99-127); an age when the only conversation in Indies society was 'coffee and sugar, sugar and coffee' (D'Almeida 1864, II:292).

What price then for a mystic prince in such a universe? Not much judging by the terse obituary notice published in Dutch colonial and national newspapers. But what of the Javanese, what did Diponegoro mean for them?

---

5   These were the F.L. Tobing (Minister of Information) (1899-1962) and Muhammad Yamin (Minister of Education) (1903-62).

A pivotal figure in the history of modern Java, his death occurred mid-way between the treaty of Giyanti (1755) and the declaration of Indonesian independence (1945). But how much of this was his own doing and how much the times in which he lived?

What if he had been born a hundred years earlier in 1685 or a century later in 1885? The first would have placed him in the Kartasura period (1680– 1742) which, if he had survived, might have seen him emerge as one of the luminaries of Pakubuwono II's (reigned 1726–49) court writing the same Sufi-inspired Javanese-Islamic literature favoured by the court elite (Ricklefs 1998a:39–91, 106–26, 254–60, 253–309). The second would have situated him at the heart of the founder generation of the Indonesian 'national movement', a contemporary of Dr Tjipto Mangunkusumo (1885–1943), Raden Mas Soetomo (1888–1938), and Ki Hadjar Dewantara (1889–1959). Given his great personal abilities, deep root of faith, and administrative and financial acumen, he would have made his mark in some capacity on modern Indonesia. But in neither case would he have been quite the same crucial figure as he became during the Java War.

The unusual epoch in which Diponegoro lived is vital for an understanding of his life. Karl Popper's dictum that history is the struggle of men and ideas, not just of the material conditions of their existence (Popper 2003, II:307), is relevant here. Had it not been for the peremptory violence visited on the south-central Javanese courts by Daendels and Raffles between 1808 and 1812, violence which tore the heart out of the Yogya *kraton*, one can imagine Diponegoro living in relative obscurity at Tegalrejo, attending to his religious duties and dying in mid-century as a quirky *santri* prince, scourge of the Yogya aristocracy and the *kafir* Dutch.

The fact that he rates not a single reference in the British reports (1811– 16), a period when he was supposedly a key adviser to his father, the third sultan, and mentor to his younger brother, the fourth sultan, indicates that he was not quite the prominent figure in pre-war Yogya he sought to portray in his *babad* (Carey 2008: 375–7). Nahuys probably had his measure better when he described the prince and his uncle, Mangkubumi, as men who 'stood quite neutral and were universally considered as good quiet persons without the least ambition' (p. 199).

The agrarian crisis of 1823–5 and the ineptitude of the pre-war Dutch Yogya officials changed everything. Once cast in a leadership role, however,

Diponegoro brought to his task a competence and charismatic appeal greater even than that of his great-grandfather, Mangkubumi. A devout Muslim, he personified the 'mystic synthesis' in Java (Ricklefs 2007:8), a Javanese Muslim who saw no problem with meeting the goddess of the Southern Ocean, undertaking pilgrimages to holy sites associated with Java's spirit guardians and rulers, and drinking vintage Cape wine.

Part of the 'long shadow of Sultan Agung' (Ricklefs 1998b:469-82), Diponegoro fought both for the restoration of an idealized Javanese past, and the establishment of a new moral order in which the teachings of Islam, especially its legal precepts, would be upheld. This was the essence of his popular appeal for the religious communities and his importance for the future, his style of 'mystic synthesis' forming one of the key strands of Islamic piety in post-1830 Javanese society (Ricklefs 2007:30-83).

His insistence on Javanese language, dress and etiquette also cast him in the role of a proto-Javanese nationalist. Here was a man who was in Engelhard's phrase 'in all matters a Javanese and followed Javanese custom' (p. 9). But one cannot take this too far. There is no indication that he entertained any notions of national independence, not even for his native Java. Another century would have to pass before such ideas gained currency amongst the Indonesian elite. The most Diponegoro could conceive was a return to the seventeenth-century status quo, an era when the Dutch had been confined to the northeast coast of Java as traders and avoided direct political involvement in south-central Javanese affairs. His insistence on their payment of market prices for Javanese products and land lease contracts was certainly prescient given the impact of Van den Bosch's Cultivation System on Javanese society.

That this was an impossible dream is self-evident. Despite the insecurities of Holland's transition from patrician republic to nation state between 1785 and 1813, there was no possibility of retreat. Daendels' mailed fist and the insufferable arrogance of the English were proof enough that a new form of European power had been unleashed and was now being applied to colonial affairs. The importance of Java for the post-1830 Dutch domestic economy was argument enough that a Dutch exit was not on the cards.

For Diponegoro this would mean summary arrest and exile, an exile in which Dutch fears, intensified by the Belgian revolt, dictated an increasingly restrictive regime which would keep the prince and his family prisoners in Fort Rotterdam. His pitiful death in Makassar points to the human tragedy at the heart of this tale: the waste of a life, the suffering of a family, the ruin of a society. The policies imposed by Van den Bosch might have saved the Dutch state, but they spelt disaster for the Javanese. After 1830 a new world was born. It was a turning point as significant as any in colonial history. But it would exact a terrible cost.

Bibliography

à Campo, J.N.F.M. (1992). *Koninklijke Paketvaart Maatschappij: Stoomvaart en Staatsvorming in de Indonesische Archipel 1888–1914*. Hilversum: Verloren.
Atlas (1990). *Atlas van Tropisch Nederland*. Landsmeer: Gemilang. [Facsimile reprint of first edition, Batavia: Nederlandsch Aardrijkskundig Genootschap, 1938].
Babad Dipanegara (2010). *Babad Dipanegara*, 4 vols, ed. Nindya Noegraha. Jakarta: Perpustakaan Nasional Republik Indonesia.
Bosma, U. and R. Raben (2008). *Being 'Dutch' in the Indies; A History of Creolisation and Empire, 1500–1920*. Singapore: National University of Singapore Press.
Carey, Peter (1981). *Babad Dipanagara; An Account of the Outbreak of the Java War (1825–30); The Surakarta Court Version of the Babad Dipanagara with Translations into English and Indonesian Malay*. Kuala Lumpur: Art.
Carey, Peter (1982). 'Raden Saleh, Dipanagara and the Painting of the Capture of Dipanagara at Magelang", *Journal of the Malaysian Branch of the Royal Asiatic Society* 55–1:1–26.
Carey, Peter (2008). *The Power of Prophecy; Prince Dipanagara and the End of an Old Order in Java, 1785–1855*. Leiden: KITLV Press, second revised edition.
Carey, Peter (2009). 'Raden Saleh: Dipanagara dan Lukisan Penangkapan Dipanagara di Magelang (28 Maret 1830)', in Harsja Bachtiar, Peter BR Carey and Onghokham, *Raden Saleh: Anak Belanda, Mooi Indië & Nasionalisme*. Ed. J.J. Rizal. pp. 85–162. Jakarta: Komunitas Bambu.
Carey, Peter (2010). 'Revolutionary Europe and the Destruction of Java's Old Order, 1808–1830', in David Armitage and Sanjay Subhramanyan (eds), *'The Age of Revolutions' or 'World Crisis': Global Causation, Connection and Comparison, c. 1760–1840*, pp. 167–88. Basingstoke: Macmillan.
D'Almeida, W.B. (1864). *Life in Java with Sketches of the Javanese*. London: Hurst and Blackett. 2 vols.

De Nieuwsgier (1955). 'Diponegoro Noemde Niemand Heiden', 10 January 1955.
Dick, Howard, Vincent J.H. Houben, J. Thomas Lindblad and Thee Kian Wie (2002). *The Emergence of a National Economy; An Economic History of Indonesia, 1800–2000*. Crows Nest, NSW: Allen & Unwin.
Dobbin, C. (1972). 'Tuanku Imam Bondjol (1772–1864)', *Indonesia* 13:5–35.
Eerdmans, A.J.A.F. (1922). 'Algemeene Geschiedenis van Celebes', 5 vols. Manuscript Koninklijk Instituut (Leiden), KITLV H 817.
Elson, R. (1994). *Village Java under the Cultivation System 1830–1870*. Sydney: Asian Studies Association of Australia, Allen and Unwin.
Hageman, J.Jcz. (1856). *Geschiedenis van den Oorlog op Java van 1825 tot 1830*. Batavia: Lange.
Het Nieuwsblad van Soematra (1955). 'Honderdste Sterfdag Diponegoro Herdacht', 10 January 1955.
Houben, Vincent (1994). *Kraton and Kumpeni; Surakarta and Yogyakarta 1830–1870*. Leiden: KITLV Press. [Verhandelingen 164.]
Huyssen van Kattendijke-Frank, Katrientje (2004). *Met Prins Hendrik naar de Oost: De Reis van W.J.C. Huyssen van Kattendijke naar Nederlands-Indië, 1836–1838*. Zutphen: Walburg.
Kalff, S. (1927–8). 'Diponegoro's Sterfdag', *Indische Verlofganger* (Desember–Januari): 521–3.
Kielstra, E.B. (1911). 'Alexander van der Hart', in P.C. Molhuysen and P.J. Blok (eds), *Nieuw Nederlands Biografisch Woordenboek I*. Leiden: Sijthoff, p. 1030.
Knoerle 'Journal' (1830). 'Aanteekeningen gehouden door den 2e Luit Knoerle betreffende de Dagelyksche Verkeering van dien Officier met den Prins van Djocjakarta, Diepo Negoro, gedurende eene Reis van Batavia naar Menado, het Exil van den genoemden Prins', Manado, 20-6-1830. MS 391 of the Johannes van den Bosch private collection in the Nationaal Archief, The Hague.
Knoerle, J.H. (1835). 'Extract uit de Gehoudene Aanteekeningen gedurende Mijne Reis naar Menado', *De Oosterling* 2:135–80.
Marle, A. van (1971). "De Rol van de Buitenlandse Avonturier", *Bijdragen en Mededelingen betreffende de Geschiedenis der Nederlanden* 85-1:32–9.
Multatuli (Eduard Douwes Dekker) (1862–77). *Ideeën van Multatuli*. Amsterdam: Meijer, Funke.
Notulen (1877). *Notulen van de Algemeene en Bestuurs-Vergaderingen van het Bataviaasch Genootschap van Kunsten en Wetenschappen*. 15:89–95. Batavia: Bruining.
Pigeaud, Th.G.Th. (1967–80). *Literature of Java; Catalogue Raisonné of Javanese Manuscripts in the Library of the University of Leiden and other Public Collections in the Netherlands*. The Hague, Leiden: Nijhoff. Four vols.
Popper, Karl (2003). *The Open Society and its Enemies*. 2 vols. London and New York: Routledge Classics.

Ricklefs, Merle C. (1998a). *The Seen and Unseen Worlds in Java, 1726–1749; History, Literature and Islam in the Court of Pakubuwana II*. Sydney: Allen and Unwin, Honolulu: University of Hawaii Press.

Ricklefs, Merle C. (1998b). 'Islamising Java; The Long Shadow of Sultan Agung', *Archipel* 56:469–82.

Ricklefs, Merle C. (2006). *Mystic Synthesis in Java; A History of Islamization from the Fourteenth to the Early Nineteenth Centuries*. EastBridge, Norwalk: Signature Books.

Rouveroy van Nieuwaal, M.Ch. van (1928). 'Het Graf van Dipå Negårå te Makassar', *Tropisch Nederland*, 13:206–8.

Sagimun, M.D. (1965). *Pahlawan Dipanegara Berjuang; (Bara api Kemerdekaan nan tak Kundjung Padam)*. Djakarta: Gunung Agung.

Scalliet, M.O. (2005). 'Raden Saleh et les Hollandais; Artiste Protégé ou Ôtage Politique?', *Archipel* 69:151–258.

Surianto, Jimmy S. (2013). 'Teguh Budi Santoso: Generasi Penerus Empu Mageti', *Kompas*, 20 November.

Tarling, Nicholas (1963). 'The Palmer Loans', *Bijdragen tot de Taal-, Land- en Volkenkunde* 119.2: 161–88.

Taylor, Jean Gelman (2003). *Indonesia; Peoples and Histories*. New Haven & London: Yale University Press.

Wallace, Alfred Russel (1890). *The Malay Archipelago; The Land of the Orang-utan and the Bird of Paradise; A Narrative of Travel with Studies of Man and Nature*. London: MacMillan.

Wallace, Alfred Russel (2002). *A.R. Wallace's Malay Archipelago; Journals and Notebook*. Edited by M.B. Pearson. London: Linnean Society.

Wassing-Visser, Rita (1995). *Royal Gifts from Indonesia; Historical Bonds with the House of Orange-Nassau (1600–1938)*. Zwolle: Waanders.

Glossary of Javanese Words

(Note: These definitions give only those senses in which the words have been used in this book)

abdi-Dalem	royal official or retainer usually living in the immediate environs of the royal palace (namely within the walls of the *kraton*, see below)
adat	custom, time honoured practice both in social etiquette and in legal matters
Adipati	used in conjunction with *pangeran* to indicate a senior prince often with an extensive apanage and a quasi-independent position in the *kraton*
Ali Basah	title accorded by Diponegoro to the commander-in-chief of his army, Ali Basah Sentot, during the Java War. From the Ottoman-Turkish 'Ali Pasha' (the 'High Pasha'). Other senior commanders bore the title of *Basah* (Pasha), while junior commanders were styled *Dullah* (from the Ottoman-Turkish *sa'dullah*).
alun-alun	the great square or open field in front of and behind the *kraton*; it was usually planted with two boxed *waringin* (banyan) trees as symbols of royal authority
babad	Javanese historical texts written in chronicle form and divided into cantos (each with a separate metre); from the Javanese verb, *mbabad*, to clear (the jungle)
bandar	a keeper of a tollgate or customs post on the main roads and rivers in south-central and east Java before the outbreak of the Java War; the tollgate keepers were usually Chinese who farmed the rent of customs, first from the Javanese courts and later (after 1812) from the European government
batik	intricately designed wax-dyed fabric

batur	porter or coolie who carried goods by shoulder load, referred to in Javanese as a *pikul* (see below), on the main roads in Java during the nineteenth century
bupati	high administrative official: the title was used for heads of provincial areas (especially in the *mancanagara*, see below) and for the chiefs of administrative departments in the *kraton*; thus *kabupaten*, the residence, office or administrative area of a *bupati*. See also *wedana* below
cacah	household, used as a unit of measurement for land and population in Java. It was usually reckoned as the amount of land which could be worked (and provide a livelihood) for a family of five; thus the size of the *cacah* varied according to the quality of the ground and the availability of irrigation
dalem	princely residence or home of a high court official; it usually comprised an extensive central building with private apartments and a large front veranda (*pendopo*, see below) for receiving visitors, a wide yard and outhouses for servants and relations. The whole complex was usually surrounded by a wall or bamboo fence and looked like a *kraton* in miniature
demang	middle-ranking provincial official with special tax collecting responsibilities
desa	village or complex of houses with ricefields and orchards attached in rural areas
dalang	puppeteer in the *wayang* theatre; he is the key figure in *wayang* performances having the task of moving the puppets, reproducing the speech of the various characters, telling the story of the plot, singing snatches of song and making jokes. He also has the duty of ensuring that the performance (which starts at about 9 p.m.) is over and complete before the break of day (at about 5.30 a.m.)
dhikr/zikir	repetitive short phrases for the glorification of God's used during prayer and military engagements by Diponegoro's forces.

Glossary of Javanese Words

emban	guardian or nurse of a young child or youth below the age of majority, which in Java is sixteen years
Erucokro	title of the Javanese 'Just King' (*ratu adil*, see below) who is believed to make his appearance after a period of economic decline and moral decadence. The characteristics of his reign are low taxes, fair justice, cheap food and clothes, and feelings of common brotherhood. The origin of the title Erucokro is unclear, but may be connected to the Hindu god Wisnu's sun disc (*cakra*) weapon (see cover image)
gamelan	Javanese orchestra comprising mainly percussion and wind instruments
Garebeg	thrice-annual Javanese-Islamic feasts, consisting of the *Garebeg Mulud* in celebration of the birth of The Prophet Muhammad; *Garebeg Puwasa* to celebrate the end of the fasting month; and *Garebeg Besar* in commemoration of Abraham's willingness to sacrifice his son (Ishmael/Isaac) and of the pilgrimage to Mecca
gunung	mountain or large hill (usually over 600 meters in height); it was also a title used in Surakarta for police and tax officials in the villages who were answerable to the *patih* (in Yogya, they were known as Tamping). The title probably derived from the *gunungan* (large mounds of decorated rice) which these officials had to bear in procession during the *Garebeg* ceremonies (see above) in Surakarta
guwo	cave, grotto
haji	the title of a pilgrim who has been to Mecca; the *haj* (pilgrimage to Mecca) is one of the five central obligations of a Muslim, the others being: the *shahadat* (the confession of The Faith: 'There is no God but God and Muhammad is His Prophet'); *salat* (five daily prayers); *zakat* (the giving of alms) and *puwasa*, the observation of the fast during the fasting month
insan kamil	the 'perfect man' in Sufi Islamic teachings

jimat	amulet or talisman (usually small pieces of different sorts of metal, wood or paper with writing in Arabic script containing secret formulae) which are believed to ward off sickness and danger, and provide invulnerability in battle
jung	a unit of land measurement (usually about 600 square feet): like the *cacah* (see above) it varied in size according to the quality of the ground. In some areas it is reckoned as being four times the size of the *cacah* and enough to provide a livelihood for four families of cultivators
jurukunci	doorkeeper or guardian of the keys of a grave or holy place (see *pradikan* below)
kadaton	inner part of the court (*kraton*) where the ruler's private apartments or (*Proboyekso*) are located (see also *Keputren*)
Kadipaten	residence of the crown prince (Pangeran Adipati Anom) at the south-central Javanese courts
kali	a large river; also 'Bengawan' in the case of the Solo river
kampung	village or urban settlement, the latter often occupied by a particular ethnic group or community, hence Kampung Melayu, Kampung Cina, the Malay and Chinese quarters of a town
Kapitan Cina	head of the Chinese community in a town or provincial area
kasepuhan	the party of the 'old' sultan (Sultan Sepuh or Hamengkubuwono II), which backed the claims of Pangeran Mangkudiningrat to the Yogya throne over and above those of the Crown Prince (later Hamengkubuwono III)
karajan	the party of the Crown Prince (Hamengkubuwono III or Sultan Raja), which took its name from his title 'Raja Putro Narendro Pangeran Adipati Anom Amangkunegoro' and was also sometimes known as the *kanoman*

Glossary of Javanese Words

kauman	strict religious community in the court cities who resided in the area near the Great Mosque (Mesjid Ageng)
kebatinan	Javanese spiritual and mystical disciplines which can range from varieties of Islamic mysticism to magical practices. In general *kebatinan* is the science of the soul or the inner man (*batin*) and is concerned with providing methods for spiritual growth and the unity of man with his Creator
kecu	robber, bandit or thief (see *wong durjono* below)
Kepatihan	office and residence of the chief administrator (*patih*, see below) at the Central Javanese courts
Keputren	special quarters for the court princesses, ruler's wives (official and unofficial), daughters and other female relatives within the inner part of the court (see *kadaton* above)
khalifah	Protector of the community of Believers (*ummat*) throughout the Muslim world, a title revived in the late eighteenth century by the Ottoman Sultan Abd al-Hamīd I (reigned, 1773–87)
kromo	'High Javanese', one of the two basic forms of Modern Javanese (see also *ngoko* below): used to address superiors in age or social standing
kraton	royal palace, court and residence of a ruler. This comprises the royal apartments and meeting halls etcetera, and also numerous houses inhabited by the families of royal retainers. The whole complex, which in Yogya contained between 10–15,000 people in 1812 and extended three miles in circumference, is surrounded by a large defensive wall
kris	Javanese dagger or small stabbing sword often considered to possess supernatural powers. The blade can be straight or undulating and the metal is inlaid with meteoric iron. This damascening (or *pamor* in Javanese) produces many different shapes and figures and gives each *kris* a unique character
kyai	honorific title for old men or country gentlemen, especially teachers of religious and spiritual disciplines see

	ulama below. The title is also used to refer to special *kris* and other *pusaka* (see below)
lakon	a plot which is enacted in a *wayang* drama (see *wayang* below)
lelono	pilgrimage to places of spiritual and religious significance to seek spiritual knowledge
lurah	chief or head, especially used as a title for village leaders; also the head of any administrative branch or group (hence *kyai lurah*, the title of the *patih* amongst court officials) *mancanagara* the outer regions or distant provinces of a kingdom (as distinct from the inner areas near the court, see *nagara agung* below). These outlying regions, which were originally added to the royal patrimony by conquest, were administered directly by their own *bupati* as opposed to the *nagara agung* which was governed in the name of the sovereign by the *patih*. The *mancanagara* areas to the east and west of the princely territories were finally annexed by the Dutch in 1830
mantri	title of an official of lower rank in the royal administration
mas	title of nobility, used for distant relations (male) of the royal families
mesjid	mosque or place of worship; hence Mesjid Ageng ('Great Mosque') at the courts
nagara agung	the core regions of a kingdom, the lands in the vicinity of the court used as crown lands (*narawita, bumi pamajegan-dalem*) for special types of produce, taxes and labour services for the court, and as apanages (*lungguh*) for members of the royal family and high court officials, see below *nayaka*
Nayaka	Eight senior advisers of the rulers at the south-central Javanese courts, comprising the *patih* and the heads of *kraton* administrative departments, namely the four Inner and four Outer *bupati*, known in Javanese as *wedana jero* and *wedana jaba*

Glossary of Javanese Words

ngoko	'Low Javanese', one of the two basic forms of Modern Javanese (see *kromo* above); used to address close equals or inferiors (in age or social standing)
panakawan	intimate retainer of a ruler, nobleman or official: these retainers occasionally had something of the humour and wisdom associated with the clown-servant advisers in the *wayang* theatre
panatagama	protector of religion, a title used by the south-central Javanese rulers
panembahan	high princely title usually reserved for respected, older male members of the close royal family, for example, the uncles and elder brothers of a ruler
pangeran	prince, male offspring of a ruler by official and unofficial wives
panji	young man of high nobility; a title given to youths who served as intimate retainers of the rulers and to military commanders at the courts
pasisir	coast, in particular the north coast of Java, also used to indicate regions not in the heartland (princely territories) of south-central Java
pathok negari	centres for the *ulama* (experts in *fiqh* or Islamic law) who acted as the advisers of the *pengulu* (chief religious functionary) in the religious courts. Before they were abolished in circa 1830, there were four *pathok* (alias 'pillars') at both Yogya and Surakarta answerable to the *pengulu* at the centre, thus recalling the five pillars of Islam or the traditional Javanese four-five cosmic system (*mancapat-mancalima*)
patih	chief minister of the Javanese kingdoms: his full title was *patih jaba* (prime minister dealing with affairs outside the court) to distinguish him from the *patih jero* who had primary responsibility over matters within the *kraton* (see *nayaka* above). The title was also used more generally for

	the head of an administration, hence *patih kadipaten* the head of the Crown Prince's establishment
payung	state umbrella, used as an insignia of rank or royal birth
pegon	Javanese written in Arabic characters (usually unvocalised), often used by the more self-consciously religious members of the south-central Javanese communities, for example, the *santri*, see below
pendopo	large covered audience hall or veranda in front of a Javanese house for receiving visitors *pengulu* head of the religious hierarchy in the court towns who also played a leading role as an interpreter of Islamic law codes in the religious courts (*surambi*) of the south-central Javanese *kraton*
pesanggrahan	pavilion, overnight stopping place or royal hunting lodge
pesantren	religious boarding school comprising dormitories, places of instruction and adjacent ricefields, which were frequented by students of religion (see *santri* below)
pikul	a weight (usually about 62 kilograms) which is carried in two baskets, weighted evenly and borne on a carrying pole slung across the shoulders
pondok	small religious boarding school set up on the same lines as a *pesantren* but on a much smaller scale
pradikan	tax-free areas given by the courts and usually set aside for those engaged in religious pursuits or for guardians of graves and holy places (see *jurukunci* above); hence *pradikan ageng*, the head of such a tax-free area
prajurit	soldier, member of the palace guard
prang sabil	holy war; a war waged for (Islamic) religious ideals, which is one of the obligations of a Muslim
primbon Jawa	Javanese divination text or almanac
priyayi	member of the official class in south-central Java, literally *para yayi*, the 'younger brothers of the ruler'
pusaka	holy regalia or heirloom handed down from one generation to the next in a particular family; often considered to have supernatural powers (see *kris* above)

Glossary of Javanese Words

raden	title of middle nobility given to persons distantly related to the main royal families
raden mas	title of high nobility given to close male descendants of the main royal families
ratu	principal official wife or consort of the ruler: in the south-central Javanese courts the rulers usually had four such principal wives, one for each point of the compass. The one for the southern quarter (Ratu Kidul) was the queen of the spirit kingdom in the southern ocean (see below)
Ratu Adil	see above under Erucokro
Ratu Kidul	the goddess of the southern ocean. According to popular Javanese beliefs, she rules over a court inhabited by spirits. The rulers of the south-central Javanese courts are expected to enter into a spiritual marriage with the goddess in order to ensure the support of the spirit kingdoms during their period of rule
santri	a student of (Islamic) religion, follower of a religious way of life, pupil at a *pesantren* or *pondok* (see above)
sawah	wet ricefield
seh (syeh)	title given to high religious dignitaries, especially to teachers and scholars who were Arabs from the Hadhramaut or who claimed descent from the family of The Prophet (Arabic Shaykh)
selir	unofficial wife of a prince or ruler
senopati	commander-in-chief of an army
sentono	member of the sultan's family, usually a distant relative such as a second or third cousin
Serat Centhini	comprehensive encylopaedia of Javanese manners, history, traditions beliefs, society and sexual mores compiled in the early nineteenth century (1815) under the aegis of the Crown Prince of Surakarta (later Pakubuwono V, reigned 1820–23) and written by the court scribe, Carik Sutrasno
sharif	title of a religious scholar (*ulama*) deemed to be a descendant of the Prophet

surjan	Javanese jacket with high collar made from thick locally made cotton cloth (see *lurik* above)
tapa	to engage in asceticism: an ascetic, mystic, man of religion. See also *tirakat*
tarekat	Sufi Islamic mystical brotherhood led by a Seh (Syeh) (see above)
tembang	verse; scanned verse used in chronicles etcetera
tirakat	to go on retreat and practice meditation and asceticism. See also *tapa* above
tumenggung	title of high administrative rank usually given to *bupati* (see above)
ulama	Muslim scholar especially applied as a title to those learned in Islamic law (*fiqh*)
wali	early apostle or saint of Islam in Java; the *wali* are usually said to have been nine in number
wayang	Javanese puppet theatre of several types. Those mentioned in this study are as follows: *wayang kulit*, shadow theatre with flat leather puppets; *wayang purwa*, plays dealing with ancient mythology (principally the *Ramayana* and *Mahabharata* cycles); *wayang wong*, theatre performance using dancers, and *wayang topeng*, a masked dance
wedana	high administrative official; the title, like that of *bupati*, was used both for officials within the *kraton* and for those in charge of extensive administrative areas such as the eastern and western *mancanagara* where the senior official was known as *bupati wedana*
wong cilik	common people
wong durjono	robbers, tramps, bandits, or 'evil folk' in general (see *kecu* above)
wong putihan	students of religion or religious officials living a communal life (see above *pradikan*, *santri* and *ulama*)

Index

(Abbreviations: d. = daughter; DN = Diponegoro; HB = Hamengkubuwono; PB = Pakubuwono; RT = Raden Tumenggung)

Abbas, Lieutenant (HB IV's Malay tutor) 161
'Abd al-Hamīd I, Ottoman Sultan (1773–87) 60, 337
Abdul Kadir I, Sultan of Bima (1621–40) 8
see also Datuk Suleiman
Abijoyo, Kyai (DN's heirloom *kris*) 41, 229
Abubakar, Prince Muhamad (Dipowijoyo I) 49
Aceh xxvii, 266
see also Sumatra
Adinegoro (DN's younger brother) 80, 93
Adinegoro, Prince (HB IX's younger brother) 28
Ageng, Ratu (Tegalrejo, DN's guardian) 8–12, 14–15, 17, 20
death and burial (17 Oct 1803) 13, 47, 53
religious devotion of 17
Ageng, Ratu (mother of HB IV) *see* Kedaton, Ratu
Ageng, Ratu (consort of HB II) *see* Kedaton, Ratu
Agung, Sultan 5, 53, 58, 220, 265, 328
lunar era of xix
as model ruler 63, 218, 246
prophecy of 5, 59
as *wali wudhar* 220, 223

Aji Soko (tales) 60, 185
aksara pegon (Javanese written in Arabic characters) ix, xix, xxvii, 26, 276, 314, 320, 340
see also Danukusumo, Raden Ayu
alcohol consumption (by Javanese elite) xvi, xvii, 32, 171, 178, 190, 328
see also Nahuys, wine
Ali Basah (title) xxxviii, 60, 261, 333
see also Sentot
Alip, Raden Mas (DN's son by secondary wife) 27, 53, 198, 227
Al Quran see Qur'ān
Amangkurat I, Sunan (1646–77) 121, 241, 251, 257
see also Plered, *santri*
Amazon Corps (*prajurit èstri*) *see* women (*prajurit èstri*)
Ambon 296, 307
Diposono exiled to (17-02-1823) 189
DN II and brothers exiled to (1840/51) 50, 321
HB II exiled to (1817–24) 299
troops at Jati Ngaleh battle (16-09-1811) 120
amok 120, 143, 229–30, 292
see also British, Joyosentiko, Meester Cornelis, Rawabangke
Angger Gunung (Police Code, 1808) 82

Angger Sepuluh (Agrarian Code, 1818) 177
Angreni see Serat Angreni
Ansari, Syekh Abdul Ahmad bin Abdullah al- 27, 49, 249
  see also Jeddah
Antang, district (east Java) 115–6
  see also Malang
Antwerp 316
Anyer xiv
apostates *see kapir murtad*
Arabia, Arabs xxxviii, 27, 35, 49, 160, 185, 228, 249, 331
  Arab-Javanese 293, 319
    see also Saleh (Raden, Syarif Bustaman)
  Arab sailing vessels 319
  Arab-style clothes 27, 230
  Arabic language 35, 185, 266, 320
  Arabic literature 29
  Arabic prayers 28
  see also aksara pegon, Ansari, Hadhramaut, Hejaz, Wahhābi
Ari Kiyamat (Day of Judgement) 58
Arjuna (Arjun) xxiii, 37, 61, 63, 158, 218
  see also Pasopati, Sarutomo, *wayang*
Arjuna Sasrabahu 160
Arjuna Wijaya ('Arjuna's Victory') 29
Arjuna Wiwāha ('Arjuna's Marriage') xxiii, 29, 61, 63, 218
Arkio, DN's elite regiment 60
  see also Barjumungah, Bulkio, Turkio
Arriëns, Pieter (captain of frigate *Bellona*; tutor to Prince Hendrik) 318
  see also Bellona, Hendrik
Arsip Nasional Republik Indonesia *see* Indonesian National Archives
Asmoro Supi see Serat Asmoro Supi 30, 321
Austen, Jane 40

Babad Bedhah ing Ngayogyakarta ('Chronicle of the Fall of Yogyakarta') 38, 80, 128, 130, 134, 142, 149, 156, 159
  see also Panular
Babad Dipanagara Surya Ngalam 25
Babad Diponegoro (DN's autobiography, Manado, 1831–2) xxvii–xxviii, 75, 122, 127, 158, 301, 305, 312
Babad Diponegoro Keraton Surakarta (Surakarta court version) 9, 18, 27, 175, 201, 252
Babad Ngayogyakarta (Yogya court chronicle) 80
Babad Pakualaman (Pakualam court chronicle) 9, 75, 78, 81, 91, 94–5, 98, 108, 124, 126, 130
Badarudin, Haji (DN's religious adviser) 17, 276, 310
  see also Ngiso, Suranatan
Baderan, Kyai 253
  see also Baderan, Mojo
Baderan, *pesantren* (religious school) 18, 249
  see also Mojo, Pulo Kadang
Bagelen 18, 71, 156, 184, 264
  annexation planned 71, 182
  Chinese communities in 244
    see also Jono, Wedi
  DN in jungles of xix, 36, 158, 264, 272, 274, 276–8
  Dutch mobile column commanders in 294
    see also Cleerens
  fighting capacity of 249
  Fort Cochius 260
  Gunung Kelir ambush (21–09–1829) 264
  Kroya victory in (Oct 1828) 262
    see also Sentot
  Pengalasan as commander in 273, 322

Index

Tan Jin Sing's Bagelen apanage in (6-12-1813) 156
ulama from 18, 250
Bahwi, Kyai Muhamad 17
Balad, Kyai (head *jurukunci* Imogiri) 53
Bali, Balinese 33, 133, 242, 256
  see also Mojo (Raden Ayu), *prang puputan*, Suropati
bandar (tollgates) 152, 180–83, 333
bandits xxxvi, 116, 121, 131, 179, 181–2, 189, 207
  DN's dealings with 27–8, 241
  see also Kali Progo, Kamijoro, Mangiran, sepoys
Banjarsari (*pesantren*, Madiun), Kyai guru 250
Bangil, district (east Java) 186
  see also Ellinghuisen
Bantengwareng, DN's *panakawan* (personal retainer) xxi, 158, 264
  see also Roto
Bantul 15, 17, 148, 182, 241
  battle of (4-08-1826) 257
  see also Secang, Selarong
Banyumas 71, 158, 182, 249, 260, 264, 272
  see also Remo, Sudirman
Banyusumurup, traitors' graveyard (Gunung Kidul) 108, 122
  see also Danurejo II, Prawirodirjo III
Barjumungah, DN's elite priestly regiment 249, 272
  in Saleh's DN arrest painting (1857) xx
  see also Arkio, Bulkio, Munadi, Turkio
Basah, Muhamad Ngusman Ali *see* Ngusman
Batavia xxi, xxxiii, xliii, 30, 86, 101, 128, 150, 275, 277, 317
  Batavian Legion 69
  see also Daendels

Batavian Society of Arts and Sciences 297, 314
  see also Vinne
British landing in (4 Aug 1811) 119
cholera epidemic in (June 1821) 188
HB II returns to (Aug 1816) 173
J.P. Coen and 73
political relations with princely states xxxiv–v, 69, 72–7, 86
Saleh's painting unveiled in (March 1857) 294
Tanah Abang landowner 150
  see also Tiedeman
Bataviaasch Genootschap van Kunsten en Wetenschappen *see* Batavia
Baud, J.C., Minister of Colonies (1840–8) 320
Bayly, C.A. 113
Bedono 282, 295
Bedoyo, Nahuys's villa/estate on Mt Merapi (1817–23) 177, 204, 229
  compensation for (July 1823) 208–9
Belgian Revolt (1830–31) 300, 315–6, 318, 328
  see also Gérard, Kock, Roeps
Belgians xiv, xviii, xxxv, 204, 244
  De Kock considers worse than Javanese 275
  see also Bus, Cleerens, Payen, Thierry
Belgium 315–6
Bellona, frigate 318
  see also Arriëns, Hendrik
Bendoro, Ratu (HB I's d.) 148
Bendoro, Ratu (HB II's d.) 157–8
  see also Sumodiningrat
Bengal, Bengali xv, 37, 118, 125, 130, 133, 142, 162, 163, 181, 183, 275
  see also Bentinck, Calcutta, Minto, Nurngali, sepoys
Bengal Light Infantry Volunteer Battalion 133, 162

see also Dalton, sepoys (plot/conspiracy)
Bengawan Solo (Solo River) xii, 07, 152, 243, 336
 British abolish tolls on (Feb 1815) 181
Bengkung (Imogiri) 52–3
benteng stelsel xxviii, 260
 see also Cochius
Bentinck, Lord William (Viceroy of India, 1828–35) 163
 see also Palmer & Co, sepoys
Bik, A.J. xxviii, 297
Bik, Pieter Vreede see Vreede Bik
Bima, Sumbawa island 8, 10, 54
 see also Abdul Kadir I, Sumbawa
Bima, Pandawa brother in *Mahabhārata* 54
Bima Raré, cycle of wayang plays (*lakon*) 54
birds' nest rocks (South Coast) 147
 see also Portier
Blitar, district (East Java) 186
 see also Iman Sampurno
Blitar I, Prince (son of HB I) 27, 212
Blitar II, Prince (son of above) 273
Boedi Oetomo ('Noble Endeavour', 20-05-1908) xli
Bonang, Sunan (apostle of Islam) 184–5
 see also Umar Mahdi
Bonaparte, King Louis (of Holland, 1806–10) 72, 116
 see also Orde van der Unie
Bondoyudo, Kyai Ageng (DN's heirloom *kris*) 41, 61, 277, 300, 323
Bonjol, Tuanku Imam 311
 see also Padri War
Borneo see Kalimantan
Bosch, Johannes van den, Governor-General (1830–4) xxxiii, 31, 265, 275, 298, 322

Cultivation System (1830–70) xxxiii, 265, 274, 326, 328–9
DN's capture and exile 275–6, 281–2, 286, 292, 295, 298–300, 309–10, 316–7
Bousquet, Isaac (Raad van Indië, father of below) 298
 see also Goldman
Bousquet, Reinier de Fillietaz, Governor of Makassar (1834–41) 318
 see also Hart, Perez, Vreede Bik
Bojong, Residency (Semarang) 295
Boyolali 101, 115
Braam, J. A. van, Resident of Surakarta (1808–10/1811) and President *Hooge Regeering* [Supreme Government] (1810–11) 75, 79, 83, 100, 114, 121
 and Ronggo 84–5, 101
 tiger-buffalo fight (Oct 1808) 83–4
 see also Veeckens
Bratayuda ('Brothers' War') 30, 218
 see also *Mahabhārata*
Breda, Royal Dutch Military Academy at xxi, 269
 see also Nypels
Britain see England
British see English
Brosot (Kulon Progo) 42
Buddha, Buddhism 33, 142, 162, 302
 see also Ceylon, Hindu-Buddhist
Bugis 317
 pirates 300
 see also Makassarese
Buku Kedung Kebo ('Chronicle of the Buffaloes Watering Hole') xiii, xvii, 28, 32, 53, 178, 248, 252
Bulkio, DN's elite regiment 60
 Mojo surrenders with 500 (12-11-1828) 255
 see also Arkio, Barjumungah, Turkio

Buminoto, Prince 19
bupati dongkol (prematurely dismissed *bupati*) 152
Bus de Gisignies, L.P.J. du, Commissioner-General (1826–30) 258–9, 265
Buschkens, Major H.F. xix, 262
  see also Kroya
Bustaman, Raden Saleh Syarif
  see Saleh, Syarif Bustaman

Cakradiningrat I, Panembahan (Pamekasan) 7
  see also Madura, Madurese, Pamekasan
Calcutta (Kalkuta) 134, 143, 146, 163
  see also Bengal, Bentinck, Minto, Palmer & Co, sepoys
caliph, title 337
  see also Abd al-Hamīd I
Cambier, J.P.C., Resident Manado (1831–42) 311, 312
Cape Colony (South Africa) 120, 163
  see also Constantia, Janssens
Capellen, G.A.G.Ph. van der, Governor-General (1816–26) xxxv, 164, 169–70, 182, 191, 198–9, 203, 227
  land-rent 205–6
Capellen, Baroness Jacqueline Elisabet (*née* Tuyll van Serooskerken) (wife of above) xviii
Capellen, S.S. van der (steamship) 295–6
  see also Davidson
Cauwer Wetan, district (west Java) 115–6
  see also Galuh
caves see under Guwo
Cemoro Tunggal 55
  see also *lalembut,* Ratu Kidul
Centhini see *Serat Centhini*
Cephas, Kassian, photographer (1844–1912) 77
Ceylon 33, 103, 163

  see also Buddhism
Chevallier, Pierre Frederic Henri, Assistant-Resident Yogya (1823–5) 37, 199–200, 203, 209, 296
  erotic energy 211–3
  see also women
Chinese xvii, 325
  anti-Chinese feelings 129, 168, 239
  attacks on (1812) 144
  attacks on (1825) 180, 184–5
    see also Jono, Kedu, Ngawi, Yudokusumo
  Chinese War (*Prang Cina*, 1740–2) 131
  clothing xvii
  Diposono's rebellion (Feb 1822) 189
  DN's attitudes towards 239, 244–6, 266
  DN's mistress 37, 39, 105, 246
    see also Kedaren
  DN's official wife (1807) 25
    see also Notowijoyo III, Retnokusumo, Supadmi
  east Java communities and Ronggo's rebellion 104–5, 107
  inhabitants of Yogya xvii, 325
    see also Prawirodirjo III
  Kampung Cina 336
  Kapitan Cina (Captain of the Chinese) 104, 132, 143–4, 156, 160, 204, 207, 336
    see also Tan Jin Sing
  landrenters 177, 179, 180, 206
  legal codes and 153
  moneylenders 152, 179
  opium suppliers 183–4
  santri and Islam 246, 249
  south-central Java communities 105, 132
  Surabaya, Bangil, Pasuruan communities 186

Tan Jin Sing appointed *bupati* (6–12–1813) 156
tax-farmers 99, 156
timber felling monopoly (east Java) 95
tollgate keepers 105, 152, 180–3, 333
cholera (1821 epidemic) xxxvi, 186–8, 191, 202
  see also Batavia, Oosthoek, Pacitan, Schillet, Surabaya
Christians, Christianity 60, 174, 251, 291, 308, 317
  see also Manado, Minahasa
Chronicle of the Fall of Yogyakarta see *Babad Bedhah ing Ngayogyakarta*, Panular
Cleerens, Colonel Jan Baptist xix, 264, 273, 294, 317
  negotiations with DN (Feb 1830) 272–9, 289, 291
cloth trade see Chinese, Jono, Kali Lereng, Wedi
Cochius, Colonel Frans David 257, 275
  benteng stelsel 260
Coen, Jan Pieterszoon 73
coffee 177, 180, 183–4, 188, 206, 207, 208, 326
Cokronegoro, Raden Adipati, Surakarta *patih* (1810–12) 127
Constantia wine (South Africa) 40, 204, 328
  see also Smissaert (Clara Elisabet)
Coromandel (India) 163
Crawfurd, John, Resident Yogya (1811–14/1816) 128, 133, 147, 149, 161, 171, 301
  compromise with HB II 123–6
  and DN 32, 129, 150–1, 170, 301
  see also Schillet
criminals see bandits
Cromwell, Oliver vi, xxvii

Crown Prince's title (Raja Putra Narendro Pangeran Adipati Anom Amangkunegoro) 115
  see also Hamengkubuwono III
Crown Prince's establishment see Kadipaten
Crusade, First (1095–9) 33
Cultivation System (1830–70) xxxiii, 265, 274, 326, 328–9
  see also Bosch

d'Abo, R.C.N., Assistant-Resident Yogya (1817–23) 172, 203
Dadapan, village/religious school 25
Dadapan, Kyai Gede (DN's father-in-law) 25
  see also Madubrongto
Daendels, Marshal Herman Willem xiv, xvi, xxxiii, xxxv, xlii, 59, 61, 79–83, 91, 93, 117–9, 122, 125, 134, 141, 177, 327–8
  annexationist policies 69–86
  Ceremonial and Etiquette Decree (28 July 1808) 49
  DN's views of 226
  Jan 1811 treaties 113–6
  July 1809 Yogya visit 93–4
  plots Notokusumo's murder 118
  postweg (trans-Java highway) xiv, 83, 97
  replaced by Janssens (May 1811) 119
  Ronggo's rebellion (1810) 79–81, 94–101, 105–8
  view of *prajurit èstri* 9, 94
  Yogya indemnity (Jan 1811) 91–3, 151
  see also *postweg*
Dalton, Major Dennis Harman (C.O. Light Infantry Volunteer Battalion) 133
  see also Light Infantry Volunteer Battalion, sepoys

Index 349

Danukusumo, Raden Ayu
  (DN's great-aunt) 26, 201
Danurejan (family) 17, 26, 147, 261, 272
  see also Danukusumo, Danurejo II,
    Kepatihan, Melangi
Danurejo, Raden Adipati Abdullah, DN's
    wartime *patih* (1828-30; uncle of
    below) 262, 264, 273-4
Danurejo II, Raden Adipati (Yogya *patih*,
    1799-1811) 12, 26, 80, 83, 116-7,
    147, 161
  murder (28 Oct 1811) 122
  see also Danukusumo, Melangi
Danurejo III, Kyai Adipati (Yogya *patih*,
    1811-13; uncle of above) 149, 155
Danurejo IV, Raden Adipati (pre-1813,
    RT Sumodipuro; Yogya *patih*,
    1813-47) xvii, 147, 160, 178, 199,
    203-4, 207, 209, 211
  appointment (2 Dec 1813) 155-6
  corruption and sexual affairs 209-13
  gunung (police officials) of 175, 335
  rebuked by DN (1816) 178
  stakes out Tegalrejo road 228-9
Danurejo V, Raden Adipati (pre-1847,
    RT Gondokusumo; Yogya *patih*,
    1847-79) 283
Datuk Suleiman, Kyai Ageng (alias Kyai
    Suleiman Bekel Jamus; son of
    Sultan Abdulkadir I of Bima) 8
Davidson, George Frank 296-7
Deans, John, Yogya Residency Secretary
    (1811-13) 133, 209
Dekso, DN's first Kulon Progo HQ
    (1825-6) 257, 263
  gunpowder manufacture at 242
  see also Into-Into, Kota Gede,
    Samen
Delanggu xiii, 18, 37, 102, 174, 249
  battle of (28-08-1826) 257

  see also Baderan, Kepundung, Mojo,
    Murmo
Demak 52, 55, 99, 243, 248
  great mosque at 51
  Raden Patah 32
  sultans of 254
  Sunan Bonang 185
  see also Serang
Demak, Sunan *see* Demak
Dento, Sunan Ngampel (Gresik) 6
  see also Gresik
Derpoyudo, Kyai Ageng (father of Ratu
    Ageng Tegalrejo) 8
  see also Majangjati, Sragen
Dewantara, Ki Hadjar
  (Suwarsih Suryoningrat) 327
dhikr (litanies from *Qur'ān*) 33-4, 132,
    159, 186, 250
Dickens, Charles xxviii, 40
Dietrée, J.G., Yogya Residency Interpreter
    (1796-1825) 204, 209, 211, 296
Dipokusumo, Prince (joint administrator
    eastern *mancanagara*/ Madiun,
    1811-22) 116
Dipokusumo, Prince (DN's second son,
    circa 1805-pre-March 1856) 281,
    299, 321
Diponegoro, Prince (husband of Ratu
    Bendoro; died 1787) 148
Diponegoro, Prince (1785-1855) *see under
    relevant entries*
Diponegoro II (DN's eldest son; pre-1825
    Raden Mas Ontowiryo II, circa
    1803-post-Mar 1856) xii, 19, 25,
    50, 58, 158, 248, 281, 299, 321
  see also Ambon, Sumenep
Diponingrat, Prince (DN's third son, circa
    1807-post-Mar 1856) 26, 299
Diposono, Prince, rebellion (Feb
    1822) 187-9

Dipowijoyo I, Prince *see* Abubakar
Dipowiyono, Pangeran (son of HB II; father of below) 149
Dipowiyono, Raden Tumenggung (husband of below) 297, 311–2
Dipowiyono, Raden Ayu (DN's sister) 311–2
Djamhari, Saleh As'ad, military historian xxvii, 272
Djojohadikusumo, Hashim xxix
dual function *see dwifungsi*
dukun (magic practitioner / herbalist/ clairvoyant) 159
  as DN's personal physician 37, 163
  see also Nurngali
  in Diposono revolt (Feb 1822) 189
Dulkabli, Raden Mas 312
Dutch *see* Dutch East India Company, Netherlands East Indies
Dutch East India Company (Vereenigde Oost-Indische Compagnie [VOC], 1602–1799) xxxii–xxxv, 9, 69, 74, 94, 100, 114–6, 128, 144, 163
  bankruptcy (1799) xxxiv
  officials at courts 69, 94
  requests military support from courts (1793) xxxv
  Residents as envoys of 74
  political reports from Residents 100
  soldiers fight subversive factions 274
Duymaer van Twist, A.J., Governor-General (1851–6) 324
dwifungsi, debate (1829) 262–3
  see also Java War, Joyokusumo (Ngabehi), Sentot

East Timor (Timor-Leste) xxvii
Eeg, Captain Christiaan (*Pollux* commander) 300, 310
  see also Pollux
Ellinghuijsen, J.C., Resident Pasuruan, Malang and Bangil (1818–25) 186
Elba 308
  see also Napoleon
élèves voor de Javaansche taal (pupils for the Javanese language) 119
  see also Javanese language
élèves voor het civiele (pupils for the civil service) (20-07-1811) 119
  see also Janssens, Javanese language
Elout, C. Th., Minister of Colonies (1824–9) 250–1, 259
Engelhard, Nicolaus, Governor of Java's NE Coast (cousin of below, 1801–8) xxxv, 71, 76
  and Daendels 70
  DN's Javanese values 9, 328
Engelhard, Pieter, Resident of Yogya (cousin of above, 1808/ 1810–11) 75, 77, 80, 82, 91, 114, 122–123
  health problems 117, 122
  negotiates with HB II 117–8
  Rojowinangun military review (1 June 1808) 77–8
  Ronggo rebellion 85, 98–102
England xxxiv, 113, 275, 316
English 118, 127, 143, 191, 309, 316, 328
  anti-Chinese feelings sparked by 144, 156–7
  archive of interregnum (Yogya) 150, 189, 203, 210
  see also Valck
  attack on Yogya (20 June 1812) xlii, 59, 61, 78, 91, 108, 113, 117, 266
  British Raj (India) xxxiv, 135, 144
  see also Plassey, sepoys (plot/ conspiracy)
  Daendels 69, 118
  death of HB III 159

see also Garnham
DN's links with 61, 129, 149–51, 210, 224, 301, 327
East India Company (EIC) 142
economic liberalism 154, 164
exile of HB II (July 1812) 146
  see also Pinang
interregnum in Java (1811–16) xxxiv–xxxi, 29, 32, 37, 91, 93, 141–63
  see also Crawfurd, Raffles
invasion of Java (Aug 1811) xv, xxxiv–v, 83–4, 94, 98, 117–21, 130–5, 141–2
handover to Dutch (19 Aug 1816) 164, 169, 190
HB III's appointment (21 June 1812) 61, 143–5
legal reforms (1812) 29, 153
navy 316
  see also Procris
naval blockade of Java (1804–11) xxv, 238
negotiations and compromise with HB II (Dec 1811) 123–5
Notokusumo / Pakualam I relations 124, 130, 143, 145–6, 160
opium imports 183
Panular's diary of 38, 47
  see also Babad Bedhah ing Ngayogyakarta
planters (coffee and indigo) 178, 206, 224
  see also coffee, Stavers
plunder Yogya court 59, 142–3, 147, 173, 203
Raffles' letters from Melaka (Dec 1810) 119–20
Royal Navy xv, 144
  see also Procris
Saleh / Sukur sent to Calcutta by (1812–15) 143, 146
  see also Suro-Adimenggolo
secret correspondence of courts against (1811–12) 107, 127–8
Sepoy Plot (Oct–Nov 1815) 162–3, 181
slavery and judicial torture abolition 149, 155
smallpox vaccination introduced by 155
tollgates and markets 152, 180–1
treaties with courts (1 Aug 1812) 151–4
Erucokro, title of Ratu Adil, xix, 52, 60, 106, 221–2, 224–5, 254, 322, 335, 341
  see also Ratu Adil
Ethical Policy (1901–29) 169
  see also Wilhelmina

Fatāh al-Muluk 29, 160
fiqh (Islamic law) 29, 228, 339
  see also *Lubāb al-fiqh*, *pathok negari*
food
  DN's liking for white bread 40, 295
  DN's shipboard fare (1830, 1833) 308
  European tastes in 78
    see also tea
  Javanese guerilla rations 257
  potatoes 40, 295, 308
  pre-Java War scarcity 182, 188
    see also rice
Fort De Ontmoeting (Ungaran) 295
  see also Imhoff. Pakubuwono II, Ungaran
Fort Nieuw Amsterdam (Manado) 311
  see also Manado
Fort Rotterdam (Makassar) xxx, xi, 31, 305
  see also Makassar
Fort Vredeburg (Yogya) 118, 145
France xxiv, 118, 163, 259
  see also Daendels, French, Napoleon
French xv, xxxiv, xxxv, 69, 102, 120
  army threatens Holland (1832–3) 315
  see also Gérard

planters 206
press 319
Revolution / Republic 69, 128, 258
tricolour flag 118
  see also Daendels, France,
    Napoleon, Paris

Gading, *pesantren* (Yogya) 50
Gading Temahan (Bantul) 189
  see also Diposono, Lipuro
Gajali, Kyai 212
Galuh, district (west Java) 115–6
  see also Cauwer Wetan
gambling 80, 171, 181
  see also Nahuys, Sumodiningrat
Gamelan, sub-district (Gunung
  Kidul) 54
gamelan (Javanese orchestra) 14, 48,
  101, 335
  captured by Ronggo in Ponorogo 98
  HB IV enjoys listening to 161
  taken by British from Yogya court
    (20-06-1812) 142
Gandhi, Mahatma xli
Garebeg 19, 100, 115, 161, 178, 205, 252, 335
Garebeg Besar 19, 335
Garebeg Mulud 19, 95 (27–04–1809), 98
  (18–04–1810), 100 (20–04–1811),
  102 (18–04–1810), 335
Garebeg Puwasa 19, 97 (13–11–1809), 100
  (30–10–1810), 178 (12–07–1820),
  205 (9–06–1823), 212
  (21–05–1825), 335
Garnham, Captain Robert Clement,
  Resident of Yogyakarta
  (1814–15) 159–60
Gawok, battle of (15 Oct 1826) 39, 226,
  245, 254, 258
Geen, Major-General Joseph van
  (1775–1846) 228
  scorched earth tactics and
    torture 258, 266

  see also Bone
Genowati, Dewi, guardian spirit 54
  see also Guwo Seluman, Ratu Kidul
Gérard, Marshal (1773–1852) 315–6
Germany, Germans see Knoerle, Prussia
Gezelschap, Hendrik Willem, Yogya Res-
  idency Secretary (1809–11) 118
Gibbs, Colonel Samuel
  (1775/6–1815) 121
  see also Janssens, Jati Ngaleh
Gillespie, Col Robert Rollo (British
  commander in Yogya attack,
  1766–1814)
  loots *kraton* 142
Giri, Sunan 220
Gisignies see Bus de Gisignies
Gitayu, DN's black horse 230
  see also Java War (horses)
Giyanti Treaty (13 Feb 1755) 5, 51, 115, 156,
  172, 314, 327
Giyanti War (1746–55) 9, 28, 102, 156
Goddess of the Southern Ocean see Ratu
  Kidul
Goldman, J.C., Raad van Indië
  (1826–39) 298
Gombong (Banyumas) 260
  see also *benteng stelsel*, Cochius,
    Suharto
Gondokusumo, Basah Abdul Mahmud
  (son of Danurejo II; DN's
  commander in Remo; post-1847,
  Danurejo V) 30, 272, 283,
  284, 293
  see also Danurejo II, Danurejo V,
    Mertonegoro, Remo
Gondokusumo see Serat Gondokusumo
Graaff, Jan van de, Inspector of Finances
  and Raad van Indië (1820–6)
  170, 205–6
Gresik 6
  cannon foundries at 96
  see also Ngampel Denta

Index 353

Grobogan 99, 125
   see also Wirosari
Grojogan, *pesantren* (Yogya) 50
gunpowder 144, 250
   Java War manufacture of 241, 243
   see also Gresik, Into-Into, Kota Gede
gunung, police officials (Yogya) 154, 174–7, 189, 335
   Angger Gunung law code (1808) 82
   see also Danurejo IV
Gunung Bancak (Maospati), Ronggo Prawirodirjo family graveyard 97
   see also Maduretno, Ratu
Gunung Kelir 264, 271
   see also Joyokusumo (Ngabehi)
Gunung Kidul 54
Gunung Krakatau, eruption (1883) 155
Gunung Megamendung xiv
   see also Daendels, *postweg*
Gunung Merapi 177, 204, 218
   eruption (28–30 Dec 1822) 201–2, 217
   see also Bedoyo, Sapu Jagad
Gunung Pola (Sumedang, West Java) xiv
   see also Payen
Gunung Rasamuni (Gunung Kidul) 218
   see also Agung (Sultan), Ratu Adil
Gunung Sundoro (Sindoro), northern Kedu 281
   see also Diponegoro II, HB II, Musbah
Gunung Tambora (Sumbawa), stratovolcano eruption (April 1815) 155
Guwo Langsé, cave (south coast) 10, 54–6, 59
Guwo Secang, cave 15, 62, 148, 213, 221
   see also Selarong
Guwo Seluman, cave 54
   see also Genowati
Guwo Song Kamal, cave 51
   see also Jejeran

Guwo Surocolo (Guwo Sigolo-golo), cave 54
   see also Bima, Bima Raré, *lalembut*
Gusti, Raden Ayu (DN's d.) 272
   see also Mangokorowati

Hadhramaut 341
   see also Arabia, Hejaz
Hadith (traditions of The Prophet) 28, 210
haj (Mecca *pilgrimage*) *see* Mecca
Hakik al-Modin 29
Hamengkubuwono I (Mangkubumi), Sultan (1749–92) xxiv–v, 5, 26, 27, 28, 49, 72, 93, 113, 118, 134, 148, 188, 243
   administrative system 154–5
   attitude to Chinese 156, 245
   grave (Imogiri) 53
   inspiration for DN 5, 328
   mother of 174
   see also Kepundung
   prophecy of 5, 21
   Ratu Ageng Tegalrejo and 9
   Ronggo's family and 81, 102–4
   see also Wirosentiko
   satria lelono (wandering knight) 48
   wife-swapping 172–3
   see also Hartingh
Hamengkubuwono II (Sepuh), Sultan (1792–1810/1811–12/1826–8) 3, 16, 78–9, 245, 336
   birth on Gunung Sundoro (7-03-1750) 9
   blandhong (woodcutter) communities 95, 108, 121
   British attack and plunder of court (20-06-1812) 13, 59, 91, 128, 130–4
   Crawfurd's relations with 123–4
   Daendels' July 1809 visit 93–4

Daendels' reforms (July 1808) and
confrontation with 70, 74–7,
82–3, 108, 114–5, 121, 205
d.s by Ratu Kedaton 80
DN's mediation with 61, 126
exile in Pinang, Ambon and Batavia
(1812–26) 59, 146, 173, 299
Javanese thought patterns 7, 80
Kasepuhan party 143–4, 336
lifestyle as ruler 11–13
Mancingan visits 55
Mangkudiningrat as favourite
son 117
Moorrees' confrontation with
(July 1810) 97–8
murders Danurejo II
(28–10–1811) 122
patronage of *ulama* 19
Pieter Engelhard's Residency 80, 91,
98–9
Raffles' Dec 1810 Melaka letter to 119
Raffles' Dec 1811 visit and
treaty 124–6
Ratu Ageng Tegalrejo's death
(17–10–1803) 12–13
religious observance of 16–17
restoration by Dutch
(17–08–1826) 259
Ronggo's rebellion (Nov–Dec
1810) 59, 81, 96, 100, 101–8
Sumodiningrat's appointment
(Aug 1808) 79–80
Van Braam's visits to (Oct 1808, Nov
1810) 84–5, 100–101
Hamengkubuwono III (Raja), Sultan
(1812–14) xvi, xlii, 187
administrative reforms (1811 /
1812–14) 155
appointment (21–06–1812)
143–5
consorts 26

death (3–11–1814) 157–9
DN as adviser to (1810–14) xlii, 6–7,
59, 187
DN's marriages arranged
(27–02–1807, 28–09–1814)
25–6, 157–8
DN's title chosen (July 1812) 148
friendship with John Deans 209
see also Deans
gunung (police officials) 175–6
historian and favourite of first
sultan 5
Imogiri gravesite 198
Karajan party 143, 336
Mangkorowati as unofficial wife
of 6–7
'New Order' and reforms of
(1812–14) 147, 154–6
Pakualam relations 119
Ratu Ageng's death (17–10–1803) 13
recognizes DN's rights as eldest
son 189
regency (Jan–Nov 1811) 117, 122–3,
125
torture abolition (July 1812) 149–50
Hamengkubuwono IV (Jarot), Sultan
(1814–22) xvi, 147, 156
accession and regency (9–11–1814)
159–61
appointment of *gunung* (police
officials) 175
Bedoyo estate and Nahuys' indemnification (July–Sept 1823) 208–9
burns HB III's letter recognizing
DN's rights 189–90, 210
circumcision (22–03–1815) 161
death (6–12–1822) 189–90, 197–8
European military uniform 178
recognized as Crown Prince 61, 147
target of Diposono rebellion
(Feb 1822) 189

Index

Hamengkubuwono V (Menol), Sultan (1822–6/1828–55) xli, 127, 178, 189, 201, 273, 280
Hamengkubuwono IX, Sultan (1940–88) 28
Hamengkubuwono X, Sultan (1988–present) xli
Hamzah, Amir 321
Hare, Alexander, adventurer 151
   see also Borneo
Hart, Colonel Alexander van der, Governor Celebes (1853–55) 313, 324–5
   see also Bousquet, Perez, Vreede Bik
Hartingh, Nicolaas, Governor Java's N.E. Coast (1754–61) 172
Hejaz (Saudi Arabia) xxxviii
   see also Arabia, Hadhramaut
Hendrik, Prince ('De Zeevaarder') (1820–79) 290, 318–19
   see also Java War
Heutsz, J.B. van, Military Governor Aceh (1898–1904) 266
Hikayat Mareskalek 119
Hikayat Tanah Jawa (1838) 301–2, 320
   see also *Sejarah Tanah Jawa*
Hindu-Buddhist 142, 162
   see also Prambanan
History of Java 95
   see also Raffles
Hogendorp, Willem van (1795–1838) xviii, 10, 154, 161, 171–2, 213
holy war see *prang sabil*
Hope, Hugh, Resident Semarang / Civil Commissioner of Eastern Districts (1811–12) xvi
Hurgronje, Christiaan Snouck xxi, 265–6

Ibrahim, Kyai Pekih, DN's Pengulu (1828–30) 276, 289, 292
Ibu, Ratu see Kedaton, Ratu
ilmu firasat see physiognomy

Imhoff, G.W. baron van (Governor-General, 1743–50) 295
Imogiri, royal graveyard, 13, 18, 52, 54, 108, 122, 132, 198, 287, 318
India xxiii, xxxv, 113, 120, 135, 142, 144, 162, 163
   see also Bengal, Calcutta, Madras, Plassey, sepoys
Indian Ocean 54
Indonesia xxv–vi, xxviii–xxx, xxxix, xl, 3, 71, 169, 226, 231, 244, 260, 296, 305, 307, 328
Indonesian Army (Tentara Nasional Indonesia) 42, 262
Indonesian 'gulag' 299
   see also Netherlands East Indies
Indonesian *hulptroepen* (auxiliaries) xxxiii, 286
   see also Ambonese, Bugis, Madurese
Indonesian identity xxxviii
Indonesian independence, declaration of (17-08-1945) 42, 327
Indonesian language (*Bahasa Indonesia*) xxvii, xxviii, xxix, 314, 317
Indonesian National Archives (Arsip Nasional Republik Indonesia) xxviii
Indonesian national hero (*pahlawan nasional*) xxvii, xxxxix, 42, 326
Indonesian National Library (Perpustakaan Nasional Indonesia) xiii
Indonesian nationalist forces 163, 266, 327
Indonesian Revolution (1945–9) 240, 249, 319
insan kamil ('perfect man' in Shaṭṭārīyya teachings) 187
Into-Into, village (near Kali Progo), gunpowder manufacture at 241
   see also Dekso, Kota Gede, Samen
Islam xxvii, xxix, xxxv, xxxviii, xli, 6, 11, 26, 38, 122, 218, 226

Islamic law 29, 153, 266, 340
   Lubāb al-fiqh 29
   Muharrar 29
   Taqarrub 29
   Taqrib 29
   see also *fiqh, surambi*

jacquerie (peasant uprising) 242
Jagad, Kyai Sapu, Merapi guardian spirit 202, 218
   see also Merapi
jaman edan ('time of madness') xli, 202
   see also Joyoboyo prophecies, *kaliyuga*, Ratu Adil
jaman kalabendu ('time of wrath') 188
   see also Diposono, Joyoboyo Prophecies, *kaliyuga*, Ratu Adil
Janissary regiments 60
   see also *Arkio,* Bulkio, Ottoman, Turkio
Janssens, Governor-General Jan Willem (May–Sept 1811) 118–21
Japan (post-1838, Mojokerto) 144, 155, 186
   see also Sumodipuro
Jati Ngaleh, battle of (16 Sept 1811) 121
   see also Gibbs, Janssens, Semarang, Serondol
Jatinom, tollgate (Bantul) 182
   see also *bandar,* Bantul
Java's Northeast Coast, Government of (1749–1808) 70. 72, 125, 172
   see also Engelhard (Nicolaus), Hartingh
Java War (1825–30) xiii, xiv, xviii, xxiii, xxiv, xxv, xxvi, xxxii, xxxiii, xxxvi, xxxviii, xxxix, xli, 12, 29, 31, 71, 74, 82, 86, 109, 135, 143, 154, 155, 157, 169, 172, 176, 181, 197, 206, 265, 266, 294, 299, 308–10, 315, 323, 327, 333
   anti-Chinese sentiments in 105, 244–5
   see also Chinese
   battlefield carnage in 41
   De Kock as supreme Dutch commander in 114, 156
   see also Geen, Kock
   diet of Javanese guerrillas in *see* food
   DN chooses military commanders for 32
   see also physiognomy
   DN's clothing in 27, 36, 50, 60, 185
   DN's leadership in xxxix, 3, 6, 11, 58
   DN's mandate for xliii
   see also Qur'ān, Ratu Adil
   DN's military formations in 60
   see also Arkio, Barjumungah, Bulkio, Turkio
   DN's titles in 224, 320, 322
   DN's weapons in 41, 63
   see also Abijoyo, Bondoyudo, *kris*
   DN's wives / affairs in 17, 37, 53
   see also Chinese, Kedaren, Retno-kumolo, Retnoningsih
   Dutch sexual abuse as reason for 172–3
   Dutch tactics in 257–60
   see also *benteng stelsel*, Cochius
   dwifungsi experiment in 261–3
   see also Sentot
   financing of 10, 240
   fighting quality of Javanese troops in 251
   fiscal oppression as reason for 125, 156
   horses in 40, 230
   see also Gitayu
   impact of 265
   Javanese guerrilla tactics in 242
   Joyoboyo prophecies and 187
   see also Joyoboyo
   legal reforms as precipitator for 153
   see also Raffles
   Louw and De Klerck as historians of xxviii, 239

opium in 183–4
  see also opium
outbreak of (20-07-1825) xl, 14, 228–31, 301
Prince Hendrik's view of 319
  see also Hendrik
Ratu Kidul's visitation in 56, 58
  see also Ratu Kidul
religious character of 250–1
  see also Elout
restoration of moral order and 103, 122
rift in leadership in 253, 256
  see also Mojo, Sentot
Saleh and Sukur in 146
  see also Suro-Adimenggolo
Saleh's DN arrest painting (March 1857) 146, 294
santri / ulama support for DN in 18, 20, 33, 52, 174, 251–3
  see also Mojo
Selarong as DN's first HQ 62
Sentot as commander in 81
  see also Sentot
social/economic support base for DN in 113
Sosrodilogo rebellion in (1827–8) 152
  see also Chinese, Sosrodilogo
South Coast pilgrimages and 63
Surakarta court chronicle of xxviii
  see also Babad DN (Surakarta version)
treatment of Dutch POWs xxxviii, 247
underworld involvement in 27
women's clothes sent to commanders 38
see also benteng stelsel, Bus, Kock, Magelang
Javanese, language
  Crawfurd's skill in 32
  DN's insistence on 328

DN's addresses Dutch in Low (*ngoko*) 212, 277
Janssens' creation of pupils in 119
kromo (High) 337
ngoko (Low) 339
  see also Dietrée, *élèves voor de Javaansche taal, élèves voor het civiele*, Krijgsman, Winter
Javanese-Islamic / mystical literature 26, 35, 327
  see also Danukusumo (Raden Ayu), *Menak Amir Hamza*
Javanese literature 30, 161, 185
Javasche Courant, government newspaper (1828–1942) 289, 324
  see also Bataviasche Courant
Jeddah 27, 249, 308
  see also Ansari
jimat (amulets) 250, 336
Jimat (title), key keepers/ grave guardians (Imogiri) 52
Jimatan, mosque *see* Imogiri
Jejeran, district (Yogya)/ *pesantren* 50–2
Jipang (Jipang-Rajegwesi) 152, 248, 258
  see also Sosrodilogo
Joned, Raden Mas (DN's eldest son by R.A. Maduretno, circa 1815–37) 281, 284
  killed in brawl (1837) 321
Jong Celebes (pre-war Sulawesi youth association) 325
Jong Java (pre-war Javanese youth association) 325
Jonggo, Kyai, guardian spirit of Lipuro 62
  see also Lipuro
Jono, weaving centre (eastern Bagelen) 184, 244
  see also Chinese, Kali Lereng, Umar Mahdi, Wedi
Joyoboyo, prophecies 60, 185–7, 201–2, 225

see also Kediri
Joyokusumo, Prince (son of HB II; post-1825, Ngabehi) 60, 132, 185–7, 201–2, 225
  Chinese ancestry 245
  death (21-09-1829) 264, 271–2
  dwifungsi debate (1829) 262–3
  see also Gunung Kelir
Joyo Lengkoro Wulang, wandering knight romance 29
  see also satrio lelono
Joyosentiko, Raden Ngabehi, head (*patih*) *Kadipaten* (1810–12) 128
  murdered (20-06-1812) 143–4
  see also Madura, Wiroguno
Joyosuroto *see* Roto

Kadipaten (Crown Prince's establishment) 20, 26, 122–3, 176, 336, 340
  British attack on (20-06-1812) 130, 132
  DN's links with / *visits* 16–17, 93, 122–3
  HB III returns to 145
  military / *santri* establishment 16–17, 93
  see also Joyosentiko, Wiroguno
kafirs *see kapir laknatullah*
Kajoran, Panembahan Rama (circa 1620–80) 7, 251
  VOC soldiers defend against 274
  see also Trunojoyo
Kali Bedog (Bantul) 62
Kali Bogowonto 259, 262, 271–2
Kali Cingcingguling 276–7
  see also Remokamal
Kali Gajahwong (Papringan) 113
  see also Sindurejo
Kalijengking (southern Kedu) 260
  see also benteng stelsel, Cochius
Kalijogo, Sunan 51–2, 63

see also Parangkusumo (prophecy)
Kali Lereng (eastern Bagelen) 244
  see also Jono, Chinese, Wedi
Kalimantan (Borneo) 151
  see also Hare
Kali Opak 54, 62
Kali Oyo 54
  see also Genowati
Kali Progo 56, 272
  DN's HQ by 242
  see also Dekso
  DN visited by Ratu Kidul at 56
  ferry-crossing bandits 27, 241
  see also Kamijoro, Mangkudiningrat II, Mangir
  gunpowder manufacture at 241
  see also Into-Into
  'killing area' 259, 262, 271
  see also Bogowonto
  Metesih encampment (8/28-03-1830) xviii, 279
Kali Tuntang *see* Tuntang, capitulation of
kaliyuga (final age of disorder) 202
  see also Joyoboyo prophecies, Ratu Adil
Kamijoro, bandit centre on Kali Progo 27
  see also bandits, Kali Progo, Mangiran
Kampung Jawa (Tondano) xiii, 255
  see also Mojo, Tondano
Kampung Melayu (graveyard, Makassar) 323, 325, 336
  see also Retnoningsih, Sarkumo
kapir laknatullah (heretics / kafirs) xxxviii, 327
kapir murtad (apostates) xxxviii
Kapitan Cina (Captain of the Chinese, Yogya) 94, 132, 143, 156, 204, 207
  see also Tan Jin Sing

Index 359

Karna, Adipati (Bratayuda / Brothers' War) 218
Kartasura, court (1678-1742) 327
   fall of court (June 1742) 131, 142
   see also Pakubuwono II, *Prang Cina*
Kasongan, *pathok negari / pesantren* 17, 50
   see also *pathok negari*, Retnokumolo
Kasongan, Kyai Guru (head of *pathok negari /pesantren*) 17
Kasuran, battle of (28-07-1826) 257
Kebumen (Banyumas) 260
   see also Gombong
Kedaren 37, 246
   see also Chinese (DN's mistress)
Kedaton, Ratu (consort of HB II; post-1803 Ratu Ageng, circa 1760-1820)
   daughters / sons-in-law 80, 133
      see also Danurejo II, Maduretno, Prawirodirjo III, Sumodiningrat
   Madurese ancestry 3, 7-8
   move to Tegalrejo mooted (1803-4) 13
Kedaton, Ratu (consort of HB III; post-1812, Ratu Kencono; post-1816, Ratu Ibu; post-1820 Ratu Ageng; mother of HB IV, circa 1770-1826)
   affair with Wironegoro 26
      see also Wironegoro
   allows Smissaert to preside at *Garebegs* 205
   arranges HB IV's sexual instruction (1816-17) 161
   condones court princesses' affairs 211
   DN's contract misplaced 210
   DN's difficult relations with 176
   dream about DN 219
   guardian of HB V 198-9, 205

Nahuys' landrent compensation 207, 209
   see also Bedoyo, Nahuys
Kedu 277, 282
   annexation planned (1808) 71
   bandar abolished in (1824) 181-2
   benteng stelsel in 260
      see also Cochius, Kalijengking
   DN II in (1830-4) 50
   DN wanders alone in (Nov 1829) 158
   Diposono's revolt in (Feb 1822) 184, 189
   fighting quality of inhabitants 249
   Kedawung enclave in 96
      see also Tersono, Tirtodiwiryo
   land-tax and its impact (1812-16) 179-80
   Menoreh garrison town in 277
   Mt Merapi eruption and (28/30-12-1822) 202
   Mt Sundoro in 9, 281
      see also Musbah
   plight of Chinese in (1825) 180-1
   pradikan and *ulama* in 18, 250
   Raffles' annexation of (1-08-1812) 145, 151-2
   Valck as Resident of xx, 71, 281-2
      see also Valck
Kejiwan, battle of (9-08-1826) 257
Kemloko, old Mataram tollgate (Sleman) 114
Kemp, P.H. van der, historian (1845-1921) 147
Kencono, Ratu (consort of HB III) see Kedaton, Ratu
Kencono, Ratu (d. of Danurejo II; consort of HB IV, circa 1802-26)
   as guardian of HB V (1822-7) 198-9, 205, 211
   marries HB IV (13-05-1816) 161

psychosis / mental health 219
  in Ratu Ageng's dream (1816) 219
Kencono Wulan, Ratu (consort of HB II; post-1812, Ratu Wetan) 97, 100
  loans to Ronggo (1810) 102
  urges Mangkudiningrat's Crown Prince appointment 117
Kepatihan (Yogya prime ministerial offices) 337
Kepundung (Delanggu), *pradikan* village (birthplace of HB I's mother) 174
  see also Murmo Wijoyo
Keputren (Yogya *kraton* women's quarters) 26, 157, 337
Kertodirjo II, Mas Tumenggung, *bupati* Kerjo (Sukowati, 1812–21) 26, 210–11
Kidung Lalembut ('Song of the Spirits') 54
Kindar, Raden Mas (DN's first son born in exile, 4-01-1832) 312–3, 324
Kitab Tuhfah, Sufi ontology 28–9
KITLV Press Leiden (post-2012, Brill) xxviii
Klerck, E.S. de, military historian xxviii, 239
  see also Louw
Knoerle, Lt Justus Heinrich (1796–1833) xl–xli
  DN's stay in *Stadhuis* (8-04 – 3-5-1830) 297, 300
  lends DN books 308
  Pollux voyage to Manado (3-05 – 12-06-1830) 300–1, 307–8
  Ratu Kidul legend 58
  receives Van den Bosch's instructions (27-04-1830) 300
  reconnoitres Manado (14–19 June 1830) 309–10
  Retnoningsih's beauty 38
  as source on DN xl–xli, 31–3, 38, 40–1
  wine tasting with DN 308
Kock, Baron A.H.W. de (Resident of Yogyakarta, 1848–51; son of below) 414
Kock, General H.M. de 34, 37, 42, 49, 88, 141, 198, 259, 303, 327, 330, 337, 345–72
  see also Java War
Koninklijk Kabinet van Zeldzaamheden (Royal Curio Collection, The Hague) 288
  see also Nogo Siluman, Saleh (Raden Syarif Bustaman)
Kota Gede, as armaments centre / royal gun foundry 96, 243, 261
Kroya, battle of (Oct 1828) 262
  see also Buschkens, Java War, Sentot
Kraus, Werner 290
Kresna 218
  see also Bratayuda, Karna
Krijgsman, C.F., Translator Semarang (1803–21) 83, 131
kris 40, 125, 247, 292, 337, 338, 340
  Abijoyo (DN's *pusaka*) 41, 229
  Bondoyudo (DN's *pusaka*) xix, 61, 277, 300, 323
  DN's heirloom collection 300
  DN surrenders (20-06-1812) 133
  DN's followers surrender at Magelang (28-03-1830) 279, 288
  see also Michiels
  Java War weapon 242
  Lipuro casting 62
  Nogosiluman (DN's *pusaka*) 54
  surrendered to British (20/22-06-1812) 133–4, 142
Kudus, Sunan 52, 254
Kuto Pekik *see* Ketonggo
kyai

Index

term explained 250, 337–8
labuhan, offerings xiii, 55
  see also Parangkusumo, Ratu Kidul
lalembut, spirits of Java 54–5
  see also Cemoro Tunggal, *Kidung Lalembut,* Ratu Kidul
land tax, Raffles' fiscal scheme (1812–16) 152, 179–80, 191
  see also Raffles
Lasem 104, 146
  Sosrodilogo's rebellion and (1827–8) 245–6
Latif, First Lieutenant Hasan Nur, militia officer (Manado)
  refuses DN's marriage proposal 37, 311
law-and-order *see Angger Gunung, gunung*
Lawu, Sunan (mountain god) 218
Leberveld, Sergeant Lucas (1757–circa 1815)
  hunts down/kills Ronggo (20-11 – 17-12-1810) 106–7
Lengkong, battle of (31 July) 257
Leeuwen, Lt-Col Aart de Kock van (artillery commander, Magelang) 284
Leiden University xxi, 266
  see also Hurgronje
levée en masse 258
  see also Bus
Liebeherr, Bogislaus Friederich van, Resident Surakarta (1806–8) 204
  see also Smissaert, Clara Elisabet
Light Infantry Volunteer Battalion (LIVB)
  plate of xv
  sepoy plot/conspiracy (Oct–Nov 1815) 162
  see also sepoys
Loevestein, royal fortress (Gelderland) 316
Lombok 133

London Convention (13-08-1814) 163
Louw, P.J.F., military historian xxviii, 239
  see also Klerck

Mackenzie, Colonel Colin 125
Madiun xii, xiv, 18, 27
  Banjarsari *pesantren* in 250
  fighting capacity of inhabitants 249
  Kerjo *kabupaten* (Kertodirjo) 27
  Ketonggo gathering (July 1817) 185–6
  PKI headquarters at 325
  post-Ronggo administration (Jan 1811) 116
  Retnoningsih from Keniten in 38
  Ronggo Prawirodirjo III's rebellion (Nov–Dec 1810) 102–5
  Ronggo Wirosentiko family in 81–2, 99
Madras, horse artillery xxxiv
  in Java campaign (Aug–Sept 1811) 118
  in Yogya attack (20-06-1812) 132
Madubrongto, Raden Ayu Retno (DN's first wife) 25
  see also Dadapan
Madura 7, 50, 251
  see also Pamekasan, Sumenep
Madurese 251
  auxiliaries from 120, 257
  DN's ancestry from 8
  see also Kedaton (Ratu), Pamekasan
  Ratu Kedaton (HB II's consort) 7, 80–1
  see also Cakradiningrat, Joyosentiko, Sumenep, Trunojoyo
Maduretno, Raden Ayu (d. of below; DN's second official wife, circa 1798–1827) 38–9, 61, 219
  death (Nov 1827) 53
  see also Kawisarjo

DN's sexual betrayal of (Aug
  1826) 246
 see also Chinese (DN's mistress),
  Kedaren
given heirloom *kris* by DN 61
 see also Sarutomo
Imogiri burial 53, 287, 318
marriage to DN (Sept 1814) 157–8
restrains DN's suicide (Dec 1822) 200
Maduretno, Ratu (d. of HB II; wife of
  Raden Ronggo) 96–7, 157
 see also Gunung Bancak, Prawirodirjo
  III
Magelang xviii, xx, xl, xliii, 74, 275–6,
  299, 301
Chinese flee to (July–Sept 1825) 180
Dutch garrison at xx, 260, 275, 288
 see also Perron
'peace conference' / DN's arrest at
  (28-03-1830) 31, 41, 240, 260,
  277–94
Saleh's painting of DN's arrest at
  (1857) 146, 294
 see also Java War
Mahābhārata xxiii, 61, 218, 342
 see also *Bratayuda,* Pandawa
Mahdi, Umar, rebel (1817) 184–5, 187
Mahmud II, Ottoman Sultan
  (1809–39) 60–1
Majangjati (Sragen) 8
 see also Ageng (Ratu Tegalrejo),
  Derpoyudo
Majapahit 6, 73, 87
DN's references to 226, 314
Javanese political philosophy regarding 32, 73
 see also Pajajaran
Majasto 6
 see also Mangkorowati
Makassar xxvii, 307, 324–5, 329
DN's correspondence with Cleerens
  from (14-12-1835) 278
 see also Cleerens
DN's correspondence with mother
  from 40, 322
 see also Mangkorowati
DN's education of children in 160–1,
  320–1
DN's exile in (1833–55) xxi, xl, xliii, 7,
  15, 31, 240, 315–21
 see also Fort Rotterdam
DN's grave in 61, 323–5
 see also Kampung Melayu
DN's literary output in xli, 32–3, 60,
  73, 301, 314
 see also *Hikayat Tanah Jawa,*
  Sejarah Tanah Jawa
DN's name in (Ngabdulkamit)
  316
DN's transfer to (20-06
  – 11-07-1833) 305–6
 see also *Circe, Pietermaat*
DN's voyage to (3-05 – 12-06–
  1830) xii, 7, 40, 307–9
 see also Knoerle, *Pollux*
Governors of 10
 see also Bousquet, Hart, Perez,
  Vreede Bik
Retnoningsih's house in
  (1856–2000) xxvii, 323–4
visit of Prince Hendrik to
  (7-03-1837) 318–9
Makassarese 317, 324
malaria (DN's malarial fever) 37, 264,
  272, 278, 295, 297, 307
portrait of DN suffering effects xix
Malay, language xxxviii, 78, 85, 161
Bengal officers competent in 125
DN's view of 31–2, 212, 246, 278,
  300, 318
HB II's competence in 76, 85
Hikayat Mareskalek 119
John Deans' competence in 133
Raffles' letters in (Dec 1810) 119

Index

'Service Malay' (*Dienst Maleisch*) xxxviii
see also Abbas
Malabar (India) 163
Malang, district (east Java) 115–6, 186
see also Antang, Ellinghuisen
Manado
  DN's *babad* written in (20-05-1831 – 3-02-1832) xli, 31, 313–5
  DN's exile in (1830-33) xxii, xliii, 7, 15, 298–9, 309–15
  see also Fort Nieuw Amsterdam
  DN's journey to (map) xii, 306
  see also Minahasa
  DN's journey to (description) 31, 37, 40, 240, 297, 299–300, 307–9, 310–14
  see also Knoerle, *Pollux*
  DN's transfer to Makassar (20-06 – 11-07-1833) 316–7
  see also Circe, Pietermaat
  Dutch Residents in 10, 37, 301
  see also Cambier, Pietermaat
mancanagara (eastern and western outlying provinces) xxxv, xlii, 334, 338, 342
  Daendels' proposed annexations in (Jan 1811) 116
  DN's letters of authority sent to (1825) 248
  Kedu annexation 151–2
  Raffles' annexations of (1-08-1812) 145
  Ronggo rebellion in (Nov–Dec 1810) 99, 101–9, 141
  teak forests in 82, 94–5
  Yogya fortifications strengthened by (Nov 1809) 96
  see also Bagelen, Banyumas, Blitar, Japan (Mojokerto), Jipang-Rajegwesi, Kediri, Kedu, Keniten, Madiun, Nganjuk, Ngawi, Padangan, Panolan, Ponorogo, Wirosari, Wirosobo
Mancingan (Pamancingan) 54–5
  see also Parangkusumo, Parangtritis, Parangwedang
Mangiran, bandit centre on Kali Progo 27
  see also bandits, Kali Progo, Kamijoro
Mangkorowati, Raden Ayu 6, 343
Mangkubumi, Sultan *see* Hamengkubuwono I
Mangkubumi, Prince (DN's uncle) 4, 199–200, 203, 206, 208–9, 211, 219–20, 229–30, 240, 327
Mangkubumi, Prince (Surakarta, younger brother of PB IV) 127
  see also sepoys (plot/conspiracy)
Mangkudiningrat I, Prince (circa 1778-1824) 145, 182, 185
Mangkudiningrat II, Raden Tumenggung (son of above) 231
Mangkunegoro I (Raden Mas Said, reigned 1757–95) 48, 104, 113, 251
Mangkunegoro II (pre-1821, Prince Prangwedono, reigned 1796–1835)
  Colonel Commandant Legion (June 1808) 79
  inauguration of HB III (21-06-1812) 144
  Ronggo rebellion (Nov–Dec 1810) 99, 102
Mangundirjo, Raden Ronggo, *bupati wedana* Madiun (1784–90/1794-6, father of Ronggo Prawirodirjo III) 116
Mangunkusumo, Tumenggung (Dutch spy, Magelang) 281
Manikmoyo see Serat Manikmoyo

Maospati, Ronggo's residence
    (Madiun) 81, 97, 99, 100, 102,
    104–5, 107, 116
  see also Gunung Bancak, Madiun,
    Prawirodirjo III
Mas, Ratu (consort of HB II, mother of
    Prince Mangkudiningrat) 117
Mataram, district (Yogya) 71, 79, 114,
    144, 189, 218, 248, 257–9, 264,
    265
  DN as true man from 187
  DN's base in 253
  fighting quality of inhabitants 249
  graveyard of rulers 53
  see also Imogiri, Kota Gede
  pesantren in 250
  ruling dynasty of 5, 7, 51–2, 62–3, 73,
    109, 156, 251, 274
  Sultan Agung as ruler of 53, 218
Maulana Maghribī, Seh (*wali* from 16th-
    century Demak) 55
Mecca xiii, xix, 12, 16, 17, 214, 217, 223,
    249, 276–7, 288, 293, 335
  DN plans pilgrimage to 299, 301, 311
  Jâwah community in Mecca 34–5
  see also Hurgronje
  Prince Abubakar plans pilgrimage
    to 49
  see also Abubakar
  Rahmanudin departs on pilgrimage
    to 228
  see also Rahmanudin
Meester Cornelis (Jatinegara), redoubt /
    battle (26-08-1811) 106,
    119–20
  see also amok, British, Daendels,
    Janssens, Notokusumo
    (Pakualam), Raffles, Rawabangke
Melaka 118
  cholera reaches Java from
    (April 1821) 188

Raffles' Malay letter to HB II
    (20-12-1810) 119, 124
Melangi, *pathok negari* / *pesantren* 17
  see also Taptojani
Memory of the World, International Reg-
    ister (UNESCO) xxvii, 314
  see also Babad Diponegoro,
    UNESCO
Menak Amir Hamza 30, 185
Merkus, Pieter, Raad van Indië
    (1829–35) 298
Mertonegoro, Basah (son of Danurejo II;
    DN's army commander) 277
  at DN's Magelang arrest (28-03-
    1830) 284–5, 292
  exploits DN's daughters 321
  see also Gondokusumo
Mertosono, Prince (son of HB II; post-
    1825 Murdaningrat)
  shares HB II's exile 185
Mesjid Ageng (Great Mosque, Yogya) 218
Metesih xvii, 279–81, 285, 288, 290
  see also Kali Progo, Magelang
Michiels, Major A.V., 11th Mobile
    Column commander
    (1797–1849) 264, 273, 282, 288
  in Saleh's DN arrest painting
    (1857) xx
Minahasa xiii, xxiv, 316
  auxiliaries from 257
  Christian inhabitants in 317
  Kampong Jawa Tondano MS 255
  see also Mojo
  Manado exile of DN/Mojo 255–6,
    309–11
  see also Manado
Minto, Lord, Governor-General of India
    (1807–13) 120–1, 124, 134, 135,
    285
Moertono see Soemarsaid Moertono
Mojo, Kyai xxiv, 18, 211–2

Balinese wife of 242, 310
  see also Mojo (Raden Ayu)
  imprisoned in Stadhuis cellars (Jan 1829–Feb 1830) 297
  see also Stadhuis
  Kampung Jawa Tondano MS 255
  knowledge of *Qur'ān* xiii
  links with Taptojani 18
  links with Kyai Murmo 174
  see also Murmo
  Pajang-Mataram rivalry 248, 258
  plate xiii
  pradikan links with Surakarta 19
  Salatiga peace talks with Du Bus (Sept 1827) 259
  see also Stavers
  santri group 249, 251–5
  shares DN's Minahasan exile 256, 298–9, 309–10
  Shaṭṭārīyya adherent 33
  split with DN (1827–8) 224–6, 229
  surrenders to Dutch (12-11-1828) 262
  visits DN at Tegalrejo 20
  xenophobia xli, 244
Mojo, Raden Ayu 242–3
  brought out to Tondano (1831) 310
  see also Bali
Moorrees, Johannes Wilhelmus, Resident of Yogyakarta (1810) 96–8
Moorrees, Jacoba Margaretha (wife of above) 98
Mojokerto see Japan
Moyo, Umar 184–5
Muhammadiyah ('Way of Muhammad') 218
Multatuli (Eduard Douwes Dekker) 308
Munadi, Basah Hasan (Syarif Samparwedi; Barjumungah bodyguard commander) 249
  counsels DN (Nov 1830) 272–4

Muntinghe, Harman Warner 125, 135
Murmo Wijoyo, Kyai 106, 108, 175, 177
  attacked and exiled to Ambon (1817–24) 173–4
  death from senile dementia (1824) 174
Musbah, Basah Imam (DN's northern Kedu commander) 281
  see also Gunung Sundoro
Museum Sejarah Jakarta see Stadhuis
Mustahar, Bendoro Raden Mas (DN's childhood name, 1785–1805) 3
  see also Ontowiryo
mysticism (Javanese-Islamic) 342
  daérah (mystical diagrams) xl, 320, 337
  DN's experience xliii, 33–4, 39, 42, 159, 326
  DN's exile writings 305
  literature 29
  see also *tasawwuf*
  mystic synthesis (Ricklefs) xxix, 58, 328, 342
  mystical visions xl
  see also Ratu Adil
  ngelmu 250
  Serat Centhini 35
  tarekat / mystical brotherhoods 33–5, 321, 342
  see also Naqshabāndīyya, Shaṭṭārīyya

Nahuys van Burgst, Major H.G., Resident of Yogyakarta (1816–22) and Surakarta (1820–22) xvii, 19, 185
  Bedoyo estate compensation (July 1823) 204, 208–9
  description of opium addicts 184
  see also opium
  DN supposedly chooses (July 1816) 150–1

DN's views of xvii, 32, 171, 199
drinking and gambling 171
land rent initiatives (1817–22) 177–8, 203
as Resident 170–4, 202
saves Notokusumo / Notodiningrat (May 1811) 118
sexual mores / *ménage à trois* 172, 190
Surakarta dinner parties (1820–22) 171
treatment of *kyai* (1817) 174
see also Murmo Wijoyo
view of DN 199, 327
Nanggulan (Kulon Progo) 184
benteng at (1828–9) 263
Napoleon 113
birthday (15 Aug) 117
Daendels as marshal of 93
DN exile compared to 44, 308
Janssens and 69, 120
wars xxxiv, 70, 164, 170
Naqshabāndīyya, *tarekat* (mystical brotherhood) 34–5
see also Shaṭṭārīyya
Nasihat al-Muluk 29
Netherlands, Kingdom of the United Netherlands (1815–30) 315
Netherlands East Indies, colonial government (1818–1942) xxxiii, xliii, 64–5, 163–4, 230, 260, 266, 274, 280, 316, 318, 325
prison 'gulag' 299
Netherlands Trading Company (Nederlandsche Handels Maatschappij, NHM) 326
New Dutch 'water line' (*Nieuwe Hollandse waterlinie*) 316
New Order (*Orde Baru*, 1966–98) 326
see also Suharto
Ngabdulkamit, Prince (Diponegoro's post-1830 name) 68–9, 260

Ngabehi, Prince see Joyokusumo
Ngarip, Raden Mantri Muhamad (alias Prince Diponegoro II) 19, 25
see also Diponegoro II
Ngawi, attack on Chinese communities in (17–09–1825) 243–4
see also Chinese, Yudokusumo
ngelmu (mystical arts/sciences)
kadigdayan (martial arts) 250
kaslametan (invulnerability) 250
kawedukan (art of striking fear) 250
see also *firasat* (science of physiognomy)
Ngiso, Haji (DN's religious adviser) 310
see also Badarudin
Ngrum (eastern Rome = Byzantium) see Rum
Ngusman, Basah Muhammad see Bahwi 17
'nobility of failure' (in relation to DN) xlii
Notodiningrat, Raden Tumenggung (post-1829, Pakualam II) 100, 106, 118, 191
imprisoned in Cirebon (1811) 118–9
Ronggo's letter to (Nov 1810) 103
Notokusumo, Prince (Pakualam I, reigned 1812–29) 100, 125–6, 129, 131, 198, 251
accession of HB III 144
appointed Pakualam I 145
arrested / imprisoned by Daendels 106, 118
Crawfurd's view of 143
during British attack (20–06–1812) 132–3
enters fort and joins British (18–06–1812) 130
friendship with Raffles 143
identifies plundered MSS 142
Nahuys and 151

Index

see also Nahuys
Pakualam *babad* 81, 97, 98, 125
Pakualaman relations with Yogya *kraton* 119, 145
  regency for HB IV's minority (1814–20) 160, 198
  returns from Surabaya exile (16-12-1811) 124
  view of Chinese 245
  see also Tan Jin Sing
Notoprojo *see* Papak
Notowijoyo III, Raden Tumenggung (*bupati* Panolan; DN's father-in-law) xii, 25, 82
  see also Panolan, Retnokusumo
Nurngali, *dukun* / herbalist (DN's Bengali Muslim physician) 37, 163
  see also sepoys
Nypels, George 264
  see also Breda

Ontowiryo, Raden Mas (DN's first adult name, 1805–12) 16, 47, 77, 123
  appointed as Prince Diponegoro (July 1812) 147
Ontowiryo II, Raden Mas (eldest son of above) *see* Diponegoro II
Oosthoek (Eastern Salient) xiv
  cholera in (1821) 188
Opera Diponegoro (Sardono W. Kusumo, 1995) xl, xli
  see also Sardono
opium 99, 105, 106, 156, 181, 204, 245, 257, 273
  see also Chinese, Danurejo IV, Java War, Purwodipuro
opium farm 183–4
Orde van der Unie (post-1810, *Orde van de Reunie*) xvi, 116
  see also Bonaparte, Louis
Ordnance on Ceremonial and Etiquette (28 July 1808) 90

see also Daendels
Ottoman Sultanate xxiv, xxxviii
  administrative practice 17, 60, 333
  Sultan Rum legends 184–5
  see also 'Abd al-Ḥamīd I Janissaries, Mahmud II

Pacitan 18, 184, 187
  cholera in (1821) 188
  bupati's view of Europeans 174
  see also Jogokaryo
Padri War (1821–38) 35
  see also Bonjol, Imam
Padangan, district (east Java) 82, 107
  see also Sumonegoro
Pajajaran 32, 73
  see also Majapahit
Pajang, district (Surakarta) 7, 18, 71, 174, 248, 258
  fighting quality of inhabitants 249
  Mojo's loyalties in 253, 255
  see also Mojo
  pesantren in 249
Pakualam I *see* Notokusumo
Pakubuwono II, Sunan (1721–49) 115, 144, 295, 327
Pakubuwono IV, Sunan (1788–1820) 19, 98, 106, 162
Pakubuwono V, Sunan (1820–23) 206, 341
Pakubuwono VI, Sunan (1823–30) 200, 258
Pakubuwono VII, Sunan (1830–58) 79
Paku Nataningrat, Panembahan of Sumenep (1811–54) 143
  see also Raffles
Palmer & Co, Calcutta bank 163
  see also Bentinck, sepoys
Panarukan xiv
Pandawa (brothers in *Mahabhārata*) 158
  see also Arjuna, Bima, Yudistira

Pangurakan, public gibbet (crossroads, northern *alun-alun*) 108
 see also Prawirodirjo III, Sumonegoro
Panolan, district (east Java) xii, 25, 36, 82
 see also Notowijoyo III, Retnokusumo
Panular, Prince (DN's great-uncle) 38, 134, 149, 159, 172, 187
 see also *Babad Bedhah ing Ngayogyakarta*
Papak, Raden Mas (Prince Notoprojo, grandson of R.A. Serang) 52
 see also Serang (Raden Ayu)
Papringan 113
 see also Kali Gajahwong, Sindurejo
Parangkusumo xiii, 54–5, 158
 prophecy (circa 1805) vi, 5, 59–61, 69, 77, 85, 103, 113, 129, 134, 164, 197, 264, 326
 see also Kalijogo, Sunan
Parangtritis 54–5, 59
 see also Mancingan, Parangkusumo, Parangwedang
Parangwedang 54–5
 see also Mancingan, Parangkusumo, Parangtritis
parchment 26
Paris 259, 319
 see also France, Saleh (Raden, Syarif Bustaman)
Pasuruan 186
 see also Ellinghuijsen
pathok negari 18–19, 57
 Dongkelan 18
 Kasongan 18
 Melangi 18
 Papringan 18
 see also *santri*
Patriot Revolt (1786–7) 69
 see also Daendels
pegon see aksara pegon

Pengalasan, Basah Kerto, DN's eastern Bagelen commander 226
 DN suggests brings mother to Makassar (1849) 322
 writes letter as though from DN (31–12–1829) 273–5
pepper 188, 208
Perez, P.J.B. de, Governor of Celebes (1841–8) 318, 322–3
 see also Bousquet, Hart, Vreede Bik
Perié, Major Johan Jacob, 7th Hussar Regt commander 285
 in Saleh's DN arrest painting xx
Perron, Lt-Col Louis du (Magelang garrison commander) 282, 286, 288
 in Saleh's DN arrest painting xx
physiognomy, science of xii, 225
Pieneman, Nicolaas (painter) xix, 293
 painting of DN's capture 290–4
Pietermaat, D.F.W., Resident Manado (1826–31) 37, 309, 311
 arranges DN's Makassar transfer (June 1833) 316
 inceptor of DN's *babad* 313–4
pilgrimage (*haj*) see Mecca
Pinang, Pulau
 British naval base xxxiv
 cholera arrives in Java from (April 1821) 188
 HB II's exile at (1812–15) 146, 173
Pisangan (Sleman) 114
PKI (Partai Komunis Indonesia) 325
Plassey, battle of (23–06–1757) 135
 see also Bengal, sepoys
Plered, Amangkurat I's kraton (1646–77) 142, 251
 DN's strongpoint captured (June 1826) 241, 257
 see also Cochius
police see *Angger Gunung, gunung*

Index 369

Pollux, corvette-of-war (Dutch navy) xii, 31, 300, 307–8, 310, 322
Ponorogo 100, 107, 250
  benteng stelsel in 260
  Ronggo's incursions in (1810) 97–8
Popper, Karl 327
Portier, Lt Paulus Daniel, inspector of birds' nest rocks (Rongkob) 247
  see also birds' nests
postweg (trans-Java highway) xiv, 83, 97
  see also Daendels, Gunung Megamendung
Power of Prophecy xxiv, xxv, xxvi, xxvii, xxix, xliii
pradikan, tax-free villages / men of religion from xiii, 6, 18, 19, 174, 249, 336, 340, 341
  see also Kepundung, Majasto, Mojo, *pathok negari*
prajurit èstri see women
prajurit kadipaten see Kadipaten (military establishment)
Prambanan 17
  see also Hindu-Buddhist
Prampelan, Kyai Ageng (ancestor of DN's mother) 6
  see also Mangkorowati
prang puputan ('final battle'; Bali, Lombok) 133
prang sabil xxxvi, 18, 244, 248, 253, 340
Prangwedono see Mangkunegoro II
Prawirodirdjo III, Raden Ronggo, *bupati wedana* Madiun (1796–1810) xiv, xlii, 12, 38, 59, 79, 80, 113–4, 121–2, 141, 158, 241
  administration changed (Jan 1811) 116
  see also Dipokusumo (joint administrator)
  buried at traitors' graveyard 106, 122
  see also Banyusumurup
  character and ancestry assessed 80–1
  at Daendels' military display (June 1808) 78
  death of beloved wife 96
  see also Maduretno (Ratu)
  DN marries d. (Sept 1814) 157
  see also Maduretno (Raden Ayu)
  father of Sentot 261
  see also Sentot
  map of rebellion (Nov–Dec 1810) xii, 92
  rebellion: antecedents 91, 95–6, 97–8, 99–101
  rebellion: course (Nov–Dec 1810) 102–9
  timber logging issues 82
  see also teak
Prawirosentiko, Raden Ronggo, joint acting *bupati wedana* Madiun (1811–26, uncle of above) 116
Prehn, Rijck van 171, 206
primbon 35, 188, 320, 340
Prins, Bart de (historian) 259
  see also Bus
Probolinggo, district (southern Kedu) 180
  see also tobacco
Procris, HMS (sloop-of-war, plate of) xv
prostitution see women (prostitutes)
Prussia, Prussians 249
  see also Germany, Sudirman
Pulo Kadang, *pesantren* (Yogya) 18, 50
  see also Baderan, Mojo
Pulo Waringin (DN's meditation island, Selorejo) 15, 221
  see also Tegalrejo, Selorejo
Purwodipuro, Raden Tumenggung (Yogya *Nayaka*; commands Yogya force against Ronggo) 102, 106

Puspodiwiryo, Mas Ngabehi, *patih* of Raden Ronggo Prawirodirjo III, 107

Qur'ān xiii, xl, 28, 29, 33, 142, 153, 159, 210, 216–18, 221, 226, 250, 252, 289, 296, 298, 320
see also *dhikr, fiqh, tafsir, Hadith*, Raffles

Raden Ayu (court princesses), sexual exploitation of 173
Raden Patah 32
Raffles, Thomas Stamford, Lieutenant-Governor of Java (1811–16) xxxv, 29, 82, 94–5, 105, 108, 113, 122–3, 128–30, 152, 161, 161, 169, 177, 191, 327
   appoints HB III (21-06-1812) 144–5
   attack on Yogya (20-06-1812) 130–1, 133–5
   cautions Crawfurd 123–4
   collects manuscripts 142–3
   creates Pakualaman (22-06-1812) 145
   see also Notokusumo
   Dec 1811 visit to Yogya 75, 125–6
   HB IV's regency (1814–20) 160
   land-tax scheme 152, 179
   legal reforms 153, 225
   Melaka letters from (Dec 1810) 119, 124
   mistakes DN's position 129
   opens correspondence with future HB III 128
   plight of wood-cutter population 95
   plunders Yogya *kraton* 142
   Sepoy Plot (1815) 162
   Suro-Adimenggolo as informant of xvi, 143
   see also Suro-Adimenggolo

   treaties with courts 113, 125, 141, 145, 151–3
Rahmanudin, Kyai Pengulu of Yogya (1812–23) 210–11
   advises DN on *wali wudhar* dream 220–1, 228
Raib, Raden Mas (DN's second son by Raden Ayu Maduretno, born circa 1816) 281, 284, 321
   see also Joned
Rama, Panembahan see Kajoran
rampog macan (tiger spearing) 94
   see also tiger and buffalo fight
Ratu Adil (Just King) xxiv, xxxvi, xl, 18, 41, 50, 52, 185–6, 219–20, 231, 316, 335
   DN as 63, 223–5, 262
   DN's vision of (19-05-1824) 213–8, 223
   Joyoboyo prophecies and 202
   Ketonggo gathering (1817) 185–7
   Ronggo as 106
   see also Joyoboyo, Erucokro, *jaman kalabendu, kaliyuga*
Ratu Ageng, see Ageng, Ratu (Tegalrejo)
Ratu Ibu see Kedaton, Ratu (consort of HB III)
Ratu Kidul 37, 61, 62, 63, 64, 65, 66, 67, 87, 262
Ratu Mas see Mas, Ratu
Rawabangke ('swamp of the corpses') 120
   see also amok, British, Meester Cornelis
rechtstaat (rule-of-law state) xlii
Rembang 91, 146, 172
   Ronggo's rebellion (Nov–Dec 1810) 104
   Smissaert as Resident of 203
   Sosrodilogo's revolt (Nov 1827 – Jan 1828) 248, 258
   see also Saleh, Raden Mas

Index

Remokamal, village (Banyumas) xix
  Cleerens' meeting with DN at
  (16-02-1830) 276-7
Rendra, W.S. 28
Retnokumolo, Raden Ayu (wife of
  DN, 1827-30; d. of *kyai guru* of
  Kasongan) 17
  see also Kasongan
Retnokusumo, Raden Ayu (DN's official
  wife, married 27-02-1807) 27
  see also Chinese, Panolan
Retnoningsih, Raden Ayu (DN's last
  official wife, circa 1810-85,
  married 1827) xxvii
  death and burial in Makassar (1885)
    325
  DN's marriage to (1827/8) 38
  in Batavia (8-04 - 3-05-1830) 297
  in exile with DN (1830-55) 305, 312
  in Saleh's DN arrest painting
    (1857) xx, 293
  plate of xxi
rice, ricefields 117, 186, 177-8, 206, 230-1,
  263, 274, 324, 340-1
  bumper harvest of 1815 155
    see also Gunung Tambora
  DN eats rice-cakes 308
  DN's Makassar family sells 324-5
  DN participates in harvest xxxix, 10
  expansion of ricefields 8
    see also Tegalrejo
  gunungan rice offering at *Garebeg* 335
    see also Garebeg
  pre-war prices soar xxxvi, 93, 182,
    187, 202
Ricklefs, Merle Calvin xxix, 36, 58, 60,
  72, 144, 328
Rijck van Prehn *see* Prehn
rite de passage 47
  see also South Coast (pilgrimage)
rivers *see* Bengawan, Kali

Robison, Captain William (ADC to
  Lord Minto) 121-2
  see also Surakarta
Rochussen, Governor-General J.J. van
  (1845-51) 323
Roeps, Captain Johan Jacob (infantry
  officer; Military Interpreter for
  Javanese)
  at DN's capture (28-03-1830) 284,
    292
  distributes DN's *pusaka*
    weapons 300
    see also kris
  escorts DN to Batavia (28-03 -
    3-05-1830) 278, 284, 287,
    289, 295
    see also Stuers
  reports to Van den Bosch in Bogor
    (27-04-1830) 298
  in Saleh painting (1857) xx
  takes DN's family letters from Batavia
    (3-05-1830) 30
Roest, Lt-Col Willem Adriaan (De
  Kock's chief-of-staff) 284, 286
  in Saleh's painting (1857) xx
Rojowinangun, royal estate
  compensation for (1823-4) 207, 209
  military review at (1-06-1808) 77,
    79
Ronggo, Prince Ario (uncle of DN, exiled
  to Ternate, June 1849) 322
Ronggo Prawirodirjo *see* Prawirodirjo III
Roto (Joyosuroto), DN's *panakawan*
  (personal retainer) 40, 158
  accompanies DN in wanderings /
    exile 264, 292
  pun on potatoes 295
    see also Bantengwareng
Rowo (Tulung Agung), district (east
  Java) 186
Rubicon 231, 301

Rum, Sultan (tales of peopling of Java by) 60, 184–5, 218
  term explained 60
  see also Ottoman, Turkey
Rusche & Co (Surakarta publishers of *Babad DN*, 1908–9/1917) xxviii

Sagimun MD, biographer of DN xxviii
Said, Raden Mas *see* Mangkunegoro I
Salatiga xiii, 77, 130, 287–8, 292
  peace negotiations (Sept 1827) 254, 259, 287
  see also Bus, Mojo, Stavers
Saleh, Raden Malikan *see* Pakubuwono VII
Saleh, Raden Mas (son of Suro-Adimenggolo) 143, 146
  see also Suro-Adimenggolo, Ternate
Saleh, Syarif Bustaman, Raden (painter) xiv, xvi, xx, 54, 147, 288, 319
  painting of DN's arrest (1857) 284, 290–1, 293–4
  Pieneman's work 290, 293–4
Sambiroto (Kulon Progo) 184
  see also Umar Mahdi, Umar Moyo
Samen, village (Bantul), gunpowder manufacture at 241
  see also Dekso, Into-Into, Kota Gede
Sampurno, Kyai Iman ('The Sage of Perfect Faith'), prophecies (1819) 186–7
  see also Blitar
santri (students of religion) xxxvi, 6, 11, 341, 342
  as abusive epithet 174
  DN as *santri* prince 256, 327
  DN's *santri* dress 36, 50
  DN's supporters from 249–51, 252–3
  Dutch fail to exploit rifts 266
    see also Hurgronje
  Dutch treatment of 256
  see also Mojo
  Kadipaten establishment 20
  paras Nabi / head shaving 50
  social order of xxv, 251–2
  Surakarta patronage of 19
    see also Buminoto
  tensions with DN's court supporters 19, 224, 231, 239, 251–4, 256, 266
  visitors to Tegalrejo 9–10, 14, 16, 18, 20–1
  wanderers 50
  Wironegoro as 26
  see also Islam, Islamic law, *pathok negari*
Sapu Jagad ('Sir Sweeper of the World'), Kyai, Merapi guardian spirit 202, 218
  see also Gunung Merapi
Sardono W. Kusumo xl, xli
  see also Opera Diponegoro
Sarkumo, Raden Mas (DN's son, born in Makassar, 1834–49) 312, 322
satrio lelono (wandering knight) 15, 29, 48
  see also Joyo Lengkoro Wulang
Saxe-Coburg-Gotha, Grand-Duke Leopold (post-1831, King of the Belgians) 315
  see also Belgium
Schillet, Dr Hermanus (ship's doctor *Pollux*; cholera expert) 300
  see also cholera
Scotland, Scots
  Crawfurd as 123, 150–1, 170
  George Frank Davidson 296
  Hugh Hope plate xvi
  regiment (78th Regt of Foot/Ross-shire Buffs) 133
  see also Crawfurd, Hope, Mackenzie, Minto
Secang, Guwo (cave) *see* Guwo Secang

Index 373

DN given land as apanage
  (July 1812) 148
  see also Bantul, Selarong
Secodiningrat, Raden Tumenggung *see*
  Tan Jin Sing
Sejarah Ratu Tanah Jawa (24-01-
  1838) 301-2, 320
  see also Hikayat Tanah Jawa
Sekaran 104
  see also Prawirodirjo III
Selarong xix, xl, 10, 15, 17, 20, 27, 29, 62,
  80, 211, 213, 221, 225, 229-30, 240,
  248-9, 253, 261
  DN given land as apanage
    (July 1812) 148
  see also Bantul, Secang
Selo, grave of Ki Ageng Selo 115
Selo Gilang (holy black stone,
  Lipuro) 62
  see also Lipuro, Senopati
Selorejo, DN's retreat (Tegalrejo) 15,
  219, 221
  plate xiii
  see also Pulo Waringin, Tegalrejo
Semarang xliii, 27, 95, 97, 99, 128, 146,
  173-4, 185, 228, 258, 281
  cholera in (April 1821) 188
  see also cholera
  Daendels in (1808, 1810) 76-7, 83,
    95, 98, 107, 114
  DN detained in (29-03 - 5-04-
    1830) 40, 282, 287, 289, 295-6
  Janssens moves government to
    (Sept 1811) 120
  see also Janssens
  DN plans Dutch confined to 75, 273
  Dutch troops in (June 1825) 227
  Jati Ngaleh battle at (16-09-1811) 121
  see also Gibbs, Janssens, Serondol
  Javanese Interpreter in 83, 131
  see also Krijgsman

Pengalasan in (1849) 322
sepoy troops in 130
Suro-Adimenggolo family in xvi,
  143, 146, 180, 319
  see also Saleh (Raden, Syarif Bus-
    taman), Saleh (Raden Mas),
    Suro-Adimenggolo, Sukur
  Von Winckelmann as Military
    Division commander 100-1, 120
  see also Government of Java's NE
    Coast
Senopati, Panembahan, ruler of Mataram
  (1575-1601) 6, 55, 58, 62, 242
  see also Kota Gede, Lipuro
Sentot, Ali Basah Prawirodirjo xli, 275
  ancestry 109
  as army commander 257, 261
  breakdown in relations with DN
    (1828-9) 239
  contemplates extra-Java
    conquests 226
  death in Bengkulen (17-04-1855) 256
  disastrous *dwifungsi*
    experiment 261-4
  inherits father's good looks 81
  see also Prawirodirjo III
  meaning of name/title 261, 333
  plate of xiv-xv
  see also Ali Basah
sepoys
  attack on Yogya (20-06-1812) 130
  capture DN and father (HB III) 133
  Crawfurd's escort (Nov 1811) 123
  cut off HB II's diamond buttons 134
  Jati Ngaleh battle (16-09-1811) 121
  see also Gibbs, Janssens, Serondol
  military review for HB III
    (21-06-1812) 144
  plates of LIVB/grenadier sepoys xv
  plot/conspiracy (Oct-Nov 1815) 152,
    162-3

see also Mangkubumi (Prince, Surakarta), Pakubuwono IV
  plunder Yogya court 142
  private armies for *bandar*/estate leasers 181
  see also Light Infantry Volunteer Battalion (LIVB)
Sepuh, Raden Ayu (wife of Prince Mangkubumi, DN's uncle) 219
Sepuh, Sultan *see* Hamengkubuwono II
Serang, Nyai Ageng *see* Serang, Raden Ayu
Serang II, Prince (son of below) 52
Serang, Raden Ayu (mother of above) 52, 243
Serat Asmoro Supi 30, 321
Serat Angreni 30
Serat Centhini (1815) 35, 341
  see also Pakubuwono V
Serat Gondokusumo 30
Serat Manikmoyo 30
Serimpi, female court warrior dance 94
Serondol (Semarang) 121, 162
  see also Jati Ngaleh, Semarang
Seselo, Ki Ageng, Javanese Prometheus 115
Setomo, Kyai (cannon) 73
Setomi, Nyai (cannon) 73
Sevenhoven, J.I. van, Raad van Indië (1832–9) 181
Sewon, *pesantren* (Yogya) 50
Shaṭṭārīyya, *tarekat* (mystical brotherhood)
  DN's inspired by 34–5, 58
  DN opens 'gateway of death' 321
  inspires DN's exile writings 305
  Mojo as possible adherent of 33
  see also Naqshabāndīyya, *tarekat*
Sidayu 104
Siluk, battle of (17-09-1829) 272
Simbolon, Parakitri T. (translator) xxix
  see also Power of Prophecy

Sindunegoro, Mas Tumenggung (post-Nov 1811, Kyai Adipati Danurejo III) 142, 155
  see also Danurejo III
Sindurejo, Raden Ario (Yogya commander), ambushes British, (17-06-1812) 113
  see also Kali Gajahwong, Papringan
Sleman 25
  see also Dadapan, Kemloko, Pisangan, Tempel
Smissaert, A.H., Resident of Yogyakarta (1823–5) 18, 178, 205, 210, 227
  absentee Resident 204, 229
  abuse of DN 199–200, 212, 296
  see also Chevallier, Dietrée
  appointment to Yogya 203
  DN's view of 204
  orders attack on Tegalrejo (20-07-1825) 229
  plate of xviii
  political naiveté 205
  repairs side roads around Yogya 228–9
Smissaert, Clara Elisabet (*née* Liebeherr, wife of above) 204
Soekanto xxviii
Soemarsaid Moertono, historian 47, 223
Soetomo, Raden Mas 327
Soko *see* Aji Soko
Solo River *see* Bengawan
Sosrodilogo, Raden Tumenggung Ario (Nov 1827 – March 1828 Revolt) 152, 243, 245, 258
  captures Lasem and rapes Chinese 'nyonyah' 246
Sosrodiwiryo, Raden Ayu (DN's sister) 250
South Coast of Java 10, 71, 247
  birds' nest rocks at 247

see also Portier
coastal defences of 71
DN's administrative archive captured at (June 1829) 263
DN's pilgrimage to (circa 1805) xi, xlii, 5, 21, 42, 47–63, 158, 213, 305
map of DN's pilgrimage to 48
see also Ratu Kidul
Speelman, Cornelis Janszoon, Governor-General (1655–63) 326, 323
see also Fort Rotterdam
Srimenganti (pavilion, Kraton Yogya) 98, 133
Stadhuis (Batavia Town Hall; post-2006, Museum Sejarah Jakarta) xvii, 297, 300
Stavers, William, English landrenter (1785–1862) 224, 259
Steel, Lieutenant James 162
see also Sepoy Plot
Stoler, Ann 172, 212
see also women
strandgeld (1746–1808, Dutch 'rent' for PB II's cession of north coast, 1746) 115, 121, 125
Stuers, Major F.V.H.A. de (son-in-law / adjutant to General de Kock) xx, 12
   accompanies DN to Batavia (28-03 – 8-04-1830) 294–6
   DN peace negotiation Magelang (28-03-1830) 283–4, 287, 289
   Javanese guerrilla tactics 242
   in Saleh's DN arrest painting (1857) xx
   Sketches of Java War xiii, xv, xviii, 280
   view of DN's character 33, 41
   view of Nahuys xvii
   view of Sentot 261

see also Roeps
Sufi *see* Islam, mysticism
sugar 187, 326
Suharto (pre-1972, Soeharto), Corporal KNIL (President of Indonesia, 1966–98) 260
   makes DN *pahlawan nasional* 326
Sukarno xxvi, xxx, xliii
   dwifungsi 262
   honours DN's centenary (8-01-1955) 325
Sukowati 26, 210
   see also Kertodirjo
Sudirman, General 249
   see also Banyumas
Sukur, Raden Mas 143, 146, 180
   see also Saleh, Suro-adimenggolo, Ternate
Sulawesi (Celebes) xiii, xliii, 255, 257, 272, 305, 307, 308, 316
   see also Fort Nieuw Amsterdam, For Rotterdam, Kampung Jawa, Manado, Makassar, Minahasa, Tondano, Tonsea Lama
Suleiman, Kyai Datuk *see* Datuk Suleiman, Bima
Sumarsonowati, Mas Ayu (Chinese *peranakan* / unofficial wife of HB II) 245
   see also Chinese, Joyokusumo (Ngabehi)
Sumatra xxvii, 17, 35, 255, 278
   see also Aceh, Padri
Sumbawa 8, 155
   see also Abdul Kadir I, Ageng (Ratu Tegalrejo), Bima, Datuk Suleiman
Sumenep 143
   DN II's exile in (1834–51) 50, 321
   Suro-Adimenggolo's death in (1827) 146

see also Paku Nataningrat
Sumodiningrat, Raden Tumenggung 12, 79–80
   as Yogya army commander (1808–12) 106, 114, 130
   death (20-06-1812) 133
   Ronggo's letter to (17-11-1810) 103
   secret correspondence with Surakarta (1811–12) 127
   Selarong lands of 62, 80
   strangles Danurejo II (28-10-1811) 122
Sumodipuro, Mas Tumenggung *see* Danurejo IV
Sumonegoro, Mas Tumenggung, *bupati* Padangan 82
   killed (17-12-1810) 107
   supports Ronggo's rebellion 105–7
   see also Padangan
Sundoro, Gusti Raden Mas *see* Hamengkubuwono II
   see also Gunung Sundoro
Supadmi, Raden Ajeng *see* Retnokusumo
Surabaya 104, 124, 163, 258
   cholera in (1821) 186
Surakarta 117, 124, 135, 198, 204, 287, 335
   Babad DN published in (1908–9/1917) xxviii, 314
      see also Rusche & Co
   Babad DN version xxviii, 9, 18, 27, 175, 252
   British attack on Yogya and 128, 145
   Capt Robison's 22–23 Sept visit to 121
   cultural tastes in 178
   Daendels' 1808 visit to 77–8
   Daendels' Jan 1811 treaty and 115
   DN's Gawok defeat near (15-10-1826) 226, 248, 253–4
   boundary/ police agreements with Yogya 71, 82–4

   see also Angger Gunung (26-09-1808)
   land leases in 206
   military exercises in (1809) 93
   Nahuys as Resident of (1820–22) 171, 177, 206
   see also Nahuys
   PB VI appointment in (14/15-09-1823) 200
   police in 335
   pradikan villages and *ulama* linked to xiii, 18–19, 253–4, 339
   see also Buminoto, Mojo
   Residency Translator in 28, 95, 171
   see also Winter
   Rijck van Prehn scandal in 171, 206
   see also Prehn
   Ronggo rebellion and (Nov–Dec 1810) 97–8, 102–3, 107
   secret correspondence with Yogya (1811–12) 127
   Semarang delegation to Daendels from (06-1808) 78
   Sepoy Plot (Oct–Nov 1815) 152, 162
   Serat Centhini written in (1815) 341
   see also Centhini, Pakubuwono V, Sutrasno
   Van Braam as Resident in (1808/1810–11) 75–6, 83, 101
Suranatan, religious regiment/corps (Kraton Yogya) 16–17, 122, 128, 249
   see also Badaruddin, Suryogomo
Suranatan, mosque (Kraton Yogya) 17
Suro-Adimenggolo IV, Kyai Tumenggung (Bupati Terboyo, Semarang, 1809–22) 143, 146, 157, 180
   plate of xvi
   see also Saleh (Raden Mas), Saleh (Raden, Syarif Bustaman), Sukur, Sumenep

Index

Suropati, Untung 33
  see also Bali
Suryobrongto, Prince (DN's younger
    brother) 93
  DN at circumcision of son
    (26–12–1822) 201
Suryogomo, religious regiment / corps
    (Kraton Yogya) 249
  see also Suranatan
Syria 160

Tafsir (*Qur'ān* exegesis) 29
Tale of Two Cities xxviii
  see also Dickens
Tan Jin Sing, *Kapitan Cina* (Captain of
    the Chinese, Yogya, 1803–13) 132
  anti-Chinese sentiments occasioned
    by 132, 245
  appointed Yogya *bupati*
    (6–12–1813) 156–7
  residence attacked (20–06–1812) 143
  see also Chinese, Kampung Cina
Tanah Abang, estate 150
  see also Tiedeman
Tanojo xxviii
Taptojani, Kyai 17–18, 26
  see also Melangi
tarekat 35, 342
  see also Naqshabāndīyya, Shaṭṭārīyya
tasawwuf (Javanese-Islamic mystical
    texts) xxi, 29
tea drinking
  DN's preference for black tea 289,
    308
  European tastes in 78
teak forests, eastern *mancanagara* (east
    Java) 82, 94–5, 108, 152
Tegalrejo 81, 197–8, 209, 213, 219, 239,
    248, 301, 327
  DN's childhood at xxiv, xxxix, xlii,
    5–13, 20, 28, 47, 251

DN contemplates suicide at
    (Dec 1822) 200
DN's family life at 37, 212
DN improves estate (post-17-10-
    1803) 13–14, 21, 62
DN's mosque at 15
DN's pilgrimage from
    (circa 1805) 48–50
DN returns to after
    pilgrimage 59–62
DN returns to after British attack
    (20–06–1812) 148–50
DN visits father from
    (1–11–1811) 122
dismissed officials gather at
    (1823–5) 209–10
  see also Kertodirjo, Rahmanudin
Dutch attack and burning of
    (20–07–1825) 228–31, 240, 322
family members invited to return to
    (April 1830) 299
horses / stables at 40
marriage celebration at
    (Sept 1814) 158
  see also Maduretno (Raden Ayu)
Mojo's visit to 20
Mt Merapi eruption viewed from
    (28–12–1822) 201
plan of estate xi, 4
plans for rebellion hatched at (Oct
    1824) 227
religious observance at 14–15
Selorejo retreat at xiii, 15
ulama circle at 16–17, 25–8, 49, 174
visit of HB IV to (1822) 189
  see also Pulo Waringin, Selorejo
Tempel (Sleman) 25, 114
  see also Dadapan, Kemloko, Pisangan
Ternate
  Saleh and Sukur exiled to
    (1830–pre-March 1856) 146

Prince Ario Ronggo exiled to
(1849) 322
textiles (cotton) *see* Chinese, Jono, Kali
Lereng, Wedi
Thierry, Lieutenant Jean Nicolaas de,
cavalry officer 230
see also Tegalrejo (Dutch attack and
burning of)
Tiedeman, Jan (landowner) 150
see also Nahuys, Tanah Abang
tiger-and-buffalo fights xxxv
during Van Braam's visit
(12/15-10-1808) 83-4
see also rampog macan
'Time of Madness' *see zaman edan*
Tirtomoyo, Lake 61
Tirtowijoyo, Raden, *demang* Tersono 97
Tjipto Mangunkusumo, Dr 327
tobacco 40, 180
DN smokes 40
failure of 1823 harvest (Kedu) 180
see also Kedu, Probolinggo
Tobing, F.L., Minister of Information
(1954-5) 326
Tol, Roger xxix
tollgate monopoly, *see* bandar, Yogyakarta
Tondano xiii, 316
Kyai Mojo at 256, 299, 309
Mojo manuscript from 255-6
see also Minahasa, Tonsea Lama
Tonsea Lama (Minahasa) 299
see also Tondano
Torboyo (Semarang) xvi
see also Suro-Adimenggolo
treaties with colonial government
Daendels (Jan 1811) 113, 115-6
Giyanti (13-02-1755) 172, 327
see also Giyanti
Raffles (28-12-1811) 125-6
Raffles (1-08-1812) xxxv, 141, 150-3
Raffles urges courts to abstain from
(20-12-1810) 119

see also London Convention,
Vienna
Trunojoyo, Raden 251, 265
Tuban 104, 245
Tulung Agung *see* Rowo
Tuntang, capitulation of (18-09-1811)
121
see also Janssens
Turi, *pesantren* (Yogya) 50
Turkey xxxviii, 218
see also Ottoman
Turkio, DN's elite regiment 60
see also Arkio, Barjumungah,
Bulkio
Twist *see* Duymaer van Twist

ulama see Islam, Islamic law, *pradikan*,
santri
Umar Mahdi *see* Mahdi
UNESCO, Memory of the World (International Register) xxvii, 314
Ungaran 130, 287-8
DN escorted to (28-03-1830)
289, 295
see also Fort De Ontmoeting

Valck, Frans Gerhardus, Resident Kedu
(1826-30) xx, xxvi, xxxvii, 178
DN view of 127, 129-30
Magelang negotiations with DN
(8/28-03-1830) 281-2, 284-5,
292
purloins British Residency
archive 126-7, 150
view of Java War female
commanders 242-3
Veeckens, Hendrik, Secretary *Hooge
Regeering* (1808-11) 83
see also Braam
Vienna, Treaty of (1815) 163
Vinne, Jan van der, President *landraad*
(Batavia) 297, 301

see also Batavian Society
VOC *see* Dutch East India Company
Vreede Bik, Pieter, Governor of Celebes (1849–52) 10, 323
  see also Bousquet, Hart, Perez

Wahhābi 35
wali songo (nine 'apostles of Islam') 6
wali wudhar xxiv, 217
  DN as 52, 219–20, 223
Wallace, Alfred Russel, British naturalist 309
Washington, George xxvii
Waterloo, Matthijs, Resident of Yogya (1803–8) 71, 118
Wattendorff, A.J.B., Resident of Yogya (1873–8) 283
wayang (Javanese shadow-play theatre) xxiii, 15, 30, 103, 334, 338, 339, 342
  Bima's exploits in 54
  Damar Wulan cycle (*krucil*) 161
  DN's marriage to R.A. Maduretno celebrated with 158
  DN uses imagery from xxxvi, 37, 61, 63, 320
  see also Arjuna
  Menak cycle (*jemblung*) 161
  Panji cycle (*gedog*) 61
  Ronggo and 103–4
  see also Ronggo
  wayang wong (*topeng*) 161
weapons (muskets, Javanese lances) 78, 131
  during Java War 240–42
  see also Gresik, gunpowder, Kota Gede
Wedi, weaving centre (eastern Bagelen) 244
  see also Chinese, Jono, Kali Lereng
Weleri 97
  see also Tirtowijoyo
West Coast of Sumatra *see* Cleerens, Padri, Sentot, Sumatra

Wiese, Gustaf Wilhelm, Resident of Yogyakarta (1808–10) 82, 92, 114
Wijoyo, Kyai Murmo *see* Murmo Wijoyo
Wilhelmina, Queen of the Netherlands (1901–48) 169
Willem I, King of the Netherlands (1813–40) 54, 169
Willem II, King of the Netherlands (1840–9) 320
Winckelmann, Brigadier-General F.C.P. von (Semarang Division) 100, 101
wine *see* Constantia
Winter, Johannes Wilhelmus (Residency Translator Surakarta, 1806–20) 28, 95
  dismissal (March 1820) 171
  see also Prehn
Wirogunan 26
Wiroguno, Mas Tumenggung (*patih* Kadipaten; father of below) 26
Wironegoro, Raden Tumenggung 26, 147, 175, 209, 212
Wirosentiko, Kyai Ronggo 81, 102
  see also Ageng, Ratu, Prawirodirjo III
Wiroyudo, Kyai 8
  see also Bima, Datuk Suleiman
Woerden, royal fortress (Utrecht) 316
women 326
  Chinese females slaughtered (1825) 244
  see also Chinese
  court women molested by sepoys 142
  Danurejo IV's penchant for 156, 204, 211
  see also Danurejo IV
  DN sends women's clothes to commanders 38
  see also Java War
  DN's followers in exile 300
  DN's weakness for xl, 37, 311
  Dutch officials' sexual exploitation of 172–3, 211–2

see also Java War
HB V and 190
Keputren female quarters in *kraton* 5, 26
  see also Ageng, Ratu
prajurit èstri (Amazon Corps) 9, 94, 132, 259
prostitutes (*ronggeng*) 181
Ratu Kidul's assistants 56
  see also Ratu Kidul
Saleh's depiction in DN's arrest painting (1857) 293
  see also Retnoningsih
santri followers of DN 246
  see also Java War, Mojo
sexual relations with Chinese *peranakan* 245–6
  see also Chinese
role in Java War 239, 242–3
  see also prajurit èstri
Yogya *kraton* as 'brothel' 154, 161, 213
wong durjono see bandits
wong putihan ('people in white') 55, 342
  see also pradikan, santri
Wonokromo, *pesantren* (Yogya) 50
Wonosobo 244

Yamin, Muhammad, Education Minister (1953–5) xxviii, 326
Yogyakarta, *kraton*/sultanate xii, xv, xvii, xxv, xxix, xxxv, xlii, 14, 20, 21, 47, 62–3, 108, 141, 164, 176, 189–90, 211, 212, 248, 251, 252, 257, 259–60, 261, 273, 283, 287, 289, 296, 319, 321, 323, 324, 327, 335, 336, 337, 339
  agreements with Surakarta 82
  Amazon corps in 9, 94, 132, 259
  anti-Dutch party at court 79–80
  attack on *ulama* in 174
  British attack on (20–06–1812) xv, 126–35, 266
  as 'brothel' 154, 161, 213
  Capt Robison's 24–26 Sept 1811 visit to 121
  Chinese in 244–5
  collection of statistics on 203
  civil war in 117
  court artist sketches xii, 36–7
  criminal underworld in 27–8, 96, 97, 98, 99
    see also bandits
  creation of Pakualaman in (22–06–1812) 145–6
  Daendels and 61, 70, 74–5, 78, 79–80, 82, 83, 85, 98–9, 114–6
  Daendels' July 1809 visit to 94
  dampar (throne) 205
  despoliation/plunder of 91–2, 142–3
  destruction predicted 59, 61
  DN's birth in (11–11–1785) 3
    see also women (Keputren)
  DN's female relatives in 7–9
    see also Ageng (Ratu Tegalrejo), Kedaton, Mangkorowati
  DN as landowner in xxxix, 15, 62, 148
    see also Bantul, Gowo Secang, Selarong
  DN's official marriages in (27–02–1807 / 28–09–1814) 25–6, 36, 157
    see also Chinese, Maduretno (Raden Ayu), Retnokusumo
  DN plans destruction of 154, 161, 172
  DN's recollection of events in 31
  DN's view of under HB II 10, 12, 16
  eastern *mancanagara bupati* in 82, 94–5, 101
    see also Ronggo
  French annexation ceremony in (27–02–1811) 118, 123
  gunpowder manufacture in 243–4
  HB II exiled from 146
    see also Ambon, Pinang
  Javanese-Islamic lawcodes in 28, 41

Joyoboyo prophecies and 187
Kota Gede and 242
labuhan ceremonies at xiii, 55
   see also *labuhan*
land lease and indemnities in 32, 173–4, 206–7, 209–10
   see also Nahuys
legitimation of Dutch power 72–3, 77
maps of xi, xlvii
Merapi eruption in (28/30-12-1822) 201–2
military reviews at 77, 79, 145
   see also Rojowinangun
Notokusumo returns to (16-12-1811) 124
opium retail in 183–4
   see also opium
Pengulu dismissed (Sept 1823) 210–11, 221
   see also Rahmanudin
pradikan villages in 174, 249
   see also Kepundung
Raffles and 61, 75–7
Ratu Adil movements in 184–5
   see also Ratu Adil
regency council in 179
religious community's links to Tegalrejo 15, 17–19, 25–6
religious schools and mosques in 49–50
   see also Mesjid Ageng, Suranatan
Residents in xviii, xxvi, xxxvii, 32, 71, 75, 98, 118, 123, 143, 151, 170, 172, 173, 177, 178, 202–4, 205, 211, 277, 283, 323
   see also Crawfurd, Engelhard (Pieter), Moorrees, Nahuys, Sevenhoven, Smissaert, Valck, Waterloo

road repair in 228–9
   see also Java War (outbreak of)
Ronggo rebellion and (Nov–Dec 1810) 100–1, 102–7, 109
Sepoy Plot in (Oct–Nov 1815) 162
   see also sepoys
siege of (Aug–Sept 1825) 241, 244, 250
stiff charm of 151
sultan's titles in 224
surambi religious court in 29, 153, 266, 340
Tan Jin Sing appointed *bupati* in 156–7
   see also Chinese, Tan Jin Sing
tastes in 78, 178
tiger-and-buffalo fights in 84
   see also Braam
tollgate receipts in (1816–24) 181–2
   see also *bandar*
treaties with colonial government 115–6, 151–3
   see also treaties
Van Braam's view of 76
Vredeburg, Dutch fort see Fort Vredeburg
   see also Hamengkubuwono
Yudistira, Pandawa brother in *Mahabhārata* 158
Yudokusumo, Raden Ayu 243
   see also Chinese, Ngawi

zaman edan ('time of madness') see *jaman edan*
zaman kala-bendu ('time of wrath/catastrophe') see *jaman kala-bendu*
Zeeland (the Netherlands) 300
   see also Belgian Revolt, Roeps